Hired Pens

Hired Pens

Professional Writers in
America's Golden Age
of Print

RONALD WEBER

Ohio University Press
Athens

Ohio University Press, Athens, Ohio 45701
© 1997 by Ronald Weber
Printed in the United States of America

Ohio University Press books are printed on acid-free paper ∞ ™

01 00 99 98 97   5 4 3 2 1

Library of Congress Cataloging-in-Publication Data
Weber, Ronald, 1934–
    Hired pens : professional writers in America's Golden Age of print
/ Ronald Weber.
        p.   cm.
    Includes bibliographical references and index.
    ISBN 0-8214-1204-3 (cloth : alk. paper). — ISBN 0-8214-1205-1
(pbk.)
        1. American literature—19th century—History and criticism.
    2. American literature—20th century—History and criticism.
    3. Authorship—Economic aspects—United States—History. 4. Authors
    and publishers—United States—History. 5. Literature publishing—
    United States—History. 6. Journalism—United States—History.
    I. Title.
    PS88.W37   1997
    808'.02'0973—dc21   97-16071
                                                                 CIP

Brief articles drawn from material in this book appeared in the following:
1. *The Eye of the Reporter: Literature's Heritage in the Press,* ed. Bill Knight and
Deckle McLean (Western Illinois University, 1996), 45–55.
2. *Michigan History* (November/December 1996): 53–54.

For Devery
and for
Christopher, Colin, and Kevin

. . . it is a delicious thing to write, whether well or badly

—Gustave Flaubert

CONTENTS

ACKNOWLEDGMENTS

The material of this book is drawn largely from accounts of their working lives by professional writers themselves as published in magazine articles, memoirs, and letters, the material supplemented by numerous biographies and critical studies. Behind the book, the single scholarly work to which I am most indebted is the late Russel Nye's *The Unembarrassed Muse: The Popular Arts in America.* I refer specifically to this work several times, but it is its overall approach to an historical account of what Nye calls "the arts of commercial entertainment" that I have absorbed most deeply. Nye's field is more comprehensive than mine, popular art in its several forms as against the domain of print; but his understanding of popular artists and his relish for their world, while remaining sensibly aware of its limitations, has been a continual guide.

Many friends and academic colleagues read and commented on portions of the book in manuscript or listened patiently to my accounts of it. I am grateful to them all. In the epilogue I refer briefly to the professional writer Murray Teigh Bloom, a reference that does not disclose his key role in the study. Simply put, he first got me thinking of an account of the development of the writing profession in America. As it turned out, the book is not what we first discussed in letters and during a happy meeting in his Long Island home. Book ideas, like fictional characters, have lives of their own. I hope, at any event, that he is not wholly displeased with how the plot worked itself out in this instance.

Hired Pens

Prologue

CLEVER AUTHORS OF
ACCEPTABLE WORK

Living by Words on America's Grub Street

*Democratic literature is always infested with a tribe of writers who
look upon letters as a mere trade; and for some few great authors
who adorn it, you may reckon thousands of idea-mongers.*
—Alexis de Tocqueville

one

In an article in *Scribner's Magazine* in 1893 called "The Man of Letters as a
Man of Business," William Dean Howells surveyed the history of writing in
America as a professional activity and concluded that before the Civil War
probably only Edgar A. Poe had actually managed to live by words alone. But
Poe's literary existence was precarious at best and often underwritten with
loans. The more typical author of the antebellum period, Howells pointed
out, was an amateur rather than a professional, one who had independent
means or earned the bulk of his or her livelihood as a teacher, editor, minister,
lawyer, or officeholder.

Exceptions come to mind. Poe's contemporary and friend Nathaniel Parker
Willis was a thoroughly professional writer who made his living with his pen.
So did Henry William Herbert, Ann S. Stephens, Lydia H. Sigourney, and

Willis's productive sister, Sara Payson Willis, under her celebrated pen name Fanny Fern. And such literary notables as Irving, Cooper, and Longfellow made considerable sums of money from their words. But in the main, of course, Howells was right. Only in the postbellum period did living entirely by the pen become a generally realistic possibility for American writers. Although their earnings in the period did not compare with those of successful tradesmen or professional people, they could, as Howells expressed it, "live prettily enough," and several had incomes that would seem like riches to ordinary working people. And it was not only "the famous or fully recognized authors" who produced such income, Howells added, but a whole class of writers that, "as a class, was wholly unknown among us before the war. . . the much larger number of clever people who are as yet known chiefly to the editors, and who may never make themselves a public, but who do well a kind of acceptable work."[1]

This is a book about Howells's clever authors of acceptable work—to be more exact, a book about a class of full-time independent professional writers who came into existence once there was a market for their wares and who managed to live more or less exclusively by the pen. Their writing lives depended, as Howells rightly noted, on a great expansion of publishing opportunities in the postbellum period, and this book is necessarily about that burgeoning print world as well. Irving and Cooper became the first professional writers in America in the 1820s through their books; the emergence of a *class* of professional writers required the much larger and more broadly lucrative market provided by story papers, dime novels, pulp and slick magazines, newspaper syndicates, newspaper Sunday editions, and inexpensive books.

Often the literary level I examine in the following pages is less elevated than that which Howells presumably had in mind—writers who wrote for and managed to live from the literary marketplace only in the most distant sense to which the word *literary* can be stretched. I omit writers who wrote for specialized audiences in fields such as medicine, science, law, business, agriculture, and religion or were compilers of the many forms of advice or information manuals; and, with exceptions here and there, I omit writers who toiled as salaried employees on newspapers and magazines, in advertising agencies and publishing houses. Since I am concerned with a print world, I also by and large exclude writers who during the twentieth century worked as contract laborers in radio and television or in Hollywood's dream factories. Although I give some attention to editors and publishers (especially in the final chapter), my main focus is similar to Howells's in his article. "In this inquiry," he noted, "it is always the author rather than the publisher, always the contributor rather than the editor, whom I am concerned for. I study the difficulties of the publisher and editor only because they involve the author and contributor; if they did not, I will not say with how hard a heart I should turn from them."[2]

To put the best face on it, the authors I treat were skilled literary craftsmen rather than high-culture literary artists. Less charitably, they could be described as Grub Street hacks adept at churning out—as a cynical observer once put it—"good bad stuff" in a never-ending stream. Upton Sinclair, who began his writing career in the lower depths of the popular market, vividly outlined the raucous "*commercial* book-world" in the latter sense in an article in the *Independent* in 1902 as

> composed of thousands of newspaper men, magazine editors and writers, poetry-mongers, story-tellers, novelists—for a large part people without the slightest knowledge of literature and without any idea whatever of literary tradition, but who have gone into writing as into any other trade; who study to know the "market," and who watch hungrily for any subject that will "go;" who will turn you out a biography of a great man six weeks after he is dead, and who watch the public taste in fiction and dash off a new romance, or a slum-study, or a "kail-yard" or other dialect concoction, according to demand.[3]

Herein is my territory—the world of writing according to demand. I trace the rise of the tribe of literary tradesmen in America from a shaky emergence in the generation of Poe and Willis before the Civil War down through the glory years that began in Howells's time and extended through World War II and on into the 1960s. Although the book follows a chronological course across roughly a century and a half, the individual chapters are directed to the varied and shifting kinds of work for which writers found their paydays rather than a period-by-period historical account of the writing life.

Typically the authors of the period took pride in the variety of their work, traveling with more or less ease between fiction and nonfiction, poems and articles. "Jack-of-all-letters," a phrase applied to the journalist and fiction writer Will Irwin, described these writers as well.[4] Behind their adaptability was professional competence, enormous labor, and above all the ability to be engaging, whatever the merits of the task at hand. "A professional writer," Wallace Stegner remarked about the popular historian (as well as critic, novelist, and prolific magazine author) Bernard De Voto, "cannot, like a teacher, be dull and be protected in his dullness. He must recapture his audience with every new start. He must be fascinating, bright, or pontifical, he must impress, charm, amuse, inform."[5] Added to the bottomless vitality writers brought to their several tasks was the good fortune of *having* an audience—of living and working in a period in which the word in all its printed forms mattered, a period in which newspapers, magazines, and books were actually read, fiction was understood as entertainment, and a few major figures became revered names while a group of industrious minor figures secured a decent living. It was, in fact, a golden age for writers, one in which, as Gore Vidal remarked, "writing was simply a trade that, sometimes, mysteriously, proved to be an art."[6] In the *Saturday Evening Post* for December 30, 1899, George Horace Lorimer, just beginning his long regime as editor, could confidently chart the magazine's future in a house advertisement: the *Post*, he said, was directed to the "average American" who was an "omnivorous reader" possessed of a "range of interests . . . wider than that of the average citizen of any other country."[7] Imagine.

Independent professional writers remain at work in the age of the electronic superhighway, processing words to the hum of their computers. Some still cross the boundaries between fiction and nonfiction. Some are actually read. Grub Street is alive and reasonably well, the money-machine of the old periodical world more or less replaced by a market that includes a few general magazines, many single-interest publications, genre fiction, specialized and ghost-written nonfiction, and the voracious appetite of film and television. But the great days of the writing game are but a faint memory. Gone with them is a good deal of both the bitter pain and the aura of glamor that accompanied independent writing—the possibility of either starving to death or becoming that storied figure whose "office and business is under his hat," as Jack London exulted, and who "can go anywhere and write anywhere as the spirit moves him."[8]

two

Another way of setting out my subject is to recall Cyril Connolly's remark that "the more books we read, the sooner we perceive that the true function of a writer is to produce a masterpiece and that no other task is of any consequence." This is a noble example of the romantic ideal of the artist, and perhaps in an ultimate sense what it says is true. But Connolly was quick to add to the remark, as would any author who wrote for a living, that "obvious though this should be, how few writers will admit it, or having made the admission, will be prepared to lay aside the piece of iridescent mediocrity on which they have embarked!"[9] Nearly all writers, no matter how towering their literary aim, spend time on Grub Street, pandering to public taste with pieces of iridescent mediocrity or worse. This they may regret, and as soon as possible put all tawdry work behind; yet Grub Street remains, a trap yet also a means of balancing the books, and for many writers it is the only word world they ever know. The literary artist is also a professional writer, and now and then the reverse is likewise true; the spheres overlap, and to study one without an awareness of the other—to pursue John Steinbeck, for example, to the exclusion of his hugely popular and equally ambitious contemporary Frederick Faust—is to miss the full reality of the writing game. Insofar as an argument is embedded in the story I tell of professional writing in America, it is located just here.

Few writers have had the luxury of living entirely on the proceeds of their best endeavors. The great majority have found patrons or worked at salaried jobs or, to repeat, taken a turn on Grub Street. The popular biographer James Parton once told Howells in a letter that he could not "recall one instance of an author who did no task or hack-work, that could safely live in the style of a prosperous grocer, unless he had property or a pension. No, not one, counting from Herodotus down. The one or two apparent exceptions prove not to be such when we get at the facts."[10] The argument of Jack London's fictional writer Martin Eden that "hack-work keeps me in touch with things literary and gives me time to try bigger things" is no doubt a youthful fancy, as is his plan to produce "hack-work and income first, masterpieces afterward."[11] Yet authorship, even for the most artistic of practitioners, usually turns out to be just such a mixed bag.

F. Scott Fitzgerald tried to follow London's program, first writing popular stories for money, then serious novels for art—and succeeded in the sense that during the 1920s and early 1930s his stories drew top dollar from the mass-circulation magazines, especially the *Saturday Evening Post* (where he published sixty-six of them), bringing him over $100,000 before his agent's commission.[12] The problem was not Fitzgerald's strategy but a style of living that left him continually borrowing against future magazine sales. During World War II, disenchanted with Hollywood's Grub Street, William Faulkner turned to his agent in the hope of finding some hackwork closer to home in Oxford, Mississippi. He wrote: "My books have never sold, are out of print; the labor (the creation of my apocryphal country) of my life, even if I have a few things yet to add to it, will never make a living for me. I dont [*sic*] have enough sure judgment about trash to be able to write it with 50% success. Could I do some sort of editorial work, or some sort of hackwriting at home, where living wont [*sic*] cost me so much as now."[13] Sylvia Plath's poetry is lodged firmly in the world of high art; yet, as biographers have told us, she spent a good deal of time writing popular stories aimed at mass-culture women's magazines. About one such story she noted in her diary: "Sent it off to *The Sat Eve Post*: start at the top. Try *McCall's, Ladies' Home Journal, Good Housekeeping, Women's Day* before getting blue. . . . my first good story for five years . . . a slick story but one I consider good."

A critic remarked about Plath's career that "certainly she writes high poetry, but she also writes—and very often prefers to write—low prose."[14] Such is the case for most writers with a claim to literary importance—a writing life that mingles high and low, serious work and hackwork, and at times embraces the shabby as eagerly as the grand. "For someone in love with the idea of writing," the British writer Jonathan Raban has said, "the joy of writing something hasty, derivative and bad goes as deep as the joy of writing something genuinely original. The play of words on the page, the illusion of forming a fresh pattern, crisply phrased, the heady sense of having nailed a fragment of the world with a telling metaphor, come more easily, if anything, to the bad writer than to the good one."[15]

In the opening paragraph of his *Scribner's* article Howells eloquently sets out the disdain the pure artist feels for making money from his productions. No man, he maintains,

> ought to live by an art. A man's art should be his privilege, when he has proven his fitness to exercise it, and has otherwise earned his daily bread; and its results should be free to all. There is an instinctive sense of this, even in the midst of the grotesque confusion of our economic being; people feel that there is something profane, something impious, in taking money for a picture, or a poem, or a statue. Most of all, the artist himself feels this. He puts on a bold front with the world, to be sure, and brazens it out as Business; but he knows very well that there is something false and vulgar in it; and that the work which cannot be truly priced in money cannot be truly paid in money.[16]

This lofty view established, Howells proceeds to describe an actual world of literature as business in a detailed account of royalty rates and income from magazine serialization and book publication. In such matters he was writing as an insider, a professional writer who had exploited the new market opportunities of what he called "our huckstering civilization" to the extent of becoming one of the most financially secure authors of the day. The year of his article, 1893, was one of severe hard times for most Americans, but for Howells eight new contracts recently signed would bring in nearly $30,000. A biographer has estimated that his writing income during the decade of the nineties was equal in purchasing power to an author in 1970 earning $120,000 a year.[17]

After Howells resigned as editor of the *Atlantic* in 1881 and agreed to begin serializing a novel in *Scribner's Monthly* (soon recast as the *Century*), Emily Dickinson inquired of the magazine's editor, Dr. Josiah Gilbert Holland, "Doctor—How did you snare Howells?" To which the editor replied, "Emily—Money did it."[18] For most writers the reality of the writing life embraces Howells's practical deeds as well as his vaulting words. For most, indeed, the act of writing is so demanding that—at least in the long run—only the prospect of money keeps them prisoners at their desks. The reporter, fiction writer, and popular humorist Irvin S. Cobb thought this a truth easily demonstrated: "When not giving concerts, a musician finds joy in playing for his own delectation. An actor not professionally engaged delights to take part in benefits. In his off hours a portrait painter does water-color sketches, largely to amuse himself. . . . But show me a writer who, when not writing for pay, deliberately writes for fun or for self-expression, and I'll show you one of the rarest cases of freakish misapplication in the entire dime museum of the human race."[19]

three

William Charvat's unfinished "history of American literature in terms of the profession of writing," as he defined the pioneering scholarly task he set himself, has many parallels with my account and one fundamental difference. The parallels are found in the essential nature of independent writing, the lines of which Charvat effectively sketched: "[It] provides a living for the author, like any other job; that it is a main and prolonged, rather than intermittent or sporadic, resource for the writer; that it is produced with the hope of extended sale in the open market, like any article of commerce; and that it is written with reference to buyers' tastes and reading habits."[20] The difference is that Charvat's attention is fixed on writers, as he puts it, "for whom both art and income were matters of concern," mine on writers for whom income alone was the reason they wrote. While he eliminates "private poets and hack writers," the latter category is the one I concentrate on.[21] The result is that Charvat begins his work with the familiar progression of American literary history:

the Connecticut Wits; Irving and Cooper, the two writers who first established the literary profession in America; Longfellow and Melville. I begin with Poe and Willis and go on to their Grub Street contemporaries. Thereafter my roll call of professional writers includes, in addition to those already mentioned, Gail Hamilton, Ned Buntline, Sylvanus Cobb, Jr., Gilbert Patten, Horatio Alger, Jr., Edward Stratemeyer, Howard R. Garis, Ida Tarbell, Richard Harding Davis, Zane Grey, Frederick Faust, Frank Gruber, Arthur J. Burks, Mary Roberts Rinehart, Kenneth Roberts, Edgar Rice Burroughs, Jim Thompson, John R. Tunis, James Oliver Curwood, Peter B. Kyne, Ralph Henry Barbour, William Heyliger, David Graham Phillips, Albert Payson Terhune, Hendrik Willem Van Loon, Frederick Lewis Allen, James M. Cain, Paul Gallico, John Bartlow Martin, and Ralph Ingersoll.

Of course Poe, who together with Willis heads the progression, was a hack writer most of the time and a literary artist some of the time. His literary stature earns him a chapter in Charvat's history, and his example points to the impossibility of strictly separating the professional writer and the literary artist. Other writers I mention similarly blur the distinction, among them Stephen Crane, Jack London, Upton Sinclair, Ring Lardner, Sinclair Lewis, Ernest Hemingway, and Archibald MacLeish. What I attempt is more a matter of focus than exact categorization: an account, necessarily selective and incomplete, of the development of the writing profession in America as against that of the literary profession.

As Howells suggested, the kind of writers who came into existence after the Civil War were known chiefly to editors and only now and then created for themselves a reading public. They had stature within the writing fraternity, seldom beyond it. For every Poe or London, writers for hire yet still read and studied, many authors labored in anonymity and vanished without the trace of memoir or learned reference. Consequently, I give inordinate attention to independent writers who retain some claim on our attention—Grub Street figures who managed to transcend the worst shortcomings of hack writing and find a public as well as a foothold in literary history. In *The Common Writer* Nigel Cross takes note of this problem in a study of professional writers (meaning, as he puts it, a writer located somewhere between the "genius" and the "amateur") in nineteenth-century England. He writes about his choice of subject: "For the most part I have selected writers who were relatively well known at the time and whose work is above the run of the mill. This means, of course, that they are not quite common writers, in the sense of absolutely average, but they are common enough by the standards of orthodox literary history."[22] For the most part the writers I mention were not quite common writers either, yet they were certainly common enough by the lights of most literary studies.

four

One might hold that all writers who write for their livelihood are inhabitants of Grub Street, and that critical distinctions only point to a writer's position in its high, middle, or lower reaches. So in the present word world the *New Yorker*'s self-conscious stylists are Grub Street figures of one sort, the unknown (to the public) ghost writers of celebrities' biographies simply another. In a 1906 *Atlantic* article called "The American Grub Street," James H. Collins took such a position, describing with thick irony the army of floating freelance professional authors and artists in New York made possible by the concentration of publishing interests in the city. "Greater Grub Street," as Collins called it, was a meritocracy in which aspirants soon found their level of ability. At one end of the continuum were "Art's chosen sons and daughters," at the other "her content, misguided dupes," and in between the large mass of "staid, careful burghers of the arts." By the end of the article, however, Collins reverted to the more typical understanding of Grub Street as the specific locale of mercenary hackwork. "Greater Grub Street is utilitarian," he concluded. "That which propels it is not Art, but Advertising—not Clio nor Calliope, but Circulation."[23] It is in this loose sense of Grub Street, referring to the utilitarian world of hack writers, that I use the term here.

Samuel Johnson's celebrated entry in his *Dictionary* of 1755 points to historical and metaphorical meanings of "grubstreet" and aligns it squarely at the literary level of "mean production":

> Originally the name of a street in Moorfields in London, much inhabited by writers of small histories, dictionaries, and temporary poems; whence any mean production is called grubstreet.

The term had first come into the language a century before, employed by the Augustan satirists—Pope and Swift in particular—to refer to a specific London locale, crowded and squalid and actually populated with hack writers, a locale they identified with a rising commercialization that was reducing literature to a vulgar trade.

When he penned the definition Johnson himself had spent many years as an odd-job laborer in Grub Street. Here he turned out for the periodical press biographies of noted figures, poems, articles on foreign and domestic events, book reviews, and a great quantity of political essays in the guise of parliamentary debates. In later life he declined to make a full list of his ephemeral work on the grounds, as recorded by friends, that "he then wrote many things which merited no distinction from the trash with which they were consigned to oblivion."[24] Johnson's eminent biographer, W. Jackson Bate, notes that much of what he wrote in this period—roughly from 1736 down to the *Dictionary* in 1755—was certainly hack work but "inspired hack work" that still claims our attention. The years in Grub Street also had beneficent effect, though Johnson lived during the time of the typical hand-to-mouth existence of Grub Street regulars, in that it turned him from a stage of lethargy and uncertainty and put him on the path to the famous work that would come. That enduring legacy, Bate remarks, "would necessarily have to grow from this particular soil," the scrambling life of writing for hire.[25]

Although he placed little value on his hackwork, Johnson had a lingering fondness for the society of Grub Street writers. Here he found freedom from social and professional pretension, and here was a natural regard for knowledge gained through actual experience as against passed-down learning. Among his fellow hacks he occasionally found real literary and intellectual interest. "The most literary conversation I ever enjoyed," he said in later life, "was at the table of Jack Ellis, a money-scrivener [a notary who drew up contracts] behind the Royal Exchange, with whom I at one period used to dine generally once a week."[26] But whatever its passing pleasures, the life of writing for hire remained precarious and inevitably lonely, the independent writer at the mercy of editors and his own inner resources. When he came to write the preface for the *Dictionary* Johnson put down in melancholy prose the hard terms of the Grub Street background from which his great work—by implication, any enduring work by a former hack writer—had emerged: ". . . the *English Dictionary* was written with little assistance of the learned, and without any patronage of the great; not in the soft obscurities of retirement, or under the shelter of academick bowers, but amidst inconvenience and distraction, in sickness and in sorrow."

In 1830 the actual Grub Street that Johnson had known so well was renamed Milton Street, but its metaphorical meaning lived on in common usage. By the end of the Victorian period it referred—as a student of the term has put it—to "the miseries of authorship at large: a vaguer, slightly pitying note attached to it."[27] The altered meaning was captured in George Gissing's 1892 novel *New Grub Street* with its account, at once satirical and sentimental, of the commercial web in which writers now found themselves, victims of booksellers, readers' tastes, and their own ambition. In our time the historical reality of Grub Street has been further diminished, Milton Street now largely subsumed into the Barbican complex; yet the metaphor remains, a handy way of pointing—as *Webster's International Dictionary* has it—to "the world or category of usually mediocre, needy, and disdained writers who wrote for hire: the world of literary hacks." Once again, it is in this broad sense, though tempered by Johnson's nostalgic fondness and a good deal of frank admiration, that I use the term in an American context.

five

Grub Street's existence, both as a locale of hack writers and as a metaphor of literary studies, depended on the emergence of a middle-class reading public in England together with new developments in print technology and marketing techniques. A heightened level of literacy made possible through education and leisure, especially on the part of women who found some freedom from household drudgery, did not create a relatively sizeable reading audience until the second half of the eighteenth century, and not before the end of the century could England be said to have a well-developed word culture that included printers, booksellers, circulating libraries, and professional writers.

In colonial America, with a small population scattered the length of the Eastern seaboard, events took a slower pace. Yet as early as 1690 a newspaper had made a brief appearance in Boston, Benjamin Harris's *Publick Occurrences,* and by 1735 the city was supporting five papers. With the opening of a press in Savannah in 1763, all the colonies had job printers in business, among them Benjamin Franklin in Philadelphia. In addition to newspapers, most of the work they turned out consisted of pamphlets, broadsides, and the occasional magazine. Few American books found their way into print since English works were easily imported or, in the absence of international copyright laws, pirated. When an American work was undertaken the author bore all or most of the financial risk.

In the years immediately after the Revolution, works of American poetry began flowing from local presses as well as fledgling efforts at fiction, among them William Hill Brown's *Power of Sympathy,* the first novel by a native-born American, and Susanna Rowson's immensely popular *Charlotte Temple.* At the same time the graduates of American colleges and a growing population in general were expanding the audience for print matter in all its forms. The long shadow of England persisted, as Tocqueville noted with the remark that "the literary genius of Great Britain still darts its rays into the recesses of the forests of the New World."[28] Nonetheless, by 1825 a print world, with Philadelphia and New York as its principal centers, was sufficiently established in America to allow for the appearance of a native class of professional writers.

Irving and Cooper were the first to take advantage of it, beginning the process whereby American writing, as William Charvat put it, shifted from "the gentleman-amateur-author phase of American letters to the professional and commercial phase."[29] Charvat estimates that Cooper's book earnings in the 1820s averaged $6,500 a year, while in the single year of 1829 Irving earned from books an astonishing $23,500.[30] It was nearly three-quarters of a century earlier that Johnson had declared "The Age of Authors" in England and had gone on to explain, in mocking tones, that everyone now felt in a position to take up the pen. "The province of writing," he noted, "was formerly left to those, who by study, or appearance of study, were supposed to have gained knowledge unattainable by the busy part of mankind; but in these enlightened days, every man is qualified to instruct every other man."[31]

LIGHT ARTILLERY
OF THE INTELLECT

The Emergence of the Versatile Magazinists

*Through joy and through sorrow, I—wrote. Through hunger and
through thirst, I—wrote. Through good report and through ill
report, I—wrote. Through sunshine and through moonshine,
I—wrote. What I wrote it is unnecessary to say.*
—Edgar A. Poe

one

The series of sketches with the imposing title "The Literati of New York City"
began appearing in May 1846 in an unlikely place for peevish literary warfare,
Godey's Lady's Book of Philadelphia. It was the kind of magazine for which
Edgar A. Poe had only disdain, given as it was to sentimental fiction and verse
and prized for its hand-colored fashion plates and fine engravings, but it was
also the most successful periodical of the day and paid its contributors liberal
fees. Although Poe remarked that Louis Godey, the magazine's publisher, had
as many ladies in his pay as the Grand Turk, male writers had equal entry to
his pages, among them such New England luminaries as Emerson, Longfellow, and Hawthorne. The magazine's scope was national and readership had
reached a hundred thousand, a dazzling figure for an American magazine of
the period, by the time Poe's series was launched.

Godey puffed the series with the prediction that it would "raise some commotion in the literary emporium."[1] In New York anticipation ran high in the wake of a tumultuous two years Poe had just spent in the city, one newspaper speculating that "the uproar which attended Pope's Dunciad was nothing to the stormy confusion of the literary elements which will war and rage."[2] And in fact the thirty-eight personal sketches that ran through October turned out to be *Godey's* greatest sensation. In New York, Horace Greeley reported that every copy of the first "Literati" issue had been bought up. Unable to meet demand in the city and in Boston, the magazine had to reprint the first installment of the series in the same issue as the second. Poe himself took note of the "unexpected circulation of the series" with plans to expand it into a book on American letters in general, and so "make a hit and some profit, as well as proper fame."[3] The book never materialized and proper fame and profit remained always just beyond his grasp.

A reading of the sketches today offers instruction in the time-bound nature of literary sensations. Most of the New York writers Poe included in the series are long forgotten; those still recalled exist on the dim fringes of literary memory, with only the author himself a looming presence. Some of his subjects were literary dabblers and academic scholars, but others were professional editors and writers—Charles Fenno Hoffman, Ann S. Stephens, Catherine M. Sedgwick, Epes Sargent—who labored in a variety of forms but made their mark largely in the periodicals and literary weeklies of the time. Chief among the writers of this sort was Nathaniel Parker Willis, one of the best-known and highest-paid authors of the day and now generally ranked as the first successful magazine writer in America.

Taken together, the magazine careers of Poe and Willis illustrate the first significant period of independent professional writing in the country. In addition, their early work set out many of the popular genres in which later writers would find their livelihood: impressionistic sketch, journalistic exposé, travel account, essay, book review, fictional story, poem. It was an age of the "magazinist," a term Poe coined for Willis's most notable arena of work, when a rising tide of periodicals and literary reviews first made it possible for writers to survive by the pen alone. The relative lack of opportunity in book publishing, where American authors faced competition with pirated reprints of foreign works that cost publishers nothing in royalty payments, added to the appeal of periodical publication. Here, and here nearly alone, was a paying native market for native production.

With the rise of the magazines, writing began the shift from a casual amateur activity to a business in which one could forge a professional career, or at least imagine one. Willis found in the magazines a glittering vein and made a brilliant name for himself. Poe pursued magazine prospects as an editor and writer throughout his short life, but though his name was widely known and respected his financial return was meager. For the six-part series in *Godey's* he apparently received $5 a page, hardly munificent and far less than Willis's usual fees, but the total amount of $172 was one of his better sales as a writer.[4] It was money for which, as usual, he had a desperate need.

two

Poe had returned to New York in 1844 and joined the staff of the *Evening Mirror,* a daily newspaper that also published a weekly edition, the *Weekly Mirror.* In the latter he published articles on the literary marketplace and contemporary writers as well as "The Raven," his great popular success in verse. The following year he had gone as editor and part owner to the *Broadway Journal,* a new weekly started by Charles F. Briggs, a young writer who concentrated on New York life. The *Journal* gave Poe a vehicle for essays, reviews, and reprints of his published stories and poems, and in its pages he obsessively waged what became known as the "Longfellow War," a series of articles campaigning against plagiarism, with the respected poet as chief villain.

Poe also took up the cause of magazines against charges that they debased literary and intellectual taste. In fact, he argued, a golden age of American periodicals was at hand, with articles rapidly becoming one of the most influential forms of letters. Unlike the leisurely quarterlies of the past, the new magazines conveyed thoughts in a manner that fit with the rapid pace of contemporary life. Especially as they had developed in England and France, magazines offered writers a wide range of subjects and real artistic possibilities. In America, it was true, writers still were hindered by the "paltry prices offered them by our periodical publishers," with the result that native magazinists found themselves "behind the age in a *very* important branch of literature— a branch which, moreover, is daily growing in importance—and which, in the end (not far distant) will be the *most* influential of all the departments of Letters."[5]

The main reason American writers lagged behind their European counterparts was the lack of an international copyright law. American publishers were required to pay American writers for their books and articles but not foreign writers, with the result that new foreign works were rapidly pirated in cheap reprint editions ("we unblushingly," said Poe, "pick the pocket of all Europe")[6] and American authors put at a competitive disadvantage. Poe campaigned in the *Journal* for an international copyright law and aligned himself with other writers in the American Copyright Club, organized in New York in 1843 under the presidency of William Cullen Bryant, in resisting the self-serving view of publishers that literary piracy had the benefit of providing American readers with a vast flow of inexpensive reading matter.

Through a crisis in the *Journal's* financial affairs, Poe suddenly found himself its sole proprietor. It was a situation he had long coveted, a magazine of his own in which he could print the finest American writing while critically exposing all that was shabby and overvalued. But the shaky financial state of the paper and the pressing demands of personally handling all editorial, business, and printing matters came at time when his life was in greater turmoil than usual. Even his literary allies were alienated by the notoriety of the Longfellow War; Poe was ill and depressed and had returned to heavy drinking; his young wife was dying; he could barely scrape up enough money for food and rent. On January 3, 1846, some two months after he had achieved his dream of ownership, the *Broadway Journal* closed.

From the city Poe retreated with his family to the nearby village of Fordham, and here, despite his bleak circumstances, he managed to publish his tale "The Cask of Amontillado" in *Godey's* and to vent the frustration of his New York failure through the Literati sketches. The series was intended as an exposé in which, as Poe explained at the beginning, the public view of successful writers would be set against the view of "private literary society."[7] Hawthorne and Longfellow were cases in point. Scarcely noticed by the press or the public, Hawthorne was nonetheless held in high esteem by the literary world; Longfellow, on the other hand, was considered a "poetical phenomenon" by the public but by private literary society a "determined imitator and a dexterous adopter of the ideas of other people." Poe's sketches, through giving his own "unbiased opinion" in a seemingly detached manner, would disclose what had hitherto been held in private. The particular subject, New York writers, provided a representative sampling of American letters as a whole because of their numbers and influence on the rest of the country.

The printed sketches were brief, hasty, and reportorial, little more than Poe's description of them as critical gossip.[8] They were stitched together from a blend of tribute and attack, an occasion both for repaying personal debts with praise and for pricking inflated reputations, while continuing his jibes at

Longfellow and, Hawthorne excepted, at the New Englanders in general. Although the majority of Poe's notices were favorable, what attracted most attention were thumbnail portraits of the character and physique of each author. Here in particular Poe used the series to score hits on the New York literary scene from which he seemed cruelly excluded. Otherwise attractive, Margaret Fuller's visage is marred by the unfortunate fact that her "upper lip, as if impelled by the action of involuntary muscles, habitually uplifts itself, conveying the impression of a sneer." William Gillespie "walks irregularly, mutters to himself, and, in general, appears in a state of profound abstraction." Thomas Dunn English provides the pitiable spectacle of a man "without the commonest school education busying himself in attempts to instruct mankind on topics of polite literature." Charles Briggs, Poe's former partner on the *Broadway Journal,* "has never composed in his life three consecutive sentences of grammatical English. He is grossly uneducated."

As with Briggs and several other subjects of the sketches, Poe had a personal connection with Willis. When he joined the staff of the *Mirror* in 1844 its editors were George Pope Morris, a poet and popular song writer, and Willis, then at the height of his celebrity as an author and New York dandy. Poe and Willis had corresponded in the past, Poe had reviewed Willis's work, and the two writers had developed a genuine friendship. Poe's assignment on the journal was routine newsroom drudgery, and though he performed dutifully, Willis knew his friend's accomplishments as a writer and editor qualified him for higher station than a "mechanical paragraphist" with the task of "announcing news, condensing statements, answering correspondents, noticing amusements—everything but the writing of a 'leader,' or constructing any article upon which his peculiar idiosyncrasy of mind could be impressed."[9] But for Poe the regular salary of $15 a week was a necessity, and while he kept to his editorial work he was turning out hack journalism and popular fiction for the freelance market, netting himself an estimated $425 in 1844 as against Willis's probable annual freelance earnings in the same period of some $5,000. When he came to write his Literati sketch of Willis, Poe indirectly acknowledged the gap between their earnings with the opening remark that there was no doubt that Willis had "made a good deal of noise in the world—at least for an American."

Poe's explanation for Willis's success pointed to his friend's affinity for fashion and society rather than to an outstanding literary talent. This affinity, which Poe attributed to "physical temperament," accounted for two-thirds of Willis's success, with "mental ability" providing the rest. According to Poe, early in life Willis had realized that to forge ahead as a man of letters required more than a flow of words, so he had formed friendships with influential women, traveled, and involved himself in attention-getting quarrels. The result—whether calculated or simply the result of temperament—was that his personal renown "greatly advanced, if it did not altogether establish his literary fame." With Willis's success thus explained, and from a literary standpoint narrowly circumscribed, Poe went on to develop a brief but judicious view of his former employer.

Willis was best understood as a versatile magazinist—meaning that his "compositions have invariably the species of effect, with the brevity which the magazine demands." Particularly as the author of sketches of society, rather than of poems and stories, had Willis made his mark, though his play *Tortesa, the Usurer* ranked as the best yet written by an American. (In an article in the *Broadway Journal* the year before, Poe had ranked Willis with Hawthorne and William Gilmore Simms as the most important American authors of short tales.) In the form of the magazine sketch Willis could fully indulge a style that was naturally extravagant and given to the bizarre and the whimsical. The closing lines of Poe's account were devoted to Willis's appearance, which escaped the scalpel no better than that of the other Literati. Although tall and well formed and with an air of good society about him, "neither his nose nor his forehead can be defended; the latter would puzzle phrenology."

three

Neither Willis's career as a professional writer nor Poe's can be understood apart from the explosive rise of the periodical press in the first half of the nineteenth century. In the previous century, the field of play for writers had been largely confined to newspapers. Lacking the patronage and government sinecures that offered support to a professional writing class in England,[10] native authors had little choice but to turn to the topical writing favored by the press. The papers produced in most towns of New England and the Middle Atlantic states, modeled on the English press and closely tied to local political events, accepted communications from readers bent on getting a point across in newsprint rather than in the pamphlets and broadsides that had previously dominated public discourse. Soon the offerings of poets, essayists, and clergymen, all of them amateur scribblers, became familiar newspaper features, printed without remuneration from publishers since supply was plentiful.

A few writers attempted to earn a livelihood as professional men of letters through books of prose or verse and through newspaper and magazine ownership and editing—among them Joel Barlow, Philip Freneau, and Charles Brockden Brown—but the marketplace was small, publishers were little more than local job printers, advertising and distribution were difficult, and readers were still in thrall to printed matter imported from the mother country. Joseph Dennie's disenchanted view was that to become "an author by profession in America is a prospect of no more flattering promise than to publish among the Eskimos an essay on delicacy of taste or to found an academy of sciences in Lapland."[11]

Dennie's own career illustrates the hard fate of native writers in the colonial and revolutionary periods. Harvard educated and eager for literary laurels, he tried to cast his writing life in the mold of sophisticated English literary journalism. But as he grew bitterly aware, the American situation did not yet provide the necessary ground for a writing career, let alone one so narrowly focused. "Had not the *Revolution* happened," he wrote in a letter in 1800, the year before he founded a notable weekly journal of politics and literature, the *Port Folio,* in Philadelphia, "had I continued a subject to the King, had I been fortunately born in *England* or resided in the City of London for the last 7 years, my fame would have been enhanced; and as to fortune I feel a moral certainty that I should have acquired by my writings 3 or 4 thousand pounds. But in this *Republic* . . . what can men of liberality and letters expect but such polar icy treatment as I have experienced?"

A lively and acute critic well regarded by other writers, Dennie clung to the American scene, supporting himself through the practice of law and political jobs together with writing and editing, rather than transplant himself to the richer literary soil of England. He clung as well to a notion of writing as the domain of a privileged few. He viewed Benjamin Franklin as the dark architect of a new literary situation in which print culture was increasingly available and thus certain to be degraded. In *Poor Richard,* the almanac initiated by Franklin in 1733 that had made him famous throughout the colonies, as well as in other published writings, he addressed a common reader with a literary credo that held that good prose ought to be smooth, clear, and brief. In this, Dennie fulminated, Franklin "was the founder of that Grubstreet sect, who have professedly attempted to degrade literature to the level of vulgar capacities, and debase the polished and current language of books by the vile alloy of provincial idioms, and colloquial barbarisms, the shame of grammar and akin to any language rather than English."[12]

As far as the few fledgling magazines were concerned, there was hardly a "Grubstreet sect" in America as the eighteenth century drew to a close. Editors who wished to carry original work rather than reprints found it necessary to wheedle contributions from readers by decrying inexperience as a reason for not taking up the pen and by offering prizes for submissions. But change was underway, a path of opportunity beginning to appear for writers; literature was in the process of becoming, as Kenneth Silverman has noted, "if not yet a profession, professionalized."[13] New magazines had sprung up; native-born writers were gaining notice both at home and abroad; and local copyright laws were enacted to protect authors' rights, with the Federal Copyright Act following in 1790.

The heroic figures of the Revolution also offered possibilities for support and patronage hitherto lacking in the country. Washington's name on a new magazine's subscription list or invoked in the dedication of a volume of verse gave immediate credibility. The *American Museum* of Philadelphia, perhaps the best general periodical in the country before 1800, boasted Franklin, Hamilton, Madison, and Jefferson as well as Washington on its list of subscribers, and at the end of each volume of six issues printed its entire subscription list. The publisher, Mathew Carey, also developed a flourishing book printing and selling business, with Parson Weems, one of his most zealous road agents, concocting for the firm popular biographies of William Penn, Franklin, and Washington.

With the new century and larger urban audiences, magazines rapidly increased in number—from a dozen in 1800 to nearly a hundred by 1825 and about six hundred by midcentury. Although unsystematically and often grudgingly, postmasters about the country now accepted magazines for transport through the mail, and with improvements in roads, postal routes were lengthened and service improved. Contributions of prose and poetry grew to be common but payment remained rare. In his history of American magazines Frank Luther Mott cites as an early example of payment the *Christian Spectator's* proposal in 1819 to "allow a compensation" to its contributors at the rate of a dollar a page. When the *Atlantic Magazine* was founded in 1824 it promised payment but the editor felt the need to urge its gentlemen-authors to "accept their honorarium for the principle of the thing. . . . As to false delicacy, we will obviate its scruples by forwarding every contributor's dues to any address given in his communication."[14] Editors themselves usually worked without salaries and depended for whatever payment they received on the financial health of their periodicals. Like writing, editing was typically an occasional endeavor rather than a full-time career.

In the period before 1825 the circulation of magazines remained small and essentially local, with contributions coming largely from local writers. Franklin's Philadelphia, the new nation's cultural hub, was also its magazine center. Among its several periodicals was the *Saturday Evening Post*, founded in 1821, and the first general magazine in the country to achieve enduring life. But New York, already twice Philadelphia's size, was hot on its literary heels, attracting most of the country's new mass-market book publishing, including the dominant House of Harper founded in 1817. Six years later, in 1823, two young poets, George Pope Morris and Samuel Woodworth, founded the *New York Mirror*, a central publication in the development of professional writing in the country. With several permutations, the *Mirror* would continue to publish almost until the advent of the Civil War.

Distinctively printed and illustrated, the weekly journal featured verse, original tales, biography, reviews, and light but revealing commentary on urban taste and fashion. Its editorial fare was slanted to home-grown American material and especially to the interests of women, the latter concern highlighted in its subtitle, "Ladies' Literary Gazette." Circulation figures are uncertain but by 1836 the *Mirror* claimed that it was paying out over $5,000 a year to contributors while accepting "not one communication in fifty" of those submitted for publication.[15] Morris also claimed, erroneously, the invention of the literary prize with the offer of cash amounts to aspiring poets, essayists, and fiction writers. Among those who sought a $20 prize for verse was a student at Yale, Nathaniel Parker Willis.

four

Willis came from a background of New England journalism.[16] His grandfather had been part owner of the *Independent Chronicle* in Boston and following the Revolution had founded a string of papers in Virginia and Ohio. His father began a successful religious newspaper in Boston in 1816, the *Recorder*, and later developed the *Youth's Companion*, a long-running paper for children that combined religion and adventure. After Andover and Yale, Willis carried on the family tradition by founding the *American Monthly Magazine* in Boston in 1829. Only twenty-three years old, handsome, charming, elegantly attired, he was already known for his periodical writing and had a published collection of verse behind him.

A literary miscellany, the magazine was witty, relaxed, and marked by bright writing. A good deal of each issue was turned out by Willis himself and included such light-hearted pieces as "The Philosophy of a Cigar" as well as descriptive travel sketches, modeled on Irving's popular *Sketch Book*, that eventually would become his primary stock-in-trade as a writer. Under the headings "Notes Upon a Ramble" and "Pencillings by the Way" Willis gave leisurely accounts of journeys up the St. Lawrence and to Montreal that were marked by a bemused tone, an observant eye, and—in the opinion of unamused critics—the self-conscious posturing of a stylish dilettante. Literary criticism occupied much of Willis's attention under the heading "The Editor's Table," with most of the coverage given over to verse. Here as well his approach was light, chatty, and intimate, the reader invited into an imagined study of baroque elegance and directly addressed: "We welcome you to our Table, for another year, dear Reader. It is pleasant to find ourselves here—the mahogany still spread for your entertainment. . . ."[17]

Willis could be cutting, however, in his criticism. When the young Poe submitted a poem from Baltimore called "Fairyland," the editor publicly committed it to the metaphorical fire of his disapproval: "It is quite exciting to lean over eagerly as the flame eats in upon the letters, and make out the imperfect sentences and trace the faint strokes in the tinder as it trembles in the ascending air of the chimney. There, for instance, goes a gilt-edged sheet which we remember was covered with some sickly rhymes on Fairyland."[18] (Public response to magazine submissions was common at the time, as noted in the following chapter. In the days before self-addressed stamped envelopes, publications ran "To Our Correspondents" columns as a way of indicating acceptance or rejection and offering editorial comment. Earlier in 1829 the editor of a Maine journal called the *Yankee and Boston Literary Gazette,* John Neal, a productive magazinist himself, had encouraged Poe by praising the poem—then entitled "Heaven"—of "E.A.P. of Baltimore" in his correspondents column as potentially magnificent. Poe later called the remark the "first jog in my literary career.")[19] For magazine nonfiction Willis called on contributors for prose that was "brief and crisp"—rarely his own manner, as the editorial comment on Poe's poem shows. Writers were told to be "dashing *in medias res* at the first sentence" and to "sink rhetoric. Nobody cares how you came to think of your subject, or why you wrote upon it. . . . Commence with your leading thought and avoid irrelevant digressions. You may be less scholastic, but you will be more original and ten times as amusing."[20]

Not surprisingly, the *American Monthly's* easygoing ways and worldly air did not sit well with sober Bostonians, and after two and a half years Willis gave up as proprietor and moved to New York as associate editor of the *Mir-*

ror. He left behind, a biographer notes, a legacy of lively writing, "the cackle of the tea-tables," and debts from the magazine of some $3,000.[21] Willis would maintain a connection with the *Mirror* (and its successors under various names) until his death in 1867.

Within a month of joining the paper Willis was off to Europe to continue his "Pencillings" letters with $500 in cash and George Pope Morris's promise of $10 for each published letter. For nearly five years he wandered the continent and the Near East, having adventures, cutting a dazzling social swath, all the while sending back chatty accounts to the *Mirror* that were swiftly copied in newspapers around the country. Part of the appeal of his letters was that he brought news of distant places at a time when little was available. Eventually collected in book form in such volumes as *Pencillings by the Way* (1835), *Inklings of Adventure* (1836), and *Loiterings of Travel* (1840), the work proved as popular as it had in the *Mirror.* Willis claimed that the latter book, for which he had received $500 when the sketches appeared in the *Mirror,* eventually netted him some $5,000 in its several editions. Largely through the intimate and impressionistic travel-essay form, together with the verse he continued to write and publish and his knack for self-promotion, Willis soon joined company with Irving and Cooper as celebrated American authors abroad.

The literary persona he casually shaped in his work had, however, little regard for either money or literary distinction—or for the labor of ordinary journalism. As he later styled them, his travel pieces were no more than "notes written on the road, and despatched [*sic*] without a second perusal."[22] When a London paper offered him $1,000 a year as a war correspondent he declined on the grounds that he "would much rather write about pictures and green fields."[23] In a letter from Florence during his early days in Europe he exulted in the style of life possible on his meager and undependable paychecks from America: a room for three dollars a month, breakfast for six cents, a meal with wine at a fashionable restaurant for twenty-five cents. "Three hundred dollars a year," he concluded, "would fairly and largely cover the expenses of a man living at this rate; and a man who would not be willing to live half as well for the sake of his art, does not deserve to see Italy."[24]

When he settled in London in 1834 his financial fortunes began to climb, responding to the stimulus of his polished social skills. "What a star is mine!" he gushed to his family in America. "All the best society of London exclusives is now open to me—*me!* a sometime apprentice at setting types—*me!* without a sou in the world beyond what my pen brings me, and with not only no influence from friends at home, but a world of envy and slander at my back.

Thank heaven, there is not a countryman of mine, except Washington Irving, who has even the standing in England which I have got in *three days* only."[25] The envy and slander at his back was a reference to the heat generated both in England and America by some of Willis's letters that touched on the indiscretions of English society in what seemed ungentlemanly fashion. The problems arose, a critic has suggested, from readers inclined to take Willis too seriously.[26] Whatever the explanation, and however pained Willis might have been, the effect of the critical attacks was to increase the popularity of his work in the *Mirror* and open the way into English periodicals for light fictional tales and travel sketches of the American scene under the pen name Philip Slingsby.

Willis's entry into London society was guided by Lady Blessington, whom he in turn sketched in characteristic fashion in his letters back to America. "She looks something on the sunny side of thirty," he wrote, even though she frankly confessed to forty. "Her person is full, but preserves all the fineness of an admirable shape." His explanation for a portrait that, however flattering, might appear an abuse of her hospitality was that the English, unlike the Americans, paid no attention to periodicals from across the Atlantic, so there could be "no offence to the individuals themselves in anything which a visitor could write, calculated to convey an idea of the person or manners of distinguished people to the American public."[27] In a sketch called, in its publication in book form, "The Literati of London"—a model perhaps for Poe's later New York series—Willis turned his descriptive eye on a group of writers gathered in a literary soiree in Lady Blessington's home. Bulwer-Lytton is set down as "slight and very badly put together, and the only commendable point in his person, as far as I could see, was the smallest foot I ever saw a man stand upon." Willis claimed to despair, however, of ever capturing the witty talk of the gathering in a "letter scrawled literally, between the end of a late visit and a tempting pillow."[28]

By the time Willis and his English wife left for America in 1836 he was among the most visible writers of the day. He hoped to make a permanent return to England but instead branched out within the American scene into play writing while traveling and writing for the *Mirror,* placing his articles, verse, and fictional tales in the popular periodicals of the time, reprinting his work in book form, and working as a *Mirror* editor. After a brief period of separation from Morris to become co-owner of the *Corsair,* a magazine devoted to reprinted English articles, the two again joined company on the *New Mirror* and later on the popular *Home Journal.* Criticism of the high style of

Willis's personal manner and the fluffy nature of his work continued apace. When Poe joined the staff of the *Mirror*, a rival New York magazine, the *Town*, looked forward to seeing the "columns of that paper relieved of much of the Miss Nancyism of Willis, and a more manly vigor infused into them."[29]

About Willis's stature as a professional writer there was never a question. His freelance magazine articles now commanded fees of up to $100, and by the early 1840s he was placing four such articles a month in different publications. To be seen in rough perspective, Willis's earnings must he set against the $300 that, a decade earlier, he claimed would have seen him through a year in Florence—or the $140 to $210 that Yale College estimated as an undergraduate's annual expense in 1843.[30] A biographer concludes that "Willis was at this time, beyond a doubt, the most popular, best paid, and in every way most successful magazinist that America had yet seen. He commanded the sympathy of his readers more than any other periodical writer of his day, and his reputation almost amounted to fame."[31]

Willis himself remained unconfused about the meaning of his success. Especially during his sojourn abroad he had discovered in the quick impressions and personal voice of the travel sketch an effective manner for his work, and in English and American periodicals he found a ready market; it was a writing situation he readily exploited for the rest of his career. He made no claims to artistic importance; his writing was of the moment and for the moment. Its only "extraneous value," he commented in a candid preface to an 1851 collection of his *Home Journal* articles called *Hurry-Graphs*, lay in the fact that it was "one man's imprint from parts of the world's doing at one place and time." The value of his work resided wholly in its quality as "hurry-graphs from life as it went by."[32]

After his death Willis's name quickly dipped in importance. As early as 1880 Charles T. Congdon, a newspaperman who was acquainted with him, could remark that "I do not think of any man so well known in his time, and now so utterly forgotten, as Mr. N. P. Willis." If his material as a magazine journalist had been equal to his writing style, Congdon thought Willis would have found lasting fame equal to Addison or Irving; instead he had devoted himself to such ephemeral subjects as "hats and coats, parties and receptions, and all manner of fashionable tweedledum and tweedledee." What was left to praise about Willis's lengthy career was an airy manner as a writer that Congdon thought had helped "correct the somewhat savage and coarse style of the prevailing journalism of his period."[33]

five

Poe was thinking of Willis primarily as a poet when in 1844 he offered James Russell Lowell his private view of the writer who would become his employer on the *Mirror* before the year was out. A flowery article about Willis had just appeared in *Graham's Magazine*, one in a continuing series of portraits of the magazine's contributors, each accompanied by a steel engraving of the author. Poe informed Lowell that the article was full of hyperbole: "Willis is *no* genius—a graceful trifler—no more. He wants force & sincerity. He is very frequently far fetched. In me, at least, he never excites an emotion."[34] When he came to write his Literati series Poe would give Willis full credit only as a magazinist, and especially as a "sketcher." The form allowed Willis to inject his personal character into his work, to indulge in fancy, and this in turn lent the work an edge of originality and freshness. As a sketcher, Poe concluded, Willis was simply unequaled.

Poe's own work could hardly have been more different. He excelled where he found Willis lacking, as a poet, fiction writer, and critic, and the qualities of his best work were uniquely those of force and sincerity. He endures as a significant figure in modern literature, one who, as Allen Tate remarked, "discovered our great subject, the disintegration of personality."[35] Nor could the two have been more different as character types—one a cultivated and secure social dandy, the other seething, tormented, an aggrieved outsider. Where they joined was in the need to make their way as writers amid a panoply of opportunities in the first flowering of American periodicals. Ambition and achievement in *belles lettres* aside, both were practical, market-wise magazinists who toiled "under whip and spur," as Willis said of himself, complaining of being "obliged to turn to account every trumpery thought I can lay my wits to."[36]

Like Willis, Poe was a seasoned professional when the two briefly joined company on the *Mirror* in 1844. Although he had already published stories and poems in magazines, his breakthrough as a writer had come in 1833 when the tale "MS. Found in a Bottle" received a first prize of $50 in a contest sponsored by a Baltimore newspaper, the *Saturday Visiter* [sic]. The year following, a tale of double suicide, "The Visionary," appeared anonymously in *Godey's*, his first publication in a national magazine.[37] In that same year a Richmond, Virginia, printer, Thomas Willis White, was inspired by the new popularity of magazines to launch the *Southern Literary Messenger*, a regional publication meant to revive Southern culture. Almost at once White and Poe entered into

a correspondence in which Poe, writing from Baltimore through the inter-
vention of the novelist John Pendleton Kennedy, offered advice for improving
the magazine, a matter on which he had no experience but an already well-
formed sense of what the reading public wanted. With the seventh issue of the
magazine Poe began contributing tales and reviews, and when White suggested an editorial position Poe was quick to indicate his interest "were the
salary even the merest trifle."[38]

When he joined the *Messenger* in 1835 as an assistant to White it was for
$60 a month. He took on the usual chores of an editor—revising copy, check-
ing proof, selecting type faces, dealing with authors—while writing his own
tales, reviews, and editorial comments. One of the more ticklish aspects of the
job was rejecting manuscripts from writers who were friends. An artfully
worded letter to John Collins McCabe, a Richmond minister and poet, suggests the tact Poe was able to muster for the task: "I need not speak to you of
the difficulties I have to encounter daily in selecting from the mass of MSS.
handed in for the *Messenger*. Personal applications from personal friends of
course embarrass me greatly. It is indeed almost impossible to refuse an article offered in this manner without giving mortal offence to the friend who
offers it. This offence, however, is most frequently taken by those who have
the fewest pretensions of merit. In the present instance I feel perfectly sure
that I shall neither wound your feelings nor cause you to think less of me as
an acquaintance by returning your poem—which I now enclose."[39]

Although it meant neglect of his own writing, through work on the *Messenger* Poe made a significant entry into the new world of magazines. He not
only learned the editorial and financial aspects of the business but through
correspondence made contact with some of the leading writers of the day. His
most important contribution to the magazine was to expand its critical department, much of the material for which he probably wrote himself. From
Blackwood's and other English magazines he drew on the example of acerbic
reviewing, soon developing a reputation as a fearsome commentator with
high principles. He excoriated writers for grammatical errors and slovenly
prose, matters for which he had a proofreader's eagle eye, and reveled in punc-
turing inflated reputations and spying the puffing system at work. About a
novel praised in New York's *Mirror*, whose author also happened to be one of
its editors, he snapped: "Well!—here we have it! This is *the* book—the book
par excellence—the book bepuffed, beplastered, and be-*Mirrored*."[40] His cut-
and-slash critical style had the effect, as Poe was well aware, of drawing attention to himself; when his reviews brought outraged rejoinders in other

publications, he responded in print, thereby adding to the public fuss. On the *Messenger* he not only learned the magazine business but also how a writer could use the new magazine world to advance his own name—a lesson in self-advertisement that Willis was applying at the same time through his gossipy travel letters from abroad.

Poe proved himself a capable editor on the *Messenger* and was largely responsible for its solid reputation. He later claimed that during his editorial stint subscriptions climbed from fewer than a thousand to some five thousand. His dealings with White were less successful, and in the January 1837 issue the proprietor announced that his editor had retired. The circumstances of Poe's departure are not entirely clear but may have involved White's wish to reclaim the magazine and free himself from the controversies generated by his editor's critical attacks.

Ahead for Poe was a painful period of trying to scratch out a living through literary hackwork, first in New York and then Philadelphia. Although his only book-length work of fiction was published at the time, the novella *The Narrative of Arthur Gordon Pym,* he was soon casting about for a career other than writing and editing. Even a low-level political clerkship seemed better than, as he put it in a letter, "the miserable life of literary drudgery to which I now, with a breaking heart, submit, and for which neither my temper nor my abilities have fitted me."[41] He continued, nonetheless, to peddle his work on a freelance basis. One of the markets that opened up for him was a new Baltimore magazine edited by two of his friends, the *American Museum of Science, Literature and the Arts.* But when the chance came for a small regular income for editorial work on a Philadelphia magazine, *Burton's Gentleman's Magazine,* he eagerly took the position. A biographer estimates that in the two and a half years between leaving the *Messenger* and joining *Burton's* Poe probably earned less than $150 by his pen.[42] At *Burton's* he received $10 a week with modest additional sums for tales and poems, allowing him to set up a household for his young wife, now seventeen, and her mother but not enough to free him from borrowing and furious freelance writing to make ends meet.

Philadelphia in 1839 was rivaled only by New York as a magnet for writers. It supported several daily and weekly newspapers as well as periodicals, and it was the home of the publishing firm of Carey and Lea that had earned a reputation by publishing American authors. For the magazine founded by William E. Burton, a one-time English actor turned entrepreneur, Poe plunged into another round of editorial chores that included soliciting contributions, reading proof, and tossing off articles that ranged from an account of Stonehenge (drawn nearly exactly from an encyclopedia, his always dependable source book) to "The Philosophy of Furniture," a discourse on American interior decoration. When Willis's play *Tortesa, the Usurer* opened in Philadelphia, Poe reviewed it favorably both in the magazine and in a new Pittsburgh journal, the *Literary Examiner*. Two of his stories, later to be ranked among his finest, also appeared in *Burton's*, "The Fall of the House of Usher" and "William Wilson." But it was his many book reviews for the magazine, and especially his penchant for cutting comment, that captured most attention—and also launched a bitter quarrel with Burton that led to Poe leaving his assistant editor's job after a single year.

What followed was an ambitious plan for a literary monthly of his own, the *Penn Magazine*. Poe tried to round up support for the venture from leading writers of the day, in so doing lecturing them on magazines as an appropriate vehicle for their work. "I need not call your attention," Irving was told in a letter, "to the signs of the times in respect to Magazine literature. You will admit the tendency of the age in this direction. The brief, the terse, the condensed, and the easily circulated will take place of the diffuse, the ponderous, and the inaccessible. Even our Reviews are found too massive for the taste of the day—I do not mean for the taste of the merely uneducated, but also for that of the few. In the meantime the finest minds of Europe are beginning to lend their spirit to Magazines."[43] When his hopes for the *Penn Magazine* were dashed for lack of capital and an economic downturn in the country, he again put on the editorial harness, this time with *Graham's Magazine*. A young Philadelphia lawyer with a passion for magazines, George Rex Graham formed the periodical in 1841 by merging a magazine called the *Casket* with *Burton's*. The new publication, an illustrated monthly featuring light literary fare and directed largely at women, proved immediately popular, circulation soaring within a year from five thousand to twenty-five thousand. In addition to the high-quality engravings, an important factor in the magazine's success was a generous pay scale for contributions that attracted the notable writers of the time.

Willis, one of its star authors, would later remark that "the burst on author-land of Graham's and Godey's liberal prices was like a sunrise without a dawn."[44] *Graham's* had no fixed rate for contributions but paid roughly $4 to $12 a page for prose (with the magazine's typical page holding about a thousand words—a standard of measurement, called the "*Graham* page," eventually adopted by other publications) and $10 to $50 for a poem. This meant that an article of five thousand words received from $20 to $60—attractive amounts given the time's cost of living. George Graham often trumpeted his liberality within the pages of the magazine as a way of catching the attention of authors. He announced in 1853, for example, that he had paid out to authors some $1,500 for a single issue, "more than twice the sum that has ever been paid by any other magazine in America; while for years our minimum rate of cost, in relationship to the item of authorship alone, was eight hundred dollars per number." The figures were no doubt inflated, but in his payments to writers Graham could fairly claim to have "introduced a new era into magazine history."[45]

When Poe joined the magazine in February 1841 he had been unemployed for some eight months after leaving *Burton's*—yet his literary reputation had never been stronger. A collection of twenty-five tales had been published in 1839 by the Philadelphia firm of Lea and Blanchard as *Tales of the Grotesque and Arabesque*, bringing him no money (payment was in copies) but drawing critical praise around the country. Poe both savored the reviews and, as was his wont, shrewdly publicized them with anonymous magazine plugs for the work of "Mr. Poe." His connection with *Graham's* could with accuracy be announced by the magazine with the editorial notice that "Mr. POE is too well known in the literary world to require a word of commendation." It was for the critical department, however, that the magazine had sought him out, and the announcement continued: "As a critic he is surpassed by no man in the country; and as in this Magazine his critical abilities shall have free scope, the rod will be very generously, and at the same time, justly administered."[46]

As a magazine *Graham's* held out no more appeal to Poe than would *Godey's* when it eventually carried his Literati sketches. It was another "namby-pamby" publication, as he would come to describe it, made up of "contemptible pictures, fashion-plates, music and love tales."[47] But he needed the salary of $800 a year and he liked Graham, whom he considered a gentleman and an able businessman who might prove helpful with the *Penn Magazine*, a scheme he hoped was only temporarily "scotched, not killed."[48]

Poe's editorial role with *Graham's* was limited to checking proofs and writing reviews, the latter managed in his typically fierce manner. To the magazine he also contributed critical articles that provided standards for literary judgment while carrying on his campaign of sorting out the genuine from the dross in American writing. He carried on, too, as a self-professed master of cryptograms sent in to the magazine, challenging all comers to defeat his powers of decoding.[49] Perhaps his most important work for the magazine, certainly the area in which he was most prolific, was fiction. Nearly once a month a Poe tale appeared in *Graham's*, among the series "The Murders in the Rue Morgue," his path-breaking story of locked-room murder and brilliant detection. The first of his "tales of ratiocination" was exactly what he would later term it, "something in a new key," opening the way to the most popular of literary genres and leaving future generations of mystery writers in his debt. Although he well understood the novelty of what he had done, Poe downplayed the demands the new genre placed on the writer. He said in a letter: "I do not mean to say that they [the tales of ratiocination] are not ingenious— but people think them more ingenious than they are—on account of their method and *air* of method. In the 'Murders in the Rue Morgue', for instance, where is the ingenuity of unravelling a web which you yourself (the author) have woven for the express purpose of unravelling? The reader is made to confound the ingenuity of the supposititious Dupin [the story's masterful detective] with that of the writer of the story."[50]

Graham's flourished during Poe's time with the magazine, circulation rising to some forty thousand copies a month, and Poe flourished as well. For prose pieces in the magazine he received $4 to $5 a page in addition to his regular salary, which meant that financially he was doing better than ever before. His reputation as a critic and imaginative writer was also at a new high. Still, he chafed under *Graham's* light yoke. He received less for his freelance work for the magazine than did such contributors as Lowell, Cooper, and Willis, and he felt his regular salary should have been higher given the magazine's rapid success. There was also a grating sense of the insipid character of the publication and the fact that, at the owner's urging, he had to modify some of his critical comments. He continued to search for some steady employment that was, as he put it, "independent of letters for a subsistence." Although he now had a significant background as an editor with the *Messenger, Burton's,* and *Graham's,* the fact remained that "to coin one's brain into silver, at the nod of a master, is to my thinking, the hardest task in the world."[51]

After some thirteen months on the staff—slightly extending his usual time limit of a year in editorial harness—Poe resigned from *Graham's* in April 1842. The hope of a magazine of his own was resurrected but with a new name free of local connotation, the *Stylus*. According to a prospectus printed early in 1843, the magazine would surpass all American literary journals, seeking out the best writing talent available and with an editorial policy guided by the highest principles of art. While Poe pursued financial support for his dream venture and struggled unsuccessfully to find a book market for his tales, he continued as a freelance contributor to *Graham's* and other periodicals. His work appeared alongside that of such prominent magazinists as John Neal, T. S. Arthur, Lydia H. Sigourney, William Gilmore Simms, and the indefatigable Willis. One important success that came his way was a $100 first prize for his tale "The Gold-Bug" in a contest sponsored by the *Dollar Newspaper,* a new weekly published in Philadelphia. Quickly pirated by other papers and widely circulated, the story added to Poe's reputation as a writer with a popular touch as well as a fearsome and learned critic.

The story was among the thirty-one Poe would manage to publish during his productive six-year stay in Philadelphia. But by the end of the period he was without regular employment, his wife's health was in sharp decline, he was drinking heavily, and his attention was fragmented by personal and literary feuds as well as his various publishing projects. His income from writing during his last full year in the city, 1843, may have been little more than $250. In March 1844 he had a streak of good luck with tales and reviews sold to *Godey's, Graham's,* and the *Dollar Newspaper* for a total of $100. Yet in the following month he and his wife abruptly put Philadelphia behind them in a second attempt to storm the gates of literary New York.

six

Before joining Morris and Willis as a sub-editor and critic on the staff of the *Evening Mirror* in October 1844, Poe churned out a steady stream of journalistic hackwork and recycled earlier publications. Among other pursuits, he became the New York correspondent for the *Columbia Spy,* a Pennsylvania newspaper, sending in letters on urban life, and to the *New York Sun* he contributed an anonymous page-one hoax—for the sum of $50—on a crossing of the Atlantic by balloon in three days. At the same time he continued to contribute to *Godey's* and *Graham's* and took up literary lecturing as a way of adding to his income.

Lambert Wilmer, a journalist and poet who was acquainted with Poe in Baltimore and Philadelphia, thought him one of the hardest-working men in the world, visiting him at various hours and regularly finding him at his desk.[52] Mornings were his usual time for composition, but he went on to late afternoon if necessary, then would wind down with reading, long walks, and, if living in the country, garden work. F. O. C. Darley, to whom read Poe read "The Gold-Bug" before it was published, recalled that "the form of his manuscript was peculiar: he wrote on half sheets of note paper, which he pasted together at the ends, making one continuous piece, which he rolled up tightly. As he read he dropped it upon the floor. It was very neatly written, and without corrections, apparently."[53]

With the *Mirror* Poe was back in editorial harness, this time in the even less congenial setting of a newspaper and with his duties limited, as Willis put it, to the drudgery of a mechanical paragraphist. There was the further ignominy of having his contributions to the paper (among the first was an account of "The Swiss Bell-ringers" with the suggestion that the popular performers were actually automatons) go unsigned. Clearly the paper was a step down for someone of Poe's stature as an editor and writer, but the minuscule monthly salary it paid was sorely needed to fill out a yearly income in 1844 that, despite a considerable writing output, amounted only to some $425.

For good reason Poe felt intensely at this stage of his life the tension between Grub Street scribbling for money and serious literary work for fame that marked his entire career. He had been reduced to publishing articles and occasional tales rather than books, he noted in a rambling letter, leaving himself "so far essentially a Magazinist" who had to accept as his return the poverty and others ills "which the condition of the mere Magazinist entails upon him in America . . . where more than in any other region upon the face of the globe to be poor is to be despised." As for his overall reputation, as a writer of ephemeral pieces he was necessarily judged by them individually unless they could be collected in book form (a project he was urging in the letter), with the consequence that his work was easily misjudged and its versatility—its serious together with lighter purposes—went unappreciated.[54]

Yet just at this low moment, as he plunged all the more commitedly into Grub Street with his pursuit of the Longfellow War in the *Mirror* and his brief involvement with the *Broadway Journal* as an editor and proprietor, both his popular and literary reputation began to climb. "The Raven" attracted widespread notice and the tale "William Wilson" was published in translation in a Paris newspaper, his first appearance in a foreign language and the start of his serious literary standing in France. Of major importance was a laudatory account of Poe's career written by James Russell Lowell and published in *Graham's* in the February 1845 issue, part of the magazine's series on contributors that had earlier featured Willis. Lowell emphasized the breadth of Poe's achievement as a poet, fiction writer, critic, and magazinist, noting that "among contemporary authors . . . we know of *none* who has displayed more varied and striking abilities." He added that through his pen Poe "has squared out blocks enough to build an enduring pyramid," but because of the nature of much of his work, written for magazines and often without credit, he "has left them lying carelessly and unclaimed in many different quarries."[55] Lowell helped lift the veil by revealing Poe as the author of such anonymous pieces as the balloon hoax and listing thirty stories written since the publication of *Tales of the Grotesque and Arabesque.*

Lowell's article was given further currency when the *Evening Mirror* reprinted it in two front-page installments. In an editorial comment Willis trumpeted the article as a "broad and honest appreciation," and added that a New York publisher ought to found a high-minded critical review and install Poe as editor. "Such a wheel of literature," he went on, "should not be without axle and linch-pin."[56] But except for his brief control of the *Broadway Journal,* this was Poe's fate for the remaining four years of his life. He continued to plan and promote the *Stylus* but nothing materialized. And he continued to work with furious if sporadic industry at the writing trade. "I put so many irons in the fire all at once," he noted in a letter soon after leaving the *Mirror* for the *Journal,* "that I have been quite unable to get them out. For the last three or four months I have been working 14 or 15 hours a day—hard at it all the time." Yet money did not follow. He was "as poor now as ever I was in my life—except in hope, which is by no means bankable."[57] Ironically, his best payday in the period following the collapse of the *Journal* came when he won a judgment for $225 in a libel case brought against the *Evening Mirror* (Willis and Morris now departed for another newspaper venture) for carrying Thomas Dunn English's vitriolic response to Poe's sketch of him in the Literati series.

At the time of his death in Baltimore in October 1849 Poe was still drumming up support for his magazine and still hiring out as a writer. He accepted without hesitation an offer of $100 from a Philadelphia piano manufacturer to edit an edition of his wife's poems. And he was regularly sending off work to a New England weekly, the *Flag of Our Union,* produced by the enterprising duo of Frederick Gleason and Maturin M. Ballou, leading figures (as noted in a subsequent chapter) in the development of popular story papers. He wrote for the paper only out of sheer necessity, he informed Willis in a letter, though it paid well for the times ($5 a *Graham* page), "for whatever I send it I feel I am consigning to the tomb of the Capulets."[58]

seven

Included in the letter to Willis was a poem previously sent to the *Flag of Our Union* that Poe was hoping would be reprinted in the *Home Journal*, the publication Willis was now co-editing in New York, and so given greater circulation. On April 28, 1848, "For Annie" appeared in the *Journal* with a prefatory comment by Willis that both praised the poem and implicitly offered a general view of Poe's career: "Money (to tell a useless truth) could not be better laid out for the honor of this period of American literature—neither by the government, by a society, nor by an individual—than in giving EDGAR POE a competent annuity, on condition that he should never write except upon impulse, never dilute his thoughts for the magazines, and never publish any thing till it had been written a year."[59] Essentially the same point, minus the suggestion of patronage, was made in a sympathetic article in the *Home Journal* shortly after Poe's death when Willis recalled that his friend had written "with fastidious difficulty, and in a style too much above the popular level to be well paid."[60]

The conception of Poe as a literary mandarin who lacked a natural feeling for the new mass-circulation periodical world of his day surfaced often during his career. Rejecting a collection of his tales in 1836, Harper and Brothers had maintained that "the papers are too learned and mystical. They would be understood and relished only by a very few—not by the multitude."[61] In a sympathetic article in *Graham's* after Poe's death, George Graham made the same point about Poe's elevated manner as a writer: "The character of Poe's mind was of such an order, as not to be very widely in demand. The class of educated mind which he could readily and profitably address, was small—the channels through which he could do so at all, were few—and publishers all, or nearly all, contented with such pens as were already engaged, hesitated to incur the expense of his to an extent which would sufficiently remunerate him."[62]

Present-day critics still ponder Poe's position as a serious writer caught up in the whirlwind of popular magazine journalism.[63] Certainly the conflict between the ambition to gain recognition as a serious author and the need to earn a living by writing for a mass audience raged with more anguish within Poe than Willis. In his work Poe often paraded his erudition, both real and affected, and placed himself on the high ground of superior intelligence, qualities hardly intended to endear him to common readers. It may also be true that a disdain for his Grub Street hackwork deeply colored his literary views, especially as he formulated plans for a magazine of his own that would uphold the highest aesthetic standards and address the "aristocracy of talent."[64] Yet as he conceived it such an ideal magazine would retain some of the qualities of popular periodicals. It would aim, as he pointed out in a letter, "to elevate without stupefying our literature—to further justice—to resist foreign dictation—and to afford . . . a remuneration to ourselves for whatever we should write."[65]

Whatever his resistance to Grub Street, Poe took pride—as did Willis—in his versatility as a writer that included a knack for stories, poems, criticism, and nonfiction pieces in a popular vein. And, as Edmund Wilson once pointed out, Poe had enough of a popular touch that he "succeeded in selling almost all he wrote to the insipid periodicals of his day."[66] In a sense Poe had no choice, given the time's climate of publication, but to work as a popular writer if he was to make his way with his pen. His financial reward remained minuscule—perhaps no more than $6,200 for his entire career as a writer, magazine editor, and literary lecturer, or somewhat more than Willis earned in a single good year. In this regard Daniel Hoffman's remark that Poe "led the most luckless life of any writer" surely rings true.[67] Nonetheless, he had his successes with the commercial editors and mass audience of his day. Although he longed for freedom from what, in a satirical article in the *Broadway Journal* in 1845, he called the prison-house of magazine writing—and no doubt would have eagerly grasped the competent annuity that Willis called for had one come his way—the new world of magazines in the 1830s and 1840s opened the way for him as a writer and he never escaped its siren song. His serious writing was mingled with hackwork, a highly personal and idiosyncratic literary manner with common speech—a mixture that linked Poe with Willis as one of the most experienced, versatile, and visible writers of the first period of magazinists. It could also be said of him—though never to the same degree and leaving out of account the inner turmoil it may have cost him—what Charles T. Congdon said of Willis's career as a professional writer: "Mr. Willis had in a large measure that best faculty of a journalist: he knew what people would like to read."[68]

In a brief comment about magazines in *Graham's* in 1846 Poe gave every indication that he not only accepted the role of a writer whose work was frequently directed to what he called the "light artillery of the intellect" but actually relished it. The comment appeared in a series of short pieces called "Marginalia" he had inaugurated two years earlier in the *Democratic Review* and presented to readers as jottings in the volumes of his personal library. It was, of course, sheer fiction: in his impoverished condition he possessed little that could be called a library, and many of his reflections were lifted from his own reviews or the work of others. It was a typical scheme of a writer for hire scratching for ways to produce income, yet here and there in the series Poe's remarks were fresh and revealing.[69] "The whole tendency of the age is Magazine-ward," he declared with an enthusiasm that fully embraced the new popular periodicals and their popular authors:

> The Quarterly Reviews have *never* been popular. Not only are they too stilted, (by way of keeping up a due dignity,) but they make a point, with the same end in view, of discussing only topics which are *caviare* to the many, and which, for the most part, have only a conventional interest even with the few. Their issues, also, are at too long intervals; their subjects get cold before being served up. In a word, their ponderosity is quite out of keeping with the *rush* of the age. We now demand the light artillery of the intellect; we need the curt, the condensed, the pointed, the readily diffused—in place of the verbose, the detailed, the voluminous, the inaccessible. . . . The bulk and the period of issue of the monthly magazines, seem to be precisely adapted, if not to all the literary wants of the day, at least to the largest and most imperative, as well as the most consequential portion of them.[70]

Two

CACOETHES SCRIBENDI

Women Writers among the Paying Periodicals

*In this age authorship has a more substantial reward than
attends female exertion in any other walk of life, and
the privileges which a successful writer commands,
are among the highest in the gift of society.*
—Ann S. Stephens

one

The success of *Graham's* and *Godey's* in the 1840s and 1850s was a signal development for writers, both magazines paying well and searching out the best talent available. Among Poe's tasks at *Graham's* was to solicit contributions, as he did in a fawning letter in 1841 to his later adversary, Longfellow: "I should be overjoyed if we could get from you an article each month—either poetry or prose—length and subject a discretion. In respect to terms we would gladly offer you carte blanche—and the periods of payment should also be made to suit yourself."[1] Although Longfellow could only have been pleased by such an open-ended offer, the letter gives a skewed view of the magazine world encountered by writers in general during the period.

Graham's and *Godey's* set a standard in compensating writers that affected the pay scale of other publications, but the money was directed largely to writers who had already made a name for themselves and whose work had been sought by the editors. A major figure like Cooper was an instant draw with readers and received top dollar, while the compensation for a writer of lesser note like Emma C. Embury (the subject of one of Poe's most laudatory sketches in the Literati series) reached as high as $40 for a tale and up to $7.30 as a page rate.[2] For unknown writers or writers submitting work on a freelance basis any pay at all was considered fortunate. Seeing their work in print, it was assumed, was payment enough.

"Of all the American magazines," William Gilmore Simms remarked in 1845, "there is not one which pays all its contributors," and the *Knickerbocker* remarked editorially a year earlier that many of the papers it printed had been "entirely gratuitous" in terms of payment, "unless indeed the writers consider the honorable reputation which they have established in these pages as some reward."[3] Willis, who had no difficulty placing his own work but also knew the other side of the editorial desk, pointed out in an unsigned *Evening Mirror* editorial on the pay for periodical writing that "there are several of the magazines that pay for articles, but no one of them, we believe, pays for *all* its contents." The "paying magazines," he added, "pay nobody whose 'name' would not enrich their table of contents."[4]

Magazines took it upon themselves to publicly lecture beginning writers presumptive enough to expect payment. *Godey's* in March 1855 reprinted from another magazine some "plain-speaking" on the subject that "suits us as well as it does them":

> We are constantly annoyed by young beginners sending us poetry and asking us to remit our usual price. We may add that we do not return poetry; those sending must keep a copy. One thing more while we are upon the subject. It is all folly for writers who have made no name to think of receiving payment, especially heavy payment, for their productions. An article may be fit to publish, without being entitled to compensation. A young writer should have a little modesty, and be thankful that he has the opportunity of displaying his talents before some half-million readers, without asking more or less pay in addition. If he write with unusual ability, he will be sought out, and his contributions solicited; and then will be the time to put a price on the productions of his brain. A little plain-speaking at this time, when we scarcely open a letter offering a prose contribution without a request to know 'our terms,' will probably prove a blessing to other publishers as well as to ourselves.[5]

New writers were regularly advised to make their mark in smaller and local publications before sending off work to the grand national magazines. But even with a background of publication they faced stiff competition in trying to place their work, whether they sought payment or not. What Willis called the *cacoethes scribendi*, the writing itch, seemed to affect nearly everyone, and he recalled an editor once telling him that a good living could be made from people willing to pay for the privilege of seeing their work in print. The major periodicals, Willis estimated, rejected fifty pieces for every one they accepted,[6] and they often rejected them in full public view.

Some periodicals of the day responded to submitted material in a column addressed to contributors, therein announcing editorial decisions and now and then giving explanations. Ordinarily, rejected material was not returned and writers were advised to keep copies of their work or send to the magazine for it, though by the 1850s writers were being reminded to include stamps with submissions if they wished to have material returned. A typical correspondents' column was one in *Godey's* in September 1856, given here in abbreviated form:

> TO CORRESPONDENTS.—We have accepted the following articles: "The Grave of the First-Born"—"Sonnet"—"Oh, Sing to me!"— "Lines to E.S.H."— "Life's a Sad . . ."—"Sacred Memories"—"Stanzas"—"Jam Moriturus . . ."—and "To a Frost-Bitten Flower."
>
> The following articles are declined for lack of room and for other reasons: "Bury me in the Forest" (will the author send a corrected copy?)— "My dear Reader . . ."—"To an absent Friend"—"To Mabel"—"Crochet"—"Twilight Thoughts" (pretty, but imperfect)—"Stray Leaves from a Journal"—"Nearer, brother, nearer"—"Wit" (but little in the article) . . . .

As the final parenthetical remark shows, editorial comment at times turned caustic, as it did again in the above column when it was advised that "J.C.G. had better forego the ambition of ranking as a writer of poetry than to appear in stolen honors. The poem he sent us as "original" for the "Lady's Book" was written years ago by Levi Frisbie." In a column in *Godey's* in August 1844 a rejected item called "My First Serenade" was followed with the remark that it would be the "last, we hope," and in June of that year "Old Maids" was turned down with the comment that it "must have been written by a *very* old bachelor."

The sprightly *Knickerbocker*, responding to submissions under the heading "Gossip With Readers And Correspondents," took pleasure in sparring with its writers. An item in January 1842 began with an emphatic rejection, then turned playful:

> We say *No*, at once, to "Philo-Franklin," and very willingly take hold of the dilemma's *horn* with which he thought to gore us. Our correspondent is *too* mat-

ter-of-fact, and errs on the other side of Carlyle. We think of an illustrative example at this moment:

> 'Tis morn, but scarce you level sun
> Can pierce the war-cloud, rolling dun,
> Where furious Frank and fiery Hun
> Shout in their sulph'rous canopy

Will "Philo-Franklin" contend that there would have been more poetry in this sublime-obscuro scene, if the sun had shone full upon the awful picture? Guess not!

The following month "J. P." was told by the *Knickerbocker* that his story *My Grand-Mother's Mystery* would appear only if he "will allow us to curtail the last two chapters." The author of "Phocion," on the other hand, was notified that the editor had no notion of its "drift":

> We thought, in trying to read his essay, that he must be some delegate from the "inworld" of Boredom. We would wager a ducat that if he were asked to explain what he intended to convey in the paragraph beginning "And thus *my* life indwells with Nature," he would be compelled to answer with Richter, "When I *wrote* that passage, God knows that I knew the meaning of it. Possibly God knows now; but I have forgotten!"

A further stumbling block for writers hoping to break into the major magazines was a system of exclusive arrangements with prominent writers that limited space available to newcomers. *Godey's* went out of its way to deny such commitments, pointing out in the July 1844 issue that it believed the field should be "open to all":

> We have had several applications lately to write for us exclusively. We now say to one and all, that we do not wish to make any such arrangements; and our reason we think is a good one. Let the field be open to all. It is impossible for a writer to vary from month to month, from year to year, to please the patrons of a particular work. The better plan is to write for different publications. . . . Again we say, we are averse to any exclusive arrangements.

The remarks may have been intended for new writers rather than the magazine's regulars. One of the innovations at *Godey's* major competitor, *Graham's*, and therefore presumably at *Godey's* as well, was to actively seek, and get, exclusive arrangements with writers such as Bryant, Longfellow, and Cooper, thereby adding the luster of famous names to its cover. While Poe was an editor at *Graham's* and trying to develop support for his own proposed magazine, he followed *Godey's* example and solicited exclusive rights. Irving was told that the literary department of the *Penn Magazine* would carry "contributions from the most distinguished pens (of America) *exclusively*." Poe went on to spell out exactly what this meant: "It will be necessary that an agreement should be made for one year, during which period you should be pledged not to write for any other American Magazine." The result of such exclusivity, as Poe clearly intended, was that his periodical would "admit *few* articles from other sources"—hardly an appealing prospect for writers still unpublished or with only modest name recognition.[7]

The situation facing new writers was summed up by Willis in a letter to one of his sisters, probably written in 1851. Sara Payson Willis was trying to break into the writing trade and from Boston had sent some sample articles to her celebrated brother, then an editor of the *Home Journal* in New York, hoping for his aid in placing them. Although his sister was in dire need of income, Willis refused all help. His indifference owed something to private feelings about his sister and irritation with what he considered the vulgarity of her work, but it also reflected his sense of the hazards confronting new writers.

> I am suffering intensely from tooth-ache, in addition to my other ills, but I will try to answer your letter. New York is the most over-stocked market in the country, for writers, as we get a dozen applications a day from authors who merely wish to have the privilege of seeing themselves in print—writing for vanity only. Besides all the country flock & send here for fame etc. I have tried to find employment for dozens of starving writers, in vain. The Home Journal pays for no contributions, being made up of extract, & so with all the papers, & many magazines.
>
> Your writings show talent, but they are in a style that would only do in Boston. You overstrain the pathetic, and your humor runs into dreadful vulgarity sometimes. I am sorry that any editor knows that a sister of mine wrote some of these which you sent me. In one or two cases they trench very close on indecency. For God's sake, keep clear of that.
>
> The most "broken reed," I know of, to lean upon for a livelihood, is amateur literature. The only chance is with the religious papers, which pay for a certain easily acquired kind of writing. Your education might enable you to do something of this. But in other literature I see no chance for you—unless, indeed, you can get employed by the editors you write for already.
>
> I am sorry that I can write no more encouragingly, but I must speak honestly, & I would not keep you on a mistaken track.
>
> I write in great pain,—you will excuse my abruptness.[8]

two

A central irony in Willis's harsh letter is that he had often lent new writers a helping hand—women writers in particular. "Females are naturally facile writers," he had declared in an *Evening Mirror* editorial, "and the attention paid to the mental culture of women in our day has set their thoughts a-flow upon paper, as the letting in of sunshine upon the dark floor of the forest draws to the surface new springs of water."[9] Such later notables as Grace Greenwood and Fanny Forrester had benefited from early publication in the *Home Journal*, and even Sara Willis's fledgling work under the pen name Fanny Fern was reprinted in the magazine before her brother learned her identity and ordered that no more of it should appear. It was, in fact, an age in which women writers seemed to have favored entry into the pages of periodicals and publishers' book lists—*The Feminine Fifties*, as Fred Lewis Pattee would later portray them. Hawthorne's well-known complaint to his publisher about the "d—d mob of scribbling women" exaggerated the dominance of women in professional writing while at the same time underscoring their considerable presence. Of the thirty-eight New York writers Poe singled out in the Literati series, twelve were women.

A revealing index to the prevalence of women writers in the period—and to a perceived threat they represented to males—is the critical scorn heaped upon them. They were said to lack craft and originality, to be given to sentimentality and wordiness; they neglected husbands and children while scribbling endlessly in the attic; to write for public consumption and be paid for it was inherently unwomanly; if they wrote at all they should confine themselves to feminine topics and avoid the manly arenas of politics, commerce, and social issues. "A remarkable work," Poe said of a new novel by a woman, "and one I find much difficulty in admitting to be the composition of a woman. Not that many good and glorious things have not been the composition of women—but, because, here, the severe precision of style, the *thoroughness*, and the luminousness, are points never observable, in even the most admirable of their writings."[10]

Despite the chorus of critical lament that often awaited them, women were quick to take advantage of a new market for the work of their pens. Between 1830 and 1860 some sixty-four women's magazines appeared, and general periodicals increasingly directed their attention to a female audience, with such mass-circulation journals as *Graham's*, *Godey's*, and *Peterson's Ladies' National Magazine* leading the way. At the same time women readers comprised the majority of the book-reading public. The demand was strong for writers who could speak directly to the concerns of women, whether through advice columns, practical articles, or the moral melodramas of domestic fiction. It was perhaps no easier for beginning women writers to break into print than men, though in the arena of popular fiction women seemed to hold a distinct edge; according to James D. Hart, publishers of the time "learned to welcome any woman who turned up at their offices with a novel in bulky manuscript under her arm."[11] Prejudice against women as authors still held firm in dim editorial corners, and for most women writers there remained the dual demands of family and career. Yet clearly the field of opportunity for female authors was vastly enlarged after 1830 with work centered, as one publisher briskly summed it up, on "Home and Jesus."[12]

In terms of popular consumption, fiction led the way. Poetry, publicly the more honored form, was far less read. Longfellow's most successful volumes of verse never came close to matching the sales of the most popular novelists, nor did his magazine earnings equal those of popular magazinists. In 1853, for example, his last year as a Harvard professor before becoming a full-time poet and nearly a decade and a half since his first book of verse, Longfellow earned a total of $1,525 from books and magazines while his academic salary for the year was $1,800.[13] Nonetheless, his work put him at the forefront of American writers, earned him a comfortable living, and opened economic doors for other poets. Though once warned by Willis that he was "not quite merchant enough" in handling his verse,[14] Longfellow learned to manage his work astutely through systematic recycling—first publishing poems in newspapers, magazines, or gift annuals, then collecting them in small volumes, finally reassembling the small volumes in collected editions. His long narrative poems summoning up figures of the native past—*Hiawatha, Evangeline, The Courtship of Miles Standish*—were his major earning vehicles, coming out in sizable first editions and remaining steady sellers over the years.

Whereas Longfellow possessed a sure popular touch yet belonged in his time to the elite of American letters, Lydia H. Sigourney of Hartford, Connecticut—second only to Longfellow in poetic success—worked solely in the literary trenches. Russel Nye has made the point that the early nineteenth century clearly distinguished two kinds of poetry—poetry as art and poetry as readable rhyming that taught, edified, or amused.[15] If Longfellow could and did compose both, "The Sweet Singer of Hartford" produced only the latter and yet occupied a respected and handsomely rewarded literary position. She

was the very definition of the "humbler poet" Longfellow sympathetically
limned in verse:

> Read from some humbler poet,
>   Whose songs gushed from his heart,
>   As showers from the clouds of summer,
>   Or tears from the eyelids start.[16]

Sigourney's first book (as Lydia Huntley), *Moral Pieces, in Prose and Verse*,
set the direction of all her pious and sentimental work. It appeared in 1815
while she was teaching school in Hartford; thereafter she married Charles
Sigourney, an older widower and Hartford merchant, but continued to write
and appear regularly in periodicals, though anonymously, at her dour husband's insistence. After his fortunes dipped she wrote frankly and copiously to
support the household, confiding to a correspondent that "as my husband has
not recently been prosperous in his business, I have felt it my duty to aid him,
by pursuing more as a trade, what had previously been only a recreation or solace."[17] In 1828 she shared a $100 prize with Willis for a poem that appeared
in *The Token*, one of the many annuals and gift books that were the rage prior
to the Civil War. Lavish gilt-edged and silk-bound anthologies of verse, stories, and pictures bearing names such as *Gems of the Season, Book of Pearls,
The Keepsake*, and *Friendship's Offering*, they usually were presented as gifts on
notable occasions and were meant to occupy a prominent place in cultivated parlors.[18] Nearly all writers of the time contributed to them, Poe and
Hawthorne included; for Sigourney, who termed them "luxurious literature,"
the books opened the way to her eventual triumph as a magazinist. They also
afforded paid editorial work, with Willis hired to put together *The Token* in
1829 and Sigourney the *Religious Souvenir* in 1839 and 1840.

In a career of undiminished productivity that extended a half century to
1865, Sigourney produced over sixty books of her own, including travel accounts, histories, and etiquette books as well as poetry collections. One, *Letters to Young Ladies* in 1833, went through twenty American editions and five
in England. During her major period in the thirties and forties something by
Sigourney appeared in nearly every issue of the leading periodicals—some
two thousand articles in all, most later recycled into her books. Magazines
also vied to list her name as an editor, a guarantee of success for their endeavor. From 1840 to 1842 Louis Godey paid her $500 a year for use of her
name on his title page while the magazine's columns kept readers informed of

her comings and goings. "We perceive it stated in several of our papers," an item noted, "that one of our editors, Mrs. Lydia H. Sigourney, is attracting much attention in Paris, and is deservedly very popular. In a letter to ourselves, dated at Paris, she mentions her intentions of publishing Pocahontas and other poems in London."[19]

For her material, the poet relied on the flow of daily events, tossing off a dozen highly-decorated stanzas recounting a story and adding one or two more invariably to specify a moral. She readily produced lines to commemorate public or private occasions, and she had a particular fondness for poems about death (whether a local infant or a missionary in Burma) that, as a reader put it, made one feel sad while not unhappy. She also shamelessly promoted her work in ways that might have caused even Poe or Willis to blush. At the start of her career she dispatched "a few verses called forth" to utter strangers on the occasions of deaths or other dire events, and later she regularly sent presentation copies of her books to the famous and the powerful (the profits of some of her books, according to a biographer, were wholly absorbed by copies she bought for presentation). If magazines to which she contributed failed to notice a new book she swiftly sent out polite but pointed letters of inquiry. With publishers she learned over the years to take a firm line in business affairs. A publisher who wanted a new book was given a response that was direct and devoid of her usually over-ripe prose: "I cannot do justice to myself, to compose a work of this nature (and which I have no doubt will be saleable) for less than 15 cents per copy, on an edition of 2000, one half to be paid (as I have been accustomed to receive it) on the reception of the manuscript, and the remainder, in six months, or a year after publication."[20]

three

Ann S. Stephens, Sigourney's friend and a writer equally adept at literary promotion, once called the poet a "pure impersonation of an American literary lady."[21] If the remark implied a tribute to economic success, it applied to Stephens herself, Sigourney's counterpart in the field of fiction as one of the first woman writers to exploit the new professional opportunities. Unlike Sigourney, Stephens's path as a writer was smoothed by the fortunate fact that her merchant husband was publisher of a magazine in Portland, Maine, where the couple moved after their marriage in 1831.[22] She was installed as editor of the *Portland Magazine* while also becoming a major contributor of poems and tales. In 1836 she branched out by editing the *Portland Sketch Book*, an anthology of regional writing that included work by Willis, Longfellow, Joseph Neal, and, naturally, Stephens herself.

After she removed to New York with her husband in 1837 she became an associate editor of the *Ladies' Companion,* a local version of *Graham's* and *Godey's* that emphasized popular fiction. The editor and publisher, William W. Snowden, took pride—apparently with some justification—in opening the magazine to new writers as well as established names. Among his major accomplishments in a literary vein was the publication of Poe's tale "The Mystery of Marie Rogêt" in three issues in 1842 and 1843. Stephens's stories began to appear in nearly every issue, and when one of them won a $200 prize from the magazine her reputation as a fictionist took a leap forward, this despite the fact that the prize had gone to one of the magazine's own in-house writers. (In a largely favorable treatment of Stephens in his Literati series,[23] Poe said she made her first "sensation" with the story and put the amount of the prize at $400. Presumably he was following a *Graham's* "Our Contributors" article about Stephens in November 1844 that also put the figure at $400 and claimed the prize "immediately placed her in the first rank of American authors.")[24] The story, "Mary Derwent. A Tale of the Early Settlers," played to a mass-audience fascination, compounded of both romanticism and dread, with the mingling of cultured white pioneers and savage Indians. So did "Malaeska," a three-part serial that followed in 1839 and was to become her most popular work of fiction.

Stephens's first-hand knowledge of forest life was limited to Pennsylvania and Ohio as seen on a visit to family members. But it hardly mattered; she was able to conjure up a colorful frontier world as a backdrop for her main interest in heavily-plotted domestic drama. In "Malaeska" an Indian princess and wife of a white hunter comes in conflict with Dutch settlers in the familiar literary ground of the Hudson Valley, Stephens finally steering the novelette-length account of intermarriage through to the pathos of a cemetery ending in which racial prejudice remains unresolved. In 1860 the tale found renewed life when it became the first of the Beadle dime novels as *Malaeska; The Indian Wife of the White Hunter,* the writer promoted in the publisher's notice as an "eminent author" and the story loftily described as "pure in its tone, elevating in its sentiments."[25]

For the right to reprint her twenty-year-old serial Stephens received $250, then watched as sales soared and the book launched a new industry of mass-produced cheap fiction—a major boon, as noted in the following chapter, for hack writers. It is estimated that in its various printings *Malaeska* may have sold a half million copies. For Stephens the sale of her rights to the novel was only a minor misfortune, and six more of her magazine serials eventually were resurrected as Beadle novels. She had behind her now a steady stream of work and an enviable publishing arrangement. In 1841 she was lured to *Graham's* with the promise of "more money and less work,"[26] and the following year she also began a long association with the magazine's Philadelphia rival, *Peterson's*. For a number of years *Peterson's* carried her name on its masthead, implying it had a woman as editor as a way of attracting female readers, but her sole job was to spin out articles and serial fiction. Each January a Stephens novel began; the following December it reached its end. In 1854 she added to her stature by striking an arrangement with the book publishing firm of T. B. Peterson (a brother of the magazine proprietor) to have the novels promptly brought out in book form after the magazine installments. The arrangement continued for the rest of Stephens's career, with T. B. Peterson adding a uniform fourteen-volume edition of her work in 1869 and a new twenty-three-volume edition in 1886, the year of her death.

While writing her tales with numbing regularity, Stephens took on editorial positions that included running her own magazine, *Mrs. Stephens' Illustrated New Monthly,* for a two-year period and later editing a weekly paper, *Brother Jonathan,* started by her husband. She also turned out guides to needlework and a two-volume pictorial history of the Civil War. But she remained a figure of note for her fiction—domestic dramas that shifted over the years from rural to urban settings but were always, as her publisher boasted, "suitable for the Parlor, Library, Sitting Room, Railroad or Steamboat."[27]

Following her death the work slipped quietly into oblivion, with only *Malaeska* having lingering life in Beadle reprints. But Stephens's industrious pen had provided her with a comfortable lifestyle that in later years allowed summers in Newport, winters in the Saint Cloud Hotel in New York, foreign travel, and a full social calendar with friends the like of Mrs. Cornelius Vanderbilt. Although her work was dismissed in literary circles as hasty and trivial, she was not without the gratification of critical praise. In his Literati portrait Poe found her given to the melodramatic and her work overwritten to the point of the turgid and bombastic; at the same time he found it praiseworthy for delineations of character and picturesque qualities. The portrait of Stephens in *Graham's* likewise drew attention to descriptive powers that quickly captured persons and place, maintaining that "no writer, since Sir Walter Scott, has excelled her in this."[28]

four

Stephens was but one of the many immensely popular feminine fictionists who followed in Scott's accommodating wake in the middle decades of the nineteenth century, and by the end of the century a writer in the *Saturday Evening Post* would declare the twilight of poetry and the age wholly given over to fiction.[29] Susan Warner's *The Wide, Wide World*, published under the pen name Elizabeth Wetherell, earned its impoverished author $4,500 in a semiannual royalty payment in 1853, three years after its original publication by G. P. Putnam (following rejection by most New York firms, including Harper's, which returned the manuscript with "Fudge!" scrawled by an unimpressed reader on one of the pages).[30] Elizabeth Oakes Smith's *The Newsboy* went through twelve printings in 1854, and Maria S. Cummins's *The Lamplighter* sold forty thousand copies in its first eight weeks in 1856.[31] Among writers specializing in serial fiction, May Agnes Fleming—like Stephens a Beadle author—received a retainer of $15,000 from the *New York Weekly* for two stories a year,[32] and the queen of the form, E.D.E.N. Southworth, could practically set her own prices.

In the nonfiction market, women writers had almost equal success with columns, articles, and book collections. Here two figures loom large, Fanny Fern and Gail Hamilton, both pen names of writers who found enthusiastic audiences in the supposedly masculine preserve of topical journalism.

Despite her brother's warning that she was on a mistaken track, Sara Willis's metamorphosis into Fanny Fern was accomplished with much the same dispatch as his own triumphant career. The circumstances surrounding the two writing lives, on the other hand, scarcely could have been more unlike. While he was fixed as a professional writer by the time he left university life, she took up the pen in later years and out of grim necessity. Five years the younger, Sara was equally well educated at the best schools of the time for women, but after finishing Hartford Female Seminary she returned home to Boston and domestic life. At age twenty-six she married; nine years later she was left a penniless widow with two children to support. A second marriage ended in divorce in 1852. Unable to earn a living through the acceptable avenues of sewing and teaching, and given only small and grudging support from relatives, she turned to the family pursuit of writing.

As Fanny Fern she began writing articles for local publications, peddling them in person to editors while existing on bread and milk with one of her daughters in a Brattle Street boardinghouse. "Many a weary tramp I had," she recalled; "much pride I put in my pocket, and few pennies." Her first published article, "The Model Husband," prefigured the direction of much of her later work, written from the viewpoint of a woman and dissecting in barbed yet humorous fashion male shortcomings. The article catalogued an ideal husband's behavior: his pocketbook is never empty when his wife wishes money; he feeds a child at night while his wife sleeps; he never reads the newspaper before his wife and never leaves clothing on the floor.[33] Payment for the article was fifty cents, for which she had to wait two weeks; only the fact that the article was immediately pirated by a prominent Boston newspaper encouraged her to further work.

Soon she was regularly publishing articles with titles such as "Thoughts on Dress" and "Deacons' Daughters and Ministers' Sons" in the *True Flag* and the *Olive Branch*, both small Boston periodicals. By the spring of 1852 she was turning out five to ten articles a week for earnings of some $6; the articles circulated in copied form in newspapers throughout the country, and her true identity was becoming a matter of public speculation. It was at this time that she wrote her brother for help in enlarging her market; after his curt refusal she broke off relations with him and plunged with all the more energy into her work. Later she would have her revenge in thinly-veiled satirical portraits of N. P. Willis in her work.

Oliver Dyer, the publisher of the *Musical World and Times* in New York, contacted the still-unidentified Fanny Fern in the summer of 1852 with the offer that she write for his paper at double the money she was getting from the Boston papers. It was the break she needed. To prevent losing her contributions, the Boston papers increased her payment, bringing her in some $13 a week together with what she was paid by Dyer. In the fall of 1852 the *Musical World and Times* and Boston's *True Flag* began featuring columns by Fanny Fern (making her the first woman newspaper columnist in the country),[34] both papers trumpeting the popular appeal of the work. Soon a book publisher, J. C. Derby of Derby and Miller, came forward with an offer to produce a collection of her newspaper pieces, and in 1853 *Fern Leaves from Fanny's Portfolio* appeared. Success was instant. Shrewdly promoted by the publishing firm, the book in its first year sold over eighty thousand copies,[35] and the critical response generally was favorable, with particular attention to a crisp writing style. "Fanny Fern is a voice," one commentator said, "not an echo."[36]

Amid the often fussy prose of the time Fanny Fern's manner was indeed different. Self-consciously free of the propriety expected of women writers, she spoke without frills in blunt and satirical tones. In a mock review of another collection of her columns published in 1857, *Fresh Leaves*, she characterized her prose as written by a woman more at home in a boxing audience than a parlor, an "antagonistic, pugilistic female" wielding a "scimitar blade of sarcasm."[37] Readers who were uncomfortable with her many controversial subjects (pompous husbands, female jealousy, social issues such as prostitution and venereal disease) nevertheless found themselves attracted by her pungent prose. Even Hawthorne set her apart from the scribbling women who had darkened American writing. In 1855 he wrote his publisher that Fanny Fern "writes as if the devil was in her; and that is the only condition under which a woman ever writes anything worth reading. Generally women write like emasculated men, and are only distinguished from male authors by greater feebleness and folly; but when they throw off the restraints of decency, and come to the public stark naked, as it were—then their books are sure to possess character and value.[38]

Hawthorne had just read *Ruth Hall*, the novel Fanny Fern published in 1855. She was now firmly established as a writer, thanks to her articles—including for some months articles in the *Saturday Evening Post* of Philadelphia —and another book collection, as well as a juvenile work with the syrupy title *Little Ferns for Fanny's Little Friends*. J. C. Derby estimated that within two years of publication she had earned a total of $10,000 from her nonfiction works.[39] The novel was meant to capitalize on her name recognition, and did. Widely advertised by the firm of Mason Brothers, the book sold fifty thousand copies in its first eight months, sales stimulated by the revelation of Fanny Fern's true identity and by a plot that paralleled her own life as a writer. N. P. Willis became the foppish Hyacinth Ellet in her story, and readers were treated to an acerbic portrait of the celebrated author as well as harsh accounts of other family members. When Hyacinth comes across Ruth's first published articles he writes indignantly to a third person and asks that the letter be read to Ruth, "alluding very contemptuously to Ruth's articles, and begging her to use her influence with Ruth to desist from scribbling, and seek some other employment. What employment, he did not condescend to state; in fact, it was a matter of entire indifference to him, provided she did not cross his track. Ruth listened to the contents of the letter . . . and went on writing."[40]

Critics were hard on the book, carping about an unwomanly lack of decorum in dealing with autobiographical matters. Sarah Hale, the influential co-editor of *Godey's*, even refused a review in the magazine. Nonetheless, *Ruth Hall* ushered Fanny Fern into her most dazzling period as a writer. For the unprecedented sum of $100 an installment Robert Bonner persuaded her to write a serialized novella for his *New York Ledger*, a wide-ranging literary weekly devoted, as it declared on page one, to literature, romance, the news, and commerce. The *Evening Mirror* immediately gushed that it did "not know which to admire most, the ability and perseverance of the lady in making a reputation that commands such un-heard-of remuneration for the labors of her pen, or the enterprise of the publisher who pays for it."[41] "Fanny Ford; A Story of Everyday Life" ran for ten weeks in the *Ledger* with considerable success, earning Fern the grand total of $1,000. Bonner followed up by signing her to an exclusive contract to write a weekly column for his paper, the length and subject to be of her own choice. It was a profitable arrangement on both sides, bringing Fern a steady income over the next sixteen years and bolstering the *Ledger's* circulation as the column developed a faithful readership.

five

Living now in New York and married to her third husband, the magazine writer and popular biographer James Parton, Fanny Fern wrote her weekly pieces for the *Ledger* and published popular collections of her work for the rest of her life. It is estimated that her annual income from her pen amounted to a comfortable $5,000. She was just one, however, of the star figures in Bonner's literary firmament. Quick to capitalize on the drawing power of name writers, he recruited for the *Ledger* the continuing work of E.D.E.N. Southworth and that of the adventure writer Sylvanus Cobb, Jr. Among prominent figures contributing articles, poems, and occasional pieces were Edward Everett, Horace Greeley, William Cullen Bryant, George Bancroft, and Harriet Beecher Stowe. Work came from such leading magazinists as N. P. Willis and Alice and Phoebe Cary, and from England, Dickens and Tennyson weighed in with contributions.

Bonner's recruiting methods were straightforward: he paid generously, then heaped praise on his writers and generally spun around them a web of considerate attention. Everett was paid $10,000 for articles, Dickens $5,000 for a story, Henry Ward Beecher $30,000 for a novel.[42] To a continuing writer like Southworth (thirty of her novels would appear over a forty-year period in the *Ledger*) he gave five-year contracts that toward the end of her connection with the paper brought her as much as $7,800 a year.[43] Cobb struck a similar deal with Bonner: he would maintain the furious pace of a fiction factory in return for what amounted to a weekly salary. The first "article of agreement" between the two, written by Cobb and signed by Bonner, read: "I promise to write exclusively for Bonner; and to write to the amount of one novelette once in eight weeks and two short sketches a week, and more if at any time he may need. In return he is to pay me fifty dollars a week, payable weekly. This agreement to continue for five years."[44] It was the first of many such agreements between the two. At the end of his long career Cobb, a writer who kept meticulous accounts, sent Bonner a record of his work:

> Thirty years I have written for you; and for nobody else. . . . I have a record of every scrap, and every page, written.
> I have written 122 Novels, or Long Stories.
> Also, 862 Short Stories.
> And—2143 of Short Scraps, Making of my large pages—Eighty-nine thousand, five hundred forty-four (89,544).
> There, Robert, is the record. There may be another like it, but I doubt it. Thirty years is about a human age—about an average. At all events, it is a good long season for such a contract as has existed between you and me.[45]

To Fanny Fern, Bonner occasionally sent an extra check as a show of gratitude for sustained work. One such came in a letter marking her fourteen years of writing for the *Ledger*: "Can it be possible that it is as long as that? . . . I enclose a check to remind you of the event; no, not exactly a present, for you might not like to receive it that way; but as compensation for some anonymous paragraphs which I want you to write for the *Ledger* whenever you feel like it."[46] Fanny Fern reciprocated by dedicating a collection of her work to Bonner—and noting, with a reference to the publisher's love of horseracing, that "the team of Bonner and Fern, has trotted over the road at 2.40 pace, without a snap of the harness, or a hitch of the wheels.—Plenty of oats, and a skilful rein, the secret."[47] When Bonner learned that a popular *Ledger* poet, Godfrey Saxe, was unwell, he sent a hefty check and encouragement: "Cheer up!—my friend. Why should *you* despond? You have the faculty of making others cheerful and happy. *Turn your attention to that now.* I herewith enclose a check for $500, and by the time you shall have sent me poems amounting to that, I have no doubt you will feel better. At any rate, keep the money in remembrance of the past, whether you can write any poems or not."[48]

Of course not all the *Ledger* contributors were on the receiving end of extended contracts or solicitous personal attention. A writer familiar with the paper during its later years, James L. Ford, sketched a satirical account of poets gathering in an outer office of the paper on Fridays to sell their wares and waiting breathlessly for the editor's judgment. On the other side of a glass partition they could see the shadow of the editor contemplating their work while moving back and forth in his private quarters. When a work was acceptable Bonner opened the door and handed the writer payment—typically

$10 a poem—then retreated into his office. According to Ford, experienced wordsmiths could already detect from the movements of the shadow through the glass whether a poem would be taken or not: "If the editor walked from his desk to the remote corner of his private office they knew that he did it in order to place a poem in the drawer of an old bureau in which he kept the accepted manuscript; but if, on the other hand, he came directly to the door a horrible feeling of anxiety came into every mind, and each poet uttered a silent prayer—while his heart literally stood still within him—that the blow might fall on some head other than his own."[49] Entirely new writers were put on notice within the columns of the *Ledger* that their contributions were an unwanted nuisance. One example: "Writers other than those whose contributions we have at some time published, will please not annoy us with their articles, however good they may be. We have too much to do now, and are out of patience with receiving *hundreds of applications* every week. Spare us!"[50]

The material Bonner wanted from his favored authors was directed to a family audience composed—as Ford cynically remarked about the *Ledger's* readership—of "farmers, midwives, gas-fitters' daughters, and the blood-relations of janitors."[51] It was "good bad stuff," and Ford—cynically again—put into the mouth of a *Ledger* poet the remark that "there are plenty of people who can write good good stuff, but there are not many who can write good bad stuff."[52] To his editorial mixture Bonner added splashy advertising campaigns, among other things printing installments of serial fiction in rival papers that left readers hanging for the next issue of the *Ledger* and running full-page ads with the single repeated sentence "Fanny Fern writes only for the Ledger." The result was circulation that during the paper's heyday reached the giddy heights of four hundred thousand copies a week.

The Irish-born Bonner, who made his way into publishing through ownership of a New York print shop, was one of a new breed of magazine owners who in the 1850s and 1860s replaced the Grahams and Godeys as major patrons of professional writers. The financial panic of 1857 thinned out the ranks of magazines and other publishing ventures; yet the *Ledger* prospered during the period, and such major new outlets appeared as the *Atlantic Monthly*, *Harper's Weekly*, and *Frank Leslie's Illustrated Newspaper*. The *Ledger* proudly publicized its spectacular payouts, and the new practice of serializing book-length work gave writers payment for both magazine and book publication— even more if their work was picked up by English periodicals or publishers.

But for the most part the financial situation for writers in general was only marginally improved by the new periodicals. Smaller periodicals and professional journals continued to pay little or nothing, and the notion that writing

ought to be an avocation rather than a professional activity still lingered. So
did the habit of anonymous contributions in newspapers and magazines.
The *Atlantic* originally intended to name neither its authors nor its editors,
Emerson remarking loftily that "the names of the contributors will be given
out when the names are worth more than the articles."[53] Before her fame from
Little Women, Louisa May Alcott published a number of thriller stories in
Frank Leslie's string of publications, all written frankly for money and appearing anonymously or under pseudonyms.[54] In *Little Women* she has Jo dash
off such a story for the $100 prize offered by a "pictorial sheet"; Jo's winning
story, as "full of desperation and despair as her limited acquaintance with
those uncomfortable emotions enabled her to make it," is set in Lisbon and
ends with an earthquake. "Bent on earning more of those delightful checks,"
Jo cranks out additional thrillers with her identity hidden, and Alcott notes
that while little notice was taken of Jo's work, it "found a market."[55]

   Yet for established writers the direction of the time was clearly otherwise.
They were now celebrities whose names, as they and their publishers well knew,
were valuable commodities. A publisher like Bonner grew rich and maintained a stable of thoroughbred race-horses; at his death his estate amounted
to six million dollars. His major writers were not in that league but did well
enough. E.D.E.N. Southworth had servants and lived in a fourteen-room
country "cottage" overlooking the Potomac just outside Washington while
Fanny Fern kept a fashionable Manhattan brownstone and took long summer
vacations with her husband. Perhaps no writer of the time was more alert to
the financial rewards of popular authorship than another of the industrious
women of the period, Gail Hamilton. In writing about her, Fanny Fern handed
out the highest compliment: Gail Hamilton, she said, was "not only independent in thought and expression, but I am happy to say, in *pocket*."[56]

                              six

The comment appeared in *Eminent Women of the Age*, an 1868 volume edited
by James Parton that contained a laudatory sketch of Fanny Fern written by
Grace Greenwood.[57] Despite an inclination for "mocking mischief" in her
work, Fern was softened in her book portrait into a figure who was "pure
womanly" at the core of her nature.[58] Fern's quite different tactic in her account of Hamilton was to quote various examples of the author's prose, much
of it seeming, in the abrasive wit of its male-baiting, to have come from Fern's
own barbed pen. One example: "Make a man understand that he shall eat his

dinner like a gentleman, or he shall have no dinner to eat. If he will be crabbed and gulp, let him go down into the coal-bin and have it out alone; but do not let him bring his Feejee-isms into the dining-room, to defile the presence of his wife, and corrupt the manners of his children."[59] Toward the end of the sketch Fern gave in to the reader's interest in personal matters by providing a few scraps of information: Gail Hamilton's real name was Mary Abigail Dodge; she came from Hamilton, Massachusetts; she was unmarried; and she had become an author by choice rather than necessity.

The latter detail separated Hamilton's career from Fern's own. After finishing Ipswich Female Seminary she began a teaching career that lasted a half-dozen years and paid reasonably well. Apparently writing had always been in the back of her mind, an activity encouraged by her large and well-to-do family, and in 1856 she sent off an anonymous article and some poetry to the *National Era*, an abolitionist paper in Washington that had printed work of Hawthorne and Whittier and found fame by serializing *Uncle Tom's Cabin*. In a breezy submission letter Hamilton pointed out that she had not turned to writing for financial reasons alone but to "measure myself by a new standard." She added: "I do not ask for charity, nor for a friendly judgment, but for a just one. If you think the pieces worthless, you will not hesitate to say so and I promise not to drown myself thereupon. If you think they are good, but not adapted to your paper, I shall be glad to know even that."[60]

The editor, Dr. Gamaliel Bailey, responded with praise ("your pen is not a commonplace one") and accepted her work. But due to financial straits he could pay her only with a promise of $50 at the end of the year for contributions of "your best style of prose sketches" during the period, an arrangement Hamilton was only too happy to accept.[61] Once launched as a writer with the *National Era*, she began sending work to the *Independent*, a weekly religious newspaper in New York, where she was paid at the rate of $3 a column for articles. She also initiated a correspondence with Grace Greenwood, asking for advice about additional publishing outlets: "Suppose you were a little bit of a writer—a *very* little bit of one, without a reputation, without much experience, but with the *cacoethes scribendi* strong upon you, what should you do? That is the question." Hamilton added that her standards were high and that, though she "would be glad to get money for writing," she "would rather write for a *good* paper without pay, than for a foolish one *with*."[62]

After a period of juggling both teaching and writing she took a year off from her job and moved into the home of Gamaliel Bailey in Washington as a governess for his children. From this vantage point she wrote articles and book reviews for the *National Era* and the *Independent* and also turned out poems and children's stories. After Bailey's death she returned to her birthplace of Hamilton and took up a literary career with full concentration. Yet she was in no hurry to wring the most money from her work. "Excellence," she claimed, "is far more valuable to me than money. I want a reputation, but I want it to be for qualities which may commend themselves to the best people."[63] When the Tract Society dangled $1,200 a year before her for an exclusive arrangement to write children's stories, she refused—and described her refusal with typical independence: ". . . the very fact that I was willing to put my brain in pawn would show that my brain wasn't worth pawning, that I would write stories, and if they liked 'em they might have 'em, but I didn't believe they would, that I would not write to suit them, and I would not make any engagement, and if I did I would break it the first thing."[64]

Still, writing was her livelihood once she put teaching behind, and money matters were never far from her mind. "One ought not to *write* for money," she remarked toward the end of her life, "but I consider it a first duty after one has written to exact the highest possible price. It is not a matter which concerns only the writer, but all writers."[65] After she had been writing professionally for a half-dozen years, she informed a correspondent that on $600 a year, the money earned from her magazine articles, she could live comfortably in the country. The money from her books was saved, and already she had set aside $2,000 and was aiming for $10,000. "My disposition to become the possessor of ten thousand dollars," she added, "is simply that I may be independent."[66]

For the next quarter century Gail Hamilton balanced her freedom as a writer and thinker with considerable financial success. Her work became commonplace in newspapers and magazines, most of it in the form of articles, and she eventually published over twenty-five books, including a biography of the political figure James G. Blaine. Blaine's wife was her first cousin and she spent a good deal of time in the family's Washington household, there immersing herself in political issues and frequently writing about them. Her typical subjects in addition to politics were women's issues, religion, and rural life, all her work being highly admired in its time for the vigor, forthrightness, and tart wit of its manner. "You see," she once wrote about her work, "I only look at things on the surface. That is my weakness. My strength is that I see them as they are, and not as tradition, or prejudice, or popular opinion, represent them."[67]

In "My Book," an article in the *Atlantic* in 1864 that was later included in a collection called *Skirmishes and Sketches*, Hamilton celebrated her life as a writer and defended herself with characteristic self-confidence against charges that her work was only frothy "ginger-pop beer" as against enduring "Madeira." She was content as a periodical writer to "flash and fade in one moment of happy daylight"; the likelihood of literary oblivion did not trouble her. "The overwhelming majority of names will turn out to be chaff, and be blown away. I shall be forgotten, but I shall be forgotten in very good company." She went on: "When I am dead, I shall be no deader than the rest of you, and I shall have been a great deal more alive while I *was* alive."[68]

seven

A lively dispute over money provided the basis for Hamilton's most controversial book. Her first work, a collection of rural articles called *Country Living and Country Thinking*, had been published in 1862 by the prestigious Boston firm of Ticknor and Fields, the publisher of Longfellow, Holmes, Mrs. Stowe, and other New England notables. Thereafter she maintained a close relationship with the firm and its successor, Fields, Osgood and Company, publishing seven more works with them over the next half-dozen years, and she counted James T. Fields and his wife as friends. "He [Fields] gets my books up himself," she noted in a letter, "—proposes to have them as books, I mean,—and is strenuous that I write only for them [the publishing firm], to which I am myself also as strongly inclined."[69]

An article in the *Congregationalist* on authors' pay caused her, nonetheless, to question the royalties she was receiving from the firm. As she retailed the story in *A Battle of the Books* in 1870, the article said most new authors received ten percent on their books while she calculated that, as an established writer, she had been getting from seven to eight percent on her work. For her first book she had been paid royalties at the ten percent figure, but thereafter Fields had paid her fifteen cents a book on the basis of an oral contract; as the price of her books was raised from $1.50 to $2 her percentage of payment had consequently dropped.

A mild letter of inquiry to Fields about the royalty payments ballooned into a full-scale argument between author and publisher. Fields took the position that Hamilton's book were more expensive to publish than others and he spent more on advertising them—legitimate reasons, he held, for her reduced royalties. Hamilton in turn wrote to other writers published by the firm, disclosing her story and soliciting support, and from other publishers she drew information on typical royalty payments—all adding to her sense of shabby treatment. In a letter to Fanny Fern's husband, James Parton, she vented her anger with ungenteel directness: "They [Fields's firm] pay well perhaps where they can make a noise about it . . . but where they think it is safe to screw—pardon the word—they screw unmercifully."[70]

Eventually the dispute went to arbitration and Hamilton, arguing her own case before a three-member tribunal, won a judgment of $1,250 for back payment on books published without a written contract and ten percent royalties on their continuing sales. She was far from satisfied. In *A Battle of the Books* she rehashed the quarrel in sarcastic and thinly-veiled fiction, maintaining that the work—as she put in the lengthy subtitle—was "For the the Use of Authors and Publishers: To the First for Doctrine, To the Second for Reproof, To Both for Correction and for Instruction in Righteousness." Published at her own expense, the book went through three editions of 500 copies each and ignited a modest controversy in the press, yet left her with a debt of $750.

Whether her "incendiary publication," as she called it, had any meaningful effect on the general tenor of writer-publisher relations is uncertain.[71] But it served the purpose of bringing the financial aspects of writing under public scrutiny, in so doing putting to rest vestiges of the notion that publishing was a polite activity carried on through the agency of gentlemanly editors and publishers and with money matters a distant consideration. Although the book was set a century earlier, the publishing milieu it depicted was clearly that of a profit-minded world of mass-circulation periodicals and large-scale publishing enterprises. It called for a firm business-like attitude on the part of writers in their dealings with equally business-like publishers. The author writing for money, Hamilton argued, becomes in reality a "business partner" of the publisher; if the author fails to pay close attention to his accounts he "shows himself to be shambling and shiftless, and puts a direct temptation in his publisher's path." Confidence and trust between writer and publisher were well and good "but never more excellent than when they have a solid basis of paper and ink." Women writers in particular were urged, in the book's hard-eyed closing lines, to realize that in the world of writing for money "there is no sex, no chivalry, no deference, no mercy. There is nothing but supply and demand; nothing but buy and sell."[72]

For the rest of her career Hamilton wrote regularly for such periodicals as the *Independent*, *Harper's Bazaar*, and the *North American Review*. As for her books, the connection with Fields, Osgood and Company, needless to say, was over; she established a new and impersonal relationship with Harper and Brothers with conventional royalty contracts of ten percent. Her treatment by her first publisher remained a sore spot, and although she considered her royalty fight a step in the direction of fair treatment of writers, she had no illusions about lasting results. When the Society of American Authors asked her to join in 1891 as a vice president, she responded that her earlier book showed she had been "fighting for your Authors' Club while you were all rocking in your respective cradles." She pointed out that she had recently published a book that had been well reviewed and even reprinted in a deluxe edition for private circulation; she expected, nevertheless, only modest rewards. She wrote: ". . . speaking as a wise man confidentially to the Authors, I confess that in spite of your efforts and mine, I shall be surprised if the author receives as much money for the brain-work of the book as the publishers receive for the de luxe work."[73]

eight

Lydia H. Sigourney, Ann S. Stephens, Fanny Fern, and Gail Hamilton had careers that lived up to authorial dreams: their work was readily accepted by periodicals and publishers; they made money; they received at least a measure of critical approval in their day and hold still faint places in literary memory. The majority of ambitious scribblers were, to repeat, far less fortunate. One can imagine their frustration when confronted with *Godey's* for May 1864 and finding under "Literary Notices" Stephens's latest novel, *The Wife's Secret*, praised in an airy manner that assumed its superiority: "We need say little of the writings of a lady whose productions are so well known and so universally admired. The story before us is one of exceeding interest; full of romance, yet with delineations true to nature." Immediately above on the page was the "To Our Correspondents" column, and here the ordinary reality of the writing situation revealed itself. Five articles were listed as accepted, twenty as rejected. Parenthetical comments about some of the rejected pieces could only have added to the frustration level: "well written for a composition"; "we have not time to write particular criticisms to our contributors"; "well written"; "worth publishing if we had room."

There was scant consolation, from the writer's point of view, that this issue of *Godey's* did not administer the sort of lengthy "plain-speaking" lecture that had appeared in the correspondents column nearly a decade earlier. Here the magazine simply added a curt preface to its list of rejections:

> These articles are not needed. Some are worth publishing, but the greater portion are not suited to our "Book." "First productions" are rarely found fit for general reading. Young writers must be willing "to work and wait."

As if that were not enough, the column went on to introduce would-be authors to the logistics of manuscript handling in tones that coldly underscored the impersonal nature of the writing life:

> We return a number of articles as requested. Those who desire this service from us must send stamps in advance, or *a stamped envelope directed*, that we may let them know we do not need the MS. . . .
>
> We do not undertake to return MSS. even if stamps are sent. Authors must keep a copy. This may appear singular to many; but if they consider the vast amount of MSS. we receive it will not be in any way peculiar. A manuscript sent us was declined in the March number, 1863. The author sends for it in December, 1863. It may be a matter of some moment to the author, but it is not to us. We cannot keep a record of the writers. Every three months we make an *auto da fe*.

Three

LAYING PIPES

Fiction Factories at Full Throttle

*"'Crack! Crack! Crack! Three more redskins bit the dust'—there's
your opening situation. Now go on and write the story."*
—Prentiss Ingraham

one

Cheap fiction was already a staple of the American book market when Ann S. Stephens's *Malaeska* launched the Beadle dime novels in 1860. Better printing technology along with developments in machine-made paper and falling prices for paper supplies had made it possible to turn a profit on books selling for far less than the stately volumes of the past. From 1845 onward there was a vast expansion in publishing as upstart enterprises and old-line houses competed in turning out inexpensive books, paper- and cloth-bound, directed to a new mass audience of readers.

For writers, the advent of cheap books meant fresh opportunities. Pirated foreign books in inexpensive editions still preempted a sizable portion of the market, allowing publishers an escape from payment of any sort while bringing down the curses of writers on their heads. With Rudyard Kipling this was literally the case. In Japan he came across his work put out in pirated editions by the Seaside Publishing Company, an American firm, and called down the furies on both the house and the country: "Because you steal the property of a man's head, which is more his peculiar property than his pipe, his horse or his wife, and because you glory in your theft and have the indecency to praise or criticize the author from whom you steal . . . you shall be cursed with this curse from Alaska to Florida and back again. Your women shall scream like peacocks when they talk, and your men neigh like horses when they laugh. . . . You shall be cursed State by State, Territory by Territory, with a provincialism beyond the provincialism of an English country town."[1] Yet despite the heavy toll taken by pirating, it is estimated that seventy percent of the work launched on the new seas of cheap books was that of native writers who were duly compensated for their labors.[2]

Many found their publisher in the several houses formed in Boston by Frederick Gleason and Maturin M. Ballou in the 1840s and 1850s. Writers themselves, adept at reading the new public taste for sensational material that was yet primly moral, and equally adept at establishing a network of agents for mass distribution, Gleason and Ballou paved the way for the successful publishing ventures later in the century of Beadle and Company and Street & Smith. After early success with adventure novelettes about the sea written by Ballou under the name Lieutenant Murray (one, *Fanny Campbell; or the Female Pirate Captain*, sold eighty thousand copies in a few months),[3] the two created what was in effect a fiction factory, hiring as staff writers the likes of Ann S. Stephens, Henry William Herbert, Alice B. Neal, Horatio Alger, Jr., T. S. Arthur, A. J. H. Duganne, Edward S. Ellis, and E. Z. C. Judson to grind out engrossing "steam literature," so-called because the material rolled off newly-developed rotary steam presses.

Individual books first appeared as "shilling novelettes" priced at a shilling and containing fifty pages illustrated with vivid woodcuts, later as twenty-five-cent stories of a hundred pages. Beginning with the *Flag of Our Union* in 1846, Gleason and Ballou branched out into a line of weekly story papers that included *Ballou's Dollar Magazine* and *Gleason's Pictorial Drawing Room Companion,* the publications anticipating the popular papers of Robert Bonner and Frank Leslie (who under his real name, Henry Carter, worked on one of the Gleason-Ballou combine's illustrated publications). To meet increased demands for material, additional writers were recruited through prize contests, with *Flag of Our Union* trumpeting in 1847 that "we do not offer prizes like some of our contemporaries, retaining the liberty of keeping *all* manuscripts and stories, awarding pay *only* to the premium one. We do not wish to publish

anything in the FLAG that we are not willing to pay for, and that liberally.
LOOK OUT FOR THE PRIZE TALES."[4]

Gleason's Pictorial Drawing Room Companion, one of the country's earliest
illustrated weeklies, ordinarily carried a serial in each issue, several shorter
pieces of fiction, some poems, and an editorial miscellany. Often the illustrations preceded the creation of the fiction. "Received a letter from Mr. Gleason,"
Sylvanus Cobb, Jr., Gleason and Ballou's most popular writer, noted in a journal entry, "with several pictures from which to write a sea story."[5] Gleason
repeatedly emphasized that his publications carried no reprint material; his
authors were Americans, as were most of his lusty fictional heroes and heroines.
"Domestic stories, so-called, are not exactly of the class we desire," contributors to the *Flag of Our Union* were informed, but rather "tales—of the sea and
land—of the stirring times of the Revolution—or of dates still farther back."[6]

Most of the writers originally turned up by Gleason and Ballou were lured
away eventually by the better pay of New York story papers and especially by
the appearance on the cheap-fiction scene of the Beadle dime novels (most of
which, during the firm's top period in the 1870s, sold for a nickel). They carried with them the melodramatic adventure formulas established by Gleason
and Ballou as well as the accompanying, and compensatory, moralism that
marked the combine's work. Dime novels of blood-and-thunder adventure
appeared, in their original form, in orange wrappers with black woodcuts on
the covers illustrating the hundred pages or so of quick-paced prose within;
yet for prospective writers Beadle and Company[7] issued a set of instructions
that were high-minded in the extreme:

> Authors who write for our consideration will bear in mind that
> We prohibit all things offensive to good taste in expression and incident—
> We prohibit subjects of characters that carry an immoral *taint*—
> We prohibit the repetition of any occurrence which, though true, is yet better
> untold—
> We prohibit what cannot be read with satisfaction by every right-minded per-
> son—old and young alike—
> We require your best work—
> We require unquestioned originality—
> We require pronounced strength of plot and high dramatic interest in any
> story—
> We require grace and precision of narrative, and correctness in composition.
> Authors must be familiar with characters and places which they introduce and
> not attempt to write in fields of which they have no intimate knowledge.
> Those who fail to reach the standard here indicated cannot write acceptably for
> our several Libraries, or for any of our publications.[8]

While holding to an air of strict moral propriety, Beadle authors had to grasp the reader's interest at the outset, then keep the pages flipping to the end. Because of the demands of the form the firm's stable of writers was nearly always made up of seasoned professionals. Ann S. Stephens, who eventually had fourteen dime novels to her credit, was typical; so was John Neal, the prolific Maine writer who had encouraged Poe as a poet, and Elizabeth Oakes Smith, an author with nearly thirty years of work behind her when she published her first dime novel in 1867. The Irish writer Mayne Reid, a one-time drinking companion of Poe during his Philadelphia days, had published a number of stories based on his own Western adventures when he entered into an agreement with Beadle and Company in 1868 to write a series of dime novels. For *The White Squaw* Reid received what was said to be the highest price for a dime novel exclusive of serial rights, $700, and he never was paid less than $600 for his other contributions.

The usual fees for Beadle novels, from $75 to $150, were enough to attract a ready supply of writers. A decent livelihood from the pen was possible, with rapid and unstinting productivity the stern requirement. Few practitioners were as accomplished as Edward S. Ellis, a New Jersey school teacher, who in 1860 sent Beadle and Company a novel called *Seth Jones; or, The Captives of the Frontier*. Accepted for $75 and widely advertised, the eighth dime novel put out by the firm became one its most popular, eventually selling a half-million copies and setting Ellis on a long writing career under a mystifying number of pen names.

But when it came to speed and productivity no one outdistanced Ned Buntline, the celebrated pen name of Edward Zane Carroll Judson, who also managed to squeeze in a life as far-fetched as any of his fictional creations. Judson began writing as a magazine contributor to the *Knickerbocker* in the 1830s, and with the Gleason-Ballou publications he was identified primarily as an author of sea stories. After a meeting with William F. Cody in Nebraska in 1869 he wrote fourteen Buffalo Bill novels, giving rise to the most celebrated of dime-novel western stalwarts. All told, Judson hammered out some four hundred novels in his career, one of which, over six hundred pages long, he claimed to have written in sixty-two hours. As he described it, his working method was to start with a title, then invent the story as he sped along: "I never lay out plots in advance. I shouldn't know how to do it, for how can I know what my people may take it into their heads to do? First, I invent a title. When I hit on a good one I consider the story about half finished. It is the thing of prime importance. After I begin I push ahead as fast I can write, never blotting out anything I have once written and never making a correction or modification. . . .

If a book does not suit me when I have finished it, I simply throw it in the fire and begin again without any reference to the discarded text."[9]

In 1872 Judson brought Cody and his friend, Texas Jack Omohundro, to Chicago, here taking—so he said—four hours' time to write for them a play called "The Scouts of the Prairie" (Prairie later changed to Plains) in which the action consisted largely of shooting Indians. The play turned out to be handsomely successful, with Judson appearing on stage himself, a necessity of casting since he could improvise dialogue when his two scouts forgot their lines.[10] Toward the end of his career Judson, using a strategy of selling exclusive rights to the work of Ned Buntline while writing for other publishers under other names, was earning $20,000 a year and living in splendor as a country squire.

Romance, crime, piracy, historical deeds—such was the stuff of dime novels. But always topping the list in popularity was the western. Prentiss Ingraham, himself the son of a novelist, was so adept at the form that he effortlessly carried on the Buffalo Bill stories after Judson's death. Like Judson, he lived a life of high adventure, numbering William F. Cody, Wild Bill Hickok, and Pawnee Bill among his Western companions, and like Judson he was hugely productive as a writer. He could whip out two short novels in a month, and once threw together a story for Beadle and Company in a day and a night. "It was a hurry order from the firm," he explained about the feat, "and it had to be done. I drew my trusty fountain-pen, placed a ream of foolscap on my desk in my room, locked myself in, working from breakfast to breakfast, and completed my task."[11]

Toward the end of his life Ingraham placed the total number of his books, written under a wealth of pen names, at over six hundred. His tried-and-true formula was to begin with a dramatic situation, create suspense, then keep the action speeding along by placing his central figure in peril after peril and rescuing him through brave deeds. Improbabilities and coincidences rarely gave him pause. Ingraham's mighty labors brought an income of $15,000 to $18,000 in his better years and underwrote the life of a Southern gentleman with a home near Georgetown and the attentions of black servants.

two

Edward L. Wheeler, the creator of Deadwood Dick and his feminine counterpart Calamity Jane as well as of a youthful urban detective known as Broadway Billy, identified himself on his letterhead as a "Sensational Novelist" writing out of a "Studio" in Philadelphia.[12] The frank designation fit all the authors of cheap fiction in the halcyon years after the Civil War, though their workplaces bore more the air of assembly-line factories than arty studios. All of them wrote to Ingraham's rough formula, and there were ready outlets for their concoctions among the many imitators of Beadle and Company.

Starting with the *New York Weekly*, a story paper modeled on Bonner's *Ledger* that carried the first of Ned Buntline's Buffalo Bill tales in 1869, the firm of Street & Smith produced a host of regular publications (usually called libraries) and eventually overtook Beadle as the prime purveyor of cheap fiction. Stories of urban crime and detection, loosely following in the vein Poe had originated, were already a house specialty when John R. Coryell, an author of detective yarns for the *Weekly*, dreamt up Nick Carter. Since Coryell had other writing assignments, Ormond Smith of the firm eventually assigned the weekly series to another experienced hand, Frederick Dey. A Columbia-trained lawyer turned writer, Dey had written for Beadle and Company before he was engaged by Street & Smith. In book form the Nick Carter stories, twenty-five thousand words in length and issued weekly, sold for a nickel and brought Dey $75 each for all rights. He claimed to be able to toss off two and three a week with no difficulty. "I go ahead," he said, "and get myself into the most impossible snarl I can; and then I get out of it."[13] Although he would number, according to his own estimate, over a thousand Nick Carter tales among his varied writing credits, Dey ended up impoverished and took his own life in a New York hotel room.

Like Dey, many authors started with the cheap fiction of Beadle and Company and naturally gravitated to that of Street & Smith. But for Horatio Alger, Jr., the path began with high ambition as a serious writer, though his inaugural efforts were directed to the popular publications of the day. After graduation from Harvard in 1852 he fired off verse and fiction to *Peterson's* in Philadelphia and made regular appearances, under his own name and pseudonyms, in Boston's *True Flag* and *Flag of Our Union*. In 1854 alone he published stories and poems in five different Boston publications under three different names. His local reputation as a writer was soon established, but when the compensation that followed was meager Alger turned to teaching and later to the ministry to support himself.

When his second book of poetry appeared in 1857 Alger followed Poe's practice and inserted an item in the *True Flag* that announced publication of the unsigned work and added some self-serving promotion: "The poem is written in a sparkling and lively style, and indulges in much well-deserved satire upon what is generally called 'our best society.' We confidently predict for it a wide popularity. The author's name is not apprehended, but, if rumor be correct, he is already known as a contributor to our best periodicals."[14] After finishing preparation for the ministry at Harvard Divinity School in 1860 Alger followed Willis's practice and sent back chatty letters about a grand tour of Europe for readers of the *New York Sun*. On his return to the country he became a regular contributor of stories and poems to *Harper's Weekly* and *Monthly*, and in 1863 he prepared an essay for the stately *North American Review*. It was his most demanding effort as a writer and the most prestigious place of publication, appearing to launch him at last on the literary career he longed for. But when payment turned out to be only a dollar a printed page, far less than the $5 a page for prose and $10 for each of his poems he was drawing from the House of Harper, ambition gave way to need and he put his pen determinedly in the service of Grub Street. Henceforth, as he put it, he would devote himself to a "humbler department which would pay me better."[15] The particular humble department he would soon dominate was juvenile fiction.

Stories for the young as a device for teaching pious virtue and prim behavior went back to the end of the eighteenth century. By Alger's time the field had greatly expanded both in subject matter and publishing outlets. Joseph Holt Ingraham, the father of Prentiss, turned out rip-roaring boys' tales of the West and the high seas, and with the advent of dime novels the thrilling world of cheap fiction threatened to overwhelm the juvenile markets. When parents and educators objected to the sensationalism of such stories, a compromise literature emerged that combined accounts of derring-do with proper moral and social attitudes. Harry Castlemon, Oliver Optic, and Edward S. Ellis soon established themselves as leading lights of the genre, but Alger was to become—in the phrase of Russel Nye—the Homer of the new style of juvenile fiction, eventually turning out some 125 books for the young that worked and reworked a middle ground between the racy world of dime novels and the bland moralism of Sunday-school tales.[16]

After a brief stint as a Unitarian minister in Brewster, Massachusetts, Alger came to New York in 1866 and plunged into the risky life of freelance writing. The following year he made his great step toward fame and fortune with the serial publication in *Student and Schoolmate*, a juvenile monthly, of *Ragged Dick; or, Street Life in New York*. With the immediate success of the series, for which he was probably paid $30 an installment, came book publication in 1868 by the Boston firm of A. K. Loring and a contract for five more works in a *Ragged Dick* series. For the books Alger drew on his observation of the street urchins who roamed the city—boot-blacks and newsboys and match-stick vendors—and stitched together the story formula he would use for work after work: through diligence, moral virtue, and a healthy dose of luck a poor boy rises in the world to respectable station. To this Alger added practical information about city life, in so doing giving the young a guide of sorts to the new urban environment. At age thirty-five Alger had found his subject and method. He would make sporadic efforts to write for adults, and he clung to his hope of literary success; but in a writing career that spanned another forty years he would never escape the juvenile confines of *Ragged Dick*.

Critics of the tales have long marveled that a Harvard graduate with literary ambition was capable of Alger's notoriously sloppy prose in his tales of luck and pluck. One maintains he "was one of the most careless writers ever to drive a publisher to frenzy," and through sad experience editors learned to go over his copy with special care to prevent gross errors in the handling of characters and details.[17] Alger's method of composition called for little advance planning. He started in with an incident and invented often tortuously complex plots as he went along, writing in pencil on cheap paper while consuming black coffee. He was capable of ten-hour stints at his writing table that allowed him, in the case of his boys' life of President Garfield, to produce a complete work in thirteen days. [18] One of his short novels could be finished in two weeks. Toward the end of his life he relaxed his work schedule, allowing himself long seaside vacations, yet stayed remarkably productive, tossing off thirty-nine serials in the final decade of his writing career.

For all his efforts Alger managed little more than the respectable life that was the goal of his young heroes. He estimated that in all his years as a writer in New York he earned only about $100,000, a considerable sum nonetheless for a bachelor who lived frugally in boardinghouses where room and board seldom ran more than $10 a week. He was, however, famously generous with money and as his life wound down was constantly troubled by financial matters.

Following his death in 1899 Alger had an odd rebirth as a writer. When he left New York in 1896 for residence in Natick, Massachusetts, he took with him a half-finished novel; two years later, unable to bring it to completion, he cast about for a ghostwriter. A younger writer of juvenile serials in Street & Smith's stable, Edward Stratemeyer, seemed to fill the bill, and Alger solicited his help in a letter: "Can you take my story and finish it in my style? You will be left to your own discretion pretty much. By way of compensation, if satisfactory to you, you shall take the story & sell it to some periodical under *my name*. You will divide the proceeds *equally* with me but I shall retain the copyright and it will appear as my book. . . . If this proposal suits you I will send [the manuscript] out by express. I fancy it would be *easy* work for you as you have a fluent & facile style."[19]

Stratemeyer accepted the offer and, after reading two hundred manuscript pages, sent Alger an outline for future chapters. In failing health, Alger never responded. After Alger's death Stratemeyer finished the book, published in 1900 with Alger's title, *Out for Business; or, Robert Frost's Strange Career*, and under Alger's name. He went on to write ten more Alger novels, all produced in the Alger manner—even, so the publisher maintained at the time, actually written from Alger's notes.

The decade and a half after his death was the period of Alger's greatest popularity. Street & Smith and other firms began issuing his tales in dime-novel format, vastly increasing his young readership. Frank Luther Mott estimates Alger's total sales during his lifetime at around eight hundred thousand, the figure given in some of his obituaries. Counting the later dime-novel issues, sales may have reached sixteen or seventeen million.[20]

three

As a boy in Maine Gilbert Patten consumed the dime-novel yarns of Prentiss Ingraham, and his first writing effort for money (a short story with a straightforward dime-novel title, "A Bad Man") was sent to the *Banner Weekly*, a story paper published by Beadle and Company.[21] Orville J. Victor, Beadle's veteran editor, accepted the story along with a second one written while Patten was waiting for a response to the first, and sent an encouraging letter together with a check for $6. Patten quickly repeated his success with sales to Beadle of a long story for $50, published as *The Diamond Sport; or, The Double Face of Bed Rock* in the Half-Dime Library in 1886, and a second long story for $75. With the money he felt himself a "bloated bondholder" and abandoned all thoughts of college in favor of a writing career.[22] Although he harbored an ambition to write serious novels and become an American Dickens, Patten would produce—by his own count—almost a thousand novels under one of the best-known pen names in cheap fiction, Burt L. Standish.

Eventually Patten made his way from Maine to New York and the offices of Orville Victor in the Beadle building at 98 William Street. For a period of thirty years Victor was the presiding genius of the firm, selecting and editing its stream of publications and holding together a collection of writers with kindly attention while providing them with story formulas that could both be mass produced and altered as popular taste shifted. Often, coming across something in a manuscript that suggested a catchy title for another story, Victor would place an order with one of his writers for a "dime" to fit the title. Writers were so adept at the form ("any one of them," one remarked, "could have built up a 70,000-word novel from a comma, if required")[23] that they invariably came through. Patten remembered that Victor's "advice, guidance and editorial aid, which he gave in abundance, helped many a faltering author to make the grade. He was an editor whom writers swore by, not at."[24]

Edward Bok, then the editor of the *Ladies' Home Journal*, might have had Victor's thriving operation in mind in his satire on "Literary Factories" carried in the *Boston Journal* and reprinted in *Publishers Weekly* in 1892. In New York a staff of thirty girls and women busily ransack newspapers and magazines for story ideas, then plot outlines are developed and dispatched along with a standard form to one of a hundred writers listed in an address book:

To _____:
    Please make of the inclosed material a _____ part story, not to exceed _____ words for each part.
    Delivery of copy must be by _____ at the latest.
    A check for $_____ will be sent you upon receipt of manuscript.
    Notify us at once whether you can carry out this commission for us.
    Very respectfully, _____

Inspecting the address book, Bok finds it contains "the names of twenty writers . . . which the public would never think of associating with this class of work—men and women of good literary reputation, whose work is often encountered in some of our best magazines." Writers are eager for the assembly-line work since the pay is good (the willingness of authors to work, Bok is told, outstrips the capacity to supply them with plots), and the material produced is quickly snapped up by "sensational weeklies . . . boiler-plate factories . . . publishers of hair-curling libraries of adventure."[25]

As a writer for hire Patten quickly established a sparkling publishing record with Beadle and soon was advising other authors about dealing with editors. Above all, he cautioned patience when sending out manuscripts. A letter of inquiry he had once sent to an editor about a story held for three months had ended with the line, "If I do not hear from you within three weeks, I shall send the story elsewhere." At once the story was returned, Patten later learning that the magazine had planned to use it. He also preached persistence in the face of rejection. One editor took the first poem Patten sent him, then rejected the next six; finally, Patten sent him another poem, enclosed no stamps, and wrote: "Please read this, and throw it into the waste basket." Within two weeks he had a check for his verse.[26]

Despite warm feelings for Victor, Patten eventually broke with Beadle and Company in a dispute over money. The particulars of the situation shed light on the financial problems that beset even thriving writers of cheap fiction. The most Patten received for a story of seventy thousand words was $150, and after his move to New York his price dipped to $100. When it slipped further on one occasion, to $90, he drew the line. Beadle's policy was to pay authors on publication, but Patten, short of rent money for his Harlem flat, asked for his $100 ten days before a novel was to appear. Victor was sympathetic but sent him to see the head of the firm, William Adams, who broke the rule against advance payment but deducted $10—a dollar for each day prior to publication. Then and there Patten decided he was through as a Beadle writer. Most of those who stayed on with the firm, he recalled at the end of his career, ended up poverty-stricken, including some, finding themselves finally unable to earn a living writing fiction, taking their own lives.

After his break with Beadle, Patten began writing for the rival cheap-fiction publications of George Munro, a former clerk at Beadle and Company. He became a regular contributor to the firm's *Golden Hours* but was never placed under contract, as were some writers, and was limited to a sixty-thousand-word serial every six or eight weeks for a price of $250. Wanting more, he decided in 1895 to try his luck with the publications of Street & Smith.

Edward Stratemeyer was then editing Street & Smith's *Good News*, a competitor of *Golden Hours*, and to test Patten's skill he gave him the title for a story, *The Boy from the West*, with instructions to write two opening installments of four chapters each. Stratemeyer accepted the work when Patten turned it in but they disagreed on a price for the finished serial. Patten finally compromised, accepting $150 as a way of getting his foot in the door of the firm. The story was the first of some twenty million words he would write for Street & Smith.

Because he had written for Beadle publications under his own name, Street & Smith wanted Patten to adopt a pen name and they settled on Burt L. Standish, the surname coming from Patten's youthful reading of Longfellow's *Courtship of Miles Standish*. Thereafter Ormond Smith of the firm proposed that Patten shift from the westerns he was writing and develop a juvenile series built around a young man at a boarding school who would eventually have some travel adventures and finally enroll in a college such as Yale. Patten liked the idea and two weeks later sent in a story called "Frank Merriwell; or, First Days at Fardale." Ormond Smith, responding at once, was thoroughly pleased:

> We are entirely satisfied with this story, and satisfied that you can do the work we require. As previously stated, it is our idea to issue a library of school adventure, and we fully expect that this library will be successful. We are willing to make a contract with you for the entire work, assured that you will be able to please us. It must, however, be borne in mind that each story should be complete in itself.
>
> We shall not care to start the library until we have at least ten numbers in hand, so that we shall be in no danger of running bare of material.
>
> You have selected a good name for the hero of the story. It is understood that this name is to be one of the firm copyrights and trade marks, just as Nick Carter is.[27]

The first of the Frank Merriwell stories appeared on April 18, 1896, and thereafter they were a regular feature of Street & Smith's *Tip Top Weekly*. Patten's first contract covered a three-year period and paid him $50 for a twenty-thousand-word story. Although the money was modest, the contract meant a regular income and Patten reasoned that at the rate of five thousand words a day he could finish a story in four days and have two left over for other work.

As it turned out, the stories were more demanding than he anticipated. There was the necessity of reading and note-taking to give his work a "color of verity," a quality he defined as "the atmosphere of being written by one who knew all about military-school life, college life, railroad life, the sea, woods, horses, dogs, wild animals, birds of the air, trees, plants, sports of all kinds, America, foreign lands, and a thousand other things with which no one man could possibly be familiar."[28] Nonetheless, working on a typewriter at his home in Maine and with plots developed to some degree in advance, he pounded the stories out on schedule. He agreed with Ned Buntline that a good title was crucial, and when he had one he felt a story was nearly half written; he was never, however, up to Buntline's speed. His best stint produced fifty thousand words in one week, with twenty thousand his normal output.

Trying to lighten the pressure of the work, Patten took to dictating. He would plot out two or three chapters by the time a stenographer arrived at nine o'clock in the morning, then pace the floor while he dictated—according to a pedometer he kept, accumulating four miles. He kept working until noon or one o'clock; after a nap and a walk he spent late afternoons and evenings revising typed transcriptions, making chapter plots, and doing his background reading. But the work remained an "awful job" of "grinding copy." There were times, Patten recalled, when he "felt like a horse in an old country treadmill. I ground and I ground and I ground, and it seemed as though there never would be an end to it."[29]

Patten believed the strength of the series was located in character more than action. "Get your mind off action," he told his publishers, George and Ormond Smith,[30] trying to explain his approach. "Action is what killed the old dime novel. It is all right for a few pages, but it gets pretty tedious unless there is some character mixed up with it that you can get interested in." With boys' stories character could not be taken from life but had to be drawn from the imaginative world in which boys lived. Patten thought this exactly the secret of Frank Merriwell: "When I conceived Frank, I think I hit on approximately the boy that every kid would like to be. Not, mind you, the boy that every kid ought to be. That was the Horatio Alger idea—a moral in every story. But my boy pointed no moral; he was just every boy's ideal picture of himself."[31]

In time Frank acquired a half-brother, Dick, and matriculated at Yale, Patten reading up on the college and traveling to New Haven for football games to give the stories touches of local color. Patten also acquired the help of John H. Whitson, an experienced writer of Beadle westerns, who in 1900–1901 turned out fifty-two Merriwell yarns while Patten took time off for other work. The Merriwell series continued on to 1914 when Patten devoted himself to Street & Smith's *Top Notch Magazine* (with Burt L. Standish given credit as editor for the sake of the name's drawing power) and a string of other writers took over.

Patten estimated the circulation of *Tip Top Weekly* at two to three hundred thousand during the peak popularity of the Merriwell stories. In fifteen-cent book form, three stories to a book with some added filler matter linking the stories together, the Merriwells had even more success.

four

Patten prospered on Grub Street while the publisher grew rich. Sold outright to Street & Smith, his stories brought him no royalties; he remained what he was, a contract writer whose price rose from $50 a story to a high of $150. Even his celebrated pen name was a property of the firm. It was left to Edward Stratemeyer to reap the profits from juvenile series fiction by becoming in effect a middleman between author and publisher. His business acumen and unflagging industry garnered him a steady $50,000 a year, and at his death in 1930 he left an estate of a million dollars. "As oil had its Rockefeller," a magazine remarked of him, "literature had its Stratemeyer."[32]

It is said that at age twenty-five Stratemeyer scribbled his first story on a piece of brown wrapping paper while working at his brother's tobacco store in Elizabeth, New Jersey, the city of his birth. The story was eventually sold to *Golden Days*, a boys' magazine in Philadelphia, for $75 and Stratemeyer was launched as a writer for the young. During his editing days at Street & Smith's fiction factory his skills were sharpened by contact with Alger, Dey, and Patten, but it was after he had left the firm and begun the Rover Boy books in 1899 under the pen name Arthur M. Winfield that he settled into his major period. A variation on Patten's Merriwell stories, Dick, Tom, and Sam Rover were students at a military academy in New York State, Putnam Hall, though they found ample time for worldwide adventures. Unlike the Merriwells, the Rover books bypassed magazine publication and appeared directly in book form from Grosset and Dunlap, with Stratemeyer eventually writing thirty works in the series and selling some five million copies.

Other popular Stratemeyer series followed, including the Motor Boys and the Bobbsey Twins. In 1906 Stratemeyer proposed to another of his book publishers, Cupples and Leon, that it price hardcover series novels at fifty cents as against current figures that ranged as high as $1.25, the idea being to gain in volume what was lost in price. In starting up a new series, three books would be produced at once; if an audience was attracted, seven more volumes followed—the point at which a series was well underway and profits came rolling in. The pricing worked and the fifty-cent novel rapidly became the norm in the juvenile market. But the endlessly inventive Stratemeyer had yet another scheme in mind, one prompted by the extent of his success.

Unable to keep up with the demand for his work, he formed the Stratemeyer Syndicate,[33] doing for himself what Street & Smith had done as a publishing firm. He continued to write under his array of pen names while farming out series work to contract writers. The syndicate came up with titles and three-page plot outlines; writers were then paid from $50 to $250 to produce a two-hundred-page book within a week to a month. Manuscripts were revised and edited in the syndicate offices, given to Stratemeyer for approval, then shipped to one of the syndicate's publishers. All rights were retained by the syndicate, which in the beginning allowed publishers to see only electrotype proofs of finished works and leased them printing plates.

The key to the syndicate's success was a smooth-running assembly line that spun out standard products in short order. From initial conception to typeset book was said to take forty days. Stratemeyer himself commuted from a conventional Newark, New Jersey, home to the syndicate offices in Manhattan and kept a rigorous nine-to-five work schedule. His contract writers produced rapidly because they knew precisely what was expected of them. Outlines they worked from gave necessary details about characters, story, and time elements, and there were in-house guidelines in the form of other books in a series. One of the syndicate writers during its later days and eventually a partner in the firm, Albert Svenson, described its well-worn formula as "a low death rate but plenty of plot. Verbs of actions, and polka-dotted with exclamation points and provocative questions. No use of guns by the hero. No smooching. The main character introduced on page one and a slambang mystery or peril set up."[34] To this was invariably added at a book's end a teaser for what would come next in a series. A book in the Tom Swift series, among the syndicate's long-running properties, concluded with a typical preview:

> When newspaper reporters, interviewing Tom Swift on how he had accomplished the work, asked him what invention he was going to turn out next, Tom replied:
> "It's a secret I haven't told my wife or my business manager."
> So naturally it cannot be revealed here. That Tom had something in mind need not be doubted, and a future book may disclose what it was.[35]

It was important that the syndicate keep hidden the real identity of its authors so that familiar pen names—Victor Appleton, Clarence Young, Roy Rockwood, Laura Lee Hope, Carolyn Keene, Franklin W. Dixon, May Hollis Barton, Alice Emerson—could carry on through the years, free of the certainty of death and taxes. One of the most productive writers hidden behind the names was Howard R. Garis, a newspaperman with the *Newark Evening News* who wrote many of the Motor Boys, Baseball Joe, and Tom Swift titles. His original agreement with Stratemeyer called for $100 for each book and no royalties; in return Garis agreed never to claim authorship of the books nor use the pen name under which they were written for any other work.

Garis set out on a writing career at age nineteen when, after piling up rejections, he sold a story to a magazine called *Happenchance* about a writer who had been rejected so many times he decides to inject a manuscript with a deadly drug that is released when inserted into a return envelope, killing the editor. Outside the Stratemeyer Syndicate he wrote, beginning in 1910, the hugely successful Uncle Wiggily Bedtime Stories (that he also read over the radio and to large audiences on tours around the country) as well as many series sold directly to publishers. Garis's wife, Lillian, was a Stratemeyer writer, as were two of their children. Together, the Writing Garises turned out more than a thousand books and likely had a hand in producing titles in all of the popular juvenile series that appeared between 1905 and 1935.[36] Roger Garis remembered the authorial preoccupations that gripped individual writers during family outings:

> My father might be planning his next series of Uncle Wiggily stories, helping the rabbit gentleman with the tall silk hat and barber-striped rheumatism crutch escape from the Skeezicks. . . ; my mother might be setting the stage for Barbara Hale's Mystery Friend; my sister could be plotting one of her girl mystery books— *Missing at Marshlands,* or *Mystery of Jockey Hollow,* or *The Orchard Secret.* I might be seeking a solution to getting Warren Finn and Terry Blondel, of The Outboard Boys, off the drifting houseboat before it reached the rapid.
>
> These silences could last an hour or so. We had sort of an unspoken agreement that no one would interrupt while any of one of us was obviously still immersed in plotting. Once in a while we would get in the car, start off for an outing, say at Eagle Rock, and no one would speak until we were in front of our house again.[37]

The Garises knew that in addition to dreaming up plots with plenty of action Stratemeyer authors had to be adept—in an expression of Howard Garis—at "laying pipes." This meant knowing when and how to insert elements in a story that later could be picked up in what would seem the inevitable movement to the story's big climax. It was well-laid pipes that made a story hang together, and these along with the "hooks" that propelled readers from chapter to chapter and book to book were the central tricks of the craft.[38]

From the standpoint of Stratemeyer's syndicate, writers like the Garises, no matter how skilled, were merely cogs in a well-oiled machine that could never be publicly recognized as a machine. It was said that Stratemeyer carefully scheduled appointments with his authors so they would never glimpse each other coming and going from the syndicate's offices. One of his series writers, Josephine Chase, complained that "the only time people will ever know I am a writer will be when I die and they write my obituary."[39]

After Stratemeyer's own death his family continued to deflect attention from the syndicate and its writers by refusing to authorize any accounts of the founder's life. Stratemeyer's two daughters, Harriet and Edna, shifted the firm to East Orange, New Jersey, but kept operations in full swing. Two new series that had just been launched, Nancy Drew (the first three volumes written by Stratemeyer himself) and the Hardy Boys, were to prove its hottest properties. By 1935 the syndicate was juggling fourteen series. In a newspaper interview in 1968 Harriet Stratemeyer Adams said she put in nine-to-five days at the syndicate's offices, dictating over seven thousand words a day and supervising a staff of eleven employees. She had written about a hundred books herself and developed outlines for several hundred more.[40] By the middle 1980s the syndicate had five series in progress and was still busy updating and reissuing old works that now had the stature of national institutions.

five

Gilbert Patten thought that movies caused the decline of the dime novels, with pulp magazines finishing them off altogether. From another point of view, cheap fiction, after going under in the deluge of juvenile tales, resurfaced in the pulps as thrilling reading matter directed both at adults and at adolescents. Whatever the chain of events actually may have been, the advent of inexpensive rough-paper pulp magazines, as distinguished from the smooth-paper slicks, offered popular fictioneers yet another ready market for their wares.

The father of the pulps, Frank Munsey, began his rags-to-riches publishing career with a juvenile magazine, the *Golden Argosy*, that ran the first install-ment of an Alger serial in its initial issue in 1882. Deciding there was more money in the adult field, Munsey created *Argosy* in 1888, then in 1896 turned it into a plump all-fiction adventure magazine printed on rough wood-pulp paper that qualified for second-class postal rates. Within a few years Street & Smith and other publishers followed suit, abandoning the cheap fiction of dime-novel books for a magazine format of seven-by-ten inches that featured flamboyant covers and some 120 densely-printed two-column pages. Sold on newsstands for a dime to a quarter, the pulp magazines bore names such as *Adventure, Western Story Magazine, Blue Book, Detective Fiction, All-Story Weekly, Action Stories, Popular Magazine*, and *Ace-High*. With its soaring pop-ularity and the possibility of starting a publishing venture with shoestring financing,[41] the genre rapidly subdivided into mainline pulps and scores of publications catering to specialized tastes trumpeted in the titles: *Railroad Stories, Sea Stories, Oriental Stories, Sky Birds, Weird Tales, Amazing Stories, Jungle Stories, Fight Stories, Ranch Romances*.[42]

The pulps were a gaudy feature of the major expansion of markets for writ-ers as the nineteenth century came to an end and competition from radio and movies was still in the future. The critic Hamilton Wright Mabie, writing in the *Forum* in 1892, felt himself nearly overwhelmed by a period of what he termed "almost unrestricted book-making": "The author no longer seeks the publisher with the faint hope that some Ollier or Cottle will befriend his un-recognized genius. It is now the publisher who searches for the author as for hid treasure. Never before in the history of book-making has there been such scan-ning of the horizon for the first faint gleam of a dawning talent for any kind of writing."[43] What was true of book-making was true of the print world in gen-eral; newspapers flourished and, in Frank Luther Mott's words, among maga-zines there was a "spectacular enlargement and increase in effectiveness."[44]

Magazine expansion was fired both by developments in printing technol-ogy and by the economic depression of 1893 that caused newsstand prices to tumble from the usual twenty-five or thirty-five cents an issue. *McClure's* began publication in June of 1893 at fifteen cents, and when *Munsey's* shortly there-after went to a dime other general-circulation magazines followed suit. In the field of weeklies a nickel became the standard—the price of the *Saturday Evening Post* after it reemerged in 1897. The result of the price cutting was a huge new audience for magazines, with *Munsey's*, *McClure's*, and *Cosmopolitan* each claiming some half million readers by the turn of the century and the *Ladies' Home Journal* even more. Still in the background, upholding literary and intellectual standards though with an aggregate circulation that roughly matched one of the popular journals, were the three prestigious illustrated New York monthlies, *Century*, *Scribner's*, and *Harper's*, and their down-at-the-heels Boston cousin, the *Atlantic*. Yet nothing approached the combined cir-culation of the pulps. By the 1920s and early '30s, the high-water mark of a period of popularity that finally trickled away in the '50s, they were consumed at a rate of some twenty million a month.[45]

Experienced pulp writers commanded rates of two cents a word, meaning $100 for a 5,000-word story, $1,200 for a 60,000-word novel to appear in in-stallments. New hands drew about half as much. Payment was usually on ac-ceptance, with a regular payday set aside each week or month. According to Harold Hersey, the editor of a string of pulps, the most skilled writers—he placed the number at around fifty—had yearly incomes in five figures. What was required was an ability to deliver the "goods"—to give editors the kind of never-a-dull-moment adventure yarns they wanted, and to supply them with speed and relentless regularity. This meant writers had to plunge in, plotting as they went along and rarely bothering with the niceties of editing and rewriting. Allan R. Bosworth, a newspaperman who produced hundreds of pulp stories, thought the main trick for all the pulp masters was writing a crampacked opening paragraph that established a character, a setting, and a situation and closed with a "narrative hook" that snagged the reader's attention. This done, storytelling took care of itself.[46]

Rejection slips that came in had to be looked upon as minor irritants along a path, given the plentiful world of pulps, to quick and certain publication. And there had to be the ability to withstand a daily grind that few other desk workers would tolerate. The idea that a professional writer possessed independence was in the opinion of Harold Hersey simply a delusion. A writer could choose where to live and what hours to work, but there was no escape from the steady toil. "He is his own producer," Hersey noted, "his own manufacturer, often his own middleman. . . . He is a complete entity to himself from all outer appearances; in reality, he is laboring under a schedule and an authority that only the professional is able to sustain and obey."[47]

Since the money was reasonably good—very good during the Depression thirties—some writers spent the bulk of their careers happily pounding out stories for the pulps. Others—among them, the likes of Upton Sinclair, Mary Roberts Rinehart, and Rex Stout—earned their writing spurs in the pulps, then escaped as quickly as they could to the upscale forms of smooth-paper magazines and books.

Sinclair was a seventeen-year-old student at the City College of New York when he sold a story to *Argosy* for $25. At once he began turning out children's tales for various papers and writing jokes for comic papers that paid a dollar a joke. The latter he circulated to editors in batches of ten; when a batch came back with one missing he knew he had made a sale. With a fellow student Sinclair collaborated on an adventure novel that they promptly took to Street & Smith; an editor refused it but suggested they try writing a novel more in line with the firm's needs. When the two students came back with the finished novel in a week they realized their mistake: the editor refused to take seriously anything written with such speed.

After graduating from the City College, Sinclair supported himself as a special student at Columbia by becoming a contract writer at Street & Smith. In 1897 the firm started a new five-cent juvenile magazine called *Army and Navy Weekly;* the editor, Henry Harrison Lewis, was to write a story every other week about cadet life at Annapolis and Sinclair would write on alternate weeks about West Point. Sinclair journeyed up the Hudson to gather local color, then, back in New York, began producing the Mark Mallory stories (the Naval Academy hero was Clif [sic] Farady), novelette-length tales under the pen name Lieutenant Frederick Garrison for which he was paid $40 each. With the success of the stories he considered his literary career launched. When Ormand Smith inquired whether the new writer had been through West Point, Lewis told him, "Yes, he went through in three days."[48]

Sinclair later replaced Lewis as the author of the Annapolis tales under the name Ensign Clarke Fitch, producing some thirty thousand words a week for another $40. With the coming of the Spanish-American War Sinclair was advised by an editor that readers of *Army and Navy* would expect to see Mark Mallory and Clif Faraday on the battlefield, so the two were quickly graduated and dispatched to Cuba for their country. Sinclair's method of preparation was to soak up atmosphere by reading a book about Cuba and by learning some expletives for lending verisimilitude to the speech of his Spanish villains. In his autobiography he recalled that "from that time on my occupation was killing Spaniards. 'What are you going to do today?' my mother would ask, and the answer would be, 'I have to kill Spaniards.' I thought nothing of sinking a whole fleet of Spanish torpedo boats to make a denouement, and the vessels I sank during that small war would have replaced all the navies of the world. I remember that I had my hero explode a bomb on a Spanish vessel and go to the bottom with her; in the next story I blandly explained how he had opened a porthole and swum up again."[49] When Street & Smith started up another war publication, Sinclair added to his workload with stories featuring Hal Maynard of the U.S. Army. For some months he was turning out eight thousand words a day, Sundays included, dictating to two stenographers. He did the work in afternoons and evenings, leaving mornings free for attending lectures at Columbia and practicing his violin.

His years as a potboiling author, Sinclair mused in his autobiography, had both good and bad effect on him as a serious writer in later years. He learned to shape stories and write swiftly, but he also developed a fondness for phrasing that was both commonplace and exaggerated. While he was engaged in it he enjoyed his adventure work; besides paying well it was fun. But he could please his audience only so long as the stories pleased him. At age twenty-one he wrote a serious novel and began looking down on his hack writing, with the result that he was never again able to do it with quite the same aplomb. Economic need, however, kept him in thrall to the pulps for some time. While his novel was declared in reviews to be "tremendous, thrilling, brilliant, remarkable, original, noble, a masterpiece, and so on," sales were another matter: ". . . at the end of eight months the publisher submitted to me the royalty

account, and it appeared that the book had earned me just $325. If anything
be needed to complete the climax it may surely be found in the royalty state-
ment of the next six months following. It showed that the book had sold to
the extent of two copies more, and with it was inclosed a check for thirty
cents."[50]

Mary Roberts Rinehart began her hugely successful career at age twenty-
seven with a story in *Munsey's*, the flagship of Frank Munsey's fleet of publications. Since her marriage to a busy medical doctor at nineteen and the coming
of children she had suppressed a desire to write; finally she sold some children's poetry, and when she and her husband lost money in the stock market
she began writing in earnest.[51] She remembered waiting with a sinking heart
for the postman and recognizing at a distance the look of an envelope containing a returned manuscript. She did her writing in scraps of time, most
often in the evenings while her husband was making his rounds. "To bolster
up my faulty craftsmanship," she remembered, "I resorted to plot, that crutch
of the beginner, that vice of the experienced writer. I devised weird and often
horrible plots. I could think faster than I could write, devise plots and put
them on paper with amazing speed."[52] In her first writing year she managed
to place forty-five stories and poems and earn a total of $1,842.50.

Looking back, she recalled that her beginning years as a professional writer
seemed wonderfully simple: "I could get an idea while making a cake, write it
in the afternoon, get it typed—I had a little Jewish girl who lived around the
corner for that—and send the story off the next day. When, or if, it came
back, I sent it off again to another magazine. It was as simple as that." [53] When
a story about the Spanish-American war was rejected for the twelfth time, she
did a rewrite and promptly sold it to *Scribner's* magazine—a breakthrough,
she later decided, in that it taught her to slow her pace and reflect on her
work. In an earlier period of her writing she had met Willa Cather, who had
been a journalist and high school teacher in Pittsburgh, and Cather had told
her she put stories away for months, then returned to them to make thorough
revisions. At the time it was an approach to writing the energetic Rinehart was
unwilling to emulate, though later in her career she would present herself as
obsessed with rewriting while disappointed by all her work.[54] For her Grub
Street material she deliberately turned away from life as it is in favor of escape:
"I wanted escape from remembering, for remembering frightened me. I turned
to romance, to crime, to farce, to adventure; anything but reality. I was amaz-
ingly happy, but I felt that happiness was not the normal lot, and that my
hold on it was tenuous in the extreme."[55]

At the suggestion of *Munsey's* editor Robert H. Davis, who would develop a number of popular writers in a lengthy career,[56] she switched to serial mystery novels handled with a humorous touch. For *The Man in Lower Ten,* which appeared in 1906 in another of Munsey's pulps, *All-Story,* she got $400. Davis remembered her bringing the manuscript of another mystery, *The Circular Staircase,* to New York and his telling her—this in a simpler age of writer-editor relations—that he would read it that evening and have a decision by morning. [57] He bought the work for $500 and it appeared in *All-Story* in 1907–08. Rinehart realized she had stumbled on a formula of sorts for mystery novels, one that could be reduced to a diagram that she would later sketch in an article in *Ladies' Home Journal.*[58]

Two stories run concurrently, but one, the "surface story," the reader follows while the "buried story," the real story of the crime, is held only in the writer's mind. At various points in the narrative the buried story emerges—there are "outcroppings"—yet only in bits and pieces. Only at the end, the "denouement," do the two stories wholly mesh.[59]

With several years of pulp publication behind her, Rinehart shifted to books. As she embroidered the story in her autobiography, at a bindery she had the tattered edges of the carbon manuscript of *The Circular Staircase* trimmed and the pages put in a flexible cover with the title in gilt letters, then shipped off to Bobbs-Merrill in Indianapolis. She had little hope of its acceptance.[60] Book writing was for serious authors and she considered herself only facile; when she read something well written she halted her own writing in despair. But Bobbs-Merrill bought the book and also sent an editor to the Rinehart home in Pittsburgh to read and buy two other mystery serials. It was, she believed, the turning point in her career. She was now set in the direction that in the 1920s and '30s, especially in the stories she published in slick magazines such as the *Saturday Evening Post* and in her book-length work, would bring her a fortune as one of country's most popular writers.

Rex Stout's affair with the pulps was brief but intense. In 1912 while living in New York he began full-time professional writing, publishing thirty-two stories and four novels over the next five years, most of them in *All-Story.* His pay ranged from a penny a word to an experienced hand's two cents. With

"Justice Begins at Home" in a December 1915 issue of *All-Story* he produced the first of the crime stories with which he would eventually make his mark; but Stout also harbored ambitions as a serious writer and had decided to put the pulps aside and strike out for a career in literature when a successful business venture intervened. It was not until 1929 that he returned to writing with a group of serious novels that drew some critical notice but sold few copies.

With *Fer-de-Lance* in 1934 Stout went back to popular fiction in the form of a detective novel featuring Nero Wolfe, the character who turned out to be his ticket to long-term success. His explanation for the move displayed the professional writer's allegiance to common sense: "I might write another dozen or even two dozen novels and they would all get pretty good reception but, two things, they wouldn't make any large amount of money and they wouldn't establish me in the first rank of writers. So, since that wasn't going to happen, to hell with sweating out another twenty novels when I'd have a lot of fun telling stories which I could do well and make some money on it. So I did." Experience taught him, Stout added, that only two kinds of books could be written with the expectation of realizing a living from them—cookbooks and detective novels.[61]

Four

THAT PRECIOUS
OVER-NOTE

Fictioneers among the Pulps, Slicks,
and Paperback Originals

Worked hard today again, eight hours, twenty-three pages. The
novel grows apace. I shall be lost presently. I feel the gathering
weight of passion. I shall write like a white flame.
—Zane Grey

one

About the same time Rex Stout was breaking in with detective stories Zane
Grey stumbled upon western fiction, rediscovering a territory previously
worked over in cheap books and pulp magazines. Before he was through he
would develop the western not only into another certain moneymaker for
professional writers equal to Stout's duo of cookbooks and detective novels
but in fact the most golden of all genres of popular storytelling.

Born in the Middle West and in his youth an avid outdoorsman who took
pride in Indian blood inherited from his mother's family, Pearl Zane Gray
turned to the east when he decided to follow his father into the profession of
dentistry. After finishing his education at the University of Pennsylvania he
set up an office in New York City. His shingle read "Dr. P. Zane Grey, D.D.S."
(Pearl Gray, for evident reasons, now shifting from his Christian name and altering his surname), but it was only a stop-gap career; his real ambition, stirred

by early reading of the dime-novel thrillers of Edward L. Wheeler and Prentiss Ingraham, was to become a writer.

While he worked halfheartedly on teeth during the day, at night Grey scribbled—first outdoor articles, then a trilogy of historical novels set in Ohio that publishers rejected. The first of the three, *Betty Zane*, he published himself with borrowed money and personally peddled to New York bookstores; the next two, according to a biographer, he "practically gave away."[1] At the end of five years of work, increasingly underwritten by money from his wife and a brother, Grey had ample reason to feel he had gotten nowhere. "Disappointments had multiplied," he recalled, "until their combined weight was crushing. Moreover, my wife's money was about gone, and a baby boy had come. My situation was indeed serious."[2]

The West beckoned as a subject when he chanced to meet C. J. "Buffalo" Jones, a Western adventurer who was in the East lecturing and showing motion pictures of wildlife in an effort to raise money for an experiment in crossbreeding buffalo and cattle to produce "cattalo."[3] Grey proposed to join Jones on a trip to Arizona and record the Westerner's exploits. After reading a copy of *Betty Zane* to assure himself Grey could write, Buffalo Jones agreed, and Grey was off on a journey financed with money from his wife. "Something tells me this trip West," she told him, "will be the turn of the tide for you."

She could hardly have been more prescient. "No boy suddenly dropped into the West could have had a more magnificent adventure than I had," Grey later wrote about the experience. "That wild, lonely, purple land of sage and rock took possession of me." Back home in the East, he wrote *The Last of the Plainsmen*, a book an editor at Harper's (the house that had rejected Grey's earlier work) turned down by telling the author to his face that "I don't see anything in this to convince me you can write either narrative or fiction." It was the darkest moment of Grey's life—yet a moment only. He recalled that "suddenly, something marvelous happened to me, in my mind, to my eyesight, to my breast. That moment should logically have been the end of my literary aspirations! From every point of view I seemed lost. But someone inside me cried out: '*He* does not know! *They* are all wrong!'" Galvanized to energy by his epiphany, he sent *Plainsmen* on a round of other publishers (after a dozen rejections it was taken by the Outing Publishing Company in New York) and set to work on a romantic novel drawn from his Arizona experience, *The Heritage of the Desert*.

Earlier he had abandoned New York and dentistry for full-time writing, living in a cottage near the Delaware River in Lackawaxen, Pennsylvania, on savings and his wife's small inheritance. Conditions were grim: "Cold weather came early in November: rain, snow, sleet, ice, and the shrill winds of winter. I wrote in a little bare room with a stove, a table, and a chair. The time came when I had to put my hand into the open stove every quarter of an hour to keep it from freezing. But I kept on writing." Along with his western novel he cranked out juvenile stories, verse, sporting articles, and a baseball novel drawn from his youthful days on the diamond. Most of his production was immediately rejected but he kept working, all the while devouring writing manuals ("I had an insatiable craving for them") that he hoped might open the door to success. His son remembered that Clayton Hamilton's 1916 manual, *Materials and Methods of Fiction,* was "father's bible. It had a greater influence on his writing than any other work."[4]

When *Heritage of the Desert* was finished he took the book to the same Harper's editor who had rejected *Plainsmen.* "You've done it," the editor reported. "You've made me eat my words. It's a fine novel."[5] At the same time the story was accepted for $1,000 for serialization in Street & Smith's *Popular Magazine.* Grey, at age thirty-eight, had his first real success. He had fixed as well on his literary landscape—an idealized West yet, he insisted, a West that was not unreal. His reading of frontier history and his own exploration of what he characterized as the "lonely and hidden wildernesses of the West" had proved to him that "hard men of the open also climb to the heights of nobility and sacrifice, to a supreme proof of the evolution of man, to a realization of God."

His next book, *Riders of the Purple Sage* in 1912, was his most famous— after Owen Wister's *The Virginian,* arguably the most famous Western novel of all. It had, nonetheless, a rocky start, with no magazine willing to serialize it and Harper's balking at publication in book form. When Grey went to see a vice president he was told that some of the firm's readers thought the book too "bludgy," a critical term Grey failed to recognize. Eventually Harper's relented, the book appeared, and in 1912 it reached the best-seller lists. Grey was on his way. In a career that extended to 1939 (and continued with posthumous publications for many years) he wrote over eighty books and scores of stories for pulp magazines and articles for sporting publications. From 1917 through 1925 he was never absent from the best-seller lists—according to James D. Hart, an unequaled record[6]—and an enormous income followed: $300,000 to $400,000 a year in the 1920s and $575,000 in 1925, his best single year. His published wordage is estimated at over nine million—or some three hundred thousand words a year, all produced in longhand and usually while settled in a Morris chair in his study and working in pencil on a lapboard.

Grey wrote swiftly and seldom bothered with more than a single draft of a book. Editing chores were turned over to his wife, who also came to his defense when critics took him to task. "A lot of these second-rate reviewers and writers would give their immortal souls to do what you're doing," Dolly Grey wrote him in the mid-1920s. "What if you're not a high-brow? If you were, thousands & thousands whom you are delighting & helping would never read you."[7] Grey wanted to believe her yet fretted continually over his literary standing, and despite his vast output his work was often produced in anguish. In his diaries he bemoaned the pain of authorship and revealed sharp swings of mood between extravagant elation and black depression. "There is always," he wrote in a typical entry, "an extreme difficulty in the taking up again the habit of writing. I wonder if this is because a relapse from literary work forms another habit. At any rate I am tortured before I can begin to write. This morning I had no desire to write, no call, no inspiration, no confidence, no joy. I had to force myself. But when I mastered the vacillation and dread, and had done a day's work—what a change of feelings. I had a rush of sweet sensations."[8]

two

While living in New York and trying to break in as a writer, Grey submitted work to pulp magazines and personally called on editors at Street & Smith and the Munsey Company, all to no avail. *Munsey's, All-Story, Argosy,* and *Cavalier* repeatedly turned him down. For his successor as king of the westerns, Frederick Faust, the pulps were always easy pickings. He started there, an instant success, but in his own eyes the great misfortune of his career was an inability to ever put pulp success entirely behind.

The statistics of that strange career have epic proportions. Faust is said to have published some twenty-five million words of fiction under at least twenty pen names plus his own. As Max Brand, he produced 170 Western novels and had enough short tales in magazines to fill some fifty more volumes. As a Hollywood film writer he had a hand in more than seventy pictures, seven of them once released in a single twelve-month period. A quarter century after his death his books were still selling at a rate of a million copies a year. Equally legendary was the speed of Faust's production. He set himself a goal of twenty typed pages a day, every day, and often surpassed it. According to one student of his work, "he could turn out a full-length book manuscript in four days, a 50-page novelette in a single evening, an average-length short story in an hour—all on a battered Underwood standard, two finger hunt-and-peck style. No dictaphones. No secretaries. He did it alone."[9]

Money rolled in. In the late 1920s Faust was commanding top-of-the-line fees of a nickel a word from pulps such as *Argosy* and *Western Story,* where he often appeared under different names in a single issue. His yearly earnings from his pen in these lush years were at the $100,000 level. When he eventually turned to the slick magazines at his agent's urging, he got $30,000 for serial novels in *Collier's* and hefty sums for short stories in the *Saturday Evening Post, Liberty,* and *Cosmopolitan,* where he launched the Dr. Kildare stories that would have a long tenure in motion pictures and television and bring in even more money.

"Three lines verse, 28 pages prose," Faust wrote from his villa in Florence in 1927. "A perfectly beautiful day."[10] The remark captures the fractured nature of his writing life—fluency and vast success on Grub Street coupled with dedication to classical poetry (he learned Greek, he said, so he could read Homer, Italian for Dante) and to the laborious and unremunerative business of trying to write it. He had begun writing poetry as an undergraduate at the University of California at Berkeley and never stopped; in the beginning, fiction was merely a way to make money while he got on with his verse. "I have just made the discovery," he wrote in a notebook in 1915, "that a short story can be manufactured out of an episode and a bunch of exposition, a la *Saturday Evening Post,* etc. However, the hell with prose. . . . Have recently sent 38 poems to our leading magazines and received 38 poems back from our leading magazines. However, Goliath shall yet be walloped amid the ivory brow."[11]

Settled in New York the following year and trying to eke out a bohemian existence, he continued with a string of rejections until William Rose Benét, poetry editor of the *Century* magazine, bought a poem for the surprising sum of $50. At the same time the mother of a college friend who happened to be a sister of Mark Twain and wife of a former staff member of the *New York Sun,* a Munsey property, provided him with an introduction to Robert Davis, the editor who had launched Mary Roberts Rinehart's career, had worked with Zane Grey, and was a major presence in the pulp field. What happened next became another part of the Faust legend.

Davis gave Faust a plot sketch ("Two young crooks, one male, one female, are converted to honesty by love and the kind deed of a man who is about to be robbed of the assay papers describing a certain mine") and directed him to a room with a typewriter and ream of paper. Six and a half hours later Faust emerged with a 7,800-word story, deftly plotted and of publishable quality. The astonished editor bought the work for the beginner's rate of a penny a word. Thus in February 1917 Faust's poem, "The Secret," was given prominent play in the elegant pages of the *Century,* and the following month the story about reformed crooks, "Convalescence," appeared in Munsey's pulp *All-Story Weekly*.[12] After two more stories for Davis, Faust made his first use of the name Max Brand. Davis wanted something less Germanic and literary for a western writer than Frederick Faust—and Faust wanted to reserve his real name for what he considered his real work.

The possibility that hack writing ("this horrible, dragging, walking prose")[13] would harm his poetry caused him some misgivings, but he seems not to have anticipated the long and demanding golden road it was opening for him. He went from story to story, his mind a total blank after he finished each one, believing himself incapable of dreaming up another.[14] Still, he continued to rise to each occasion, cranking out new work to sustain the steady flow of money he lavished on high living and generous gifts to friends and down-on-their-luck writers. After his marriage in 1917 at age twenty-five, the need for money increased and he branched out with work in *Argosy* as well as *All-Story*. His first novel, *The Untamed*, appeared as a six-part serial in *All-Story* before it was put out in book form by Putnam's in 1919.

The book fixed Faust's course as essentially a writer of westerns, though one who gave only cursory attention to actual Western settings, relying instead on the action-action-action plot manner of cheap fiction, a heightened tone that shaded his work toward the fantastic, and a fondness for mythical allusion. The opening of *The Untamed* is typical Faust—or Max Brand—in its mood-creating description of a timeless landscape:

> Even to a high-flying bird this was a country to be passed over quickly. It was burned and brown, littered with fragments of rock, whether vast or small, as if the refuse were tossed here after the making of the world. A passing shower drenched the bald knobs of a range of granite hills and the slant morning sun set the wet rocks aflame with light. In a short time the hills lost their halo and resumed their brown. The moisture evaporated. The sun rose higher and looked sternly across the desert as if he searched for any remaining life which still struggled for existence under his burning course.

The western figure, when he makes his appearance, must contend with impending death. "Perhaps he runs from death," Faust said about his usual manner of presenting his chief character, "and the poor sucker does not know that he is carrying it with him all the time. Or else he stays where he is for reasons and the readers see death closing in around him."[15]

"I think in this type of man you have the proper hero," Davis told Faust in urging him to follow in the western wake of Zane Grey. Grey had left the pulps for better-paying magazines and Davis was hunting for a replacement. He had given Faust a copy of Grey's *Riders of the Purple Sage* as a model. "This is it," he told Faust when he read *The Untamed.* "I think you can be the new Zane Grey."[16] Though the novel eventually sold a million copies in all editions and was twice made into films, Faust himself held the book—and the West itself—in small regard. When at Davis's suggestion he made a trip to the Southwest to gain a firsthand feeling for ranch life, he took along a volume of Sophocles' plays as well as his own poetry. "This ranch life is worse than being in the Army," he reported back. "Stinking cowpunchers, rides in all sorts of weather—and all the stuff that hundreds have done before me—and which in reality is so discouraging."[17]

"Daily I thank God in three languages that I write under a pen name," he told his wife.[18] Faust took pains to conceal his real identity as a writer, avoiding interviews and photographs and, as his popularity soared, letting others attend to fan mail. His eye was still on building a reputation as a poet, and he still believed he could turn out potboilers with his left hand. "Of course if you go after the mechanics of Western stories as such," he said, "you'll find that it's a simple group of rules by which one may cut the pattern for any number of yarns. And your bank account need never fail if you follow the rules, and clip carefully along the marked lines."[19]

Faust was making the writing life look easy. Not only was his work appearing regularly in the pulps and then in book form but he was selling motion picture rights to Hollywood. *The Adopted Son,* based on an *All-Story* novelette, appeared in 1917 with Francis X. Bushman and Beverly Bayne in the leads; the following year, when Faust was briefly in military service, two other films appeared. In 1920 Tom Mix starred in a popular film version of *The Untamed,* the first of several Max Brand stories in which he would appear while ushering in the vogue of western films. For the rest of Faust's writing life films based on his work would appear virtually every year, with *five* appearing in 1922.

Despite his success the need for money was constant and Faust kept churning out pulp stories at a prodigious rate. He had switched his main publishing base from Munsey's publications to Street & Smith's *Western Story.* The firm's spartan office building struck him as "a queer shop. . . . Looks like a prison and has a prison atmosphere inside. It is, literally, Grub Street. But the money they pay is a noon-day fact if there ever was one."[20] In one thirteen-day period in 1920 he outdid himself with 190,000 publishable words. He was working at the time in a rented office on Columbus Circle in New York and using the steady clatter of his typewriter to drown out the noise of the city. Although he found the lively pace of urban life stimulating as a writer, he wrote equally well in any circumstances.

During a long European trip in 1921 he rigorously kept to his schedule of twenty typed pages a day, and when in 1926 he began a princely, servant-attended life in a Florentine villa nothing interfered with his production. Poetry still remained uppermost in his mind, and when Putnam's issued his first collection, *The Village Street*, in 1922 he seemed to have accomplished his aim: potboilers for money, verse for fame. The book made him no money, but there was no need of it; that year he published prose in six magazines under six different names, plus eight short detective novels (a new field of endeavor), while Hollywood made the twelfth film from his work.

His writing routine in Florence gave priority to a vision of himself as a poet in a classical mold. After breakfast in bed and medicine for serious heart trouble he went to his tower study overlooking the city. He wrote seated at a vast antique table that had come from a Benedictine monastery, using a quill pen on long and heavy sheets of white paper, hoping to produce three to six lines of poetry in a four-hour stint. After an elegant lunch and a nap he turned to prose at about three in the afternoon, writing now in an easy chair with a typewriter on a specially built stand between his knees. After about two hours he had finished his twenty pages and was free for entertaining guests at the villa's tennis court and swimming pool, drinks, and a formal dinner at eight-fifteen. Late in the evening he and his wife would go to the tower study and work until the early morning hours, she reading proofs and sorting manuscripts while he made notes or finished some writing. At eight-fifteen the next morning the routine of the day began anew.

Despite his dedication to verse, after *The Village Street* Faust published only two more poems during his lifetime, both in *Harper's,* and the long classical epic on which he labored, *Dionysus in Hades*, had to be privately printed. Walter Morris Hart, a University of California professor to whom the poem was dedicated, told him frankly that "interest in antique poetic themes is at a low ebb, and the fact that no one has tackled yours for at least twenty-four hundred years is not going to help." Faust was discouraged but undaunted; he continued in his verse to devote himself to the ancient world ("It isn't really a preference for those themes," he responded to Hart, "but a lack of all other themes that determines my choice")[21] while turning out his popular prose. It was typically Faustian that he and Hart, who admired the younger man's success in the pulps, joined in writing a story that they promptly sold to *McCall's*. And typical, too, that as he was failing to find a publisher for his epic poem he published *Destry Rides Again*, among the most popular Western novels of all time.

Plot-making now seemed to him an easy matter. He spotted stories "in the air, flying out of conversations, out of books." One way he did it was to invert situations, such as eating dinner with a rich man and then imagining him suddenly broke and entertaining for the last time. Another was to read some-one else's story halfway and then finish it in his own imagination. "Often you will find that you have a totally new final half of a story. Fit in a new begin-ning and there you are." Or he would take a theme from classical literature and change the setting. "Once I wrote the story of Troy, with Priam, Hector, Paris and Helen, Achilles and Patroclus, etc., and I merely established it in the West and it served pretty well—if only I had known enough West to make it real."[22]

In the Depression thirties Faust spread his wings into spy stories, South Sea stories, historical stories, and the first of his Dr. Kildare tales. As the pulp mar-ket weakened, he made the transition to slick magazines. It was not a question of writing better, he maintained, but one of different attitudes and ideas. When the *Saturday Evening Post* finally bought a story of his in 1936 they paid $750, modest by Faust's standards, but it was a prestige publication and he took the rare step of signing his own name to the work. Soon he was a major supplier of fiction to various slicks as he had been to the pulps. "They want my stuff, now, and they want lots of it," he noted happily. "*Post, Liberty, Col-lier's, Cosmopolitan*—all are vigorously in the field."[23] But artistic satisfaction remained as elusive as ever. "I'm dissatisfied with everything I'm doing," he wrote his agent, Carl Brandt, with a reference to a recent novel of John Stein-beck. "Listen, Carl, the only guy that ever had a right to write *Of Mice and Men*, without a let-down ending, is Heinie Faust. Why the hell can't I do something? Why can't I see you and talk about something except cheese to fit the *Collier's* market? I'm sick. I don't like life. All I want to do is to write verse which makes everybody else sicker than I am. Just now, I think I'm writing better than Milton. Which means that I need a brain doctor."[24]

The lure of a regular salary brought Faust to Hollywood in 1938 at $1,000 a week and with an arrangement that his mornings would be free for verse and fiction while afternoons were given over to films. In the MGM Writers Building, which also housed F. Scott Fitzgerald and Aldous Huxley, he once again dazzled everyone by the speed with which he spun out story ideas. And once again he was a considerable success, both with the stories he worked on and with films made from his work such as the Dr. Kildare series and a popular remake of *Destry Rides Again* with James Stewart and Marlene Dietrich. When he moved to Columbia he wrote the story for *The Desperadoes*, the studio's first technicolor hit; at Warner Brothers, where he joined a stable of writers that included the English author Richard Aldington and William Faulkner, his salary rose to a star writer's $2,000 a week.

Although he worked constantly, Faust gave generously of his time to other writers. Steve Fisher, a pulp veteran who joined the writing staff at Warner Brothers, credited Faust with pushing him to finish a novel: "He saw in it powerful things that had never remotely occurred to me. He said it was an opportunity to write with my guts, the way I should. He hounded and tormented me to start the book, then came in every day to see how many pages I'd done. It was published, and I sold it in addition as a serial, but I don't think Heinie liked it. I could never have come up to the expectations he had for me." For his own work Faust would accept no help—and no praise. Fisher remembered that "the most he ever said about his stories was once, about one thing: 'Junk, sheer junk. Gibberish.' Yet when he talked stories (and when he wrote them, too, never fear) he was a wild man, tender and passionate and fierce, and his ideas soared!"[25]

Film writing satisfied Faust no more than writing for the pulps and the slicks. "Nothing I have done has been any more shameful than this Hollywood work," he told his wife, "and on it as a basis your life cannot be happy."[26] He was drinking heavily, his heart problem was a constant concern, and though the villa in Florence was closed he was still living in high style and usually hard-pressed for funds. During his Hollywood years Faust actually produced little fiction, and though his agent sold a serial to the *Saturday Evening Post* for $15,000, there were disappointing rejections. An air novel was turned down and a serious Civil War novel into which he put four years of research and writing found no takers. With the coming of World War II he longed for involvement, and finally through a studio contact reached the Italian front in 1944 as a correspondent with a plan to accompany a platoon of combat infantrymen and report their story from firsthand knowledge—a hazardous scheme and wholly outside his experience as a writer.

He died at age fifty-one from injuries inflicted by shell fragments during a battle on the Italian front. With his death, the public became more aware of the man behind the many pen names. "Frederick Faust, who thrilled millions with his fiction of adventure under the name of Max Brand," the Associated

Press reported, "died in the forefront of battle within thirty minutes after the Allied offensive opened last Thursday night, the seventeenth war correspondent killed in the war."[27] In accounts of his death and editorial tributes in newspapers and magazines around the country and abroad he was called the "King of the Pulps" and identified as the author of the Dr. Kildare stories and films. His work, meanwhile, continued to come off the presses. Dodd, Mead announced that enough Max Brand material was in hand, largely serials that had appeared in pulp magazines, to permit publication of two books a year well into the future, and there were still unpublished manuscripts in the possession of Faust's agent and family. The legend of the Fabulous Faust—a name acquired back in his college days for the man who would become perhaps the most productive of all Grub Street writers—was still in the making.

three

Faust has maintained a legacy of sorts on the edges of literary memory, the subject now and then of scholarly notice. The more typical suppliers to the fiction pulps had their day on Grub Street—lengthened, if nimble enough, by the carryover of the pulp tradition into paperback books, radio, the movies, and comic books—and were heard from no more. There was W. Bert Foster, who specialized in westerns about Homer of the Lazy D Ranch, and who effortlessly pounded out a million words year after year; Hugh Cave, who in a twelve-year period wrote for a hundred different pulps while trying to average two sales a week; H. Bedford-Jones, who appeared regularly in the pages of *Western Story* with Max Brand, working on two and three novels at the same time, switching from typewriter to typewriter as he amassed his average of ten thousand words a day. Others in the coveted two-cent-a-word class included Walt Colburn, Allan W. C. Macdonald, Ray Nafziger, Walter Gibson, Carroll John Daly, H. P. Lovecraft, George J. Brenn, and Arthur J. Burks—all capable of repeatedly sounding what pulp editor Harold Hersey called "that precious over-note" that separated their pulp creations from run-of-the-mill productions.[28] The literary agent Paul R. Reynolds thought Bedford-Jones, who was said to have an income of $30,000 to $40,000 a year and one year was reported to have reached $75,000, "could scarcely write literate English," yet he possessed "something undefinable, some quality which readers relished."[29]

Burks, considered by his peers the speed merchant of pulp fictioneers, had a brief respite from the anonymity of the trade when he appeared in an amusing *New Yorker* Talk of the Town item in 1936. A Marine officer in both world wars, Burks was thirty-eight at the time and living with his wife (who acted as his literary agent) and an Underwood typewriter in the Knickerbocker Hotel during the winter, then taking both with him to Connecticut for the summer. He estimated he had written 1,200 stories for 140 magazines since his first story in 1924, using his own name and a litany of pseudonyms. His specialty areas were detective, western, mystery, fantasy, terror, airplane, world war, adventure, pseudo-science stories—and, he added, "weird." As for the quality of his work, Burks took the usual position of the professional writer: he had readers and made money. "I don't feel like apologizing for writing to an audience of 25 million people," he said, and went on: "A pulp writer who can't make four hundred a week isn't worth his salt."

The *New Yorker* reported that Burks never bothered to reread his work, either in manuscript form or when published, and had no concern with changes made by editors. (One remembered that Burks wrote so quickly and heedlessly that "he would write right past the end of the story and keep going for another couple of pages with almost a new plot starting. You just had to edit that out. . . . one time I bought a story from him and as a joke I sent back the last two pages and told him, 'We only want to buy up to page 20.'")[30] He found his challenge in dreaming up stories, and claimed he could find an idea in anything. "We tried him out," said the magazine, "on a lampshade in the room":

> "It's the shape of a coolie hat," he said, "and there's a little nick that looks like a bullet hole . . ." "All right," we said, handing him an ashtray. "Reminds me of a machine-gun part," he said. "I'll just put a crew of three men in No Man's Land . . ." We pointed at a picture in a gold oval frame. "A wound of that shape with a gold edge around it," he muttered. "By George," he said suddenly, slipping a piece of paper into his typewriter. "*The Gold Kiss,* by Arthur J. Burks," he wrote, as we watched. "The body was half in and half out of the shadow cast by a huge samovar. The detective stooped over the corpse and gasped in amazement. The gaping oval wound had not bled at all. More than that, it was surrounded by a thin film of what, at first glance, looked to be gold dust . . ." As we tiptoed away, we heard the hum of the Underwood rise in a fierce, white-hot crescendo.[31]

An aspiring young pulp writer of the period, Frank Gruber, recalled that the *New Yorker* profile caused Burks some grief because few writers actually were earning $400 a week during the Depression, Burks included. Although Burks could easily crank out two hundred thousand words a month, selling that many was another matter. Gruber nonetheless considered Burks a master of the pulps and sat as his feet for instruction. "The life of a pulp writer is seven years," he remembered Burks declaring. "At the end of seven years you've got to go on to better writing, or go downhill."[32]

As Gruber later recounted his own career in a memoir, his start in the pulps was in sharp contrast to Frederick Faust's instant success. When he arrived in New York in 1934, a half-dozen years of writing already behind him, there were some 150 pulp magazines in existence and, by his estimate, three hundred professional pulp writers in and around the city who regularly made the round of editors and maybe another thousand in the country who mailed in their work. In addition, hard economic times caused others—all rank amateurs, in Gruber's view—to write for the pulp market, with the result that new writers faced stiff competition. For Gruber this meant a stream of rejections that would have caused most writers to ponder another line of work.

He began storming the gates by poring over publications for writers like *Writer's Digest* and *Author and Journalist* to get a line on what magazines wanted, the names of editors, and rates of pay. He also got involved in the American Fiction Guild, an organization of pulp writers (five pulp sales needed for membership) that had Burks as president of its New York chapter. At lunch meetings in a New York restaurant Gruber and other neophytes rubbed shoulders with editors and successful writers, heard the shop talk, and saw writers displaying checks from their weekly paydays. One contact made during the sessions was with the editor in chief of a pulp house, and from him Gruber learned the typical system of accepting stories. The editor himself never read stories; they were read instead by three readers, and if all three approved the story was purchased; if one disapproved the story was rejected. The editor encouraged Gruber to submit stories of detection, love, and adventure, but when he did all were turned down.

Gruber's break came when the editor of a pulp called *Operator #5* told him a 5,500-word story was needed to fill out an issue. Could he supply one overnight? The next morning Gruber's eighteen-page spy story was ready; it was accepted, and he was asked to supply another for the following month. "The tide," he remembered, "turned that quickly."[33] In 1934 his income from writing had been $400, a figure that included some money from stories sold before he came to New York. In 1935 he sold fifty-five stories and made $10,000, an impressive figure in a time when he could get an apartment in Greenwich Village for $25 to $30 a month, eat well on $10 a week, and buy himself a Buick for around $750.

He had four regular outlets now but knew it was important to keep expanding his market. Magazines could become overstocked and stop buying for two or three months, and there were always magazines closing down. He hammered away at the Munsey publications and tried to crack what he considered the most prestigious pulp, *Black Mask*. The latter's editor, Joseph T. Shaw, met with Gruber in his office, treated him with courtesy, and encouraged him to submit work to the magazine, which he in turn read, discussed with Gruber in detail, but never bought. "He encouraged you to do revisions of revisions," Gruber remembered, "and when he finally rejected your story, it was always with great regret, a hand on your shoulder, a pat on the back. 'Try again, old man. *Please!*'"[34]

Black Mask was founded in 1920 by H. L. Mencken and George Jean Nathan as a pulp home for quality detective fiction, but it was after Shaw took over the editorship in 1926 that it gained a reputation for cool, cleanly-written, hard-boiled crime stories. Shaw wanted rapid pacing and plausible plots; above all he insisted on a realistic atmosphere and strong characterization that was revealed through action. Writers like Raoul Whitfield, Paul Cain, Carroll John Daly, Dashiell Hammett, and Raymond Chandler set the magazine's style, in so doing shifting the mystery story from puzzles solved by the elegant reason of Poe's Dupin or Doyle's Holmes to a dark-hued, humanly-flawed world of urban private eyes. As Shaw described it, the magazine's fiction "was simple, logical, almost inevitable" and emphasized "character and the problems inherent in human behavior over crime solution."[35]

Black Mask's success spawned many imitators, and one of them, *Detective Fiction Weekly*, a Munsey publication, became a market for Gruber. But he had no luck breaking into *Argosy*, which ran four serials simultaneously each week, many of them written by Max Brand, George Owen Baxter, George Challis, and Evan Evans—all, Gruber learned later, pen names of Frederick Faust. The editors Gruber dealt with were mostly young, in their twenties and thirties, and a varied lot. John Nanovic of Street & Smith was a Notre Dame graduate and deeply religious; Duncan Norton-Taylor, editor of *Detective Fiction Weekly*, was a learned man who later worked at *Time* and *Fortune;* Norton-Taylor's successor, Charles Ingerman, was a philologist who spoke several languages; Shaw, considered the most demanding of pulp editors, had won an Olympic fencing medal. Other editors were former pulp writers who preferred a steady income to the uncertain life on the other side of the desk. Gruber learned it was important to be knowledgeable about editors and cultivate their company, but it was equally important to keep them in the dark about one's backlog of work. All stories were supposedly hot off the typewriter and expressly meant for a particular editor.

Gruber branched out into novelettes and became a regular writer for *Ranch Romances, Short Stories,* and finally *Black Mask,* his pay rate now at two cents a word. But real advancement as a writer meant leaving the pulps for the slicks, and in 1938 he finally sold a story to Fulton Oursler, the editorial director of *Liberty;* then he turned to book writing. He picked his genre by considering the competition: there were fifty good mystery writers turning out novels but only two good western writers. He invested $200 in books about the West, studied the region, and in three weeks turned out *Peace Marshall.* When an agent told him the novel was hopeless he took it in person to *Adventure,* a pulp magazine he had never tried before, and within a week it was purchased for $1,200—Gruber's best sale as a writer—and eventually brought out in book form by William Morrow. Shortly thereafter Gruber turned his hand to a mystery novel.

He read a number to see how they were done, then cranked out *The French Key* in seven writing days over a two-week period. The book won an honorable mention in the first Mary Roberts Rinehart Mystery Novel Contest and, with a modest $250 advance, was published by Farrar and Rinehart in 1940. Five years later the novel sold to Hollywood for $14,000. In the meantime Gruber kept up a furious pace of writing westerns and mysteries for the pulp magazines and as books—sixty to seventy thousand words a month. "I flogged the typewriter day and night," he remembered. "I flogged it in the early hours of the morning, I beat at it, late at night. I worked Saturdays and Sundays." He developed a formula for mysteries that involved eleven elements (hero, theme, villain, background, murder method, motive, clue, trick, action, climax, emotion), working out "each element at a time, concentrating on one until I had licked it, then going on to the next." He maintained that a "perfectly salable mystery story" might include seven or eight of the elements, "but get them all into a story and you cannot miss." For westerns he concluded that there were seven basic stories in the genre (Union Pacific story; ranch story; empire story—meaning a story about a vast spread like the King Ranch; revenge story; Custer's Last Stand story—meaning a Cavalry and Indian story; outlaw story; marshal story—meaning a dedicated lawman story), and "once I had these classifications worked out thoroughly it was of great help to me. I could go over them, decide that I had written stories in one or another of the groups only recently and it might be easier to do one of the others."[36]

After he left New York for Hollywood in 1943 Gruber became acquainted with Faust, a writer he considered the most prolific of all time—and the biggest drinker he had ever known. According to Gruber, Faust could write only after taking a few drinks "to transport him into that world of fantasy of which he wrote so well."[37] Gruber also found that Faust had nothing but contempt for Hollywood and for screenwriting. He was only able to write for the screen in the sense of writing original stories; he had neither interest nor skill in turning his work into screenplays. Gruber had both, with the result that, in addition to selling twenty-five of his novels to Hollywood (including his first, *Peace Marshall*, that became a popular film as *The Kansan*) he eventually wrote sixty-five screenplays and some one hundred television scripts, and created three series for television. To his staggering productivity Gruber added a brief biography of Horatio Alger, Jr., and a full-length study of Zane Grey.

four

As Grey led the way with westerns, a fellow Midwesterner and near contemporary, Edgar Rice Burroughs, did the same with science fiction, expanding Poe's early experiments into a full-blown genre that, while never matching the popularity of westerns or mysteries, became a durable earning vehicle for writers. From a prosperous Chicago business family, Burroughs had tried working for the American Battery Company, his father's firm, and for Sears, Roebuck, but nothing satisfied him; when he tried his own business he failed. In 1911, in his middle thirties, married, eking out a living in a small enterprise selling pencil sharpeners, he began work on a science fiction novel with a Martian setting. He knew nothing of the world of authors and publishers but, as he later recalled, he had read the all-fiction pulp magazines "and it suddenly occurred to me that people were probably paid for writing such rot."[38]

The first half of the story complete, he mailed it off to the Munsey Company's *All-Story* under the insistently ordinary pen name of Normal Bean ("I was sort of ashamed of writing as an occupation for a big, strong, healthy man, so I kept it a secret")[39] together with a letter summarizing the plot: "The story is supposedly from the manuscript of a Virginian soldier of fortune who spends ten years on Mars, among the ferocious green men of that planet as well as with the highly developed and scientific race of dominant Martians, who closely resemble the inhabitants of Earth, except as to color. It is a member of this latter race which gives the story its name and at the same time infuses the elements of love into the narrative."[40] The response to the narrative of his space explorer, John Carter, was heartening. Thomas Newell Metcalf, *All-*

Story's editor, told him the story was too long and leisurely for magazine purposes but encouraged him to revise and hold the manuscript to seventy thousand words. Burroughs went back to work and finally the story was accepted
for $400 and published in the February 1912 issue of the magazine as "Under
the Moons of Mars."

Burroughs was pleased but cautious, figuring that with the time spent on
the story he had earned only about $100 a month. He had a family to support,
he was not young, and he had a history of business failures. But he turned to
more writing while keeping his business options open. His next novel, a historical romance featuring a heroic outlaw, was rejected by Metcalf and under-
went a good deal of revision before it was purchased by Street & Smith's *New
Story* in 1913 for $500. In the meantime Burroughs turned to a work that he
termed "improbable" but which flowed easily from his pen. Metcalf was given
a preview in a letter: "The story I am on now is of the scion of a noble English house—of the present time—who was born in tropical Africa where his
parents died when he was about a year old. The infant was found and adopted
by a huge she-ape, and was brought up among a band of fierce anthropoids."
Metcalf, no doubt to his lasting delight, responded with enthusiasm: "I think
your idea for a new serial is a crackerjack and I shall be very anxious to have a
look at it."[41]

"Tarzan of the Apes, A Romance of the Jungle," for which Burroughs received $700 for serial rights, appeared in the October 1912 issue of *All-Story*
under Burroughs's own name, with his pen name following in parentheses.
The story was an immediate success with pulp readers. Although Burroughs
had scant knowledge of Africa, it scarcely mattered; he possessed instead a gift
for building suspense and dreaming up memorable characters, including various jungle creatures. Alva Johnston once theorized in a tongue-in-cheek article in the *Saturday Evening Post* that Burroughs early in his career recognized
the "folly of research" for a popular novelist. He placed his first novel on Mars
because so little was known about it, and he cast the Tarzan stories in Africa
largely for the same reason. "He knew," Johnston wrote, "that nobody could
trip him up on the psychology, customs and language of his own private
anthropoids." Johnston added that Burroughs's career revealed a number of
lessons for writers of popular fiction, one being to avoid subjects you know
anything about.[42]

Tarzan would become one of the great popular creations of all time, perhaps second only to Mickey Mouse. Yet when Burroughs first tried to find a
book publisher for his magazine saga he found no interest, and it was not

until 1914 that A. C. McClurg and Company brought out a hardback version. In the meantime Burroughs went back to his Martian chronicles with a five-part *All-Story* serial, "The Gods of Mars," in which John Carter returns to earth, informing a nephew that he has the secret of space journeys between the two planets.

Burroughs was riding high, certain now his future was in writing. Yet when his next work, a Tarzan sequel, was rejected by Metcalf on the grounds that it lacked balance, he plummeted into despair. He wrote the editor: "There is so much uncertainty about the writing game—the constant feeling, for me at least, that I don't know how my stuff is going to hit you that I am entirely discouraged. I certainly can not afford to put months of work into a story thinking it the best work that I had ever done only to find that it doesn't connect. I can make money easier some other way." And he added: "I probably lack balance myself—a well balanced mind would not turn out my kind of stuff. As long as I can't market it as it comes out it is altogether too much of a gamble, so I think I'll chuck it." But he had too much invested as a writer, and too much confidence in his ability, to give up entirely; he mailed off the Tarzan sequel to *New Story,* where it was promptly accepted for his best payment to date, $1,000, and published as "The Return of Tarzan."

By 1913, job abandoned and writing full time, Burroughs swiftly progressed from a rank amateur to a complete professional. He patched up relations with Metcalf, accepting an offer from *All-Story* for two cents a word for first serial rights to all of a year's production, and he began to master the intricacies of newspaper syndication (of which more in the following chapter). With his fertile imagination he spun out story after story, and with his business background he marketed his work with a firm hand. He was shrewd enough to realize that the John Carter Martian chronicles and Tarzan were hot properties, allowing him to bargain with editors for prices. With his third Tarzan story he played the editors of *All-Story* and *New Story* off against each other (in the course of negotiation a manuscript was lost and Burroughs asked that the editors share the remaining one; astonishingly, they agreed), with Metcalf coming out on top for $2,500, probably *All-Story's* biggest payout for a serial.

While "The Beasts of Tarzan" was serialized in 1913–14 Burroughs ventured into another lucrative avenue for his work, film rights. Eventually forty Tarzan stories would reach the screen, there would be popular radio versions, and the jungle hero would be widely merchandised in comic strips and book reprints. By 1921 Burroughs's writing income had climbed to $100,000 a year and the money kept coming in. In 1923, ever the man of business as well as a writer, he incorporated himself for tax purposes, possibly the first professional writer to do so. To Edgar Rice Burroughs, Inc., he granted all current and future literary rights, he and family members taking shares of stock in return. Until his death in 1950 at age seventy-four Burroughs operated as a salaried employee of his corporation.[43]

Russel Nye has pointed out that the Tarzan stories were essentially science fiction, Burroughs creating an Africa of his copious imagination and using themes of a superbeing, lost worlds, and utopia, and drawing on the device of the time warp.[44] The Tarzan stories alternated with work in a direct science-fiction vein in the Martian series and in a number of "Pellucidar" stories about life in the earth's core, together with a few books in a realistic manner and with contemporary settings.

Although Burroughs published fifty-nine novels in all, twenty-four featuring Tarzan, his primary publishing outlet remained the racy world of pulp magazines. After Metcalf left *All-Story* Burroughs came into the editorial hands of Robert Davis of the Munsey organization and began appearing in *Argosy* as well as *All-Story.* Later he became a prize property of another star editor, Ray Long, who orchestrated *Red Book* (renamed *Redbook* after the McCall Corporation bought it in 1929) and later *Cosmopolitan.* Hugo Gernsback, considered the founding father of a more reality-based science fiction that developed in the twenties (and whose term "scientification," by which he meant romantic fiction mingled with scientific fact and prophetic vision, became "science fiction"), attracted Burroughs to his *Amazing Stories,* a twenty-five-cent magazine with a circulation of a hundred thousand, high in both areas for a narrowly aimed periodical. For his *Amazing Stories Annual* in 1927 Gernsback commissioned a novel from Burroughs, *The Master Mind of Mars,* and paid him $1,250, this despite the editor-publisher's reputation in pulp quarters as a poor—and slow—paymaster. It was a shrewd investment, as it turned out, since the *Annual,* with a stiff fifty-cent cover price, nearly sold out a print run of a hundred thousand copies.

five

Burroughs discovered with John Carter and Tarzan what pulp and cheap-book writers had known for some time—the lure of recurring characters when it came to drawing regular paychecks from the fiction market. When a character caught the public fancy, he or she could be marketed again and again with plots that were only slight variations on the original, reader interest continually nourished by the very familiarity and predictability of the figures. While the possibilities were seemingly endless, older figures drawn with warm humor were particular favorites—like Norman Rockwell covers for the *Saturday Evening Post,* presumably appealing to nostalgia for an earlier age of simplicity and common-sense sanity.

Peter B. Kyne shared with Burroughs a business background and liked to think of himself as a businessman in literature. While working for a wholesale lumber and shipping firm he learned the ways of the San Francisco waterfront, a locale that provided characters and incidents for his fiction; later he operated a shop in San Francisco and worked as a lumber broker. When money began coming in from his fiction he invested in schemes from gold mines to manufacturing, bought racehorses, and ran a farm on which he profitably raised purebred cattle.[45] Ray Long, among the magazine editors who eagerly bid for his work, described Kyne as having the "face and figure of a well-fed priest."[46]

Kyne broke into the slick magazines in 1909 with a shipping story in the *Saturday Evening Post,* "A Little Matter of Salvage," and with his third novel in 1916 he found a profitable groove with *Cappy Ricks.* The breathless two-page dedication saluted Kyne's business background, embracing American sailors, shipowners, Pacific coast lumbermen (Kyne noting his own abandonment of "lumber for literature"), and marine insurance brokers. Cappy Ricks, who would appear in another of Kyne's twenty-five novels and in some fifty out of a thousand published stories and articles (this considerable output achieved despite a working method in which he produced material rapidly but also went months without writing at all), is a vigorous bantam-rooster tyrant—rough on the outside, soft-hearted inside—who has made a fortune in shipping and lumber, then turned over the businesses to managers but meddles, usually shrewdly, in their affairs. Kyne had success with other fictional ventures through the 1920s and 1930s, including westerns, romances, and hunting, racing, and sea stories.[47] Still, Cappy Ricks remained Kyne's prime creation.

Irvin S. Cobb made his first appearance in the *Saturday Evening Post* in the same year as Kyne, 1909, with a story called "The Escape of Mr. Trimm." At the time Cobb was a jack-of-all-trades journalist and budding humorist with the *New York Evening World;* he had written stories before ("every reporter has—fiction masquerading as the lighter side of the news," he said later) but

"Mr. Trimm" was his first effort at "avowed fiction."[48] After two more stories were accepted by the *Post,* George Horace Lorimer encouraged Cobb to give up newspapering for freelance magazine work, offering the enticement of a check every two weeks as advance payment for future production.[49] Thereafter, Cobb was a regular contributor to the *Post* and later *Cosmopolitan.*

A story in the *Post* in 1911, "Words and Music," introduced the character who, as Cobb put it, "became a mainstay and a breadwinner for the Cobb family over a stretch of thirty years or longer."[50] Judge Priest was modeled on figures Cobb had grown up knowing in Paducah, Kentucky—a rumpled, courtly Southern sage who enjoys his bourbon and corn-cob pipe, reminisces about the still vivid Civil War, spends a good deal of time hunting and fishing, and feigns an uneducated and even simple-minded manner while managing to outwit all who enter his courtroom. Cobb thought the first story an "isolated and individual yarn" but went on to write—by his own count— nearly seventy stories[51] along with a novelette and a novel-length mystery story, *Judge Priest Turns Detective,* featuring the circuit-court country jurist and a recurring cast of cronies.

During World War I Cobb reported from Europe for the *Post* in impressive fashion, and later won acclaim as a magazine humorist, platform wit, and radio performer. Renowned for his speed at turning out copy, he was said to have written six hundred thousand words in longhand from a courtroom while covering the Stanford White murder trial in 1907—and Robert Davis claimed that Cobb was the only writer of his acquaintance who could turn out a story and hold a conversation at the same time. Such productivity resulted in hundreds of stories and nearly sixty books in a life crammed with activity. But as with Kyne's Cappy Ricks, it was the Judge Priest tales that stuck as Cobb's major popular accomplishment. In 1934, age fifty-eight, he moved to Hollywood to work on a screen version of the stories. Directed by John Ford and with Will Rogers in the lead role, the filmed *Judge Priest* added another notch to Cobb's success.

Mary Roberts Rinehart worked an effective variation on the appealing-elder type, creating in Letitia Carberry—Tish—a comic spinster figure who in foolhardy fashion embraces every new fad and technology of the modern world, from golf to airplanes to outdoor camping. Like Cappy Ricks and Judge Priest, Tish was drawn from actual experience, in Rinehart's case three spinsters who during a summer vacation happened to catch her attention with their ineffectual efforts to rid themselves of a stray dog. The first story, "That Awful Night," introduced the two other characters who would appear in all the Tish tales—Lizzie, who narrates Tish's misadventures, and Aggie, in lengthy mourning for a dead fiance. Sent first to *Harper's*, which had requested a story from her, and turned down with a rejection slip, the story was taken by the *Saturday Evening Post*—with the sequel, as Rinehart recalled, that when it appeared in the *Post* in 1910 *Harper's* wrote her that "they had not yet had the manuscript I was to send them, and there was a tale of mine in *The Post* which was precisely of the sort they would like to have!"[52]

A second story, "Three Pirates of Penzance," appeared in the *Post* a few months later, the magazine now fixed as Tish's home for the next thirty years. Although Kyne and Cobb would defect to *Cosmopolitan*, taking Cappy Ricks and Judge Priest with them, Rinehart remained loyal to Lorimer's magazine. She noted in an autobiography in 1931 that "*Tish* still belongs to *The Post*. I have determinedly remained a free lance in my work, sending it where it belongs, but *Tish* is for *The Post* so long as they will have her."[53]

The character did not wear out her welcome until after 1937, the year of Lorimer's retirement as editor in chief, when the magazine carried "Tish Marches On." When Rinehart wrote another Tish story in 1941 the magazine turned it down on the grounds that the character had become outdated, a view Rinehart unhappily accepted with the comment that with war-time "the world is in so grave a mood that even humor seems out of place." (In a revised edition of her autobiography she said further that with the *Post's* rejection she lost confidence in the character and was never able to revive her.) Just a few years earlier a reviewer in the *Boston Evening Transcript* had concluded about Rinehart's work that "it is to be doubted if, when the final judgment is made, her serious volumes . . . will weigh as much as a straw against the not always so naive adventures of Tish"—and the character retained enough popularity with readers that in 1955, three years before her death, Rinehart published a collection of twelve stories as *The Best of Tish*.[54]

six

If mass-circulation slick magazines operated in a middle range between pulps and high-culture monthlies and quarterlies, so too in the arena of book publishing did the paperback originals or "made books" that, after sporadic appearances earlier, gushed forth in the 1950s. For popular fictioneers the timing was fortunate, providing a crucial survival line as pulp markets dried up or were transformed into a demand for male adventure in magazines such as

Stag, Male, and *True.* "Writers drifted into the men's magazines," one Grub Street figure of the time remembered, "and fiction writers into paperback originals. If you weren't a name writer there was no place else to go."[55]

At first regarded solely as reprinters of successful hardcover books, paperback houses like Pocket Books, Lion, Ace, Ballantine, and Bantam began putting original novels on their lists to circumvent bidding wars for hardcovers. Gold Medal Books from Fawcett Publications was the first entry in the field, launched in early 1950 as exclusively originals. Most of the offerings were male adventure novels—western, mystery-detective, thriller—together with a sprinkling of light romances. Other publishers had doubts, thinking writers would resist first publication in paperback, but Fawcett's idea rapidly gained a foothold. In a year and a half Gold Medal issued over eighty titles, with sales averaging 150,000 copies each.[56]

Writers received advances of $2,000 against royalties based on print runs of 200,000, upped to $3,000 when print runs were boosted to 300,000, and retained all subsidiary rights.[57] The contract terms were appealing, in many cases adding up to more money than writers could make from combined hardcover royalties and paperback reprint rights, and there was pleasure in working with the gentlemanly editor in chief, William Lengel, who had once been a magazine editorial assistant under Theodore Dreiser. Rather than return manuscripts with suggestions for revision, he often invited writers to the firm's editorial offices to work directly under his or another editor's guidance.[58] "By taking some books turned down by hardcover publishers," an editor at a rival house added, "Gold Medal has built up considerable good-will . . . tending to draw more mystery and western writers. Publishers don't do a thing for mysteries and westerns as far as advertising and promotion are concerned and this fact makes it easy for Gold Medal to persuade writers to come to them directly—once the prestige factor can be disposed of."[59]

But not only rejected books turned up as originals. Wade Miller, a successful mystery-writing team of Bob Wade and Bill Miller, switched from an arrangement with Farrar, Straus for hardcovers and New American Library's Signet for paperback reprints to Gold Medal originals with first printings that averaged 450,000. Others writers who turned out paperback originals, whether redirected from hardcover publishers or dusted off rejections, were—among names that still survive—Sax Rohmer, Bruno Fischer, John D. MacDonald, Chester Himes, Louis L'Amour, Ed McBain, Isaac Asimov, and E. Howard Hunt, later of Watergate notoriety. Hunt was recruited for Gold Medal by Jim Bishop, an editor who would become the author of such best-selling books as *The Day Lincoln Was Shot* and *The Day Christ Died,* with an offer of $2,000 advances and royalties on books printed rather than sold. Hunt was publishing hardcover thrillers with major houses but he jumped to originals, works he approached as "spare, gutsy, action-suspense books with not too many plot complications to slow the reader and lose his interest."[60] Later he wrote for other paperback houses under his own name and pseudonyms.

By the middle of the 1950s one-third of all mass-market titles issued by book publishers were paperback originals produced by inexpensive high-speed manufacturing, widely distributed through local wholesalers, and generally priced at twenty-five cents. Complaint about lowered standards issued from critical quarters (Bernard De Voto said of Fawcett's early offering that "what Gold Medal has proved is we didn't know how lousy novels could be"),[61] but for toiling writers, the well regarded and the unknown, quarter originals had the drawbacks only of the "prestige factor" and the absence of continuing life on library shelves. Tipping the scales the other way was the good money and the fact that it was quick money. Publishers of originals depended on volume; they had to make publishing decisions more rapidly than hardcover publishers, with the result that advance money came swiftly and, if the writer was riding a hot streak, often.

Jim Thompson's career in originals is a case in point—and illustration, too, of how such careers could be as fleeting as they were rewarding. In 1952 Thompson, in his forties and a professional writer with a broad background with newspapers, trade magazines, true-crime pulp magazines (as discussed in chapter eight), and a published hardcover novelist, had just left an editorial job with the *Police Gazette* in New York when he was taken by his agent to meet Arnold Hano, the editor of Lion Books. Hano had announced in *Publishers Weekly* that his firm, primarily a reprinter, was in the market for paperback originals. At that meeting Thompson was introduced to how Lion Books planned to generate its originals. "We handed him about five synopses or so," Hano remembered. "Bryans [Jim Bryans, an editor with the firm] had this one about a New York City cop who got involved with a prostitute and ends up killing her. It was kind of a cheapo suspense novel. Jim looked it over and said, 'I'll take this one.'"[62] An agreement was struck that Thompson would draft the opening forty or fifty pages of the novel and work up an outline for the rest; on that basis Lion Books would decide whether to go ahead. The pay, Hano recalled, was $1,000 if the sample was adequate, another $1,000 on completion.

Two weeks later Thompson returned with almost half of *The Killer Inside Me* written and a transformed synopsis that relocated the story from New

York to the West Texas oil country he had known in earlier years. Hano was stunned by the changed characterization and gripping quality of a chilling plot, and after a second novel for Lion Books, *Cropper's Cabin,* Thompson never again started off with a synopsis. "Very early on," said Hano, "I realized that what Jim needed was encouragement more than anything else. As far as I was concerned, he was inventing a new genre for us. You unleash a guy like that, you simply don't try to direct him."[63] In a concentrated period of writing over the next two years Thompson produced a string of originals—among them, *A Swell-Looking Babe, The Nothing Man, The Criminal, Savage Night*— whose violence, obsessive characters, and surrealistic tones surpassed anything previously seen in crime fiction.

Discounting his serious alcoholism, Thompson, a family man with an aversion to violence, seemed an unlikely figure as a black-hued crime writer. Some of *The Killer Inside Me* was written while on a visit to a daughter in what was an equally unlikely location—the Marine Corps base in Virginia. He worked all day in a tiny upstairs room that, the daughter recalled, was rocked with the noise of construction trucks going by; but when she looked in on him "you'd never know anything was happening around him, he was so deep into that book. He'd write ten pages every day. Each night I'd read the ten pages, and I was horrified all the way through, but I never said so. I did ask him finally, where in the world did you get all this? He said that he had acquired a lot of it from reading, from research and looking things up."[64]

Lion Books also published as originals Thompson novels written earlier and, oddly, given the firm's emphasis on fiction, two autobiographical volumes, *Bad Boy* and *Roughneck.* "Jim wanted to do them, and he assured us they would be stories," Hano said about the two works. "We cheated on the packaging—we didn't scream 'autobiography' or 'nonfiction.'"[65] All Thompson's novels sold well in printings of two hundred thousand copies and more, and the autobiographies did well enough; with the advances he pocketed (in one year, 1953, there were five), Thompson was flush with money for the first time in his writing career. Even some critical approval came his way from Anthony Boucher, who took enthusiastic note of most of Thompson's originals in his "Criminals at Large" column in the *New York Times Book Review.* (Boucher was a ray of light for many authors of originals. Vin Packer, the author of popular Gold Medal mysteries, said she began writing originals "solely because I'd heard that *The New York Times'* mystery columnist, Anthony Boucher, would review paperbacks." Encouraged by his notices of her work, she stayed with originals for a decade.)[66]

Then, at the top of his game, everything went sour for Thompson. Hano decided to switch from editing to freelance writing and Lion Books abruptly ceased publishing originals. Thompson kept writing but had difficulty finding new publishers, despite his success and the fact that Fawcett and other paperback houses were doing well with crime fiction. In 1955 alone some three hundred originals appeared. Thompson's agent was bewildered, writing Boucher that she "couldn't understand why such a good writer should go begging. He has built up a following—thanks partly to you—and that should count for something with a publisher."[67] Not, as it turned out, enough. Thompson picked up money writing for crime magazines, including the true-crime pulps, and men's adventure magazines; and for a short time he returned to newspaper work. But the market for paperback originals remained closed to him. "Nineteen fifty-four, fifty-five was the worst time of all," his daughter remembered. "After the paperback market dried up for him Daddy kept writing, but he didn't know where to turn."[68]

Thompson drifted from New York to Hollywood and film writing by committee. Eventually he published more paperback originals, and for money produced novelized versions of successful films and television shows. There were high points, especially with the novel *The Grifters* in 1963, but he never regained the success of the white-hot period from 1952–54 with Lion Books, when he wrote more than half of his lifetime output of novels. It was a decade after his death in 1977 that his originals began taking on the aura of underground classics and there were well-regarded film adaptations. The belated shift in fortunes had the quality of a bitter Thompson story. "This whole revival is pretty amazing," said the crime writer Donald E. Westlake in 1990 when a film version of *The Grifters* got Academy Award nominations and there were adaptations of two other Thompson novels. "I think you'd have to say that it somehow matches Jim's view of life, that he gets his fifteen minutes of fame thirteen years after his death."[69]

Five

SUBLIME TRAMPS

Newspaper Journalism and the
Dream of the Writing Life

"To become a reporter now, just as my style is taking form,
crystallizing, would be to commit literary suicide."
—Jack London

one

In 1888, Julian Hawthorne, an active magazinist of the time, estimated that
five thousand Americans might earn their living by writing. A rough guess at
best, it was a figure that included book and magazine authors and fictioneers
of all stripe but no newspaper journalists.[1] Hardly a friend of newspapers,
Hawthorne took the position that they so infected the writing of the time as
virtually to rule out the possibility of serious literature;[2] all the same, he himself held a dozen newspaper positions in the course of a long writing career
that included unblushing labor on Grub Street. The exclusion of journalists
from his aggregate of authors, together with the division about the press evident within his own career, points to the curious and essentially ambiguous
place of newspapers in the world of professional writing.

Typically, daily and weekly papers were the first medium in which aspiring
writers were able to break into print and begin to forge a name for themselves.

Established writers found publishing outlets there as well, especially in contributions to pages set aside as literary departments and, beginning with their introduction in the 1830s and '40s , in Sunday editions. But taking a staff position on a newspaper as a reporter or editor was another matter entirely. It meant exchanging precious independence for the routines of an employee and fitting words into ready-made forms that could be hard if not impossible to escape in future work. A salaried journalist was a writer, but a writer in captivity.

Early newspapers in the American colonies were put together by a single editor-publisher with scissors and paste pot, news and features largely clipped from other papers and the foreign press. Contributions from subscribers of essays, poetry, political articles, and satirical pieces became more important as the feature content of papers expanded following the Revolution, with Philadelphia's *Gazette of the United States* in 1800 (a daily paper at that point, having begun as a semiweekly) promising "seven or eight columns a week to the motley tribe of miscellany readers" and providing even more.[3] But with the turn to the nineteenth century the newspapers' function as something of a literary miscellany became increasingly absorbed by magazines, with papers settling into the role of a medium for more or less current news. Only with the rise of the penny press in the 1830s and '40s and a new emphasis on local coverage and journalism for the masses did the in-house staff reporter make an appearance.

When Mark Twain took his first reporting job on the *Virginia Daily Territorial Enterprise* he was told to "go all over town and ask all sorts of people all sorts of questions, make notes of the information gained, and write them out for publication." It seemed a straightforward task, and after a day on the job he got the hang of it and decided he was "peculiarly endowed" as a reporter. From Twain on, through Bret Harte, Stephen Crane, William Dean Howells, Theodore Dreiser, Sinclair Lewis, Ernest Hemingway, James Thurber, John O'Hara, and hosts of others, young writers pursued reporting jobs on the way to the literary life. The idea was to get the benefits newspaper work offered as, in Howells's phrase, a "university of the streets and police stations" and then move on before being sapped by its limitations.[4] In an article in 1888 James Parton, a former newspaperman himself, viewed such a course as fraught with more danger than reward and advised the ambitious young writer occupied in journalism always to be "on the lookout for a chance to escape." The wisest course was to avoid the profession of journalism entirely. That world, Parton allowed, "has its fascinations and its ecstasies. The most honest man in the

world may find congenial work in it, and it offers a few prizes of a truly dazzling character. Nevertheless, upon the whole, I say, leave it to the left-outs;
leave it to the adventurers; leave it to the good fellows who have been educated out of the ordinary vocations, but not into the extraordinary. Leave it to
the sublime tramps of the intellectual world."[5]

For some writers their days as sublime tramps were colored in retrospect
with a romantic glow. Norman Hapgood, who became the reform-minded
editor of *Collier's*, happily recalled the course that turned him from a Harvard-educated lawyer and literary aspirant into a New York reporter enlivened
by the "zest, adaptability to circumstance, and that almost insolent audacity
which is not undersupplied in the American press."[6] Sam Blythe, one of the
country's top political writers in the World War I period, put together a
lengthy bill of particulars against his own field ("the grind saps strength; . . .
the life has a tendency to invite the forming of ruinous habits; . . . young men
become old in it quickly and . . . old men become useless") yet insisted that
"newspaper work in his country offers an exceptional advantage to the young
man who has an aptitude for it."[7] A. B. Guthrie, Jr., who after twenty years
abandoned the newsroom for western fiction, regretted "the loss of that community intimacy that is a newspaperman's special possession, that knowledge
of subjects and men and associations and stresses that lie underneath news."[8]
Still, the more common view of daily journalism for writers was James Parton's:
largely a misspent youth with little profit and much loss. Twain set the stage
here as well with the speedy discovery that the reporting job for which he
thought himself peculiarly endowed gave no "rest or respite" and left him "un-
speakably tired of it."[9]

Thereafter writers fired off a steady barrage of criticism of their newspaper
days. Willa Cather excoriated journalism as "the vandalism of literature": "It
has brought to it endless harm and no real good. It has made an art a trade.
The great American newspaper takes in intellect, promise, talent; it gives out
only colloquial gossip. It is written by machines, set by machines, and read by
machines. No man can write long for any journal in this country without for
the most part losing that precious thing called style."[10] Gertrude Stein made a
similar point in a celebrated remark in the 1920s, telling the young Hemingway
that "if you keep on doing newspaper work you will never see things, you will
only see words and that will not do, that is of course if you intend to be a
writer."[11] A short while later Hemingway decided to leave his reporting job
with the *Toronto Star*, telling Stein: "I am going to chuck journalism I think.
You ruined me as a journalist last winter. Have been no good since. Like a bull

or a novillo rather, well stuck but taking a long while to go down."[12] Howells, on the other hand, bemoaned the hurly-burly world into which journalism cast him rather than the work itself: "If all my work could have been the reporting of sermons, with intervals of sketching the graduating ceremonies of young ladies' seminaries, such as that where once a girl in garnet silk read an essay of perhaps no surpassing interest, but remained an enchanting vision, and the material of some future study in fiction; if it could have been these things, with nothing of police-stations in it, I might have tried longer to become a city editor."[13]

But whatever the testimony of others, aspiring writers had to experience for themselves both the enchantment of journalism and its suffocating embrace. Through World War II, when classroom writing programs overtook newsroom apprenticeships, they continued to try out their literary wings as reporters. What most of them discovered was that the "great grind of a daily paper" was hard to put behind, as Dreiser grumbled in his column in *Ev'ry Month* magazine in 1896, and that literary talent "often lingers and wears itself out in journalism unheard of."[14] But if there were seldom triumphs of the sort envisioned in the mythical scenario of the reporter turned artist, figures like Crane, Dreiser, and Hemingway seemed to make the transition from journalism to literature easily enough. And there was the larger-than-life figure of Richard Harding Davis, who worked both fields simultaneously with ease.

His first day on the job in 1889 on Charles Dana's *New York Evening Sun*, Davis fell into a street adventure with a confidence man, wrote it up as amusing farce, and saw it run in the paper as a front-page report under the heading "Our Green Reporter."[15] Instantly, Davis's name was made as a reporter. Nearly as swiftly he became known as a fiction writer when his tale of newsroom adventure, "Gallegher," appeared to great acclaim in *Scribner's* magazine in 1890. A month after the sale to *Scribner's* he made a second to *Harper's* and was summoned to the office of its editor, Henry Mills Alden, who praised the story as "light in a grand and noble way." Alden then added: "We have had no such writer in this country. The French have them but America has wanted them for years and you are the man." Dazed by the praise, Davis had to ask if the editor was talking about him. It is easy to understand why his contemporaries believed that Davis, both as journalist and storyteller, had literally become famous overnight.

The reality was slightly different. From his first newspaper job, on the *Philadelphia Record*, Davis was summarily fired, and when he began trying to place stories and articles with national magazines during his brief student days at Johns Hopkins he expected and got rapid rejection. Behind the success of "Gallegher" was over a year's tinkering with the manuscript, and before *Scribner's* accepted it, after first requesting revisions, it was turned down by three major periodicals. But there was no denying the rapid ascent of Davis's star. At the ripe age of twenty-six he found himself fully established as both a metropolitan reporter and a man of letters.

two

Now and then newspaper work offered a writer some direct benefit, as it seemed to do for Hemingway when writing feature-story journalism from Paris encouraged a narrative bent. The same was true for other writers, and more often writers of the Grub Street sort, when they were freed from reporting and allowed to work in the more open forms of columns, features, and fiction serials. When Howard Garis began turning out juveniles for the Stratemeyer Syndicate he was still with the *Newark Evening News* and did his writing after a full day's work on the paper. His Uncle Wiggily stories began when the paper's publisher suggested he try some stories for children that could be published daily. "Maybe stories about animals," the publisher suggested. "Children love animals." Later, pondering an approach, Garis noticed a rabbit in a park and Uncle Wiggily was born. He went on to write six stories a week for a half century, the stories seven hundred to a thousand words each, appearing in the Newark paper and syndicated around the country.[16]

David Graham Phillips's career was more typical in that, rather than finding his subjects within the confines of the daily newspaper, he used the paper as a stepping-stone to an honored career as a popular novelist and muckraking journalist. After an apprenticeship on Cincinnati newspapers Phillips joined the *New York Sun* in 1890; three years later he had moved over to Joseph Pulitzer's *World*, his career marked by steady advancement from reporter to special assignment writer, foreign correspondent, and editorial writer. But from the start he also contributed on a freelance basis to publications such as *Harper's Weekly*, and in 1901 he branched out even further with his first novel, *The Great God Success*, a work that drew directly on his own newspaper days.

The main character, a Yale graduate named Howard, follows Phillips's own upwardly mobile career on a New York paper, eventually becoming its publisher until, greedy for success, he alters an editorial for financial gain and appointment as Ambassador to the Court of St. James. Early in his career

Howard is introduced to an established journalist, Kittredge, who voices the familiar view that "journalism is the dragon that demands the annual sacrifice of youth" and that one must abandon it quickly for fear of being trapped forever. Journalism, Howard is told, is not a career. "It is either a school or a cemetery. A man may use it as a stepping-stone to something else. But if he sticks to it, he finds himself an old man, dead and done for to all intents and purposes years before he's buried." Kittredge announces that he himself is "getting out of it as fast as ever I can. I'm writing books." Good as his word, he writes a successful novel, then goes abroad for two years of travel and writing. "I'm my own master," he tells Howard. "Why, I can't begin to fill the request for 'stuff.' I can go where I please, do as I please."[17] Howard manages some outside writing but fails to heed Kittredge's example of a quick exit from the paper, and so begins the process of moral descent revealed at the book's end.

Phillips himself did heed his spokesman, setting aside newspaper work for independent writing after his novel's appearance. Thereafter stories and articles appeared regularly in the *Saturday Evening Post, Cosmopolitan,* and other leading magazines of the time while he also produced twenty novels in a nine-year period. Phillips's work habits, as described to a friend, followed a nocturnal schedule and were marked by the professional writer's disdain for literary inspiration: "I write *every* night, from about eleven until about four or five or six in the morning. Sometimes seven or eight. . . . Let me urge you to work *the same hours* every day and *never, never, never* to let anything or anyone interfere between you and working at those hours. I write every night—seven days a week. I don't wait for mood or inspiration, and I don't give up because I don't begin right or am writing rubbish. I think it's fatal to give way to moods. And I'm not a bit afraid to throw away everything I've written, or to edit my stuff to the bone."[18] Only a deranged assassin waiting outside New York's Princeton Club in 1911, convinced that he and his family had been vilified in Phillips's fiction, could finally stop the writer's dogged pen.

three

Although Albert Payson Terhune professed to despise his long newspaper career, it had more direct links than Phillips's with his eventual success as a fiction writer.[19] After Columbia University and a tour of Europe and the Middle East, Terhune began a $15-a-week reporting job in 1894 on Pulitzer's *Evening*

World. He had some background as a writer—his mother wrote fiction under the name Marion Harland and he had published a travel book about the Middle East—but Terhune found himself ill-equipped for reporting. He did better when he was shifted to the editorial and magazine department where in addition to editing chores he wrote reviews and eventually serial fiction. Among his tasks was turning the scripts of unsuccessful plays into serials. He found newspaper fiction (known on the paper as Oh-my-Gods!) "laughably easy to grind out, calling for little more than reflex action of the hand," and managed to write two-thousand-word chapters in the gaps between other work.[20]

These were days of frenzied competition in New York journalism. William Randolph Hearst had taken over the *Journal,* established an *Evening Journal* to compete directly with the *Evening World,* and raided Pulitzer's staff of some of its best people, hiring the accomplished Arthur Brisbane as the *Journal's* editor. For reporters it was an unrivaled period, with top men commanding salaries of $3,000 to $5,000 a year in return for ten- to twelve-hour workdays and six-day weeks. Irvin S. Cobb, who joined the fray of New York journalism in 1904, eventually drew $150 a week on the *World* and was said to be the highest paid newspaper writer in the land. With added pay coming from work for the *Evening World* and *Sunday World* his monthly income was often over $11,000.[21] Name reporters as well as celebrated writers also were lured away by the magazines for special assignments. Stephen Crane was hired to report on vice in New York and Mark Twain to cover Queen Victoria's Diamond Jubilee in London. Richard Harding Davis was paid $500 for an account of a Yale-Princeton football game. When news coverage of the Spanish-American War further fired the circulation struggle, the *Evening World* produced as many as nine editions a day, adding to an already voracious appetite for material. Terhune was recruited by Brisbane to join the *Journal* but stayed on at the *World,* working in a variety of positions on the paper that included the sports and rewrite desks as well as the editorial and magazine departments.

Among Terhune's more colorful tasks was ghosting fiction serials for the magazine. A ten-installment story by "Ten Beautiful Shopgirls," an inspiration of the advertising department, was turned out by Terhune. "I used to stare at the ten retouched photographs of the literary beauties," he recalled, "and wonder if I were really as compositely lovely as all that; or if the bulk of our readers actually believed that the silly serial was the combined work of those ten beauties; instead of being ground out by a prognathous-jawed hack-writer who stood six-foot-two and tipped the scales at two-hundred-and-twenty."[22]

A serial by "Ten Popular Actresses" likewise came from his hand, as did a prizefight serial by Jim Jeffries and numerous other stories and articles by figures of passing renown.

By 1899 Terhune was making $40 a week on the *Evening World* (each raise requiring a note of thanks to Pulitzer, a gray eminence the writer glimpsed only twice during his newspaper career) plus added money for writing chores on the Sunday and morning papers. For a dollar apiece he contributed to the morning paper anecdotes supposedly written by well-known New Yorkers, the items meant to brighten the news columns, with Terhune cribbing the material from a joke book with the subjects' connivance. For fifty cents apiece he peddled two- and three-line fillers to the paper's editorial page; for another $8 a week he wrote "Up and Down with the Elevator Man," a humorous monologue supposedly delivered by one of the operators in the *World* building, the feature appearing each week for nearly a year. Yet another source of income were stories rewritten or translated from foreign papers. From the *Sunday World* alone Terhune earned $60 a week for his extra hack writing.

But money worries persisted and to bolster his income he turned in earnest to fiction, setting up a schedule of writing five hours a night, five days a week, following long days on the newspaper. Within two months he had a 60,000-word serial that he sold to Robert Davis at Munsey's *All-Story* for $125. A second serial was taken by *Argosy* for $180.

Terhune was now on his way as a writer for the pulps, turning eventually to historical serials, writing both for *All-Story* and *Argosy*, his pay rate rising to $500. At the same time he cranked out short stories for the two pulps at $50 each. When he began writing for a third pulp, Street & Smith's *Top Notch*, he farmed out stories to another writer, revised the finished product, added material of his own, and split the proceeds.

Once Davis called him to his office to discuss a story Terhune had submitted to *All-Story*. The story was flawed in ways the editor could not put his finger on but found apparent; he suggested Terhune rewrite it from a different angle. Terhune retrieved the story but left it unread and unchanged for ten days before returning it to Davis. The story was promptly accepted, the editor pointing out the wisdom of revision after allowing a tale to settle for a time.

With Street & Smith publications Terhune moved up to *Ainslee's* and *Popular Magazine*, his rates reaching $100 for stories and $1,400 for serials. He was now hammering out some twenty stories and five serials a year. Although the quality of his work had improved from the serial by Ten Beautiful Shop-girls, he thought of his fiction as "a billion miles from anything approaching literature," finding solace only in the fact that "the stuff was making money for me."[23] He now had a bank account, a country estate near Pompton Lakes, New Jersey, and a flat for the winter in New York. With his outside work bringing in three times what he earned on the newspaper, he longed to cut free of his day job. "Always I had detested the newspaper business in all its branches," he later remarked. "Always I had yearned to get out of it and to be able to make a living by writing."[24] But he was not yet confident enough as a freelancer to abandon the security of a salary.

One of his outside writing schemes involved the popular novelist Winston Churchill, who had been approached to write a serial for newspaper syndica-tion. Since the writer was busy, it was assumed he would more likely accept the assignment if he was provided with a synopsis, and Terhune was hired to write one with the title *Caleb Conover, Railroader.* When Churchill declined to take on the work, Terhune jumped in to write sixty thousand words in thirty days. The book stalled, however, over the details of a political conven-tion and campaign, and Terhune turned to Irvin S. Cobb, at the time a top correspondent on the *World,* who supplied the book with two chapters. As a bound book the serial with its ghosted chapters sold fairly well, considerably helped along by the fact that another side of Terhune's work was writing glow-ing reviews of it for syndication.

Before World War I Terhune had branched out, writing $75 stories for *Smart Set* about an underworld character called Aloysius Raegan and striking a connection with the Chicago magazine *Red Book* for stories and serials in a milder vein. When *Red Book's* editor, Ray Long, visited Terhune's New Jersey estate the writer stumbled upon the material that would lead to his leaving newspapering for good. Terhune and his wife raised collies, and Long sug-gested a story about one called Lad after Terhune told him of one of the dog's exploits. "What's the use?" Terhune responded. "For ten years I've been beg-ging editors to let me write dog stories. I know dogs—or think I do. I've been studying them all my life. I want to write about them. But not an editor on earth will let me do it. Editors tell me the public isn't interested in dogs, and that all animal stories are out of date. Not one of them will give me a chance to tackle a dog yarn. What would be the sense of scribbling such a story and then having it rejected everywhere?"[25] Nonetheless, he wrote the story, relat-ing Lad's struggle with another collie and the wooing of Lad's mate, Lady, and

Long printed it in the January 1915 issue of *Red Book*. For the 6,000-word story Terhune got $200—a figure that soon jumped to $2,000 for work of the same length.

Editors now came clamoring for dog stories. By 1916 Terhune's yearly income had reached nearly $30,000 and he felt able to put newspapering behind. His last five years on the *Evening World* had been, as he put it, "incomparably less horrible to me than had been their sixteen gloom-ridden predecessors," while the number of writers he had seen leave journalism and fail as independents had given him reason to question the wisdom of the move. Nine out of ten "limped home to the jail, begging to be taken in again. Henceforth they plodded hopelessly on, at the news treadmill, bereft of the one meager comforting belief that they could make good elsewhere."[26] Terhune was willing to allow that three years spent on a newspaper were good training for a writer, teaching literary virtues of economy and concentration; thereafter newspapering had a negative effect on a writer's style, making it hurried, slovenly, and devoid of distinction.

Terhune relinquished any dreams of serious writing at the same time he put newspaper work behind, resigned to the fact that he could "make much more money as a scrawler of second-and-third rate stuff." The audience he aimed for was "frankly lowbrow," "the whole army of my fellow nonliterary roughnecks," and he took comfort—together with the comfort the money from the work brought in—in giving "more happiness to a farm hand in Kansas on a snowy night—not always a farm hand, either, nor always in Kansas —and lift him further out of his deadly-dull daily life than would *Arrowsmith*."[27] He modeled himself on Trollope, keeping rigid desk hours and viewing his work as that of an old-fashioned artisan. He retained an admiration for writers of a more literary cast, but for himself he felt it impossible to overcome the limitations of a journalistic background even though "doughtily and futilely I have tried to correct the incorrectable blemish."[28]

At the time he left daily journalism Terhune was pulling in good outside money by turning popular motion-picture serials into serial novels, a variation on his earlier hackwork of turning failed plays into newspaper serials. Using the pictures' synopses and continuity as a guide, and seeing previews of filmed episodes, he wrote 3,000-word installments in half a day, bringing in $3,200 for a finished serial. But it was his dog stories that provided his future as a writer. In 1919 he published a collection called *Lad: A Dog*, the book going through many editions. Other dog books followed at regular intervals together with serials that had dogs, usually collies, in passing roles. Although

Terhune's work appeared in adult slick magazines of the level of *Harper's* and the *Saturday Evening Post,* he found his dog stories cast him largely as a writer for children. This he accepted as a necessary feature of the swelling popularity that, by the 1930s, caused him to hire Amy Vanderbilt as a press agent and to seal off his country estate from incursions by fans.

four

During his early fiction-writing days Terhune once turned for help to Sinclair Lewis. The year was 1914 and Lewis wrote two or three chapters of a serial called *Dad* for Terhune as part of a straight-out business arrangement, Lewis getting twenty-five percent of all proceeds. Lewis also sold Terhune a plot for a short story—a service he had performed earlier for Jack London—and, the story published, happily received as further recompense a check for $40.[29]

Terhune and Lewis became acquainted in New York where Lewis was working for a publishing house and scrambling to gain a foothold as a writer. They used to debate where big money was to be found in writing, magazines or books. "From my own experience, up to then," Terhune remembered, "I held that it was all in the magazine end of the game—if it were anywhere at all." Lewis, on the other hand, "believed there was more money in one successful book than in an armful of magazine work. It was his ambition, he said, to write best-seller novels, rather than well-paying magazine yarns, and he was certain that one day he could do it. . . . Lewis had a queerly unswerving faith in his star."[30] Before Lewis was proven correct with his triumphant string of novels in the 1920s, he, like Terhune, served an apprenticeship in newspaper journalism, though one that was far shorter and notably less successful.

After finishing Yale in 1908, Lewis, bent on a writing career, found a full-time position on an Iowa paper, the *Waterloo Daily Courier,* a jack-of-all-trades job that included editorial writing. He had done part-time newspaper work on his hometown weeklies in Sauk Center, Minnesota, and on a paper in New Haven during college years, but the experience had given him only a thin veneer of journalistic skill. He would later give himself credit as a feature writer but observe that he "never saw the news or heard the news or brought in the news."[31] Eight weeks into his Iowa job, his limitations apparent, he was fired.

Before he landed another job, Lewis tried to make his way as a freelance writer in New York. He placed a story with *Red Book* for $75, but the sale was

followed by few others and he returned to scratching out a living as a journalist, this time on the copy desk of the *San Francisco Evening Bulletin.* "Gee!
This newspaper work is plumb hard," he soon complained in a letter. "Working most every evening—long hours & no chance to write at stories."[32] Two
months into the job he was fired again. His next position was with the Associated Press as a night wire editor, but here he found the routine all the more
stifling, writing to his father that "it is about the same as a stenographers [*sic*]
place. Every day just the same old stunt."[33] And here, just before he could be
fired yet again, he resigned.

In California Lewis had come to know Jack London (at Yale Lewis had
been outraged when students booed London during a lecture), and the two
soon entered into a business relationship. Strong on mood and atmosphere in
his fiction, London found it hard to come up with story plots. "Dam [*sic*]
plots; I don't think I could construct a decent one to save my life," he fumed
in a letter.[34] Lewis, troubled more by developing his ideas than by dreaming
them up by the dozen, had organized an extensive plot file, and London went
through it, buying fourteen plots for the sum of $70. Two became published
stories and one the start of a novel. Later London purchased nine more plots
for about $5 apiece, and later still bought seventeen more. For Lewis it was
found money that bought time for writing, as he pointed out to London in a
letter urging the purchases: "I hope to gawd that you will feel like taking a
considerable part of them, because, if you do, it will probably finally give me
the chance to get back at the free-lancing—nothing but writing—which I
haven't done for over a year; can the job and really get at decent work." To
which London replied: "Your plots came in last night, and I have promptly
taken nine (9) of them, for which same, according to invoice, I am remitting
you herewith check for $52.50. Some of the rejected ones were not suited to
my temperament; others did not suit because I am too damn lazy to dig up
requisite data or atmosphere. . . . Be sure to send me plots from time to time,
with prices attached, and for heaven's sake, remember the ones I take, so that
you won't make the mistake of writing them up yourself some time." Lewis
informed London that he need not worry about duplication since the notes
for each story were destroyed when Lewis sold them to the writer. The notes
were brief, ranging from 60 to 240 words; the following is a typical example:

GODIVA OF TODAY

Tho' a socialist, she is the wife of a rich manufacturer. He, laughing at her theories,
says he will make a certain reform she greatly desires if she will, not ride naked thru
the streets, but, say, lecture on socialism at st. crossings and corners. Tho' rather

sensitive, and regarded by the socialists themselves with suspicion because she is connected with the disliked mgfr. she pulls it off.[35]

From the wreckage of his California newspaper career Lewis bolted across country to the position of subeditor of a Washington journal for teachers of the deaf, a subject—as he later noted—about which he knew less than radar, even though radar had yet to be invented. Though the job on the *Volta Review* drained his time for freelance work and he was soon writing to London in hopes he would buy more plots, the one thing certain to him was that he would not return to newspapering. He told his father that his present job, "though taking a fair number of hours a day, does not have that tearing, wearing, tissue destroying quality of newspaper work. In any case, I can't do newspaper work; am a less excellent newspaperman every year. The only way I can write a story is to polish; think it out; rewrite. . . . I can always make a living in newspaper work—but that's about all; and it's at the expenditure of tremendous nervous energy."[36]

From Washington, Lewis fled in 1910 to New York, the place he wanted to be as an aspiring writer, and a job in the publishing house of Frederick A. Stokes Company, as first a manuscript reader and then a publicity writer. Here he stayed for a little over two years, performing well. One of his efforts, unsuccessful as it turned out, was to draw London from the publishing house of Macmillan to Stokes. Lewis also cautiously inquired into how much money London had made from the plot outlines he had purchased, and further suggested that as a collaborator he might be due "some modest per cent of your profits on 'em."[37] London replied that he had made $1,200 on one of the stories, though it was a come-down from his usual fees, and he closed the door on any thought of a percentage for his young friend.

For his employer Lewis dashed off in three weeks a Tom Swift-like boys' adventure book, *Hike and the Aeroplane*, under the name Tom Graham, in return for two months' paid vacation and a three-percent royalty. He used the time to work on *Our Mr. Wrenn*, a book for which he had serious commercial hopes. Waldo Frank remembered Lewis at the time as torn between high literary ambition and the wish to make money from his work: "He did not seem to be sure of himself as a writer—I mean, as a writer of value and stature. Perhaps, therefore, he pretended he was a hard-boiled 'commercial.'"[38] Neither was he sure of what work to pursue while writing on the side.

In 1912 he left Stokes for a $30-a-week editing job on the pulp magazine *Adventure,* there working in a office a few steps from one housing Dreiser. Lewis handled everything on the magazine, from reading manuscripts to dummying pages, enjoying the range of the work and the freedom he was given. Nonetheless, he was off in 1913 to the Publishers Newspaper Syndicate where he helped put together a book review page that was circulated around the country. Here he began the lifelong habit of wearing a newspaperman's green celluloid eyeshade while he wrote. With the coming of war in Europe the syndicate was shut down and Lewis retreated to book publishing, this time at the George H. Doran Company, where he served as an editorial assistant and advertising manager. Again he worked seriously and well while holding on to his ambitions as a writer.

After it was turned down by three publishers, *Our Mr. Wrenn* appeared in 1914 and *The Trail of the Hawk* the following year, the latter work scribbled in mornings before work, while on commuting trains, and during weekends. Both books were frank attempts at commercial success, but while they drew applause for their realism, sales were poor. Undaunted, Lewis turned to a third novel, *The Job*, while at the same time he reversed the position he had argued with Terhune, that real money lay in books rather than in magazine writing, and produced a humorous short story, "Nature, Inc.", that was taken by the *Saturday Evening Post* for $500, his first big sale. He dug into his plot file and quickly wrote three more stories for the magazine, the last for $1,000. Certain now he could wrest a living from magazine writing ("I am a good trained hack, and I know almost instinctively how to write for George Lorimer"),[39] he resigned from his job with Doran and he and his wife left New York on a motor trip of indefinite duration, free at last of the routines of journalism, editing, and publicity.

In the years before *Main Street* in 1920 Lewis kept working the lucrative slick market with stories and articles for the *Woman's Home Companion, Metropolitan, Popular,* and *Hearst's* as well as the *Post*. His biographer, Mark Schorer, estimates his magazine income in the period at nearly $34,000. Just before the publication of *Main Street*, a book he knew was important (it would sell 180,000 copies in six months) and into which he poured a fierce effort of ten- and twelve-hour writing days, he made yet another sale to the *Post*, this one for $1,000. Two more novels appeared as well, *The Innocents* and *Free Air*, both written as magazine serials, and neither a great success but adding to the growing Lewis coffers, as did a play, *Hobohemia*, that was panned by critics but ran for eleven weeks in New York in 1918. Years later, looking back on his career and using a lordly editorial "we," Lewis would measure his triumphs in light of Poe, a hack writer who had not been so fortunate: "We of an older generation have done well. Indeed, in a great many cases we have received, both in money and in praise, so much more than we have ever deserved that if we were to run into Poe in the club, and he were to scoff, 'I hear you're doing very well, my lad!' we would blush distressingly, in memory of his struggles."[40]

five

When Sinclair Lewis knew him in California, Jack London was already a glamorous literary personage. Lewis regarded him as the Master, and one of London's biographers has suggested that the plot-buying scheme was actually charity on the part of an established writer directed to an aspiring and impoverished one.[41] What the two shared were apprenticeship days on Grub Street, an experience London had recently dramatized in his autobiographical novel *Martin Eden* and Lewis was just beginning.

Surprisingly, London had studiously avoided the confines of the newsroom in a period of hack writing and desperate poverty during which he had embraced nearly every other way of making money with the pen. His first publication at age seventeen was for a newspaper, a sketch drawn from his experience as a seaman that won a $25 contest for young writers in the *San Francisco Morning Call* in 1893. Later he contributed freelance work to newspapers and covered foreign wars as a special correspondent; but from the beginning of his career he understood that a regular position, no matter how badly he needed a paycheck, would rein in the freedom he prized as a writer. A series of ten articles commissioned by the *San Francisco Examiner* in 1901, work that London considered an exercise in yellow journalism, had the effect of obliterating all other writing. "My whole life has stood still for ten days," he maintained. "During that time I have done nothing else. Why, so exhausting was it that my five and one-half hours would not suffice and I had to sleep over seven."[42]

When *Cosmopolitan* offered him an editorial job at about the same point early in his career, London turned it down because—as he reported to a friend and fellow writer, Cloudesley Johns—"I do not wish to be bound. . . . I want to be free, to write of what delights me, whensoever and wheresoever it delights me. No office work for me; no routine; no doing this set task and that set task. No man over me."[43] It was a view of the hazards of in-house newspaper and magazine employment he never relinquished. "Don't you see, my boy," he would complain in 1913 to the editor of a socialist paper who had written a flawed article about him, "hell and the newspaper offices are full of men who do careless work such as you did, and who are as insular and provincial as you are."[44] There was also the matter of the harmful effects of newspaper work on writing style. When it is suggested to Martin Eden that, given his ambition to become a writer, he take a reporting job for a while, he replies: "It would spoil my style." When it is further suggested that his hack fiction writing might have a similar effect, he insists that "the cases are different. The storiettes were ground out, jaded, at the end of a long day of application to style. But a reporter's work is all hack from morning till night, is the one paramount thing of life."[45]

Where newspapers were vital to London was as source material. The supposedly weak imagination that sent him to Lewis's plot file also caused him to ransack papers for story ideas, a working method he stoutly defended—when a question of excessive borrowing was raised—as the common practice of authors, and indeed one recommended by instructors in the art of fiction. His own art, he said, involved turning "journalism into literature," and to this end he freely "used material from various sources which had been collected and narrated by men who made their living by turning the facts of life into journalism."[46]

When London began his writing life in Oakland in 1898—six years after his first publication in the *Call*—he had behind him a wealth of personal experience that included tramping across the country, a brief prison stay for vagrancy, one semester at the University of California, his celebrated adventures in the Klondike gold rush, and a furious effort of omnivorous reading to turn himself into what he called a "brain merchant." He immediately adopted a professional's workaday approach to his craft: he studiously examined the newspaper and magazine markets, wrote in every sort of genre, and mailed out his work, resubmissions following rejections and what he called "trailers" or follow-up letters sent to publications that failed to respond at all.

In a notebook he recorded the results. Between August 1898 and May 1900 he had fifteen acceptances on a first try while eighty-eight pieces were rejected a total of over four hundred times. According to a biographer, his mounting rejections slips, skewered on a piece of wire, soared five feet high. Rejection became so familiar that the process seemed to operate with the mechanical certainty of "the working of a soulless machine. I dropped the manuscript into the mail box. After the lapse of a certain approximate length of time, the manuscript was brought back to me by the postman. Accompanying it was a stereotyped rejection slip. A part of the machine, some cunning arrangement of cogs and cranks at the other end (it could not have been a living, breathing man with blood in his veins) had transferred the manuscript to another envelope, taken the stamps from the inside and pasted them on the outside, and added the rejection slip."[47] Later, in *Martin Eden*, the impersonal workings of rejection would assume the form of a slot machine "wherein one dropped pennies, and, with a metallic whirl of machinery had delivered to him a stick of chewing-gum or a tablet of chocolate or gum. And so with the editorial machine. One slot brought checks and the other brought rejection slips. So far he had found only the latter slot."[48]

Despite failure, London refused the pleasure of self-pity. He sought a civil service job in the post office, yet when one was offered he decided not to trade the dream of becoming an author for security. A 21,000-word juvenile serial, returned by the *Youth's Companion* in Boston with the suggestion that he not make writing his means of livelihood, brought forth a letter maintaining that "some day I shall hit upon my *magnus opus*."[49] When San Francisco's *Overland Monthly* finally took a tale drawn from his Alaska adventures for $5, then agreed to take seven more at $7.50 each, London groused about low pay from a magazine that had once been edited by Bret Harte but recognized nonetheless the greater importance for a new writer of beginning to make a name for himself.

By the standards of most independent writers, London's daily work routine was restrained—at least a thousand words six days a week. But the work was meant to be in finished form and launched upon the magazine seas with no hesitation. He would write up to two hundred words in longhand, read the material over, then "slap it through" the typewriter.[50] To a fellow California writer, Elwyn Hoffman, he gave a further account of the brisk mechanics of his writing day: "Let me tell you how I write. In the first place I never begin a thing, but what I finish it *before* I begin anything else. Further; I type as fast as I write, so that each day sees the work all upon the final MS. which goes for editorial submission. And *on* the day I finish the MS. I fold it up and send it off without once going back to see what all the previous pages were like. So, in fact, when a page is done, that is the last I see of it till it comes out in print. Of course, sometimes I have to hunt back for the spelling of the name of some character, or for just how an incident occurred; but otherwise I don't go back. I think it pays."[51]

No hack writing was beneath London as long as it paid, including fifty-cent jokes for a San Francisco weekly and a $10 prize from a local Republican club for a campaign song. Nor was any field, agriculture to socialism, beyond his range. Although his future plans called for literary masterpieces, he gloried in a sense of himself as a day-laborer with words. "Saturday night, and I feel good," he exclaimed in a letter. "Saturday night, and a good week's work done —hack work of course. Why shouldn't I? Like any other honest artisan by the sweat of my brow." In the same letter he noted that his friend Cloudesley Johns looked with scorn on such tawdry work: "He writes for posterity, for a small circle of admirers, oblivious to the world's oblivion, doesn't want money, scoffs at the idea of it, calls it filthy, damns all who write for it, etc. etc." Yet Johns's deeds, London gleefully added, failed to match his words. He had recently sold a story to *Munsey's* with the agreement that he wholly change the ending to the extent of allowing the chief character to live rather than die. "'I fell,'" London reported, "is the only explanation he has vouchsafed of his conduct."[52]

An abrupt change in London's fortunes came in October 1899 when the *Atlantic* paid him $120 for "An Odyssey of the North." Soon thereafter Houghton Mifflin offered to put out a collection of his Alaska stories, a work that came out in 1900 as *The Son of the Wolf,* his first book. London's industry as a writer was formidable but his timing was also fortunate. The turn of the century, with the Spanish war just behind, was a period of national enthusiasm for the strenuous life; popular magazines eagerly sought out tales of brawny outdoor adventure handled in a vigorous manner. London was their man. The reader's report to Houghton Mifflin on his story collection, advising acceptance, captured exactly the broad appeal of his work: "He draws a vivid picture of the terrors of cold, darkness, and starvation, and pleasures of human companionship in adverse circumstances, and the sterling qualities which the rough battle with nature brings out. The reader is convinced that the author has lived the life himself."[53]

In an article in the *Writer* in 1900 London declared that once an author had established his name it was "no more than right that he should enjoy the perquisites of office, namely: the *entree* of the first-class periodicals and publishing houses, and the privilege of continuing to supply his own reading public which he has built up by his own exertions."[54] For London himself this was just the way it happened. After the publication of *The Son of the Wolf* editors begged him for work. He dusted off rejected manuscripts, sent them out, and most were snapped up. S. S. McClure tendered a generous monthly retainer ("We will send you a check each month for five months for $100, and if you find that you need $125, why, we will do that") while London worked on a novel,[55] and his stories and articles appeared in *Harper's Weekly, Ainslee's, Cos-*

mopolitan, Saturday Evening Post, and virtually everywhere else. When London's connection with McClure was broken off, George P. Brett, the president of Macmillan's publishing company, stepped in with an offer of $150 a month for two years in return for rights to publish all of London's books.

Over the next years London's name appeared with clockwork regularity in the popular magazines, both as an author and as a swashbuckling personality who had mastered the art of self-promotion by making himself easily available to the press. In the slightly less than two decades of his foreshortened writing career before his death in 1916, he produced some five hundred nonfiction pieces, nearly two hundred stories, and twenty novels among over fifty books. Although for his most enduring work, *The Call of the Wild,* he made the worst deal of his writing life, accepting an outright offer in 1902 of $2,000 from Macmillan as against royalties (after the novel had been serialized in the *Saturday Evening Post* at three cents a word), he still became one of the first millionaire writers. Hackwork for immediate cash, however, was never left far behind. His last long novel, *Hearts of Three,* was a hired job of fleshing out a Hollywood screenplay for adventure-yarn serialization in Hearst's *New York Evening Journal*—a notable comedown for a writer of London's stature but the money was too good to ignore. Martin Eden's career plan to turn out hackwork for money first, masterpieces afterward, was London's aim as well, but for neither seasoned professional did the writing life prove quite that simple.

six

Unlike most young writers who hoped to vault from newspaper reporting to literary stardom, James Oliver Curwood was already flooding the pulp and juvenile fiction markets with contributions, and with some success, when he took up newspaper reporting to help pay expenses at the University of Michigan. In 1898 *Gray Goose* in Cincinnati had accepted a tale for $10, his first payment after years of youthful scribbling, his spirits maintained with some non-paying publication and occasional encouraging remarks. A note by Robert Davis scrawled on a rejection from *Munsey's*—"Keep at it, kid! You're bound to win"—had seemed wildly hopeful.[56]

After serving as the Ann Arbor correspondent for several papers Curwood put college behind in his third year to become a regular reporter with the *Detroit News-Tribune,* confined at first to covering funerals until he learned, as he recalled, to describe them as other than romantic features. But when he got

a name wrong in a front-page news story he was summarily fired, and he
tramped the streets looking for work before in 1902 he caught on again with
the paper's Sunday edition as a feature writer. It was an ideal job—"really not
a task at all," he remembered, "but rather a labor of love" in which the work
he turned out was "part fact but more fiction."[57] Eventually Curwood became
an editor of the Sunday edition as well as a special writer, his salary reaching
$30 a week. All the while he was soaking up material he marketed in freelance
stories and articles to magazines and other papers. When *Munsey's* took a
Great Lakes adventure yarn, "Captain of the Christopher Duggan," for $75
(with a note from Frank Munsey saying "At last—good boy!"),[58] his first appearance in a national publication, Curwood was tempted to take up full-
time writing but kept on with the *News-Tribune* even though more money
was coming in from freelance work.

In stories and articles he developed a reputation as a specialist in two areas
—the danger and romance of shipping on the Great Lakes and rugged outdoor adventure in the far north. Editors began asking for material and he
started a novel and a juvenile serial. By 1907, in his late twenties, he was selling to *McCall's, Red Book,* and *Cosmopolitan* as well as *Munsey's,* working on
books, and holding down his newspaper job while squeezing in as much time
as possible for Great Lakes and wilderness excursions. Because of his northwoods stories and articles the Canadian government hired him as a public relations writer to promote settlement in its western regions, paying $1,800 a
year plus expenses and providing free railway passes. Then Bobbs-Merrill in
Indianapolis accepted a hunting book for boys, *The Wolf Hunters,* and issued
a contract calling for five more juvenile books. "The wonderful hour had
come," Curwood later wrote, "when I could hand in my resignation and re-
tire from newspaper work, and this I did as soon as possible. There was no
thought in my mind that anything but sunshine lay ahead."[59]

Curwood returned to his hometown of Owosso, Michigan, built a house
for himself and his second wife, and settled down as a full-time independent
writer. With his Bobbs-Merrill books he followed the time's common practice
of magazine serialization before book publication—the practice that brought
him, together with numerous film scenarios, films made from his works, and
films he produced himself, a considerable fortune. His subject matter was set
as well when he followed the advice of a *Munsey's* editor that he had a "good
field in the Northern wilderness of Canada. That novel atmosphere helps sell
your stories—stay with what works for you."[60] He toiled up to twelve hours a
day at his desk while letting editors clean up his casual grammar, spelling, and

messy typescripts (later a series of hired secretaries undertook the chores). By 1911 his income from stories, articles, and book royalties was averaging $15,000 a year.

The following year Ray Long, then editing *Red Book* in Chicago, took the train to Owosso to meet Curwood, the beginning of a long, close, and profitable association for both men. Curwood had submitted a story about a part-wolf sled dog named Kazan that caught the editor's attention. Long had read stories by Curwood in other magazines but none struck him as particularly good; "Kazan," on the other hand, was the best dog story he had read, and he urged the writer to produce more.[61] When Curwood sent him a series of connected stories about Kazan, Long took them all at $300 apiece. Published in book form in 1914, *Kazan* had a slow beginning. Curwood later said of the book that he had hoped to match the success of London's *White Fang* and *Call of the Wild*, and though this failed to happen the work over the years proved one of his most enduring moneymakers. He kept writing for other magazines such as the *Saturday Evening Post, Leslie's,* and *Collier's*, and he kept up his link to *Munsey's;* but the connection with Long, who eventually switched to the Hearst publications as editor in chief, was central. With William Randolph Hearst's blessing a scheme was worked out that called for Curwood's animal stories to run in *Cosmopolitan*, novels in *Good Housekeeping,* and other stories in either *Cosmopolitan* or *Harper's Bazaar. Cosmopolitan* was also going to publish in book form a small list of its own novels, no more than six a year, and for Curwood's would pay $5,000 upon publication and royalties of a whopping 20 percent. It was a program, Long gushed, that "no publishing house has ever done before," and he promised Curwood "advertising beyond your dreams."[62]

By 1920, with nineteen books and dozens of stories and articles behind him, Curwood was entering into a decade of major popularity. His per-word rate for magazine serials was said to equal if not surpass that of any writer, this for works—as Ray Long recalled—that were "more nearly sure-fire circulation builders than almost any other thing one could publish."[63] Published in book form, such novels of northern adventure coupled with chaste romance as *The River's End, The Valley of Silent Men,* and *A Gentleman of Courage* were major best sellers.

Yet as his reputation soared during the twenties Curwood's career was winding down. Although Long described him as "tall, wiry, outdoorsy in every line and movement," Curwood's health was poor. With editors urging him to work less even while soliciting new stories, he began devoting large chunks of time to a passionate concern with conservation issues in Michigan. He was appointed to the Conservation Commission by the governor, using the position as a pulpit to rail against bad conservation practices while predicting a time when the northern part of the state would rival Yellowstone as an outdoor attraction.

In 1926 Curwood gave his recipe for good health in a fate-tempting article in *Hearst's* magazine called "I Shall Live To Be 100." A year later he was dead from kidney problems at age forty-nine. Long wrote a brief appreciation for the *Bookman* in which he recounted his friendship with the writer—and took note of the fanciful stone castle Curwood had built for himself in Owosso as a writing studio and his equally fanciful log lodge in the Michigan woods near Roscommon that, true to the primitive northwoods aura of Curwood's fiction, had no electricity or running water. Later, in a collection of stories in which he included "Kazan," Long remembered Curwood's growth "from rather an obscure writer of adventure stories to a writer who was recognized, at the time of his death, as being one of the world's foremost advocates of living close to nature." He added: "He wrote melodrama, yes; there were action and vigor and at times brutality in his stories; he was far from being the greatest psychologist who ever wrote; but he was sincere, he loved nature, he made you love nature. And that's not a bad epitaph for a writer, is it?"[64]

WRITING FOR
THE MILLIONS

Newspaper Syndicates Expand the Market

*I could give a new writer such an instrument of publicity as had probably
never been built up before. Through my newspaper syndicate I could
place him at once before a million families, the representative people
who read the leading dailies in all parts of the country.*
—S. S. McClure

one

In 1899, his career just underway, Jack London asked Cloudesley Johns for
information about S.S. McClure's newspaper syndicate: "Suppose *McClure's*
[magazine] had accepted that study of yours. Would they have published it in
the magazine, or would it have come out in some newspaper through the syndicate? I am always afraid to send *McClures* [*sic*] anything that I consider good,
for fear they will publish it through the syndicate, which syndicate I know
nothing about. Can you enlighten me?"[1] Soon enough London discovered for
himself the main thing he needed to know about McClure's syndicate and
others like it: they were a significant way of bolstering his writing income.
"Then there are the newspaper syndicates, and the newspaper short-story syndicates, and the syndicates for the Sunday supplements," he has Martin Eden

realize. "I can go ahead and hammer out the stuff they want, and earn the equivalent of a good salary by it."[2]

If writers had misgivings about journalism as an avenue to the writing life, they had reason only to welcome the benefits offered by newspaper publication with the rise at the end of the nineteenth century of syndicates specializing in literary material. Here was a major new market rather than a springboard to established markets; and here was a means of advancing name recognition through widespread newspaper readership while retaining a freelancer's freedom. Writers for the syndicates were in the world of daily and weekly newspaper journalism while happily free of its workaday grasp.

Auxiliary news services for weekly and provincial newspapers first appeared in England. In America rival services began operating in the Civil War period, supplying ready-print sheets of news, miscellaneous features, and advertising, the material pre-printed on one side with the other left blank for local printing. "Patent insides," as they were called, eventually gave way to stereotype plates, or "boiler plate," that could be shipped throughout the country and locally printed. In 1871 Ansel Nash Kellogg's Chicago-based Newspaper Company—the first syndicate independent of a parent newspaper—introduced serial fiction to syndication, and the following year illustrated articles.[3] In an advertisement in 1875 the rival American Newspaper Union listed the range of reading matter it provided the country press as "state news and legislative reports, a full summary of general news, late and correct market quotations, an agricultural department, a department for young folks, and a good story for everybody."[4]

Missing from the inventory was a poetry column, a ubiquitous syndicate offering. Although the quantity and quality of magazine poetry was said to be in decline (the *Saturday Evening Post* editorialized in 1898 on the "Twilight of Poetry"), newspaper poetry flourished during the period, with nearly every paper offering a column of popular verse and some writers achieving national reputations. Edgar A. Guest, among the best known, spent his entire career with the *Detroit Free Press*, turning out poems every day for several decades. Newspapers that did not conduct their own poetry department typically depended on syndicated material. Beginning in 1884 Ella Wheeler Wilcox, who had made her name with a faintly risqué collection called *Poems of Passion* in 1876, wrote a poem a day for newspaper syndication as part of a career in popular verse that spanned more than forty years and included over forty books. Sam Walter Foss produced a poem a week for syndication between 1887 and 1893, whereupon he began a one-a-day schedule that he kept to over the next twenty years. In Sinclair Lewis's *Babbitt,* Zenith's poetaster, T. Cholmondeley Frink, has had his poem "Poemulations" syndicated in sixty-seven leading newspapers, giving him "one of the largest audiences of any poet in the world." Another character, Vergil Gunch, adds that in terms of literary productivity even Dante "wouldn't stand one-two-three if he had to buckle down to practical literature and turn out a poem for the newspaper-syndicate every day, like Chum does!"[5]

By 1880 over 2,500 country weeklies were carrying the many forms of ready-print copy in their columns. Soon syndicates expanded by providing literary material as well as the work of popular columnists and humorists to small-city and metropolitan dailies, and it was here that Sam McClure found his niche with a literary service. As he recalled in his autobiography, his plan had the beauty of simplicity: "I could get a short story from any of the best story-writers then for $150. I figured that I ought to be able to sell that story to 100 newspapers throughout the country, at $5 each. News was syndicated in this way, and I did not see why fiction should not be."[6]

While McClure was confident a newspaper literary syndicate would succeed, others were not. An early version of his plan, this one calling for syndicating previously published juvenile stories among country papers, was broached to the Century Company in New York, publisher of the *Century* magazine. McClure, working as an editorial assistant with the firm, hoped the scheme would be his ticket to success. Instead it was rejected and he was fired.

Newspaper editors around the country took advantage of lax copyright laws and clipped what they wanted out of magazines and rival papers. Why would they pay for what they already took free? And would writers agree, despite the added income and wider circulation a syndicate would bring them, to have their work appear in lowly newspapers rather than prestigious journals? In England, George Gissing sniffed that he would "never dream of writing a *story* for a newspaper syndicate; the kind of stuff they publish, and the way they advertise it, is too ignoble."[7] McClure's college friend and later business associate, John Phillips, thought the enterprise decidedly flawed on this score. He informed McClure that the syndicate scheme "seems to me too extensive to be feasible. Even if the capital &c were secured, I doubt if the best American writers would agree to put themselves under such bonds for any length of time. . . . And then I surmise that many would object to the manner of publication—which will be quite indiscriminate. Perhaps they would prefer (not speaking of price) to publish once in a choice journal like Century to a broader circulation through the medium of 2nd and 3rd rate papers. Of course by this the writers would receive larger remuneration for stories, but that is not all they look at."[8]

McClure understood better than Phillips, and better than the Century Company, the role of remuneration in the lives of writers, and pressed on with the plan as a business venture of his own. In a circular mailed to editors around the country in October 1884 he announced his syndicate was open for business:

> I have made arrangements with a number of our most popular authors, including W. D. Howells, H. C. Bunner, J. S. of Dale, Mrs. Helen Jackson, Mrs. Harriet Prescott Spofford, Dr. William A. Hammond, and over a score of others, to furnish serial and short stories for simultaneous publication in syndicates of leading newspapers.
>
> This method of publication has been employed very successfully in England and France for a long time. . . . There is no reason why American newspapers should not reap great advantages from a similar arrangement.
>
> A dozen, or twenty, or fifty newspapers—selected so as to avoid conflict in circulation—can thus secure a story for a sum which will be very small for each paper, but which will in the aggregate be sufficiently large to secure the best work by the best authors. A small outlay will enable a newspaper to furnish its readers with stories by our most noted writers, which have not been published before, and which will be accessible to its readers in no other periodical.[9]

Rather than "over a score" of writers, all McClure had at the start were commitments from a few, together with his tireless zeal in promoting the syndicate. For capital to purchase material he planned on using money that came in from the papers buying the service; this arrangement in turn depended on the willingness of writers to accept delayed payment or a portion of their money paid on account. That several were in fact willing can be attributed in part to McClure's charm as a salesman, in other part to the access he was providing to a fresh market for previously rejected work or work in a vein unlikely to be accepted by the dominant magazines of the time. A letter McClure sent to a large number of possible contributors as the syndicate was getting underway indicated its seductive appeal to professional writers: "I shall need between 300 and 400 stories during the year, and can profitably use all the stories you will write for the newspaper press. . . . I will meet your views. Please let me know your terms, the number of stories you will write this year (1885), and the probable length of the stories."[10] To handle the costly problem of duplicating stories, McClure hit on the idea of supplying his service free to one newspaper that set material from the author's copy and then supplied the syndicate with a number of galley proofs, distributing the proofs in turn to other newspapers as setting copy. Newspapers that bought the service were guaranteed exclusive rights to material within their circulation areas.

As the names highlighted in the circular to editors suggest, the stories offered by the Associated Literary Press—its formal name until 1900 when it became the McClure Newspaper Syndicate—were regular magazine fare from the recognized authors of the day. As time went on the syndicate supplied more varied material that included stories by the new realists and naturalists. From newspaper editors who either took or rejected stories McClure had instant reaction to the material he circulated, putting him in a better position to read public taste than insulated magazine editors. What editors repeatedly told him they wanted was something fresh—and something geared to newspaper audiences. "Some of the daily stories you send out are fossil chestnuts from the antediluvian strata of literature," one informed him. "The new authors excite more interest than the old stand bys," another said. "You get more originality with the new writers. . . . A reader of a *short* story in a daily newspaper cares very little about literary polish. He only wants to be interested or amused."[11]

Howells, while recognizing the expansion of the market brought about by syndicates such as McClure's, lamented the quality of the work that was sought precisely on these grounds. "In fact," he noted, "the newspapers prefer to remain newspapers, at least in quality if not in form." What they wanted in fiction was "something sensational" rather than something artistic; "they wanted their emotions raw, or at least *saignantes* from the joint of fact, and not prepared by the fancy or the taste."[12] McClure himself had neither time nor inclination to trouble over such niceties. He had a growing business on his hands, and as he expanded the types of stories circulated by the syndicate he also branched out into material other than fiction.

The number of newspapers printed in the country was expanding; at the same time newspaper size was increasing and Sunday editions were gaining popularity. Editors, faced with filling the new space as cheaply as possible, especially the yawning pages of Sunday editions, turned to McClure and he supplied them with varied forms of nonfiction as well as stories and serialized novels. (Howells thought the fact that syndicate fiction was heavily used in Sunday papers also worked against quality material. He argued—with considerable strain—that women, "who form the largest, if not the only cultivated class among us," tended to dismiss the Sunday paper "except for its social gossip," with the result that "its fiction is mainly of the inferior sort with which boys and men beguile their leisure.")[13] When papers wanted cooking articles McClure whipped them up himself under the pseudonym "Patience Winthrop," a name he hoped conjured up a New England housewife. Popular humorists like Opie Read and Bill Nye came on board, happy to have their work copyrighted and syndicated as a measure of protection against what Nye called the pastepot-and-scissors fiends at work on country weeklies. A series of articles on Mormonism by Kate Field, a prominent Washington journalist, was one of the syndicate's early triumphs. The popular religious novelist E. P. Roe offered a series of travel articles about the West.

Three years after it began, McClure's syndicate was selling some fifty thousand words a week to over a hundred papers. McClure was also altering the familiar writer-editor relationship. By nature he belonged, as Hamlin Garland remarked, to the "conquering side of the editors' guild."[14] He refused to wait for material to appear in the mail but hunted it out, buying mostly on an author's reputation or on recommendations, while also spinning out ideas to writers and commissioning material. He had his rivals, especially a syndicate run by a former New York journalist, Irving Bacheller, and this spurred on his restless literary scouting parties. In a six-year period from 1887 to 1893 he made eight round trips across the Atlantic and an equal number of journeys across the United States—a man, as commentators on his life have noted, meant for the jet age but imprisoned in the age of steam. In his search for fresh material he met with nearly every writer of note from Ned Buntline to Henry James, and bought from virtually all of them. In England he garnered for the syndicate the work of such major figures as Rudyard Kipling and Thomas Hardy as well as the American expatriates James, Bret Harte, and Harold Frederic. His second-in-command in America, John Phillips, was advised to publicize the new stable of authors "so that Bacheller will not write to them & perhaps make tremendous offers, after they have engaged to me at quite moderate sums, as I hope." In a subsequent letter Phillips was told that "Bacheller is utterly routed & badly beaten. . . . Success, absolute & cloudless, is ours."[15]

Another rival, Edward Bok, began his syndicate by locating newspaper needs not served by McClure and Bacheller.[16] He circulated a weekly letter by the famed preacher Henry Ward Beecher, then followed it up—as the Bok Syndicate Press—with material aimed at women. He supplied a weekly letter from New York and engaged Ella Wheeler Wilcox for another weekly letter on specific women's topics; soon he had an entire page of material for women. The idea proved so popular that papers unable to get rights for what became known as a "Bok Page" had to develop women's pages of their own. Another successful feature of the syndicate was a chatty New York–based literary letter, "Bok's Literary Leaves." After he became editor of the *Ladies' Home Journal* in 1889 Bok closed his literary syndicate, leaving the field largely to Bacheller and McClure.

By its nature the business was a furious treadmill. New names and new material had to be continually injected into the operation, with at least one surprise offering each month and a spectacular offering every November when a fresh season was launched. Always new clients had to be attracted, old ones retained. As the literary syndicates became established features of daily papers and Sunday editions, their mass-production needs were prime targets for satirists. James L. Ford took aim at McClure:

> I paid a visit yesterday to the model village of Syndicate, founded by Mr. S. S. McClure for the benefit of the literary hands employed in his great enterprises, and I am bound to say that in point of neatness, order and the completeness of its sanitary arrangements it is infinitely superior to the similar towns of Pullman or any of the colonies established by the late Baron Hirsch. . . .
>
> At one o'clock the factory whistle blew again and the men returned to their work. Mr. McClure took me through one of the large buildings and explained every detail of the work to me. Every morning the foreman goes from bench to bench and gives an idea to each author. Just before noon he passes along again and carefully examines the unfinished work, and, late in the afternoon, a final inspection is made, after which the goods are packed and sent down to the wharf for shipment.
>
> I inquired whether there was any truth in the report that several authors had been taken with severe illness immediately after beginning work at Syndicate, whereupon the foreman explained that this had happened several times, but it had always resulted from giving an author a whole idea all at once—something to which few of them had ever been accustomed.

Elsewhere Ford described McClure's operation as "that Home for Literary Incurables."[17]

The need for a continuous supply of fresh material caused McClure to steadily inflate his prices, a boon to authors but a practice that kept the syndicate on the brink of financial ruin. Richard Harding Davis, then just beginning his wondrous career, turned down a $50-a-week offer to write a syndicated letter but shortly thereafter sold his tale "The Reporter Who Made Himself King" for syndication for $300. To Twain, McClure paid $1,000 apiece for syndication rights to a half-dozen letters from Europe while Howells received $10,000 for rights to a novel. To Robert Louis Stevenson, the writer McClure considered his grandest catch, he paid out even more. Eventually it became clear that something other than a newspaper syndicate was needed if McClure was to fully profit from his investments. A national magazine, with the potential for a rich stream of advertising revenue, beckoned—a publication that in later years he would think of as his "syndicate work grown up."[18]

two

McClure's Magazine had the misfortune of beginning publication in the depression year of 1893. As newspapers felt the pinch of hard times they cut back on the use of syndicates and withheld money they already owed; but despite a lack of funds McClure pushed ahead, using reprint material from the syndicate for the magazine and signing up new writers with payment in stock in the venture. Henry Drummond, a Scottish theologian and scientist who wrote popular articles on evolution, turned over a $3,000 fee for delivering the Lowell Lectures in Boston in return for stock in the magazine. When Hamlin Garland was offered stock in lieu of payment, he declined—to his lasting regret. Conan Doyle invested $5,000 in the magazine, just the sum McClure needed to pay off a debt he had run up to English authors.

A year into publication the magazine was losing $1,000 a week but gaining in circulation and reputation. It carried fiction by regional writers such as Octave Thanet (pen name of Alice French), Sarah Orne Jewett, and Joel Chandler Harris as well as the major English writers; at the same time McClure was using his interventionist manner as an editor to create a fresh kind of topical journalism. The magazine was meant to have the up-to-date quality of a "monthly newspaper"; it offered itself, as Garland put it, "as a bold and enterprising truth dispenser" to the masses.[19] To that end McClure spun out ideas for articles, found writers to carry them through, and attached the writers to the magazine as staff members or contributing editors. Unsolicited manuscripts were also welcomed, the magazine announcing in its columns that "we are glad to receive and examine contributions of any sort within the scope of the magazine—short stories and historical, scientific, and other special articles." The magazine added that it had a standing prize of a staff position for the "special writer who can prove his right to it"[20]—a right established, though the magazine left the requirement unspecified, by capturing the attention of the dynamic owner.

By the decade's end *McClure's* circulation had soared to 400,000, the McClure syndicate (which Sam McClure left largely in the hands of family members) was grossing $50,000 a year, and McClure had branched out into profitable book publishing with the creation of Doubleday and McClure. The firm offered another means of attracting the services of authors for the magazine and syndicate operations. After reading Frank Norris's novel *Moran of the Lady Letty* in serial form in a California publication, McClure brought the writer to New York as an assistant in the publishing firm, with his mornings spent in editorial work and his afternoons left free for writing. For some time fiction had been coming directly to the magazine rather than from syndicate files, and Norris was added to an impressive roster of new young writers that included Garland, London, Dreiser, Booth Tarkington, and O. Henry. McClure also showered his fiction writers with article possibilities while at the same time securing for the magazine a group of nonfiction specialists that included Ida M. Tarbell, William Allen White, Will Irwin, Lincoln Steffens, and Ray Stannard Baker (who also served for a year in the late 1890s as managing editor of the newspaper syndicate and turned out stories on scientific subjects for syndicate circulation).

The idea of a staff of fact writers was a McClure inspiration. Nonfiction was ordinarily accepted on magazines on the same freelance basis as fiction, but McClure wanted more control over articles than the prevailing practice allowed. He had firm notions about subjects and how articles should be written. To get what he wanted he set about attaching writers to the magazine on a full-time basis—uncertain at first whether they should be called associate editors, staff writers, or staff associates—then showered them with ideas and his relentless enthusiasm. Ellery Sedgwick, who toiled for *McClure's* before becoming owner-editor of the *Atlantic*, remembered what it was like: "Everyone about him caught fire and he would inflame the intelligence of his staff into molten excitement. The mood would be too hot to last but would bring results. Should anyone object that another magazine had printed an article on the very subject he was suggesting, the chief would run his hand through his electric hair and shout: 'You say other magazines have told that story. You are wrong. A story is never told till McClure tells it.'"[21]

Over the years *McClure's* gained a reputation as a magazine that valued writers and writing, and with good reason its proprietor could say that his real capital in starting the magazine had been his "wide acquaintance with writers and with what they could produce." He could similarly boast that through his syndicate and magazine he could win for new writers a public larger than that provided by any other editor or publisher in the land—"a million families, the representative people who read the leading dailies in all parts of the country."

He added: "The test of a writer's market value is, how many people will read him? I could give a new writer that test at once. The magazine and syndicate combined were the machinery I offered to get the young men in whom I believed to the people."[22]

three

And not only young men.

Few writers benefited more from public exposure through McClure's syndicate and magazine than Ida Tarbell, the first of the fact writers lured onto the magazine's staff. She once remarked that "nearly all women who escape marriage and the schoolroom try for journalism," and in following this course herself she eventually became through her association with *McClure's* one of the most prominent writers of her day.[23] Well before that, in an article in 1887 called "Women in Journalism," she had noted an observation of Thomas Wentworth Higginson that women writers were well represented in popular fiction but seldom devoted themselves to serious magazine nonfiction—a situation she singlehandedly corrected.

After a try at teaching Tarbell took an editorial position on the *Chautauquan*, publishing there her first articles and learning the ropes of the magazine business. A series of small studies of the women of the French Revolution published in the magazine got her thinking about a life of Madame Roland; what followed was a daring decision to leave her job and move to Paris, supporting herself as a freelance writer for newspapers. She was thirty-three years old, her writing experience was limited, she read but could not speak French, and friends tried to dissuade her. Nonetheless, as she recalled in her autobiography, she "plunged gaily into planning for a career in journalism, self-directed, free-lance journalism. Surely I could find subjects enough in Paris to write about, subjects that would interest American newspapers." What she in fact planned was a "syndicate of my own," with her newspaper work eventually leading to magazine pieces.[24] Beyond this was the study and research needed for a major work on Madame Roland.

With three friends she settled in Paris in 1891 and immersed herself in the daily life of the city as material for her one-writer syndicate. She had offered her work to six big-city papers and three began accepting; several weeks after her arrival in Paris she had her first check for a syndicate article—$5.[25] A few weeks later *Scribner's* bought a short story for $100. Fiction had no part in Tarbell's plan as a writer but the sale bolstered her confidence as well as her shaky finances. An article sent off to the McClure syndicate gained another sale, this for $10, and an expression of interest in more of her work. Tarbell followed up with articles that included translated pieces cribbed from French newspapers, and some were accepted—"enough," she later wrote, "to make me feel that this might be a stable and prosperous market for short and timely articles."[26]

Eventually the McClure syndicate began suggesting articles to her, including a series on French women writers that tied in with her historical interest in Madame Roland. She also was put to work translating short stories, for which she was paid less than a dollar a translation, while her articles brought in $2 to $12 apiece. In effect, she had become the syndicate's representative in Paris. Success as a freelancer meant hard work, and the diligent Tarbell was usually at her desk by eight in the morning and rarely finished a day before midnight. She did her writing in longhand and made careful final copies—so careful that John Phillips, on the receiving end of her syndicate work in New York, assumed she was a middleaged New England schoolteacher.

In the summer of 1892 Sam McClure suddenly materialized at her Paris door, announcing he had ten minutes to spare and staying over two hours. Tarbell was captivated by a youthful-looking figure who was about her own age and brimming over with energy. He held forth about his life, his wife, his syndicate, and finally a magazine he was planning. This was where Tarbell came in. What the new magazine wanted from her were articles on the work of eminent French and English scientists.

Tarbell's articles so pleased McClure and Phillips that when the magazine began publication in 1893 she was offered the editorship of the Youth's Department at a salary of $2,100 a year, which soon would be raised to $3,000. McClure also agreed to pay her return passage to America with the agreement that she could stay with her family in Pennsylvania for a few months before joining the magazine. The plan changed when McClure suddenly brought her to New York as a staff writer to begin work on a new scheme, a biography of Napoleon Bonaparte. It was the start of her long tenure (about which more in a subsequent chapter) as one of *McClure's* star authors.

four

When McClure published his autobiography in 1914—ghosted by Willa Cather, one of the magazine's finds as a writer and a valued staff editor—he paid close attention to his relationship with Ida Tarbell but sidestepped that with Stephen Crane. For good reason. While Tarbell's *History of the Standard Oil Company* was one the magazine's great triumphs, the failure to publish Crane's *The Red Badge of Courage* was a sad episode best left unrecorded.

It was through Hamlin Garland that Crane came to McClure's attention in early 1894. An unlikely friendship had developed between Garland and Crane when the young reporter covered a talk Garland had given; Crane's *Maggie: A Girl of the Streets* was just published, under the pseudonym Johnston Smith and at Crane's expense. Garland sent him to see McClure with a personal note: "If you have any work for Mr. Crane talk things over with him and for Mercy Sake! don't keep him *standing* for an hour, as he did before, out in your pen for culprits."[27] At that meeting or shortly thereafter McClure had in his hands the manuscript of *The Red Badge of Courage*. He kept it for months, temporizing, unable to buy for lack of funds. Crane was furious, writing Garland that "McClure was a Beast about the war-novel."[28] Finally, Crane took the manuscript to McClure's rival, Bacheller, who recognized it as a "vivid and powerful piece of work" though "indifferent to grammatical rules."[29] For $90 Bacheller bought a shortened version and serialized it through his newspaper syndicate.

Bacheller was a reporter for the *Brooklyn Daily Times* when he began a syndicate operation in 1884 by selling a novel by the British writer Joseph Hatton to Robert Bonner's *Ledger* for $3,500 and receiving $500 from Hatton for his service.[30] He followed up by placing a series of Hatton interviews with eminent British men and women in several newspapers. Buoyed by his success, he gave up his reporting job, opened an office, took on a partner, James W. Johnson, who added capital to the operation, and devoted himself to the syndicate, crisscrossing the country over the next several years to sell his material. By 1892 the Bacheller-Johnson syndicate was said to be offering metropolitan papers a weekly supply of copy equal in quantity and quality to a single issue of *Century;* eventually it would claim to supply copy to virtually all the leading American papers. After buying out Johnson and then in 1898 leaving the syndicate business himself under press of competition from McClure and other operators, Bacheller returned to newspaper work as Sunday editor of the *New York World*. In 1900 he published an immensely popular novel of farm life in upstate New York, *Eben Holden*, that a quarter century after its appearance was still selling some 3,000 copies a year.[31] In 1917 and 1919 Bacheller novels again reached the best-seller lists.

Bacheller prided himself on boosting the pay of authors through buying their work for syndication. He remembered that Conan Doyle had been getting about $68 per thousand words when Bacheller purchased his work at a rate of $130. Although his payment to Crane was hardly bountiful, Bacheller got the *Red Badge* into print, albeit in an abridged form of some fifteen thousand words, and notice of it followed. The editor of the *Philadelphia Press* told Bacheller that editors, reporters, and even pressmen on the paper had read the story and were eager to see Crane. Bacheller promptly delivered him for a meeting, and when he arrived "word flew from cellar to roof that the great Stephen Crane was in the office. Editors, reporters, compositors, proof-readers crowded around him shaking his hand. It was a revelation of the commanding power of genius."[32] Crane's story had appeared in the *Press*, however, only because its stock of daily installments of fiction was depleted; moreover, it was a gamble to publish an unknown writer and a story about the Civil War, a subject considered overworked.

A contract for a book version of *Red Badge* was forthcoming from Appleton and Company and for Crane there was journalistic work for syndication. For Bacheller's syndicate he traveled through the South and the West on his way to Mexico. At a stop at the *Nebraska State Journal* in Lincoln, hoping to find a check from Bacheller awaiting him, Crane met Willa Cather, then a student at the University of Nebraska who had proofread the syndicated version of *Red Badge* while working part-time in the *Journal* office. She remembered that he told her about his dual literary life in which he wrote "in the first place the matter that pleased himself, and doing it very slowly; in the second place, any sort of stuff that would sell. And he remarked that his poor was just as bad as it could possibly be." Cather added that in later years she was always astonished to hear Crane spoken of as "the reporter in fiction" for he lacked a reporter's ability to soak up surface detail and information and quickly turn it into readable copy. "The detail of a thing," she quoted him as saying, "has to filter through my blood, and then it comes out like a native product, but it takes forever."[33]

For Bacheller's needs, Crane's copy was good enough. "I sent him to Mexico for new color," he recalled. "He wrote for me a number of vivid sketches of the life he saw there."[34] Work also came Crane's way from McClure, his finances on the upswing. Crane sought him out ("Whenever you have some article or other in mind, let me know at once"),[35] and the editor bombarded the writer with suggestions ranging from stories about actual battles of the Civil War to a weekly New York letter for the syndicate. One of Crane's finest stories, "The Bride Comes to Yellow Sky," appeared in the magazine and he ground out various New York sketches for the syndicate. From the syndicate came a circular boasting that "Mr. Crane has been added to the McClure staff, and his writings will be placed before the public exclusively through the newspapers of the Syndicate and McClure's Magazine."[36]

The situation was not entirely to Crane's liking. Living in England in 1897 and spinning out hackwork to meet mounting debts, Crane pleaded with his New York agent, Paul Revere Reynolds, to "get me out of the ardent grasp of the S. S. McClure Co. I owe them [for advances] about $500, I think, and they seem to calculate on controlling my entire out-put."[37] (Jack London would go through a similar struggle with the company. When *A Daughter of the Snows,* the novel London had written on retainer, turned out to be a failure, it was sold off to other publishers and *McClure's* insisted he pay off his debt with future stories for the magazine. They "held the bread-and-butter lash over me," London bristled, wanting him to write "petty, smug, complacent bourgeois stories; wanted me to enter the ranks of clever mediocrity and there to pander to the soft, fat, cowardly bourgeois instincts.")[38] Still, McClure's operation remained an important outlet for Crane's work, and he supplied it with war reporting and potboiling occasional pieces drawn from travels in England, Scotland, and Ireland. The work, he acknowledged to Reynolds, was "a big graft to play as long as I am here in Europe,"[39] and he urged the agent to peddle it to McClure among others ("Hit him hard. Hit him beastly hard").[40] The agent was told that Crane also meant to hit up McClure for a substantial loan and was sent stories to "use as a boost for a loan," though only if and when "you see this loan in sight."[41] Crane's last novels, *The Third Violet* and *Active Service,* were serialized by the syndicate but the loan, like many of his schemes for raising money, never materialized.

Writers could, of course, bypass operations like McClure's and Bacheller's and syndicate their own work, as Ida Tarbell had done in a minor way during her early writing days in Paris, claiming all proceeds as their own. While he was a student at Columbia University following World War I, Paul Gallico learned about the business through an interim job with a syndicate. He then began writing short stories modeled on O. Henry and syndicated them himself to Sunday papers, getting space rates as high as $20 a story. For most writers, though, self-syndication was easier to conceive than execute.

His career heating up, Edgar Rice Burroughs, ever the businessman, was quick to spot the benefits of newspaper syndication. "Tarzan of the Apes" had been serialized in the *New York Evening World* through an arrangement with the Munsey Company, and with its success Albert Payson Terhune, then on the staff of the *Evening World,* had written Burroughs about future work for newspaper serialization after prior magazine publication. Subsequently, Terhune bought New York newspaper rights to the Tarzan sequel for $300. Burroughs was careful thereafter to sell to his primary publisher, the pulp magazines, only first serial rights and reserve to himself the chance for newspaper sales.

At first he handled syndication himself, then found the details overwhelming. He wrote to Terhune for advice: "I have been asked to quote on the newspaper serial rights for Cleveland, Cincinnati, Toledo, Akron, Columbus, Des Moines, Oklahoma City, Denver, Memphis, and Los Angeles; and I have no idea what to ask. I presume that the price would be governed largely by either the population of the city in question or the circulation of the newspaper. Can you help me out—I shall certainly appreciate it."[42] The solution, finally, was to turn over syndication of "The Return of Tarzan" and subsequent work to a syndicate operation, Chicago's International Press Bureau, for a percentage of gross sales, with Burroughs holding for himself all dealings with Terhune and the *Evening World*.

five

The Newspaper Enterprise Association (NEA) was a syndicate of a different order, operated by a newspaper rather than independent entrepreneurs like McClure and Bacheller and offering writers opportunities that were more strictly journalistic. Started in 1901 in the offices of the *Cleveland Press*, it serviced the needs of the Scripps-McRae (later Scripps-Howard) chain of newspapers and others who bought the service, providing a full range of editorial material from pictures and features to cartoons and editorials, the material sent out daily in the form of printed proofs and mats for stereotyping plates. When Burton Rascoe began writing for NEA in 1921 he thought that with a newspaper title and masthead added the material was so complete it "would make an acceptable adless newspaper—with no spot news in it which would be stale news two or three days later."[43]

Rascoe had been let go by the *Chicago Tribune* after eight years and numerous positions, including literary editor and drama critic, when he was hired by NEA as a freelance space-rate writer working out of Chicago. (A predecessor in the Chicago position was Carl Sandburg, who began with NEA as an Eastern Europe correspondent based in Stockholm. When he was fired in 1919, he was informed that he and the syndicate were not "hitching well together.")⁴⁴ Rascoe had first turned down a staff editorial position at the syndicate's offices in Cleveland; the salary was an attractive $150 a week but he preferred to write and believed he could easily improve NEA's usual feature fare. He made a specialty of medical and scientific stories, going to the John Crerar Library each day, reading specialized journals, then writing unsigned features and occasional news items based on the articles and mailing them at night to NEA headquarters. His first day at work yielded a story, drawn from the *Yale Review,* about life expectancy that the NEA displayed for member papers with a front-page streamer headline.

Rascoe varied his method by taking ideas from obscure journals and calling up specialists around the country and asking for comment. He also regularly contributed to the five editorials the service sent out daily, all of them, he recalled, "innocuous and platitudinous but irrefutable and readable—homilies on the seasons, the first groundhog, the first robin, the anniversary of some historical event, the pleasures of walking, famous fallacies, the future of aviation."⁴⁵ His efforts brought in $314 his first week, $268 his second, then settled in at an average $175 a week—the amount that met his needs and more than a staff position would have paid.

Rascoe had been promoted from one of NEA's writers to manager of its Chicago bureau, a shift he regretted because it limited his writing time, when he moved to New York as associate editor of *McCall's.* The money was less than he was making with NEA but the lure of New York was too strong to resist. Shortly thereafter he became the literary editor and chief book reviewer of the *New York Tribune,* a position from which he exerted considerable influence on the literary life of the 1920s. Later in the decade he reentered syndicate work with the Editors Features Service, writing a daily column about New York life.

Rascoe's chief competition came from O. O. McIntyre, whose "New York Day by Day" column was circulated by the McNaught Syndicate from 1922 to 1938. McIntyre's special angle was to view the big city through small-town eyes, portraying its racy glamor but comforting his readers with the knowledge that they were living elsewhere. Contemporaries charged that he compiled the column while hardly ever leaving a luxurious hotel apartment, that he often lifted material from other writers without credit (McIntyre responding that he thought anything printed in yesterday's newspaper was in the public domain), and that he had only a passing interest in accuracy. The column, nonetheless, was widely popular, and McIntyre at the time of his death was said to be earning $200,000 a year.[46] When Rascoe gave up his competing column after nearly three years he was appearing in over four hundred papers as well as writing a weekly book review that was syndicated in sixty-three papers.

six

In 1928, the year the McClure syndicate was sold, John M. Wheeler described in a *Saturday Evening Post* article his decision to become a syndicate entrepreneur: "Early in life I decided I could make a bigger profit by selling other men's brains than my own, and so far I don't think I have ever found myself wrong."[47] Wheeler was one of the most important of a new breed of operators who appeared on the scene as syndicates developed and matured between the two world wars, their function narrowed more to purveyors of news and feature material than fiction and poetry. He had first entered the business in 1913 when, after the *New York Herald* turned down his request for a salary increase as a sports writer, he opened a syndicate specializing in articles by sports celebrities that he ghosted himself. Another specialty was the use of literary figures to cover important events.

One of his star attractions was Richard Harding Davis. In 1914 Wheeler sent the middleaged writer to Mexico in anticipation of a war directed against the military strongman Victoriano Huerta, paying a fee of $1,000 a week for the first four weeks, $500 for each week thereafter. The Mexican work was so successful—and Wheeler so enamored of being the employer of a hero of his youth—that Davis was sent to Europe by the syndicate to cover the outbreak of war. "We met in the Lambs Club in New York," Wheeler said of his arrangement with Davis, which called for $600 a week plus expenses, "and agreed to terms. He told me how much he wished sent to his wife weekly. The rest we were to hold for his return. There was no letter, no contract—only a nod. We operated on that contract all through the war, and again it was most satisfactory."[48] Later Wheeler had the same kind of informal contract with Ring Lardner, who for a number of years wrote a weekly humor column for a new operation Wheeler launched called the Bell Syndicate.

In 1930 Wheeler became general manager of the North American Newspaper Alliance (NANA), a syndicate formed by a number of leading American and Canadian newspapers to supply feature material to supplement news reporting. To gain an advantage in an increasingly competitive market, syndicates now searched for journalistic coups by securing the services of prominent figures. The McNaught Syndicate signed up Will Rogers and Eleanor Roosevelt for regular work, and Wheeler's NANA gave General John J. Pershing $275,000 for serial rights to his memoirs. With the outbreak of the Spanish Civil War later in the decade, Wheeler went after a major name in literary circles, Ernest Hemingway.

Hemingway had been away from regular journalism since leaving the *Toronto Star* in 1923, but he was eager to get to the Spanish war any way he could, and Wheeler was just as eager to have his eye-catching byline for the syndicate. When Wheeler offered a contract calling for $500 for each cabled story and $1,000 for stories sent by mail up to 1,200 words, with Hemingway paying his own expenses, the writer immediately accepted. Hemingway sent thirty-one dispatches from Spain during three trips to the country in 1937–38, twenty-eight of which found their way into print.[49] The mailed pieces were fully written out while the cables in abbreviated cableese had to be fleshed out by editors back in New York. Frequently the editors fired off instructions on how they wanted the war covered, treating their celebrity journalist as they might any green reporter in the field, and they let it be known that, given the high fees involved, they wanted only one story a week from their expensive correspondent unless there was important breaking news to file. A particularly heated squabble arose when a NANA customer, the *New York Times,* complained that Hemingway's dispatches merely duplicated those from its own correspondent in the field, Herbert Matthews.

Although his dispatches had flashes of color and some strong battle reporting, Hemingway's journalism in the Spanish war was generally undistinguished and NANA was not displeased when the contract expired.[50] In a memoir published in 1961, Wheeler avoided particulars of his relationship with Hemingway, saying only that he did an "outstanding job" in Spain and that his reporting "worked all right for us and for him, too, I guess, for we have been pretty good friends ever since."[51] For his part Hemingway thought well enough of his Spanish journalism that he outlined for Wheeler and for Maxwell Perkins, his editor at Scribner's, a collection of recent work that included the Spanish material. Nothing came of the idea. Hemingway also thought well enough of NANA that with American entry into World War II he applied to Wheeler to report on the war for the syndicate. Despite the continuing star quality of Hemingway's name, Wheeler tactfully declined.

seven

In time newspaper syndicates grew less important as an avenue of public exposure and a source of income for writers—and with the shrinkage of newspapers through failures and consolidations the syndicates became less important
in general. Where they remained a considerable bonanza was for celebrities,
columnists, sports figures, and above all for cartoonists. One of Wheeler's first
triumphs when he got into the syndicate business in 1913 was luring away from
the Hearst organization H. C. "Bud" Fisher, the creator of the Mutt and Jeff
cartoon strip, with an offer of 60 percent of the revenue from his work and a
guarantee of $1,000 a week.[52] In his *Saturday Evening Post* article of 1928
Wheeler noted that the top syndicate pay for newspaper cartoon artists "runs
as high as $200,000 a year, without including the income from novelties such
as toys, books, and so on."[53] Remunerative as they were for writers, newspaper
syndicates were never bonanzas of quite such magnitude.

SPORTING LIFE

Field, Stream, and Playing Field as Material

Life is just a game of base ball
so win or lose with a smile.
—Ring Lardner

one

With the first Frank Merriwell stories in Street & Smith's *Tip Top Weekly* in 1896, Gilbert Patten led the way into another enriching arena for fiction-eers—tales of the sporting life. Given the volume and popularity of the work that followed, the date seems oddly late, and in fact the world of sport had for some time provided independent writers with material, though largely for nonfiction articles appearing in outdoor journals.[1] Among the first writers to tap the market was Poe's and Willis's contemporary, Henry William Herbert, a versatile Grub Street scribbler who shared Poe's eagerness for loftier literary standing.

Born and raised in aristocratic circumstances in England and given a clas-sical education at Eton and Cambridge, Herbert came to New York in 1831 at age twenty-four, perhaps in flight from gambling debts.[2] Tall, charming, hot-tempered, given to a brawling tavern life while keenly aware of his elegant background, he found companionship in a young sporting crowd, drawing on a well-honed knowledge of horses, dogs, and hunting. When his funds ran low he took to teaching Greek and Latin at a boys' school in New York, then followed the example of a fellow teacher who supplemented his income with newspaper and magazine writing and began sending contributions to local papers. All the while he pursued an active outdoor life of hunting and fishing.

Eventually Herbert turned his hand to historical fiction in the manner of Sir Walter Scott, but soon discovered that periodical editors, able to fill their columns with reprinted foreign material, were unwilling to pay for his work. His response was to drum up financial backing and start his own magazine in March 1833, giving it the same name as Willis's earlier Boston journal, the *American Monthly Magazine.* A literary venture whose anonymous contributions came largely from Herbert's own pen, including a serial novel called *The Brothers, A Tale of the Fronde,* the magazine was intended as a rival to the *Knickerbocker,* New York's popular literary miscellany. Herbert stayed on as an editor for two years before a falling-out with his then co-editor, Charles Fenno Hoffman, caused him to resign. Poe would credit the magazine under Herbert and Hoffman with one of the few early critical appraisals of Nathaniel Hawthorne's work.[3]

Herbert came away from his magazine venture a dedicated professional writer with a reputation for versatility and learning. In 1835 Harper and Brothers published *The Brothers,* though minus the author's name in the hope that anonymous publication would stir reader curiosity, and Herbert set to work on a second historical novel. *Cromwell* came out in 1838, again anonymously, but found most of its success in an edition in England, where it went through several printings. By now Herbert had given up teaching for full-time independent writing, his profession the rest of his life, turning out poems, sketches, and articles as well as historical fiction. Poe, who thought well of Herbert's poetry and considered including him in the series on the New York literati, also thought he had "written more trash than any man living, with the exception of [Theodore S.] Fay."[4] Much of this hackwork went unsigned, agreeably so in Herbert's view since he harbored serious literary hopes, especially as a historical novelist, and wanted his name to appear on only his major productions.

Translations became a central source of income, Herbert putting French novels into cheap English versions for fees that brought him an average of $3,000 to $4,000 a year. Most writers of the time would have lived comfortably on such income, but expensive tastes and the impulsive entertainment of friends kept Herbert in financial difficulty. In his search for funds he turned to writing outdoor articles for the *American Turf Register and Sporting Magazine,* a New York paper that had been founded in Baltimore in 1829, using the woodsy pen name Frank Forester. Here he drew on expert knowledge of rod and gun in articles of a practical, how-to bent that were flavored with the personality of a comfortable outdoorsman who relished the manly life. With the success of the articles he also began contributing outdoor pieces to the *Spirit of the Times,* considered the first general sporting journal in the country, and in 1845 the first collection of Frank Forester articles appeared as *The Warwick Woodlands,* modestly turned out by a Philadelphia firm in a twenty-five-cent paper edition and with the author's name given on the title page beneath his pen name.

A first edition of three thousand copies sold out within two months, surprising both author and publisher. Other Frank Forester books quickly followed, among them *My Shooting Box* in 1846 and more authoritative manuals such as *Field Sports in the United States and the British Provinces of America* (1848) and *Frank Forester's Fish and Fishing of the United States and British Provinces of North America* (1849). Realizing he had struck a vein of popular writing, Herbert gave his outdoor work full attention, even making studious woodcuts for his books. Eventually his work would be valued less for its practical sporting advice than for outlining a code of outdoor ethics—standards of fair play in the taking fish and game—that provided a basis for later conservation efforts. To define "a *genuine* sportsman," an outdoor journal noted in an editorial well after his death, it was enough to mention the name of Frank Forester, the "prince" of sporting writers.[5]

Herbert was now settled in a remote location (presently within the boundaries of Newark, New Jersey) in a cottage called "The Cedars" built with money sent from his father in England. A widower, he lived a solitary country existence of writing, reading, and walking the fields with gun and sketchbook. The path to his house was said to be lined with dog kennels, a chorus of barking announcing visitors. While to neighbors Herbert seemed a curious eccentric, to friends who paid calls he was still a warm host and convivial companion, and to editors he remained a prolific source of material both erudite and perfunctory.

Among his regular outlets was *Graham's,* where he shared billing—both as Henry William Herbert and Frank Forester—with the prominent writers of the time. In a letter to Lydia H. Sigourney in 1842 Poe informed the popular poet that she would be included in a "quite successful" future issue with such notables as Longfellow, Willis, Ann S. Stephens, Emma C. Embury, and

Herbert.[6] Herbert's pay rate from *Graham's* was $5 a page for prose, about the same as Poe's usual fee of $4–$5 but well under top rates running to $10 and $12. At one point, eager for "a little ready money," he offered the magazine a bargain-basement price of $200 cash for twelve tales of some eight pages each.[7]

While he was mass-producing magazine pieces Herbert kept on with historical fiction that he hoped possessed literary significance, and in *The Prometheus and Agamemnon of Aeschylus* he published a well-regarded translation from the Greek. But his popular success continued to reside in the guise of Frank Forester. A sporting novel in 1852, *The Quorndon Hounds*, was dedicated to George R. Graham, and the following year *American Game in Its Seasons* came out under the imprint of the new firm of Charles Scribner. The final Frank Forester book to appear in his lifetime, *Frank Forester's Horse and Horsemanship of the United States and British Provinces of North America* in 1857, revealed how far he had come as a sporting writer from the cheap edition of *Warwick Woodlands*. The new work was published in two elegantly illustrated volumes and sold at the premium price of $10 a set.

Yet for all Herbert's industry—some forty books in a career of just over twenty years—financial stability never followed. Neither did contentment. In 1858 he married a much younger woman who promptly left him; shortly thereafter he killed himself with a pistol following a seemingly pleasant dinner party with friends. He was fifty-one years old. Left behind was the unpublished manuscript of an ambitious historical book, Herbert's last full work. The manuscript, which had been turned over as collateral to a Newark money lender, eventually disappeared—a melancholy final episode in the unusual life of one of the earliest writers for hire.

two

Zane Grey broke into print with field-and-stream articles, and while his western novels became routine best sellers he also established himself during the 1920s and '30s as an outdoorsman whose name was even more prominent than Frank Forester's a century earlier. Vacillating at the start of his career between a humdrum life as a New York dentist and his longing to be a writer, Grey sold an article to *Recreation Magazine* in 1902 called "A Day on the Delaware" that was drawn from a fishing trip with his brother. It was his first publication. Soon thereafter *Field and Stream* took an article called "Camping

Out." Three years elapsed before he made another sale, but with the outdoors fixed as a magazine speciality Grey took to the woods and streams with even greater enthusiasm, and neglected his dental practice all the more.

In time, his novels huge moneymakers, he indulged a love for outdoor adventure that bordered on obsession. He fished and camped in Florida, Nova Scotia, and throughout the West; there were extended excursions to the Galapagos Islands, the South Seas, New Zealand and Australia; and he conspicuously accumulated hunting lodges, ranches, and boats. As a fisherman he became an international expert, holding at one time world records for several deep-sea catches. The Gulf Stream as well as such favored fishing places as Catalina Island, the Florida Keys, and the Rogue River of Oregon became fashionable sporting grounds because of their association with Grey, his exploits with rod and reel duly recounted in magazine pieces for *Country Gentleman, Field and Stream,* and *Sports Afield* and in a flow of books with titles beginning *Tales of . . .* (*Fishes, Lonely Trails, Southern Rivers, Fishing Virgin Seas,* etc.).[8]

Apart from providing material for his magazine articles and books, outdoor life served Grey as therapy for recurring lapses into depression linked to the difficulty he found in writing. His spirits soared on his hunting and fishing trips, and he was able to plan stories and write them in interludes between exhausting periods of pursuit. "Florida for ten weeks was, as always, good for my spirit and health," he noted in a typical diary entry during an outing in 1923. "I wrote most of the romance *Code of the West* and several outdoor stories, and fifty pages in another book."[9] (Upton Sinclair added the suggestion that Grey used the outdoors as an escape from fame: "He cannot go walking without seeing his name on billboards, nor read the papers without seeing pictures of his sturdy heroes rescuing his lovely heroines. He grows tired of them . . . so he goes after big game fish, and having caught all there are in local waters, buys him a yacht and goes crusing to New Zealand.")[10]

During the thirties Grey's major competition as a literary outdoorsman came from Hemingway, especially as he recounted his exploits in *Esquire* magazine. *The Sun Also Rises* and *A Farewell to Arms* were behind him and he had just published his nonfiction treatise on Spanish bullfighting, *Death in the Afternoon,* when Arnold Gingrich came calling in 1933 with an attractive magazine offer. The editor of *Apparel Arts* magazine in Chicago was starting a new men's magazine; he wanted Hemingway as a regular contributor at a rate of up to $250 an article (later doubled to $500), and he had definite ideas about the nature of the contributions. They would deal with hunting and fishing, forming—as Gingrich pitched them to Hemingway—"a sort of sports-man's notebook." In structure they would follow the rambling personal-essay manner of the "Pamplona Letter" that Hemingway had published in a Paris literary journal nearly a decade earlier, stringing together a variety of items in a way that would not involve a "formal composition—a major effort involv-ing gestation and labor pains."[11]

The first article in the fall of 1933, "Marlin off the Morro: A Cuban Letter," recalled an ordeal two weeks before in which Hemingway had fought a 750-pound marlin for an hour and a half across several miles of ocean before his rod splintered and the fish was lost. Except for a few articles on war and politics and some that dealt with writing, the initial letter set the tone and subject for most of the twenty-five that appeared over the next three years. Hemingway's life and opinions were center stage, and in his self-portrayal he was a virile outdoorsman with expert knowledge of rod and gun whose gypsy life took him from the American West to the Gulf Stream, from Europe to Africa. In Hemingway's eyes, the letters were eminently practical, the quality, he insisted, that separated them from Grey's outdoor writing. Hemingway in-formed Gingrich that while Grey only wanted readers to marvel at his skill, Hemingway gave useful tips that had cost him thousands of dollars to learn. (When Grey invited him in 1935 to join in a "giant world fishing cruise to make a [motion] picture," Hemingway declined, holding in private that Grey was jealous of his fishing skill and wanted to ride on the coat tails of his fame—"the silliest of surmises," according to one of Hemingway's biographers.)[12]

The *Esquire* letters served Hemingway well. Gingrich advanced him $3,000 against future articles, the money used as a down payment on a fishing cruiser he greatly desired; the articles also helped underwrite an African safari. Regu-lar magazine publication had the added benefit of boosting his public reputa-tion, bringing him the attention of a larger audience than he had yet found through his fiction while also beginning that image-making process through which the author's persona would finally overshadow the fiction. One critic has maintained that, thanks to the *Esquire* letters, no major American novel-ist before Hemingway "ever had so large an audience for such a sustained pe-riod," and "none ever had like opportunity to talk about himself and to expect admiration in return."[13]

Hemingway took pains, nonetheless, to point out to readers that writing for mass-circulation magazines was not his real work. "Your correspondent," he noted in "Monologue to the Maestro: A High Seas Letter," "takes the prac-tice of letters, as distinct from the writing of these monthly letters, very seriously."[14] Gingrich, eager to have a literary star in his magazine, made no complaint, telling Hemingway to "go ahead and write anything that comes into your head. No holds barred. If it's good journalism I'll be well satisfied. If it isn't I'll know it, as a person, but accept it and like it, as an 'editor'."[15] In later years Gingrich credited Hemingway as an important factor in the magazine's success. Despite a steep newsstand price of fifty cents at a time when the *Saturday Evening Post* and *Collier's* were selling for a nickel, *Esquire* was an immediate hit, switching quickly from quarterly to monthly publication and within three years selling over a half million copies a month. Gingrich also used Hemingway's presence in the magazine as a recruiting device that helped bring in work by John Dos Passos, Ring Lardner, and Dashiell Hammett. Even though Hemingway was paid more than the others—a gentleman's agreement with Gingrich called for payment at a rate twice that of anyone else—his stature was such that writers signed on with the magazine regardless.

three

Outdoor writing was all well and good but the trail Gilbert Patten blazed with juvenile sports fiction remained a more lucrative year-in year-out earning vehicle, as professional writers were quick to notice. Among the legion that fell in behind Patten in writing for the young was Zane Grey, with baseball stories becoming yet another arrow in his writing quiver.

As a young man in Ohio Grey was a curve-ball pitcher who attracted the attention of college and professional scouts. At the University of Pennsylvania he shifted to the outfield and became known as a star hitter. In his final varsity game he hit a home run in the ninth inning to beat the University of Virginia, the crowd showering him with roses, and newspapers acclaiming him an authentic Frank Merriwell. Later, in his dreary period as a New York dentist, he played on a New Jersey team with ex-college players ("Doc Gray," a sportswriter wrote of him, "is famous for making home runs when needed")[16] and thought seriously of turning professional, held back only by a stronger desire to become a writer.

After he began selling articles to outdoor magazines Grey tried his hand at a serial novel about baseball that he sent off to the *American Boy,* whose associate editor at the time was Clarence Budington Kelland, later to become one of the *Saturday Evening Post's* stalwart fictioneers. *The Short-Stop,* rejected by the magazine and other juvenile publications before being brought out in

book form in 1909 by A. C. McClurg, was Grey's first substantial sale, earning him about $200 beyond a $100 advance. He followed up with baseball
stories for the McClure Newspaper Syndicate, later collected in *The Red-
headed Outfield and Other Baseball Stories*, and another juvenile novel, *The
Young Pitcher*, drawn from his own college playing days. Grey's *alter ego* in the
story, Ken Ward, studying forestry while pitching for Wayne College, already
had appeared the year before in the boys' outdoor-adventure novel *The Young
Forester* and later would be featured in *The Young Lion Hunter* and *Ken Ward
in the Jungle*.

While juvenile fiction was a passing feature of Grey's work, for Ralph
Henry Barbour it was his entire career. Of Patten's many imitators, including
the various hired hands of the Stratemeyer Syndicate, his New England contemporary was one of the most successful. Launched with a novel in 1899
called *The Half-Back*, Barbour for thirty years produced a steady flow of stories of athletic heroism in prep-school settings. Although his schools bore
such gilt-edged names as Yardley and Erskine and Ferry Hill, there was no
emphasis in his work on social prestige; his typical hero, as Henry Steele
Commager remarked about Barbour's fictional world, "was always a little de-
mocrat: his mother sometimes took in wash to keep him there, or so it
seemed."[17]

Barbour's first novel grew out of a story sold to *St. Nicholas* magazine that
was expanded to book form at the suggestion of an editor at Appleton and
Company. What followed from the former newspaper reporter and editor
were some 135 boys' books, many of them series titles, as well as a few adult
novels and scores of juvenile stories for *St. Nicholas* and the *Youth's Companion*. Barbour's tales followed the annual round of the athletic seasons—from
baseball and track to football and hockey and basketball, the cycle repeating
again and again—and often centered on themes, beyond a predictable concern with physical prowess, sportsmanship, and teamwork, that emphasized
school spirit, as indicated in the title of his second novel, *For the Honor of the
School*, and such later concoctions as *The Spirit of the School* and *The School
That Didn't Care*.

To fellow writers Barbour's productions seemed as effortless as they were
enriching, supporting homes in Cambridge and Marblehead, Massachusetts,
and winters in the South and Southwest. "He lives on the fat of the land," one
remarked. "He enjoys himself all the year, and for most of the time makes no
effort to get down to work."[18] Barbour's success naturally attracted competitors,
with William Heyliger the most accomplished of the sizeable group. Another

former newspaperman, Heyliger recalled that his first attempt at what he called a "school-athletic" story was handwritten on both sides of sheets of foolscap, the sheets then tied together at the top with blue ribbon and foolishly dispatched to the *Saturday Evening Post.*[19] His first success came in 1911 with *Bartley, Freshman Pitcher*, and thereafter he turned out a string of boys' sports books at a pace of one a year. Compared to Barbour, his stories were more realistic and contained fewer heavy doses of moralizing. "Today's boy," Heyliger declared, is "keener, less unsophisticated. . . and better educated. He is coming along. He wants a hero matched in possibilities to himself, and not a prodigy or a caricature. He wants a book that will have, within limitations, the forms and depth of the adult novel. He wants characterization, and not merely the names of characters."[20]

The tide of specialized pulp publications in the 1920s and '30s was less of a boon to sporting writers than one would imagine. Street & Smith's *Sport Story* was a marketing success, as was *Fight Stories,* a competitor from Fiction House; but generally sports fiction proved to have more audience appeal in mixed than single-interest magazines.[21] In the durable realm of schoolboy stories, perhaps the greatest advance came in slick magazines and books in the 1930s and '40s from the hand of John R. Tunis. Unlike Barbour and Heyliger, Tunis arrived at juvenile fiction late in his career after many years of surviving as a freelancer in the nonfiction magazine market with work that ranged from articles in *Good Hardware* and *Charm* to a weekly sports column in the fledgling *New Yorker* under Harold Ross. As Tunis later recounted it in an autobiography, *A Measure of Independence,* the main theme of his life was the freedom he gained, burdensome yet satisfying, as an independent writer: "Mine is an ordinary American story but a happy one, chiefly because I was able to do what I wanted to do in life, and make a living so doing. Looking back I realize nobody could have lived a fuller life. I was rare among my contemporaries to be permitted freedom of choice."[22]

After graduation from Harvard in 1911 and World War I service, Tunis turned to writing without much forethought about it as a career, flooding the mail with articles and soon discovering the rueful truth of P. G. Wodehouse's remark that "I have always felt that the glamour of rejection slips wears off; when you have seen one, you have seen them all."[23] Eventually the humor weekly *Life* took a sketch and paid him $5.62, his first sale as a writer. He kept grinding away, working nights and weekends while supporting himself and his wife with a laboring job, and by the end of the year, 1919, his writing income stood at all of $19.09.

To gain a leg-up in his new profession Tunis took a correspondence course he had seen advertised in a writer's magazine, and in fact he did better in 1920, making $81. When he came into a small inheritance, he promptly moved to France as a full-time writer with the idea of creating a miniature self-run syndicate by covering winter sports along the Riviera, mostly tennis and golf, and selling short articles to a half-dozen American newspapers. Now and then the idea worked and papers bought his work at space rates; his income rose to $30–$40 a month. He played tennis—at Harvard he had made the tennis team—and chanced to meet and play with Suzanne Lenglen, a French champion and a Wimbledon winner. Back in the United States when his money ran out, he sold an article about Lenglen to the *Boston Globe* for $35, his best single payday. Another piece about Lenglen was taken by *American Lawn Tennis*.

Tunis also began making small sales to veterans' magazines, the most important being *American Legion Weekly*, whose young editor had been in charge of *Stars and Stripes* in Paris during the war. A sale to the *Weekly* brought a check for $100 and, for a struggling freelancer, a life-giving note:

> Pursuant to yours of July 26th, we will make the changes necessary in your article, and will use it on the opening pages of the August 11th issue. It's good stuff.
>   Sincerely yours.
>   Harold W. Ross, editor.

Success did not immediately follow. Although Tunis kept churning out copy, he ran into a dry spell for acceptances; when through a chance meeting he was offered an introduction to a New York literary agent, he leaped at the opportunity. Surprisingly, Erd Brandt of the successful agency of Brandt and Brandt took the young writer on as a client—more than for any other reason, perhaps, because of a shared interest in tennis—and Tunis moved to New York to be at the center of the magazine market.

Here he learned to become a salesman, calling on magazines and worming his way past receptionists to display his goods to editors. He reduced article ideas to a few sentences typed on small white cards and followed up, if he chanced to spark interest, with a one- or two-page outline. "It was like working for the Fuller Brush Company," he recalled, "and in many magazine offices I must have been no more welcome."[24] Because he had written for *American Legion Weekly*, he had no difficulty in getting inside Harold Ross's office on West 45th Street when the *New Yorker* was just underway. Although Tunis thought Ross knew "less about sport than any male American I ever met," the editor had a hazy notion that his fledgling magazine's sports coverage could be improved.[25] For $50 apiece Tunis was hired to write weekly columns up to a thousand words for the back of the magazine, beginning in April 1925. At the same time he was turning out a monthly article for *American Lawn Tennis* for $25, and when his work there caught the eye of the sports editor of the *New York Evening Post,* Tunis signed on with the newspaper to write three articles a week for $75. For the first time since his days as a laborer he now had a regular paycheck.

By the late twenties Tunis had broken into *Collier's,* the *Saturday Evening Post,* and *Harper's.* Frederick Lewis Allen, then an assistant editor at *Harper's,* had been at Harvard with Tunis and the two eventually developed a close writer-editor relationship. Tunis thought he gained intellectual depth from Allen while the editor admired the writer's willingness to work and native flair with language. With Tunis's articles Allen was willing to open *Harper's* pages to sports—a subject, he noted at the time, "which we now consider not quite respectable."[26] In later years Allen wrote an affectionate account of his association with Tunis:

> From the outset, John was like no other author of ours. After we had agreed upon a subject he would go away and hammer out a rough draft. Rough is the word; it came with many an infelicitous sentence and ill chosen adjective or adverb. I would go to work on this with a blue pencil, and send it back with suggestions for rewriting whole passages. In would come a second draft, and this, too, I would manhandle. At last came a third and the product was ready for the printer.
>
> I often used to wonder why John's manuscripts didn't stream letter-perfect from the typewriter as so many other writers' did, why he had to beat them out this way in draft after draft through many weeks. But I noticed something else. The roughest and most imperfect copy had color and clarity. You knew what he meant.[27]

Tunis switched to fiction in 1930 for his first book, a tennis novel called *American Girl* that sold out its first edition of 3,500 copies, then disappeared for twenty years until it was reborn as a Hollywood film, the generic title changed to *Hard, Fast and Beautiful.* Through the Depression he kept writing fiction while banging out a livelihood as a freelancer, earning at least $5,000 a year, and hooking up with the National Broadcasting Company to report, in fifteen-minute spots, events such as the Davis Cup matches and tennis at Wimbledon and Forest Hills. His next novel, about an Iowa boy who goes to Harvard and eventually becomes a track star, was accepted by Alfred Harcourt of Harcourt, Brace as a juvenile novel. As he remembered, the designation left Tunis "shocked, rocked, deflated": "What on earth was a juvenile? I stuttered and sputtered. He [Alfred Harcourt] paid no attention. Taking me firmly by the arm, with my manuscript under his other arm, he hustled me down the hall to a tiny cubicle where sat an alert, attractive, brown-eyed woman. Introducing her as Mrs. Hamilton, he dropped the book on her desk as though it might explode, and fled."28 Over Tunis's protests that his book was simply a book, Mrs. Hamilton explained that there was a large and ongoing market for juvenile fiction; moreover, she thought the book might be a candidate for a prize contest inaugurated by the *New York Herald Tribune.* Still unnerved, Tunis signed a contract, and in 1938 *Iron Duke* was published, won a newspaper prize, and over the years sold some sixty thousand copies in hardcover.

Though the novel pointed to a fresh direction for Tunis's work, and he followed it up with more boys' books, he did not commit himself wholly to juvenile fiction. He kept on with freelancing, though with modest results. There were fewer magazines about, especially those that were not staff-written and still open to contributors. During the winter of 1940 he sold an article to the *Saturday Evening Post* and realized it was for the same amount he had received from the magazine fifteen years earlier. The same was true of his sales to *Collier's.* It seemed, too, that the golden era of sports in the thirties was over, and with its passing was the prospect that his writing career for newspapers and magazines was winding down as well.

He turned back to Mrs. Hamilton at Harcourt, Brace, wondering if she was interested in a story featuring major-league baseball. She was, produced a modest advance, and Tunis was off to Florida to absorb the atmosphere of the spring-training camps. The result was *The Kid from Tomkinsville* in 1940, the story of a sandlot player who survives disappointments to win a position on a fictional Brooklyn Dodgers team. Three other baseball novels followed, all featuring the Dodgers and forming what a present-day critic calls "something of an American epic that helped establish a serious role for sports as a literary source."29 Serious they might be in their feeling for sport, yet they were written for a teenage audience and with pressing financial rather than literary ends in view. Tunis now eased off as an article writer and for the rest of his career dedicated himself to sports fiction, writing in addition to baseball about track, tennis, football, and basketball, a game he had to learn from the ground up. Although his work gave off an authentic, insider feel for the various games, Tunis's plots often centered on moral issues of democracy, racism, and social awareness. A continuing concern, directly expressed in his magazine pieces, was the amateur spirit in sport besieged by the corrupting values of fame and money.

four

Paul Gallico's career took an opposite tack, starting out in sports writing, then swinging to fiction while largely avoiding sports as a subject.[30] He had sold a short story to *Blue Book* for $90 at age twenty-one, but after graduation from Columbia turned to journalism with a job on the *New York Daily News* and eventually found himself on the sports desk, in time becoming sports editor and a columnist. In the latter capacity he produced a thousand words every day of the week for thirteen years. Looking back, it seemed useful training for fiction, requiring him to present dramatic material in dramatic fashion. It also was a time of vivid personalities in sports, requiring equally vivid prose to capture them on the page.

In an effort to get inside his material Gallico rode a speedboat with Gar Wood, tried to catch the fastballs of Lefty Grove and the football passes of Benny Friedman, played tennis with Helen Wills and golf with Bobby Jones, got in the ring with Jack Dempsey. He persuaded the publisher of the *News* to let him stage an amateur boxing tournament, thereby inaugurating the Golden Gloves, and promoted sports extravaganzas that included a canoe race around Manhattan Island. "It was a fast, gay, wonderful, and completely thoughtless life," he remembered. "Winter sports merged into summer sports; the seasons and the years flowed by."[31]

Gallico was also selling sports articles to magazines, drawing on the same material that was going into the newspaper but developed at the more leisurely pace of monthly publication, and after he sold several to *Vanity Fair* he was invited to join the staff as an associate editor under Frank Crowninshield. He wrote and edited sports for the magazine and also tried his hand at short fiction pieces, using several pen names as well as his own, sometimes having three pieces in a single issue. In 1931 he acquired Harold Ober as his agent, and two years later he sold a story to the *Saturday Evening Post,* his first appearance in the magazine after years of trying and failing. Thereafter he concentrated all his outside writing on fiction, with the slick magazines his main markets.

One of his stories at the time, a thinly-fictionalized account of the grim setting of a Max Schmeling training camp in Ohio he had once covered for the newspaper, was rejected by several magazines and bounced back in a special way by H. L. Mencken's *American Mercury.* After first returning the story, Mencken wrote back that he wanted to reconsider it. Gallico's hopes skyrocketed, since Mencken was one of his literary heroes and he longed to break into the *Mercury,* but after a couple months the story was returned with a note from Mencken: "Dear Gallico: I am not going to publish this story, but if you don't mind I intend to send for it and read it about once every year."[32] Gallico considered the note nearly as good as a sale until *Esquire* finally picked up the story for $100.

In 1936 a story sold to Hollywood for $5,000 and Gallico, at age thirty-nine, used the stake to cut his ties with journalism, move to England, and set up as a full-time freelance writer specializing in fiction. For material he only rarely dipped back into his sports bag. The main reason was concern that magazine editors might pigeonhole him as a single-subject writer; a mixture of material, he reasoned, would lengthen his career. Earlier, he had said as much to George Horace Lorimer. After selling a second story to the *Post,* one with a sports background, he was summoned to Philadelphia to meet the august editor, who told him the magazine was in need of more short stories about sports and Gallico had the background to write them. To his own astonishment Gallico blurted out, "But, Mr. Lorimer, I don't want to write sports stories. I want to play Hamlet." He collected himself enough to explain that he meant he wanted to write stories with various subjects. "Young man," Lorimer replied, "just you go back to New York and write us some more pieces. You tell us a good story and I don't care *what* your background is. Remember that." Gallico took the editor at his word, and was thereafter, as he recalled, "fired with the ambition to have my name a trade-mark, not on any one type of yarn, but simply of a good story."[33]

five

Another moneymaking magazine and book market for sports writers was ghostwriting, as John Wheeler found in the days before he began selling other men's brains in his syndicate operations. He was working for the *New York Herald* as a baseball writer covering the New York Giants when his sports editor wired him to sign up a top pitcher, Christy Mathewson, to cover the World Series of 1911 for a fee of $500. Mathewson agreed, and after each game pitcher and writer conferred and Wheeler wrote an article. The following winter the two joined again on a group of "Inside Baseball" articles for the McClure syndicate that sold well and were subsequently put out in book form under Mathewson's byline as *Pitching in a Pinch,* the collaborators splitting the proceeds.[34] Sales were helped along by a review written by Wheeler in the

Herald in which, as he recalled in a breezy memoir, "I let myself go, and I very much doubt whether any book ever got a more favorable review."[35]

Wheeler believed himself possibly the first newspaperman to ghost write for sports figures. True or not, the practice quickly spread, the identity of writers masked entirely or revealed in "as told to" or "with" attributions. The *Saturday Evening Post* in the 1920s reversed its earlier practice of treating sports only in fiction and began carrying ghostwritten articles by celebrity athletes, with much of the work turned out by Wesley Stout, who would succeed Lorimer as the *Post's* editor. (Stout also ghosted a book-length autobiography of Harold Lloyd, the title page listing the account as "Acted By" Lloyd and "Directed By" Stout.) Among the magazines big hits were ghosted life stories by the boxers James J. Corbett and Jack Dempsey.

After he left the *Herald* to form his syndicate Wheeler continued ghost-writing articles and books for big-name athletes too busy or illiterate to manage them themselves. For Ty Cobb he wrote a book called *Busting 'Em* and for Mathewson juvenile novels with titles like *Second Base Sloan, Pitcher Pollock, Catcher Craig*. During one World Series he ghosted newspaper copy for eight star performers. A variation on the approach was to hire writers with established name appeal to cover major sporting events. Jack London agreed to cover an Eastern yacht race for Wheeler's syndicate—for the extraordinary fee, as London recalled, of $1,100 a week plus expenses for two[36]—only to have the race called off by the advent of war in Europe. Another of Wheeler's big-name catches was Ring Lardner.

six

Lardner was a seasoned writer out of the spirited world of Chicago sports journalism when he was hired in 1913, at the age of twenty-eight, to write the *Chicago Tribune's* prestigious daily column "In the Wake of the News."[37] Over the next six years he established himself not only as a sports columnist but a major Midwestern humorist, following the vein of vernacular comedy developed by two earlier Chicago newspapermen, George Ade and Finley Peter Dunne. His leap to a larger national stage began when the Sunday editor of the *Tribune* offered him $50 for a baseball story to appear in the feature section and Lardner gave him one told through semiliterate letters from a brash rookie pitcher with the Chicago White Sox, Jack Keefe, to his friend Al back in Bedford, Indiana. When the editor decided he could not use the story

Lardner, apparently believing he had written something worth pursuing, sent it to Lorimer at the *Saturday Evening Post*.

What happened next is in dispute. Some say the story was promptly returned to Lardner, others that it was accepted at once, still others that a fellow sportswriter, Charles Van Loan, persuaded the magazine to accept it.[38] It is also claimed that Lorimer bought the story over the protest of his staff, who considered Lardner a fine sports reporter but a poor fiction writer, and that a *Post* sub-editor wanted to tidy up Lardner's artfully calculated prose. Years afterward Lardner tried to settle the matter in a letter to Burton Rascoe, who had peddled a particularly fanciful version: "The first 'busher' story was never sent back by the *Post*; it was accepted promptly by Mr. Lorimer himself. I didn't show it to . . . Charlie Van Loan first; I sent it to Mr. Lorimer at the *Post*'s office, not to his residence; I didn't write 'Personal' on the envelope in even one place; I didn't write any preliminary, special delivery, warning letter to Mr. Lorimer; no sub-editor ever asked me to correct the spelling and grammar, and I never sent any sub-editor or anyone else a bundle of letters I had received from ball players. Otherwise—"[39] In any case, "A Busher's Letters Home" appeared in the magazine on March 7, 1914, to reader response so favorable that Lorimer asked Lardner for more of the same.

Few writers were ever so sensationally launched by a single piece of work. The George H. Doran Company inquired about book rights; John Wheeler invited Lardner to write humor pieces for syndication; *Red Book, McClure's,* and *Metropolitan* magazines solicited new stories. Lardner accepted nearly every offer—though not, for the time being, Wheeler's—and by the end of 1914 he had published nine stories in the *Post* and one in *Red Book*. In 1916 six Jack Keefe stories—all using the epistolary form and setting the busher's deadpan comedy within a world of real major-league ballplayers and real teams—were published as *You Know Me Al,* and two more collections eventually followed.

With these stories Lardner opened up new territory for writers—sports fiction aimed at an adult audience rather than juveniles, concentrating on professionals rather than schoolboys, and depicting athletes not as paragons of virtue but as flawed adults playing a children's game for money. Jack Keefe, as the British author Virginia Woolf remarked with astonishing insight in a 1925 article on American fiction, is allowed through Lardner's sure touch to reveal himself as the "foolish, boastful, innocent athlete"—just the kind of athlete who would become a commonplace figure in the hands of later writers. In Keefe readers also recognized something of themselves and their fractured language; he was a figure deeply rooted in popular culture, and through him Lardner was able to bring to life the foibles of a national society. This Woolf saw as well—and recognized as a form of writing about sports that went far beyond the fleeting importance of the games themselves:

> It is no coincidence that the best of Mr. Lardner's stories are about games, for one may guess that Mr. Lardner's interest in games has solved one of the most difficult problems of the American writer; it has given him a clue, a centre, a meeting place for the divers activities of people whom a vast continent isolates, whom no tradition controls. Games give him what society gives his English brother. Whatever the precise reason, Mr. Lardner at any rate provides something unique in its kind, something indigenous to the soil, which the traveller may carry off as a trophy to prove to the incredulous that he has actually been to America and found it a foreign land.[40]

Years would pass before Lardner was taken up by critics at large as a serious literary man and cultural analyst, but at age thirty he now towered over a talented assembly of Chicago journalists and had national name recognition that allowed him to sell everything he wrote. He kept up the "Wake" column in the *Tribune* while pursuing his lucrative freelance career, in the two-year period from 1915 to 1917 publishing twenty-nine magazine pieces and making roughly $12,000. From this rich time came such enduring works as the boxing story "Champion," harsh and melodramatic—and, for just those qualities, unlike Lardner's fiction as a whole—and the genial baseball story "Alibi Ike" (with its delicious opening line: "His right name was Frank X. Farrell, and I guess the X stood for "Excuse me").

Despite success, Lardner refused to take himself seriously as a fiction writer. He sent out the originals of his stories, retained no copies, and failed to keep the magazines in which the stories appeared.[41] His public stance as a writer was always self-mocking and whimsical. The preface he wrote for *How to Write Short Stories,* for example, suggested that young writers made a mistake when they sent out stamped, self-addressed envelopes with their manuscripts. "This is too much of a temptation to the editor. Personally I have found it a good scheme to not even sign my name to the story, and when I have got it sealed up in its envelope and stamped and addressed, I take it to some town where I don't live and mail it from there. The editor has no idea who wrote the story, so how can he send it back? He is in a quandary."

By 1919, his family growing, Lardner had left Chicago daily journalism for New York and the hazards of full-time freelance writing. One stable source of income was a column for John Wheeler's Bell Syndicate, "Ring Lardner's

Weekly Letter," that was modeled on his old column in the *Tribune*. It had the same thousand-word length and Lardner filled it with the same odds and ends, including scraps of poetry, nonsense rhymes, and a good deal about his family and his travels. "More than anything else he did," a biographer, Jonathan Yardley, maintains, "writing the 'Weekly Letter' made Ring a genuinely national figure, a 'celebrity' as we now use the term," by extending his name to a reading public untouched by his magazine work and books and one that cut across all ages.[42] By the middle years of the 1920s the column was appearing in some 150 newspapers, bringing Lardner a tidy annual income of $30,000.

Rarely did the column deal with sports. Yardley suggests that Lardner's deep disenchantment with baseball as result of the Black Sox scandal of 1919 helped cut his emotional ties to professional sports in general, freeing him to write of other things. He continued covering the World Series and kept up friendships with sports journalists, but after 1919 he wrote nothing more about Jack Keefe. Several years passed before he wrote any baseball fiction. He did, however, agree to write continuity for a "You Know Me Al" comic strip the Bell Syndicate began selling in 1922, a grinding labor he kept up for three years for the money it brought him—approximately $17,000 annually. (In the 1930s Zane Grey, his magazine fees temporarily shrunk by the Depression, briefly wrote continuity for a daily syndicated comic strip called *King of the Royal Mounted*.) Along with his money from the weekly letter, Lardner's income from syndication now stood at about $50,000 a year. With money also coming in from magazine stories—eventually as much as $4,500 each from *Cosmopolitan*—Lardner's total annual income reached about $100,000, a remarkable figure for a writer who had only modest financial success with his books.[43]

With the move to New York Lardner's fictional world shifted from professional sports to suburban society at cutthroat play on golf courses, tennis courts, and bridge tables. A carryover from his Chicago days was a passion for writing popular songs for the musical theater. He turned out five musical comedies as well as a play between 1919 and 1928, with only the play, a money loser, ever getting produced. Sweet success came in 1929–30 when he collaborated with George S. Kaufmann on *June Moon*, a satire of Tin Pan Alley that had 273 Broadway performances and a road-company run across the country. Newspaper accounts of his activities now referred to him as Ring W. Lardner, author and playwright.

In 1927 he had ended his weekly letter for Wheeler's syndicate, giving up a steady income and for the first time cutting his ties to newspaper journalism,[44] and devoted himself primarily to magazine pieces and short stories, telling his friend, Long Island neighbor, and literary booster F. Scott Fitzgerald that "I am going to try to work half as hard and make the same amount of money, a feat which I believe can be done."[45] He continued covering major sporting events for the Bell Syndicate, and Wheeler had the inspired idea of having him attend national political conventions, which Lardner treated as occasions for yawning humor.

In the thirties, as physical ills and money needs overtook him, he returned to baseball with six stories in the *Saturday Evening Post* for the fee—elegant by Depression standards—of $4,000 apiece. Collected in book form in 1933 as *Lose with a Smile,* the stories recreated Jack Keefe in the milder form of Danny Warner, an outfielder with the Dodgers who corresponds with his girlfriend Jessie back in Centralia, Illinois. Danny is another rural innocent thrust into the hard world of big-league baseball, more boastful than productive and in the final story demoted to Jersey City. Danny also fancies himself a singer (his teammates call him Rudy "on account of Rudy Valet") and a song writer. "I don't see how I can mist," he writes Jessie about one of his songs, "and maybe it means that I can make more money off writeing songs than plain base ball and you know kid what that means."[46] What it means is he will be able to marry Jessie, a prospect Danny alternately offers and withdraws over the course of the stories.

Following the Danny Warner stories Lardner's last major writing project was twenty-five columns of radio criticism, for $400 apiece, turned out for the *New Yorker* in 1932–33. The surprising shift in subject was the result of illness and hospital stays in which, finding it hard to read or write, he paid attention to radio for the first time. The initial "Over the Waves" column took the form of a letter to the magazine's editor in which Lardner, after a passing and melancholy reference to his one-time fame as a sportswriter, outlined in typical fashion his new work:

> To the Editor:
> In this Home for Disabled World Series Experts they give you a *New Yorker* once a week as part of the treatment for insomnia, and in skimming over recent issues I have noticed that the publication always contains reviews of new productions on stage and screen, but hardly ever a mention of dat new davil radio which is largely responsible for the fact that there ain't more stage and screen productions to review. Now I am not a charity patient in this institution, and a man named Mr. Pest who works down in the front office claims I owe him three weeks' back rental for a concrete mattress, so I wonder how would it be if you took me on your staff

as a radio critic and perhaps you could pay enough to keep Mr. Pest from running a temperature and I could do the work in my spare time which begins at seven o'clock in the morning and ends at eight o'clock the following forenoon.[47]

seven

In an appreciation of Lardner after his death at age forty-eight, Fitzgerald argued that his friend's strengths and limitations as a writer were formed in his early years as a newspaperman covering baseball. His mind had been shaped "in the company of a few dozen illiterates playing a boy's game," with the result that "however deeply Ring might cut into it, his cake had exactly the diameter of Frank Chance's diamond." Fitzgerald concluded: "So long as he wrote within that enclosure the result was magnificent: within it he heard and recorded the voice of a continent. But when, inevitably, he outgrew his interest in it, what was Ring left with?" Whatever the merits of the argument, Fitzgerald's final assessment of Lardner, that he "got less percentage of himself on paper than any other American of the first flight," has dominated later critical views.[48] Lardner has continued to seem an original talent who wrote much but left behind little of lasting value.

Yet in the arena of writing about sports he still casts a long shadow. Especially with stories of baseball, the most written-about of team sports, he departed from preoccupation with schoolboy heroes and formulaic moral development to offer adult stories that were hilarious, illuminating, devoid of sentimentality, and technically adept. Before Lardner, an experienced pulp-magazine editor remarked, the hero of a sports story "must ever win out against every obstacle. He is denied the privilege of failure and, in consequence, the greater privilege of growth"; fashioned in the mold of Gilbert Patten's Frank and Dick Merriwell, he has to remain the "complete, utter juvenile."[49] With *You Know Me Al* and *Lose with a Smile* Lardner broke the pattern, and though this gained him little or no favor with the vast, conventional-minded audience for tales of the sporting life at the level of the pulps, it led to the directly literary uses of baseball in fiction by Bernard Malamud, Mark Harris, Robert Coover, and Philip Roth and in artful nonfiction by John McPhee, Roger Kahn, and David Halberstam.

FACTS OF THE MATTER

The Vogue of Biography, History, and Current Events

As a literary man, I love to talk about things I'm completely
ignorant of. . . . But as a historian . . . by God I hold my
peace except when I know what I'm talking about. It's
only a small decency, but mine own.
—Bernard De Voto

one

When *McClure's* sought out Hamlin Garland in 1896 to write a life of Ulysses Grant he was placed on monthly salary and given full research expenses. S. S. McClure explained the magazine's largess on the grounds that ordinary journalists of the time were not used to pursuing subjects in depth, and experts either could not write well enough or had axes to grind. He turned to professional writers and, as he put it, decided "to pay my writers for their study rather than for the amount of copy they turned out—to put the writer on such a salary as would relieve him of all financial worry and let him master a subject to such a degree that he could write upon it, if not with the authority of the specialist, at least with such accuracy as could inform the public and meet with the corroboration of experts."[1] While McClure himself flitted from idea to idea, a dynamo of energy, he insisted on fact writing that—as the pas-

172

sage suggests—got the facts straight. Ellery Sedgwick recalled that "slipshod work, even in tiny details, he would not tolerate. Strange in so romantic a man, but . . . to him, a fact was a fact to be scrutinized, attested, indubitably fixed. . . . In *McClure's,* accuracy was a moral force."[2]

One strain of the magazine's fact writing concentrated on the present and developed into science, travel, and political articles and especially into the journalism of exposure—the celebrated muckraking efforts of the magazine's trio of talented staff members, Ida Tarbell, Lincoln Steffens, and Ray Stanndard Baker. As Will Irwin remarked about the work of such writers, "*McClure's* virtually founded national journalism as contrasted with local journalism."[3] Another strain, indicated by Garland's series on Grant, turned back to the past and led to a renewed concern with biography and history. With both strains *McClure's* led the way for popular magazines, causing competitors to adjust their nonfiction contents accordingly.

History and biography had long been inviting fields for professional writers, though as Howells observed in "The Man of Letters as a Man of Business," while the work had steady value in the marketplace it did not compare with the sales of fiction. Before the great success of *The Sketch Book,* Washington Irving's *History of New York* ("a kind of freak" as a work of history, William Charvat noted, "although it is proof of the early vogue of historical writing")[4] sold 3,750 copies in its first edition in 1809 and earned Irving the significant sum of $3,000. When public interest faded after *Tales of a Traveller,* his third collection of sketches and light tales, Irving turned to history—history now in a straightforward vein—as a more dependable earning vehicle. *The Life and Voyages of Columbus* in 1828 brought him the handsome return of $25,000 and placed him among the first American historians to gain a reputation for his work in Europe.[5] Thereafter, Irving sensibly devoted his writing career to pursuing the vein of history and biography.

In the days before research libraries and research grants the fields of history and biography required building personal book collections and traveling for interviews and document research—expensive and time-consuming activities for a writer making his living with words. (Howells would make the point that usually only rich men were able to afford the luxury of historical writing while anyone could set up shop as a poet or novelist.) Even though he was able to rely on published documents, the Columbus book cost Irving two years of sustained work. His solution was to turn, with *A Chronicle of the Conquest of Granada* in 1829, to a less demanding form that was a variation on the historical romance—a "romantic history," Irving called it, that was "dressed up with an eye to the scenery of the country and the customs of the time," history that had "something of the effect of a work of the imagination."[6]

In the latter half of the nineteenth century a surge of interest in historical writing, stimulated in part by the nation's centennial, was led by the *Century* magazine under Richard Watson Gilder. Beginning in 1882 the periodical ran Edward Eggleston's chronicles of life in the original colonies, an enterprise so successful that it turned Eggleston from a career as a regional novelist into a social historian and eventual president of the American Historical Association. This was followed with a famous series of Civil War papers that began with accounts of John Brown's raid, then a parade of articles by the aging military participants on the war's great battles. For Grant's lead-off accounts of the struggles at Shiloh, Vicksburg, Chattanooga, and the Wilderness, the material later incorporated into his *Memoirs,* the *Century* paid $1,000 apiece.[7]

Running for three years, from 1884 to 1887, the war series was a source of vast excitement for the magazine's editors. "Grant one day and Beauregard the next!" Gilder exclaimed to his wife.[8] But when the first Grant article arrived at the editorial offices it was met with dismay. The material was drawn largely from the General's flat official report on Shiloh, and an editor had to be dispatched to inform him that something more personal and engaging was needed. Grant redid the article to the *Century's* satisfaction, and in fact took pleasure in doing the remaining pieces. "Why, I am positively enjoying the work," he told an editor. "I am keeping at it every day and night, and Sundays."[9]

Reader response was overwhelming. A contemporary observer declared that the Civil War articles "created in this country the greatest interest ever felt in any series of articles published in a magazine."[10] The *Century's* circulation nearly doubled, reaching the lofty figure for a thirty-five-cent magazine of 250,000, and the parent company's profits increased accordingly. As a follow-up the *Century* turned to a massive biography of Lincoln written by his former secretaries, John Hay and John G. Nicolay, for which it paid the dazzling amount for factual material of $50,000 for serial rights. In abridged form "Abraham Lincoln: A History" ran in the magazine from November 1887 to February 1890. It proved heavy going for many readers and the *Century's* circulation dipped during serialization, but Gilder professed to be pleased with the work and the reputation it continued to earn his magazine as a quality publication. In 1890 the Century Company published Hay and Nicolay's *Abraham Lincoln* in ten volumes.

Although popular magazines tended to ignore the past (with *Harper's Weekly* in 1871 offering by way of explanation that loss of "links that still connect us

with the past . . . is one of the inevitable consequences of progress and im-
provement"),[11] historical and biographical pieces were commonplace now in
stately monthlies like the *Century* and the *Atlantic*. University-trained historians had not yet appeared on the scene, and would not until the end of the
nineteenth century. For the time being, with all historians amateurs, the field
was wide open for professional writers.

two

James Parton entered biographical writing by way of magazine journalism
and eventually became the country's foremost biographer. After contributing
articles to N. P. Willis's *Home Journal,* he was hired in 1852 as an editorial assistant and took over much of the responsibility for the magazine. When he
began printing contributions from the columnist Fanny Fern, and when
Willis learned she was actually his sister, Sara Payson Willis, Parton was ordered to carry nothing more by her. The dispute that followed ended with
Parton leaving the magazine.[12] Subsequently, a chance meeting with Lowell
and Daniel Mason, brothers who ran a publishing house, turned Parton in a
new direction, writing a life of Horace Greeley, the still-active editor of the
New York Tribune and subject of a recent article in the *Home Journal.* An advance of $750 freed Parton to live in New York for a year and provided mod-
est travel funds for interviewing.

Parton developed his biographical methods as he went along—methods he
late in life set down as "my great rules":

> 1. To know the subject thoroughly myself; 2. to index fully all knowledge in exis-
> tence relating to it; 3. to determine before hand where I will be brief, where ex-
> pand, and how much space I can afford to each part; 4. to work slowly and finish
> as I go; 5. to avoid eulogy and apology and let the facts have their natural weight;
> 6. to hold back nothing which the reader has a right to know.[13]

For the life of Greeley the rules meant traveling to places where his subject
had lived, interviewing friends and relatives, examining letters, and digging
through back files of the *Tribune*. Parton checked all his findings with Greeley, who had agreed to cooperate to this extent with his biographer, and eleven
months after he began he had a manuscript ready for the printer. Published in
1854, *The Life of Horace Greeley* was a critical and commercial success. Twenty-
eight thousand copies were sold in the first six months, bringing Parton

$2,000 over and above his advance—enough to settle him on a lifelong career as a biographer.

The same year *Greeley* appeared Mason Brothers issued *Ruth Hall,* Fanny Fern's satirical novel in which she settled family scores with her brother. Parton has a walk-on part in the story as an editorial assistant, Horace Gates, "a gentlemanly, slender, scholar-like-looking person." Shortly after the novel appeared, with Fern now writing for Bonner's *Ledger,* she and Parton were married. By all accounts the marriage was a tempestuous one due to differences in age (she was eleven years older) and temperament. After Sara's death in 1872 Parton married her daughter by her first husband, an apparently tranquil union[14] that lasted until his own death in 1891.

For his second biography Parton turned to the life of Aaron Burr and an attempt to portray the shadowed career in a more balanced light. He began by making a list of Burr's descendants and those who had known him in his lifetime together with sources to be consulted and books read—the routine he would follow in setting out on most of his biographies. The book that was produced with surprising speed, *The Life and Times of Aaron Burr* (1858), was as controversial as its subject and the recipient of scathing reviews. Some thought Parton had treated Burr's misdeeds too lightly, others faulted an inflated journalistic style and a tendency to break the narrative with long quoted passages. Nonetheless, the two-volume work was a considerable success, going through sixteen editions in five years and earning Parton forty cents on each volume sold.

His next subject, a life of Andrew Jackson, was his most daunting. Materials were scattered around the country, letters were in private hands and zealously guarded, and there was no published work to guide him through the still recent experience of the Jacksonian era. Despite the demands of the task Parton managed to have the first of three volumes ready for sale by Christmas of 1859 and the remaining two the following year.

To finance the *Life of Andrew Jackson* and two works that quickly followed, *General Butler in New Orleans* and the *Life and Times of Benjamin Franklin,* Parton had returned to magazine journalism, producing a stream of varied articles, serious and frivolous. While he was writing for the sprightly *Ledger* he also was appearing in the solemn *North American Review,* contributing forty-page historical articles at a $3 page rate. The *Review's* editor, Charles Eliot Norton, praised Parton's dexterity, telling him that "men who can write as you do—articles alike for the great public and for the critical few—may be numbered on one hand."[15] For the *Atlantic* Parton did a series of reports on American cities, another—prefiguring the work of the muckraking reporters—on waste in government, yet another on new inventions such as sewing machines. A whimsical anti-smoking article deluged the magazine and the author with reader letters, causing Parton to immediately write another about drinking. In between he published a sober two-part article on "Our Roman Catholic Brethren."

"I am almost always here," Parton said about the time he spent in his study, "from 7 A.M. to 2 P.M.—and from 6 P.M. to 7 ½; often, all evening." In addition to new work he pieced together earlier publications for various pamphlets and book collections, in 1871 alone putting out three such concoctions. And he remained at work as a popular biographer, publishing in installments in the *Atlantic,* then edited by Howells, a series on Jefferson that appeared in book form in 1874 as the *Life of Thomas Jefferson.* By such diligence he managed to make ends meet and buy time for research—but just barely. Looking back on his life, he concluded that "an industrious writer, by the legitimate exercise of his calling—that is, never writing advertisements or trash for the sake of pay—can just exist—no more. By a compromise not dishonorable, though exasperating, he can average during his best years $7000 or $8000 a year. But no man should enter the literary life unless he has a fortune or can live contentedly on $2000 a year. The best way is to make a fortune first, and write afterwards."[16]

Finally, it was not his hack writing that allowed Parton to devote himself to biography so much as a tried-and-true form of author patronage, talking for hire on the lecture circuit. During the 1870s he put himself into the hands of James Redpath's speakers bureau in Boston and began lecturing throughout the East and the Midwest. The money that came in, together with magazine work and royalties from his biographies, at last bought the research freedom he needed.

In 1875 Parton moved to Newburyport, Massachusetts, and settled into what he viewed as the grand work of his career, a life of Voltaire. It was a major undertaking, and an odd one. Heretofore, he had examined American lives, and one of his main research tools, the personal interview, was not available for a figure dead since 1778. He was mentioning Voltaire as a subject as early as 1867 and could not be dissuaded by perplexed friends and editors. "Why go to the old World for a topic (even though it be such as Voltaire)," Charles Eliot Norton asked him, "while the new world affords such subjects?"[17]

Parton invested five years of work in the project. Published in 1881, the two-volume *Voltaire* met a cool reception, Parton credited with a vigorous narrative but attacked for critical failings and errors in translations of Latin and French. The book went through several editions but failed to add the final flourish to his career that Parton had anticipated. In the remaining decade until his death in 1891 he returned to occasional journalism, becoming a contributing editor of the Boston periodical *Youth's Companion* for pay of $1,200 a year and writing for a range of publications from the *Forum* and *American Magazine of History* to Bonner's *Ledger.* Although he was now honored as the father of American biography, he saw no contradiction in his continuing hack writing for periodicals—the kind of piecework in which, as he put it, "the most gifted and enlightened journalists must of necessity write to order."[18]

three

When *McClure's* in the 1890s began running historical and biographical articles together with journalistic exposures it was breaking fresh ground among the popular magazines of the day. It was innovative in another way in the choice of the writer who led the way in both areas—the relatively inexperienced journalist Sam McClure had plucked from Paris for his staff, Ida Tarbell. When *McClure's* chose to compete with the *Century* by running Tarbell's biographical series on Lincoln, Richard Watson Gilder would sniff from the editorial heights that "they got a girl to write a Life of Lincoln."[19]

Tarbell's first assignment for *McClure's,* a life of Napoleon to accompany a number of illustrations, left her amused that a popular magazine would consider such a subject. McClure remembered that the project "touched her sense of humor by its very improbability."[20] But the lure of the material, together with the possibility of returning to Paris for research, was too much to resist. As it turned out, Tarbell did her work mostly in Washington in the Library of Congress, and within six weeks had the first of seven installments ready for the printers.

Lavishly illustrated, her life of Napoleon began appearing in November 1894 and gave the new magazine's circulation a boost while helping Tarbell place her long-cherished work, a life of Madame Roland, with Scribner's, which eventually published the book in 1896. McClure's next enthusiasm was Lincoln, with Tarbell not writing this time but editing. The idea was a series of articles on Lincoln, dead just thirty years, written by several people who had known him yet had not published their reminiscences, the series edited by Tarbell, who also would fill in gaps in the material. But quickly the plan was altered, Tarbell actually writing the entire series and traveling wherever needed for interviews and research ("Out with you—look, see, report," McClure told her)[21] while drawing a salary from the magazine of $5,000 a year. The money was attractive but so was the magazine and the association with McClure and John Phillips. The new and struggling magazine, Tarbell remembered, had "something youthful, gay, natural about it which captivated me. Often, too, it achieved a most precious thing. Mr. Phillips called it a 'lift.' To be youthful, gay, natural with a 'lift'—that was an achievement."[22]

By her own count the life of Lincoln took Tarbell four years and, as McClure remembered, it "told on our circulation as nothing ever had before."[23] Yet ahead for Tarbell was even more attention-grabbing work for the magazine and the centerpiece of her long career, the series of articles that became the *History of the Standard Oil Company*. Behind the series was an impressive amount of dry, diligent, meticulous investigative reporting. McClure believed it necessary to "invent a new method in magazine journalism" in which reporters took the time to master the "highly specialized activities of modern civilization." Tarbell's series on the robber-baron practices of the Standard Oil trust was his great case in point. She had made herself, he noted with pride, "probably the greatest living expert on that subject."[24]

Tarbell had first thought of treating the predatory practices with which John D. Rockefeller assembled his monopoly as a novel, then turned to the possibility of a factual report. "Was it possible to treat the story historically," she asked herself, "to make a documented narrative?"[25] The research task was intimidating. Her chief source was the voluminous testimony that had come from state and federal investigations of the company; to this had to be added a vast amount of document search, collateral reading, and personal interviews with those Rockefeller associates willing to talk with her. An enthusiastic research assistant, John Siddall, was engaged to work in Cleveland, the headquarters of the company. To Siddall, Tarbell set out her aims in a letter: "Perhaps I should say that the work we have in mind is a narrative history of the Standard Oil Company. I am to do it, and shall go about it as I would any other piece of historical work in which I had to draw almost entirely from original sources. It is in no sense a piece of economic work, nor is it intended to be controversial, but a straightforward narrative, as picturesque and dramatic as I can make it, of the great monopoly."[26]

Tarbell's original outline in October 1901 anticipated three articles coming

to about twenty-five thousand words, but before the series began appearing
the plan was increased to six articles. Once publication was underway in November 1902 and public reaction registered intense interest in an account that
unfolded like a detective story, it was increased again to twelve articles and
finally to nineteen. The writing that went into it was as demanding as the research. As with the Napoleon and Lincoln articles, each installment of Tarbell's work was revised three times under the direction of editors; the material
was also sent to Siddall for comment and inspected by economists hired by
the magazine. "She had to fight her equals to say the least there," a *McClure's*
editor commented about the rigorous process, "and she did it with Sam Mc-
Clure and JSP [John S. Phillips] demanding that they be satisfied and thrilled;
they pounded her and her stuff to make the best of it page by page."[27] But as
the series ground on Tarbell's energy waned. Some installments came in so
late there was no time for Siddall's review.

The magazine series and the book that followed—published in two volumes in 1904 with sixty-four appendices of documentation—brought Tarbell
great acclaim. Stories about her with accompanying photographs appeared in
newspapers and periodicals throughout the country. In the *Critic* she was ap-
plauded for having "beaten upon facts rather than upon a gong, and her *History of Standard Oil* is to the present time the most remarkable book of its
kind ever written in this country."[28] Tarbell herself was overwhelmed by being
thrust into the limelight, and later in life she professed to having felt some disappointment. "I had hoped that the book might be received as a legitimate
historical study," she said in her autobiography, "but to my chagrin I found
myself included in a new school, that of the muckrakers."[29]

four

With the end of World War I and America's new prominence on the world
stage came a resurgence of interest in history and biography—indeed, in
nonfiction in general, including popularized science, current events, and criticism of the arts, that appealed to the wider interests of an increased number
of college-educated readers. Writers who could satisfy such interests still came
largely from backgrounds in journalism and literature. "Never before," John
Higham remarked about historical writing in the 1920s and '30s, "had so
many journalists and free-lance writers possessed the ability and incentive to
undertake serious historical research. Their movement into this kind of non-

fiction reflected the same broadening of intellectual interests . . . that was creating their audience."[30]

By present-day academic lights the "serious historical research" that went into such work seems limited. Freelance historians had to gather their material on the fly while juggling assignments that paid the bills and underwrote their labors. While working on *The Stammering Century,* a social history of American reformers and utopians published in 1928, Gilbert Seldes continued as a major player in New York's contentious world of literary journalism and regularly placed articles in the *Saturday Evening Post.* Looking back on this active time in his career, he characterized himself as "nothing of a scholar. I haven't ever, consciously, written to suggest that I knew much of an intricate subject when I hadn't studied it. But I've been content to be superficial."[31] Frederick Lewis Allen was another, and more notable, instance of a working journalist who pursued the rewards of historical writing without overburdening himself as a scholar.

After a try at teaching composition at Harvard, Allen had turned to a career in magazine editing by first following the advice of Frank Crowninshield, then with *Century* and later the colorful editor of *Vanity Fair,* that he begin by establishing himself as a freelance writer.[32] Allen had a reputation as the author of humorous pieces when he joined the *Atlantic* in 1914 as an assistant to Ellery Sedgwick. While his days were now taken up with editing, nights and weekends were kept for his own writing—the regimen he followed for most of his productive career.

From the *Atlantic* Allen moved to the *Century* as managing editor, then back to Harvard as its first publicity director before joining the publishing firm of Harper and Brothers, dividing his time between book work and *Harper's* magazine. The magazine was then undergoing change, following the lead of the *Atlantic* in reducing the amount of fiction and verse it carried and giving greater attention to contemporary issues and public affairs. The new direction suited Allen both as an editor and writer. In his busy freelance career he shifted from humor to social and cultural matters in thoughtful but witty magazine pieces such as "The Fetish of the Ph.D.," "The New Tories," "These Disillusioned Highbrows," and "Suburban Nightmare," the latter about urban encroachment in such leafy suburbs as Allen's Scarsdale. He also undertook his first lengthy work, a sketch of the life of Paul Revere Reynolds, a Scarsdale neighbor and one of the earliest American literary agents (as noted in the following chapter), written privately for the Reynolds family.

With the economic collapse of 1929 it seemed to Allen that a period in

American life marked by optimism, prosperity, and a happy hedonism had come to a close, a view he outlined in an article in 1930 called "The End of an Era." The subject seemed to demand more treatment and he turned to a book, working in evenings and arranging his office schedule to free himself one day a week for writing. Although the sudden death of his wife occurred during the writing of the book, Allen kept to an orderly work schedule and *Only Yesterday: An Informal History of the Nineteen-Twenties* was published in 1931 to rousing success. Eventually it sold over a million copies in various editions. Allen downplayed his sudden elevation as an historian, calling himself instead a "retrospective journalist"; as his subtitle noted, his book was meant as an informal ordering of recent events, culled largely from the newspapers and magazines of the period, not a work of original scholarship. As a historian, however, Allen was ahead of his time in the attention he paid to manners and morals as well as figures of popular culture, concerns ordinarily bypassed in accounts of the past. It was the freshness of his approach joined to a smooth and breezy writing style that caused the book to soar in the marketplace.

The book also stimulated Allen's freelance career. He was now able to wring a $1,000 fee from the *Ladies' Home Journal* for an article about the Depression, far better than *Harper's* standard rate of $250 for contributors. Although he himself was doing well in the early thirties, the reasons behind the collapse of the economic system preoccupied him and became the subject for his next book. He undertook a crash reading program at the New York Public Library, then in 1933 began writing, following the same systematic program he used with *Only Yesterday*, giving himself a ten-month period in which he took off every Wednesday from the magazine, with a corresponding reduction in pay. But *The Lords of Creation* in 1935 failed to match the success of *Only Yesterday*, and Allen found some irony in the fact that a stock he bought and sold within a few months brought in more money than two years of labor on a book about the economic system.

Since Yesterday: The Nineteen-Thirties in America, Allen's companion volume to his first book, was another best seller, enhancing his reputation as an historian of contemporary events who treated his material with broad and lively strokes. He continued freelance work—in the *Saturday Review of Literature*, for example, recounting Horatio Alger's writing career—but after 1941, when he succeeded to the editorship of *Harper's*, he devoted himself to the magazine. At the start of the 1950s he picked up his writing career and turned out another book devoted to the recent past, *The Big Change: America Transforms Itself*, *1900–1950*. Success was once more his, the work a Book-of-the-Month

Club choice and the reviews, despite some carping from the academic community, generally favorable. At his death in 1954 obituaries and articles recounted his long editorial career while saluting a body of historical writing that was still popular. Allen, said the *New York Times*, "was favorably known as Herodotus of the Jazz Age," an epitaph that seemed appropriate for a retrospective journalist whose accounts of the twenties and thirties would strongly influence scholarly historians.[33]

five

The field Allen carved out for himself was recent American history—the just-passed past, tinged with nostalgia, as recovered largely through journalistic materials. Another aspect of public interest in popular history was the reverse—panoramic world history that gave a skeleton of order to the great sweep of events. H. G. Wells's two-volume American edition of the *Outline of History*, appearing to vast success in 1920, seemed only to whet an appetite for more of the same. James Harvey Robinson's *The Mind in the Making* was published the following year, along with John Arthur Thomson's *Outline of Science* and Hendrik Willem Van Loon's epic account of *The Story of Mankind*, a nonfiction best seller in 1922.

Van Loon, a dominating figure who spoke several languages, played the violin, and dazzled with his wit and erudition (a "three-hundred-pound figure of the Renaissance," an acquaintance called him),[34] was particularly suited to history and biography of vast dimension. Born in the Netherlands, he had come to the United States at age twenty, graduated from Cornell, took a European doctorate, and returned to Cornell to teach history, developing a reputation as an authority on Dutch history. He left Cornell in 1914, apparently due to controversy over his wartime views. "No one liked me," he said of his classroom experience, "except the students."[35]

During the war he covered the fighting in Europe until the Armistice as a correspondent for the Associated Press. His career as a popular historian began when he turned to revising the first volume of a planned twelve-volume history of the world for children, a project thought up during his Cornell days. Sixteen publishing houses turned him down before T. R. Smith of the Century Company approved the work, only to be overruled by others in the firm on the dual grounds that it would be too expensive to publish and that Van Loon had no following as a children's writer. Smith then directed Van

Loon to Boni and Liveright's Horace Liveright, who immediately provided funds for four months while Van Loon completed the manuscript.

Ancient Man, the opening volume of what was called a "primer history of the world," came out in 1920 to good reviews and weak sales. Smith, who in the meantime had joined Boni and Liveright as an editor, and Liveright convinced Van Loon to abandon the multi-volume series and pull the rest of his history into a single book aimed at adults as well as children. Van Loon agreed and *The Story of Mankind* came out late the following year, simply written and brightly illustrated by Van Loon's own drawings. An edition of fifty thousand copies was quickly snapped up, and during the decade of the twenties the book went through thirty more editions and found its way into a dozen foreign languages.[36]

For his next work Van Loon, sights only slightly lowered, took on the Bible. When Burton Rascoe, then an associate editor at *McCall's,* learned of the project he tried to secure first serial rights for the magazine. Authorized to pay up to $50,000, he approached Horace Liveright for Van Loon's price. "He [Liveright] said he was Van Loon's agent," Rascoe recalled, "and he was setting the price. He said, 'The price for first serial rights is $30,000,' in such an emphatic tone that I knew that if I chose to haggle he would cut it to $20,000 or less; but . . . I knew the subject would be a sure-fire circulation builder worth more to the company than the price asked, and so I said, 'Sold, $30,000!'"[37] Published by Boni and Liveright in 1923, *The Story of the Bible* failed to match the success of *Mankind,* and Liveright would think back on Van Loon's first book, and his firm's first moneymaker, as a stunt book. "Stunt books like Van Loon's *History,*" he explained to another author, "they're the thing, my boy! I know perfectly well that you understand what I mean when I say stunt books. Something new, something new. That's the cry these days."[38]

Van Loon continued to produce big stunt books in his enthusiastic accounts of America, Rembrandt, philosophy, music, painting, sculpture, architecture, and geography. Complaints about oversimplification and a lack of historical precision he shrugged off as "pedagogical persecution," maintaining about the factual underpinning of his work that if he had believed something for years it was true.[39] (Henry Seidel Canby remembered Van Loon as "rolling a body as big and pink as Walt Whitman's and banging down every argument that was going against him with his great, if rather inaccurate, erudition.")[40] At his death in 1944 the *New York Times* estimated his total book sales at over six million copies, while the *Saturday Review of Literature* reported that, befit-

ting of a man who made no small plans, Van Loon had left ten separate books
in progress, one the opening volume of an autobiography called *A Report to
St. Peter.*[41]

six

Whether pursued on grand or small scale, history and biography were, to repeat, difficult nonfiction fields for independent professional writers to tackle,
due to the time and money needed for research and travel. When John Phillips
of the McClure syndicate in 1895 proposed to Stephen Crane a series of
sketches of Civil War battlefields, the writer indicated his interest but finally
declined because of the excessive work involved. He wrote Phillips:

> Your project it seems to me would require a great deal of study and a great deal of
> time. I would be required to give up many of my plans for this winter and this I
> am reluctant to do. I dont [*sic*] know how you would advise going about it but one
> of the first things I would want to do, would be to visit the battle-field—which I
> was to describe—at the time of year when it was fought. The preliminary reading
> and the subsequent reading, the investigations of all kinds, would take much time.
> Moreover, if I did not place the only original crown of pure gold on the heads of
> at least twelve generals they would arise and say: "This damned young fool was not
> there. I was however. And this is how it happened." I evaded them in the Red
> Badge because it was essential that I should make my battle a type and name no
> names but in your case, it would be very different.[42]

For large-scale research projects writers often turned to teaching or took on
editorial chores to support themselves until a time when, if fortune smiled,
advances or royalties would underwrite their endeavors. Bernard De Voto,
who during the 1940s and '50s produced monthly essays as the occupant of
the influential *Easy Chair* column in *Harper's,* potboiling stories and serials for
the slicks,[43] and a tide of freelance magazine journalism while working on his
sweeping narratives of Westward expansion, once complained that behind his
historical writing was "an effort whose intensity and cost nobody but me will
ever appreciate and nobody, including me, will ever think justified by the results." Professional writers needed more immediate results, and results they
could bank. They could well understand how a self-described "literary gent"
like De Voto chafed under history's hard discipline and yearned for a different
kind of writing:

I loathe research with a cold abhorrence. The routine day by day, month by month boredom of history—reading, checking, appraising, following up, sifting a ton of revoltingly dull material in order to find that one grain of viciously tiresome relevance either is or isn't there, the heaping up of triviality upon pettiness on top of inertness, the endless and cavernous abyss into which one has to heave a hundred thousand inert, colorless, lifeless, and worthless details, all amassed by the stinking sweat of one's soul, in order to achieve one single foothold, handhold, page, sentence, idea—all this, I say, makes my soul writhe. My mind yearns for the comfort of loose ideas, fantasies, things you make up, talking and writing at your ease and to hell with slave labor, the dry rot of boredom, and history.[44]

The great temptation was fiction, the writer inventing rather than recovering, employing—as Crane said about the *Red Badge of Courage*—typical rather than actual situations. But if the fiction was historical fiction—and especially historical fiction in which, disregarding Washington Irving's casual style of romantic history, realism was meant to be a central feature—the writer could find himself snared in a different kind of trap.

James M. Cain provides a telling example. After World War II, his classic California thrillers *The Postman Always Rings Twice, Mildred Pierce,* and *Serenade* behind him and working as a high-paid Hollywood screenwriter, Cain began thinking about a big Civil War novel and corresponded with a Harvard professor about background books to read.[45] Involvement with the controversial American Authors' Authority (discussed in the following chapter), screenwriting, and fresh contemporary fiction intervened, and it was not until 1948 that he picked up the thread of his research. In addition to his reading Cain toured the South to acquaint himself with locations and to visit libraries, all the while taking notes on index cards. He considered his style of research particularly demanding, "for while the historian need only concern himself with who won the battle, and how, the novelist has to know which road his character took after it was over, what he ate while stumbling along, the local names of all sorts of small things, and what the people were doing with themselves as the action proceeds."[46] In the back of his mind was an obsession with accuracy he had picked up from H. L. Mencken, a lifelong friend. When Cain was once taken to task in the *Baltimore Sun* over something he had written, Mencken dismissed the importance since things were quickly forgotten in newspaper work. Book writing was another matter, Mencken warning Cain to "never go up on your lines if it's a book you're going to do. It's on somebody's shelves forever, and for twenty years somebody'll be taking it down to show his friends, at your expense."[47]

To immerse himself in Civil War material Cain turned his back on Holly-wood and took up residence in his native Maryland. The particular story he had in mind dealt with a neglected episode in the war, the Red River cam-paign in western Louisiana led by the Union General N. P. Banks that in-volved Army-Navy conflict, the cotton business, and, as Cain told an editor, was "full of skulduggeries involving large sums of money."[48] Cain thought the tale had all the ingredients of a best seller and movie potential as well. But the research was seemingly endless, dragging on through the winter of 1948 and into 1949 as Cain trooped off each day to the Library of Congress.

After accumulating thousands of research cards he finally began writing, turning out three drafts, each with a different title, each worse than the other. "I simply could not bring it to life," he remembered. "It just lay there in pieces and I did not know why."[49] Work on other projects occupied him but Cain refused to abandon his historical novel; he kept writing—enough, he claimed, to fill ten normal books. To pep up the story he now focused on a love affair between a Union officer, Bill Cresap, and the daughter of a Southern busi-nessman, Mignon Fournet, with the latter giving her name to the book's new title, *Mignon*. But he was far from finished. There was more research, another trip to the South for local color, more rewrites.

Months and years dragged on. "God deliver me from a period book," Cain wrote to his publisher, Alfred Knopf. "But I know no way to finish them, but to finish them."[50] Finally, in early 1957 and at age sixty-six, he did, but when Knopf's response was decidedly negative Cain returned to his desk for more tinkering. He expected a rewrite to go quickly, but three years elapsed before another version of *Mignon* was ready for the publisher—only to be rejected again. Understandably, this time Cain did not accept Knopf's decision and told his agent to circulate the manuscript. When Dial agreed to publish there was more rewriting, resulting in what Cain called practically a new work, be-fore publication at last came in the spring of 1962, nearly a decade and a half after he set out on the story.

To Cain's sharp disappointment *Mignon*—by the standards of historical novels a slim work of 246 pages—made little money; nor did it sell to Holly-wood. One reason for its lacks of success, according to Cain's biographer, Roy Hoopes, is the thin treatment of the Red River campaign; despite the research effort Cain had put into it, the reader picks up little detail or atmosphere of the war. Surely another was reader expectation that linked Cain's name with hard-edged stories set in contemporary California rather than historical fic-tion. Although he was puzzled by the failure of what seemed an exciting and well-grounded story, Cain recognized the book's fate. "It was just 'a lotta god-damn research,'" he lamented, and added: "All that reading and labor and a kind of mouse is born."[51]

seven

Current events provided an alternative to factual writing about the past—and the on-the-move methods of investigative reporting could replace dry, sedentary library research, whether for factual or fictional history. Such instant history had a reduced place in mass magazines after the glory period of the muckrakers, yet it was still possible to develop a career that drew on the example of Ida Tarbell and the turn-of-the-century *McClure's* journalists. Among the leading practitioners of topical, public-affairs magazine journalism in the post–World War I period was Kenneth Roberts.

A former reporter in Boston, Roberts had joined the intelligence section of the Siberian Expeditionary Force in 1917 when he asked George Horace Lorimer of the *Saturday Evening Post* if he wanted a report from that remote region. By cable Lorimer dispatched the guarded answer he ordinarily gave to such queries: "Am very much interested in articles on social, political, economic situation."[52] As a rule the *Post* refused to commission articles; an expression of interest was all a writer could expect. Lorimer once explained his position, as well as his distaste for long-term contracts with writers, this way: "Commissioning stories is a bad practice—bad alike for the author and the magazines—that America has imported from England. Tying up authors on contract is a worse one that we have developed at home. The first means that a magazine is being edited haphazardly by fifty men, instead of consistently by one. The second usually means another headstone in some publisher's private graveyard."[53]

Finding encouragement in Lorimer's response, Roberts pushed ahead, producing a whopping 22,000-word article that, to his surprise, was promptly accepted for a fee of $1,000. It was the first of over two hundred pieces he would turn out over the next dozen years for the magazine as a roving correspondent abroad and in America. With each acceptance came warmly worded notes of appreciation from the editor, such as one that praised a careful article on immigration reform, a cherished subject in the *Post*,[54] while reminding Roberts that he was to replace Sam Blythe, who was retiring, as the magazine's Washington political and social correspondent:

My Dear Roberts:

You struck twelve, and kept right on striking up to one hundred plus in this last story. It illuminated my whole evening and reconciled me to my hard life as a farmer. Check by the treasurer on Tuesday.

Don't forget our plot to send you to Washington for the winter, with perhaps an occasional excursion into the Hinterland.

Sincerely yours,

Geo. H. Lorimer[55]

As with most important contributors, Lorimer bound Roberts to the magazine by steadily raising his rates. By 1924 he was up to $1,750 an article, bringing him an annual income of over $25,000. The following year his income surpassed $32,000. In turn, Roberts directed his work solely to the *Post* save for a brief fling with *Cosmopolitan.* When the editor of *Cosmopolitan,* Ray Long, offered a contract for a year's output of articles at $1,000 each, Roberts resisted tying himself down but sent in a piece about actions of the Japanese army in Siberia that the *Post* had rejected. Long was enthusiastic and asked for another article, then complained of its length and, as Roberts remembered, "proceeded to carve chunks from it in a manner far more whimsical than I had ever before encountered."[56] When Long rejected a third long piece, Roberts sold it to the *Post* and therewith returned to Lorimer's fold.

Despite his heady success at it, in time Roberts grew dissatisfied with magazine journalism, feeling he was "making no progress—except financially." Lorimer was making editorial changes in his work and not everything he wrote was accepted; more important, he was eager to try his hand at a long historical novel that drew on the experience of his Maine ancestors during the Revolutionary period. Lorimer's response to a switch to fiction was cool. "How long's that novel of yours going to run?" he wrote Roberts. "No, don't tell me! Anybody who writes 16,000-word articles couldn't possibly stop a novel short of 200,000 words, and that's too long for the *Saturday Evening Post.*"[57] Roberts persisted, and a draft of *Arundel* was written during a winter in Italy under a contract with Doubleday that called for a $1,000 advance. On his wall he posted a work schedule for himself: "Write a chapter every 4 days: write 1 1/3 pages (1500 words) every day for 120 days."[58] Although his heart sank whenever he glanced at the schedule, he held to a rigorous discipline (of which more in the next chapter) and within nine months had a 250,000-word manuscript.

The book sold modestly but Roberts kept on with historical fiction. Lorimer asked to see his second novel, *The Lively Lady,* and agreed to run it in the *Post* if Roberts would allow deep editing. "It's a grand book," he wired Roberts, "and by cutting some of the opening fifty pages . . . we can get a five-part serial out of it. If this is satisfactory and you are willing to trust our surgeon, confirm. Glad to have you supervise the job if you prefer." [59] Although it meant a radical alteration of the book, Roberts agreed but asked for seven installments rather than five, wanting no more money but more space. "What we print we'll pay for!" Lorimer responded. "We just haven't got the space! Well, I'll see what we can do. Now don't bother me about this any more, damn it!"[60] The novel, reduced to eighty thousand words, finally ran in six installments.

Lorimer remained generally unenthusiastic, however, about his prized journalist's fiction, considering it an experiment on Roberts's part. When Roberts sent him the manuscript of his third novel, *Captain Caution,* Lorimer dug in his heels. The novel had gone the rounds of the office, he wrote Roberts, and the verdict was unanimous: "We all think it is good, and in some ways a better story than *The Lively Lady,* but we do not feel we can run another novel that so closely parallels *The Lively Lady* for some time to come. We now have on hand at least eight months' supply of serials. Unless you have an earlier market, or decide not to defer book publication, we shall be glad to re-consider *Captain Caution* six months from now."[61] Roberts sent the book off to other slick magazines, and all declined. Discouraged, he returned the manuscript to the *Post* (and kept submitting it at six-month intervals until, on a sixth try, Lorimer bought!) while asking, and getting, the editor's okay on four nonfiction articles.

His articles, readily accepted by the magazine, continued to underwrite Roberts's lengthy forays into fiction (". . . in three weeks of February [1932]I earned more from the *Post* than I did by putting in a year writing and rewriting *Arundel,* waiting six months for its publication, and collecting royalties for two years after publication"), and although he considered reporting fun he bemoaned the difficulty of imaginative writing. It was similar to the pain of childbirth, but "while there are many rapturous moments during some of the preliminaries to childbirth, there are none whatever before or during the birth of a novel."[62] Nonetheless, Roberts now saw himself primarily as a historical novelist even though Lorimer kept him busy with articles. His fourth novel, *Rabble in Arms,* was rejected as a *Post* serial, Lorimer returning it with a curt comment on the excessive length of a ten-pound novel. He bought for serialization, however, another weighty work and Roberts's most celebrated, *North-*

west Passage, after reading only half the manuscript. He chose this as the last *Post* serial to see through publication in his long reign as editor in chief, a fact Roberts took as a personal tribute.

eight

In the post–World War II period one of Roberts's most visible successors as a magazine writer of contemporary fact was John Bartlow Martin, his work also largely appearing in the *Post* though never mixed like Roberts's with forays into fiction. After graduation from DePauw University and early newspaper training in Indianapolis, Martin shifted to Chicago in 1938 to begin a freelance career by writing mostly for a pair of local true-crime pulps, *Official Detective Stories* and *Actual Detective Stories of Women in Crime.* In time he had as many as three or four stories in a single issue of the magazines, some under pseudonyms, some ghosted for the women featured in the latter publication. "For example," Martin recalled, "a young Polish stickup man shot a man during a robbery; I persuaded his wife to tell me her life story and wrote it under her name." The woman received $50, Martin $150—his usual rate for a true-crime article. Beyond a few bare facts of a case, the articles were fleshed out with fictitious dialogue and episodes—ideal training, Martin came to think, for his later career because it taught him to think of his work as stories more than articles, stories that possessed "narrative pull—that mysterious invisible force that pulls the reader onward."[63]

Martin eventually put Chicago pulps behind and moved on and up to *Harper's,* specializing in serious nonfiction, or what he called "heavy fact." Frederick Lewis Allen printed a good deal of his work—in one twelve-month period, eight articles—but advised Martin that the magazine could not pay enough to support him as a freelancer. He recommended spreading his work around among the big-circulation slicks, and he helped Martin find an agent to represent his work, Harold Ober. For breaking into the slicks Martin's timing was fortunate. The magazines were still popular and profitable but their editorial formulas had switched from the emphasis on fiction to greater use of nonfiction. During the 1940s and '50s Martin's work appeared in *Cosmopolitan* as well as *Harper's* and so regularly in the *Saturday Evening Post* that he seemed virtually a staff writer for the magazine.

He conducted all his dealings with the *Post* through Ober, in whose New

York office he met regularly with editors in town in search of manuscripts. Unlike others who felt the magazine confined them to familiar subjects, Martin was not held to crime stories but given free rein to report on whatever interested him, including school desegregation, abortion, care of the mentally ill, and prison rioting. He was able to spend up to a year on a subject, and his reports often ran as lengthy installments in a series.

Within the *Post* Martin was known for the patient and meticulous quality of his research—and on its covers the magazine trumpeted his work and hailed him in advertisements as "One of America's Great Reporters." For a 1950 account of a criminal gang he put together a paste-up outline 130 feet long, reduced it to a rough draft of over three hundred typed pages, finally trimmed it to forty-four pages before it ran in the magazine. When the *Post* put out a sampler of its work in 1954 it included Martin's "Death on M-24," an unsparing, clinical recreation of a commonplace auto accident in Michigan that killed six people. "What caused it?" Martin asked, and supplied detailed answers. "What were its effects? Could it have been prevented? Who were the people involved?"[64] However, when Ben Hibbs, then the *Post's* editor, wanted to list him on the masthead as a contributing editor, Martin declined, wanting to hold on to a freelancer's freedom. In 1952 he met Adlai Stevenson, beginning a long involvement in Democratic politics that led to his becoming ambassador to the Dominican Republic in the Kennedy years. He capped his career with an authorized biography of Stevenson, published in two massive volumes in 1976 and 1977, that was ten years in the making, Martin supporting himself with a publisher's advance and teaching stints.

With *The Life of Adlai E. Stevenson* behind him Martin turned to a long-cherished desire to write a novel. Unlike Roberts with historical fiction, he drew on his knowledge of contemporary politics ("To feel comfortable in attempting it [the novel], I made the work as close as possible to writing heavy fact")[65] in a story revolving around television, political poll-taking, and a Senatorial campaign. In the writing he discovered to his surprise "how much material a novel chews up. . . . Into it I put a dozen political campaigns. Into it I put a lifetime of living. It was all packed down. . . . When I finished, I thought I could never write another novel—I'd put into this one everything I knew." The novel was published as *The Televising of Heller,* but two other attempts at fiction came to nothing and Martin turned with relief back to nonfiction with a memoir of his writing and political life, published in 1986 as *It Seems Like Only Yesterday.*

nine

Martin's early days with Chicago's true-crime pulps recall yet another Grub Street venture, ostensibly for fact writers yet attracting more than a few fictioneers, provided by pulp publications from the 1920s into the 1950s. A slight if racy variation on fiction pulps like *Black Mask* and *Detective Fiction Weekly*, the true-crime or fact-detective pulps first appeared in New York with the magazine magnate (and sex and physical fitness guru) Bernarr Macfadden's *True Detective* and *Master Detective*.[66] Eventually as many as seventy-five publications contended for readers. For writers the true-crime pulps offered quick and relatively easy money since material was found rather than invented, though most, like Martin (and, in crime fiction, Dashiell Hammett, Ellery Queen, Bruno Fischer, Erle Stanley Gardner, and S. S. Van Dine, among others), soon shifted to higher ground. Jim Thompson, who would find posthumous fame with his dark crime novels that appeared as paperback originals in the 1950s, was one who stayed on and on.

"Apprenticeship inside the more lurid lowlife of real-life murder inescapably stamped his mature work," a biographer, Robert Polito, remarks of Thompson, and adds that he is the only writer of significance to develop his craft largely on true-crime publications. It was the "trademark tone of incredulous horror," says Polito, that Thompson drew from such pulps, and even the rigid guidelines for style and content helped shape his later work. "All stories must be post-trial," writers were instructed, "with the perpetrators convicted and sentenced at the conclusion. . . . We also prefer that cases involve not more than three suspects. . . . Do not pinpoint the guilty person too early in the story because it kills suspense. . . . Remember that detectives probe, unearth, dig up, ferret out, determine, deduce, seek out, ascertain, discover, hunt, root out, delve, uncover, track, trace, inspect; they canvass, inquire, question, interrogate, quiz, etc."[67]

For much of his true-crime writing Thompson used an "as-told-to" manner, sharing the by-line with his source. However he approached it, the genre freed Thompson from the trying need to devise plots while at the same time allowing him some of fiction's freedom in recreating talk and interior states. Probably most important, it caused him to experiment with a variety of first-person voices, the kind of story-telling he found most congenial. "In writing for popular magazines," he held, "I have found that the first-person—as-told-to or ghostwritten—story has a far wider audience than the third-person narrative; it gives the reader a feeling of being part of things rather than an observer."[68]

From a hard-scrabble background in Texas and Nebraska, Thompson was an experienced writer when he was lured to the true-crime pulps by rates that reached, in *True Detective* during the thirties, $250 for a six-thousand-word article. He had worked for newspapers and written scores of mechanical pieces for trade publications; while a student at the University of Nebraska he had published in the well-regarded literary quarterly *Prairie Schooner*. In Oklahoma during the Depression Thompson joined the Federal Writers' Project, becoming one of the star writers in a group that included Louis L'Amour, and eventually rose to state director of the program.

He was holding down a job at a hotel in Fort Worth when he turned to writing for true-crime pulps, the work becoming a form of family enterprise. Although he turned out exacting accounts of grisly slayings and, in his later crime novels, eerily inhabited the mind of demented killers, Thompson was uncomfortable with violence; he avoided going to actual crime scenes and hunting up sheriffs for interviews, depending instead on his mother, wife, and sister for the legwork and research. Typically, they would follow a murder story through the newspapers until there was a trial and conviction, then travel to the town where the murder took place and interview everyone involved, look into court records, and take photographs. When necessary, the photographs were faked, a family member or Thompson himself stretched out on the ground, face down, recreating the position in which a body was found. Used by the magazines, the photos brought in $3 apiece. Eventually the interview and research material was dumped in Thompson's lap and he went to work, writing as if he had handled the investigation himself. When a check for a story arrived, his wife hung a white handkerchief from a porch light, a success signal to the writer returning from his day job.

Through the 1930s and '40s Thompson, by his own reckoning, wrote for all the true-crime magazines, including Canadian pulps under the name Bird E. Thompson, a variation on his mother's name, Birdie. Even after he was established as a writer of crime novels, he returned to true-crime magazines like *Police Gazette* and *Master Detective* for ready money. In 1959, his fiction market for paperback originals having suddenly dried up, Thompson circulated a proposal for "a book-length fact story" of an actual murder,[69] anticipating the spate of so-called nonfiction novels about crime unleashed with Truman Capote's *In Cold Blood* in 1965.

Nine

BRASS TACKS

How to Succeed at the Writing Game

Nor do I believe there are such abnormal creatures as born
writers, any more than that there are born wire walkers
and born concrete mixers. . . . every writer must learn
his trade just as every paper hanger must.
—Irvin S. Cobb

one

Struggling for a foothold as a writer, Jack London scoured writing handbooks for technical advice and marketing hints, an effort he also ascribed to his alter ego Martin Eden. After writing his first article for a San Francisco newspaper Martin learns from a rhetoric book "that there were such things as paragraphs and quotations marks"—and from an article on writing tips "the iron law that manuscripts should never be rolled and that they should be written on one side of the paper."[1] Quick to soak up such technical information, London was equally quick to share it. "Keep yourself wholly out of the story—I noticed a number of 'I's.—they jar," he instructed Cloudesley Johns. "Let it be all third person."[2] With other correspondents he took note of niceties of punctuation, confessed his own problems with dialogue, and stressed the importance of economical prose. "The art of omission," he said about the latter virtue, "is the hardest of all to learn, and I am weak at it yet."[3]

His own career established, London generously took the time to instruct aspiring authors who sent him manuscripts to read. He presented himself as a "brass-tack man" who gave straight-from-the-shoulder advice at how to succeed at the writing game. The analogy he frequently drew was to a trade that required a long and painstaking apprenticeship before one was able to produce marketable goods. Although he stressed the hazards of professional writing, including the often poor pay, the appeal of London's advice was that the trade could in fact be mastered. Through diligent application it was possible to enter the free-wheeling world of authors who carried their business wherever they went and worked whenever they wished.

The writing magazines not only offered advice to would-be writers but, as London learned early on, provided another market for those with a foot in the door. "Feeling rather nervy one day, I sent them a skit of 1,700 words of advice to young authors," London told Cloudesley Johns about an article called "On the Writer's Philosophy of Life" he had submitted to the *Editor*. He understood the magazine paid liberally but was uncertain what that really meant. "What I am curious about is to see what they consider liberal pay. Or will they expect me to take it out in trade?"[4] As it turned out, the article—published just before his breakthrough with "An Odyssey of the North" in the *Atlantic* —netted him only $5; nevertheless, the acceptance kept London sending the magazine more contributions and in later years he recommended that young writers take out a year's subscription. In advertisements the *Editor* reciprocated London's regard, telling readers that "if you want to follow the trail blazed by Mr. London, you should go about it by studying the profession."[5] Late in his career London was thinking about exploiting the literary how-to market with a nonfiction book that would be a "personal narrative of my whole writing experience from the time I started to learn how to write, up to the present time." He was certain there were "millions of would-be writers who would eat up that sort of stuff."[6]

A particularly useful technical manual for London was *500 Places to Sell Manuscripts*—a manual, according to the subtitle, "Designed for the Guidance of Writers in Disposing of Their Work." Compiled in 1894 by James Knapp Reeve, who published the all-story magazine *Gray Goose* in Cincinnati and in 1895 would found the *Editor,* the slim booklet listed magazines, newspapers, and literary syndicates that accepted freelance work, with brief information on the type of work used and desired manuscript lengths. The manual also listed publishing houses for books. In a preface Reeve advised readers of the special popularity of short stories; as he put it, "the recent development in this line is extraordinary." Travel articles were next in demand. Beginning writers were advised to develop material for specialized publications such as farm and religious journals where pay was poor but the chance of getting in print better.

Reeve offered an additional service of evaluating manuscripts. Charges ranged from fifty cents for poems and manuscripts up to three thousand words to twenty cents per thousand words for works over five thousand; for each manuscript clients could expect "a letter of advice as to its availability for publication, with a list of six periodicals to which adapted." For serial stories there were special services and special terms. "Whenever desired," Reeve noted, "the compiler of this book will examine such MSS. carefully and give an opinion as to what periodicals they are best adapted to. He will also advise regarding the construction, and will revise, correct and give a personal letter of criticism. Will also forward MSS. to publishers when desired. The charges for this work have been put at a moderate price, so that any who wish the benefit of experienced criticism, and advice as to the very best market, may have it without undue expense."[7] Although London acknowledged the usefulness of Reeve's market listings for professional writers (and in his copy of a 1899 edition of the work added names and addresses not included), he made clear that he himself had never drawn on the critical services. "I don't know whether a correspondence school can help a fellow or not," he told a correspondent. "In the old days I found *The Editor* and *The Editor's* '501 Places to Sell Manuscripts,' in [*sic*] great assistance to me in marketing my pot-boilers and my failures. But I never had *The Editor* people look at, correct, or revise a manuscript of mine."[8]

Subsequent editions of the work produced by The Editor Company carried an enlarged listing of outlets and bore a new title, *1001 Places to Sell Manuscripts*. By 1913, with the book then in its ninth edition, the market had changed sufficiently that the editor, William R. Kane, pointed out that stories were probably still more in demand than articles but the latter brought in larger checks. Vital articles "will always sell *eventually*," he declared, while good short stories "will often remain unsold for long periods."[9] He added that poetry could still be marketed but competition was stiff.

Other guides for authors produced by the company bore titles such as *Practical Authorship, Points About Poetry, The Fiction Writer's Workshop*, and *How to Write a Short Story. The Fiction Factory*, a guide produced by William

Wallace Cook, describes (as the title page noted) his twenty-two years of keeping a "Story-mill Grinding Successfully." Using the pseudonym John Milton Edwards and writing in the third person, Cook traced his hack career from a first $8 newspaper sale to steady production for pulp magazines and newspaper syndicates. While major success had eluded him, he proudly reported that he had "wrested more than $100,000 from the tills of the publishers"—an amount certain to catch the eye of aspiring writers. In addition to sketching his career and including correspondence with editors, Cook provided insider information on the mechanics of publication, including the seemingly life-or-death matters of preparing, mailing, and recording manuscripts: ". . . there is not a detail in the preparation or recording or forwarding of a manuscript that can be neglected. Competition is keen. Big names, without big ideas back of them, are not so prone to carry weight. It's the *stuff*, itself, that counts; yet a business-like way of doing things carries a mute appeal to an editor before even a line of the manuscript has been read. It is a powerful appeal, and all on the writer's side."[10]

two

The manuals and trade journals appearing in the 1880s and '90s sought to give authorship a patina of professional standing. Here was a world to be learned and mastered, one complete with precedents, technical information, insider jargon, marketing strategies, and even ethical considerations. The first edition of *Authors and Publishers,* put out by G. P. Putnam's Sons and subtitled "A Manual of Suggestions for Beginners in Literature," clarified the various contractual arrangements in book publishing, discussed the pros and cons of the use of literary agents, and led the writer through the steps of book production. Other "Books for Authors" advertised by Putnam's included the historical studies *Authors and Their Public in Ancient Times* and *Books and Their Makers During the Middle Ages,* both written by George Haven Putnam, the son of the founder, the firm's current head, and himself a prolific author and authority on international copyright law.

The most important and long-running periodical directed to authors was the *Writer,* subtitled "a monthly magazine for literary workers," founded by William H. Hills in Boston in 1887.[11] Two years later Hills launched a short-lived sister publication called the *Author* with essentially the same contents, though carrying more reprint material, which was meant to supplement the earlier magazine by coming out at mid-month. A newspaperman, Hills also conducted a correspondence school called the Writer's School of Journalism and Literary Training. An eighteen-page monthly priced at a dollar a year, the *Writer* declared its slant as "practical and useful" and envisioned itself as a clearinghouse for all manner of information about writing. Readers were asked to forward advice, suggestions, and accounts of their own experience, the editors seeing themselves as conducting a writing magazine more than supplying dogma about the trade. For a fee the magazine also provided editorial advice through a literary bureau that, as it advertised itself, "serves as a medium between authors and publishers, and gives honest advice and unprejudiced criticism of manuscripts when desired."

The *Writer's* initial issue carried articles on writing sermons, the art of interviewing, and the laws of libel, as well as the first of a three-part series by Hills on advice to newspaper correspondents, and a feature by one Stephen O'Meara called "Does It Pay to Be a Reporter?" (answer: No, but there are other considerations). In subsequent issues of the magazine the minutiae of newspaper work received considerable attention, most of it at the level of William J. Fowler's declaration in "Hints to Newspaper Writers" that "much more depends on proper paragraphing to make an article attractive than on any other trick of the trade in preparing literary matter for the market. It is scarcely less important than having something to say."[12]

A particularly useful function of the magazine was information about prize contests for new writers. Among the most lucrative were those offered by the *Black Cat*, a lively Boston magazine that capitalized on the appeal of short fiction and the enthusiasm of amateur writers. Its founder, an advertising man named Herman D. Umbstaetter, came up with the idea of drawing material from amateurs through a flurry of prize contests, this method of acquiring stories ultimately costing him as much as if he bought from professionals but having the side benefit of acquiring subscribers as well. The magazine quickly caught on, claiming a circulation of over 150,000 through the late 1890s. In later years it took pride in listing well-known writers who had begun their careers in its pages—among them, Susan Glaspell, Alice Hegan Rice, and Jack London.

The magazine had taken a London tale at the floundering start of his career—one he breathlessly described as "a pseudo-scientific tale, founded on hypothetical chemical, biological, and pathological laws, dealing with the diametric converse of chemical affinity and the mysteries of protoplasmic co-agulation"[13]—and he was forever grateful. The magazine's prize money was a continuing attraction, and London happily reported to Cloudesley Johns when a story was sent winging in pursuit of it: "I, at the eleventh hour, from a chance newspaper clipping, caught the motif for a *Black Cat* yarn. Behold, it is finished and off. How's this for a title: 'The Minions of Midas'? That's what I afflicted it with. 5000 words in length. I did not write it for a first second or third prize, but for one of the minor ones. I knew what motif was necessary for a first prize *Black Cat* story, but I could not invent such a motif."[14] At the height of his fame London contributed an introductory comment when Herman Umbstaetter published a collection of short stories in 1911, praising both the founder and the magazine: "To many a writer with a national reputation, the *Black Cat* has been the stepping stone. The marvellous, the unthinkable thing Mr. Umbstaetter did was to judge a story on its merits and to pay for it on its merits. Also, and only a hungry writer can appreciate this, he paid immediately on acceptance."[15]

Writing in the *Boston Evening Transcript* just after the turn of the century, Frank Norris thought the problem facing what he called the "ambitious amateur" in the marketplace for fiction was not the lack of practical information addressed by writing manuals and magazines but the immensity of competition. The numbers, as he tossed them off, were more than formidable: "At a conservative estimate there are 70,000,000 people in the United States. At a liberal estimate 100,000 of these have lost the use of both arms; remain then 69,900,000—who write novels. Indeed, many are called but few—oh, what a scanty, skimped handful that few represent—are chosen." Still, Norris, then working as a reader for the publishing house of Doubleday, Page, offered a "little seasonable advice" that parodied the orderly, just-follow-the-dots manner of the writing magazine—seventeen suggestions that begin with sensible admonitions, ranging from the need for typewritten manuscripts to a moratorium on letters of introduction from friends of publishers. As the suggestions continue, however, they become more delightfully unlike those of the writing magazines. For example:

12. Don't write a colonial novel.

13. Don't write a Down East novel.

14. Don't write a *Prisoner of Zenda* novel.

15. Don't write a novel.

16. Try to keep your friends from writing novels.[16]

With his final suggestion Norris abruptly reversed his sardonic manner, assuring his audience that all manuscripts were in fact read by publishers and that good work invariably found its way into print.

three

Another avenue of aid for aspiring writers was to beseech established authors for personal help. In 1927 Upton Sinclair decided there were 200,000 would-be writers in the country, with 10,000 new recruits each year coming from high schools and colleges—figures he arrived at "with reasonable accuracy, because they send me their manuscripts and write me letters telling the story of their lives."[17] While writers like London were often good about dispensing advice, others resisted intrusions on their time and chose to offer instruction in the form of articles and books, either of the direct how-to sort or merged, if the writer happened to be especially successful, into a full-scale memoir of the writing life. The latter had particular appeal because the writer could, at one and the same time, shape the story of his rise to prominence, showing how painful or relatively easy it had been; impart hard-won advice to aspirants; and, not least, bring in royalties at a time when his career might be on a downward slide.

Fanny Fern used her column in the *New York Ledger* in the 1850s and '60s to express exasperation with aspiring writers who sought her "candid opinion . . . as soon as convenient" on illegible manuscripts with woeful spelling and absent punctuation.[18] She considered issuing "a printed circular, embodying the above obvious difficulties in the way of 'literary aspirants,' and mail it on receipt of their epistles."[19] James Oliver Curwood devoted a chapter of his unfinished autobiography, *Son of the Forests,* to "Advice to Authors," therein taking the uncommon position for a professional writer that the key to success was a healthy body. He described in detail his own regimen of rising early, drinking two glasses of water, spending fifteen to twenty minutes on calisthenics, drinking two more glasses of water, then a cold-water bath, breakfast, and a ten-minute walk. Finally arriving at his writing studio, he portrayed himself as "vibrantly alive and eager to get to work for the sheer pleasure of it. My brain is clear and my body healthy because I have started the day right by taking the opportunity which Nature is intended all men should have."[20]

A year after Curwood's autobiography was published in 1930, the popular historical novelist Kenneth Roberts vented his frustration with youthful writers

in a *Saturday Evening Post* article. In particular he railed against three perni-
cious falsehoods about the nature of the writing life: "It appears to be the fixed
belief of these enthusiastic young people that (1) a person needs only to write
a book in order to become immediately rich and famous; (2) the work is easier and cleanlier than other forms of endeavor, and can be performed anywhere
and at any time; (3) little training is needed, and no equipment except a large
pad of paper, several pencils and a place to hang the hat." Roberts pointed to
Edith Wharton's novel *Hudson River Bracketed* as especially culpable. Here a
callow youth publishes a short story in an obscure magazine and is catapulted
to fame, publishers clamoring for his work and beautiful women his favor. As
Roberts and every other writer he knew had experienced it, the reality was far
different, and he used the writing of his first historical novel, *Arundel,* as a
lengthy case in point.

While turning out a draft, Roberts and his wife were living on a publisher's
advance in Italy—a romantic location that did nothing to ease the grind of
the work, as Roberts revealed in a detailed account of the schedule he followed, seven days a week for four months:

> 9 A.M. Retire to the workroom, wrap an overcoat around the feet to keep out
> the chill that rises from the tiled floors of all Italian buildings, sit down at the desk
> and devote one hour to revising and rewriting the work done on the preceding two
> days.
>
> 10 A.M. Dip into eleven reference books to make sure of dates, weather, cos-
> tumes and sundry other matters having to do with the day's writing, and try to go
> on with the story until
>
> 1 P.M. Unwrap the overcoat from the feet and emerge for lunch, read the Paris
> *Herald* and the morning mail, curse the clown-like antics of American legislators
> and European statesmen, and play three games of cribbage, piquet or backgam-
> mon with Mrs. Roberts.
>
> 2:30 P.M. Retire to the workroom, adjust the overcoat around the feet and work
> for five hours.
>
> 7:30 P.M. Emerge for dinner, complain about the small amount of work ac-
> complished during the day, and play three games of piquet, cribbage or backgam-
> mon with Mrs. Roberts.
>
> 9:30 P.M. To bed with an armful of reference books, to brood morosely over the
> next day's work.[21]

After the first draft came lengthy revision, then a lengthy correcting of proofs,
and finally—a year and a half after beginning the book—publication. Neither
fame nor fortune followed. A year after publication, sales stood at just under

10,000, Roberts had paid off his advance and made $1,400 more, and was under siege neither by publishers nor by women.

From the article Roberts turned to a full cautionary tale in *I Wanted to Write,* published in 1949, a book frankly addressed to the sort of "Wanta Writer" who came to him for advice. "I'd like to have it understood in the beginning," he opened the work, "and remembered until the end, that these chapters have been written solely because of the staggering number of would-be authors who seem to labor under the delusion that I know a routine, formula or diet that in a half hour's time will transform any aspiring young person who admires his own letter-writing ability into a competent and successful novelist." The only transforming tip he gives is that one must drive oneself "incessantly and ruthlessly," and to make the point the reader is taken on a tour of Roberts's own writing life from his college days at Cornell to his distinguished journalistic career with the *Saturday Evening Post* to the writing of his fifth historical novel. Along the way extensive, often numbing, use is made of diary entries, showing the painstaking effort of reading, research, writing, and revision that went into his work, the considerable amount of help he received from his close friend Booth Tarkington, and the roller coaster of elation and despair that marked his inner life as a writer.

At the end of a book of 350 pages and a hundred more of appendices Roberts reports his gloomy conclusion that writing never becomes easier nor does practice make perfect. His later historical fictions caused him more problems than the first, yet while the work was "infuriating and exhausting," he held to a belief that it was "considerably more gratifying and exhilarating than golf, tennis, poker, cocktail parties, movies or The Game—provided the person who does it really wants to write."[22]

Mary Roberts Rinehart's *My Story,* published in 1931, is a more conventional recounting of an active personal life interwoven with her hugely successful writing career. But she pauses to note her impatience with those who ask her help when magazines return their manuscripts, ascribing their failure to lack of "pull" rather than talent or effort. She compares the difficulty of writing to childbearing, only more so; and she describes her own method as writing in snatches of time and thinking "at the point of my pen." She explained: "I can think there, and there only. If throughout the hours away from the desk I were still to be absorbed in the work which lies there, it would be impossible to live a rounded life. I could be perhaps a better craftsman, more of an artist; but I would be nothing else." It was never easy, though, to switch from the introverted attitude of writing to the extroverted needs of daily life. "I am often a little dazed when I leave the desk, and certainly very tired and empty after a full day of work. . . . But this transition must be made."[23]

four

Kenneth Roberts mentions in passing in his memoir the many writers' conferences going on around the country—instructional settings he avoids because "there's no way of telling how it's done, either in a two-hour address or by any other sort of demonstration."[24] But as a young writer just starting out he was willing to sit at the feet of a writing master. In 1917 he had a job with a Boston newspaper but felt he was making no headway in his plan to become a writer; deciding he needed formal instruction, he tried to join a fellow journalist in a course for would-be playwrights at Harvard taught by George Pierce Baker. The requirements for entrance were an application and samples of original work. A week after the submission Baker returned the samples with a note saying Roberts was not sufficiently serious about writing plays to take up a place in the course.[25]

Baker's famous playwriting workshop, conducted for a number of years at Radcliffe and Harvard and later carried to Yale, was an early spark in the explosion of creative writing programs in colleges and universities around the country. An academic rather than a professional writer, Baker had been influenced by his Harvard instructor Barrett Wendell, among the first novelists to teach at an American university and an influential instructor of English composition. Baker's first Harvard class in 1905–6 for English 47, in which all the members were accepted on the basis of manuscripts, included Edward Sheldon and Van Wyck Brooks; two later students, Eugene O'Neill and Thomas Wolfe, helped to give the course and its laboratory theater, the 47 Workshop, a widespread reputation. Few of Baker's students actually went on to become working playwrights, and one of his lasting achievements—no doubt that of most instructors in creative writing—was to direct the theater-mad elsewhere. This was the case with both Wolfe and Heywood Broun, an English 47 student who later pointed to Baker's "splendid record of cures" and "the number of excellent young men who have gone straight from his classroom to Wall Street, and the ministry, and automobile accessories with all the nascent enthusiasm of men just liberated from a great delusion."[26]

Schools of journalism appeared at the University of Missouri in 1908 and at Columbia University in 1913. In 1930 Norman Foerster, a professor of English, was appointed director of the new School of Letters at the University of Iowa and there established a graduate program in creative writing. Foerster was not aiming at a professional training center that would, as he scornfully put it, give "practical shortcuts and trade tricks," nor did he envision a free-standing writing program.[27] His intention was to reform literary studies by bringing writing as an ongoing activity into a curriculum that included criticism, literary history, and language studies. The end in view was a humane education of broad scope. But out of Foerster's work came the Iowa Writers' Workshop, the leader in a nationwide movement beginning in the 1940s toward degree-granting programs for writers of fiction, poetry, and drama. By the late 1980s over a thousand degrees a year were being awarded in creative writing, divided almost equally between graduate and undergraduate degrees.[28]

For professional writers, writing courses and programs of any sort were a mixed blessing. On the college and university level they provided a wondrous patronage system in the form of student fellowships and tenured faculty positions, and on the level of workshops and conferences they provided interesting travel and attractive stipends. But they drained time and energy away from writing, and, for instructors who believed that writing in any important sense could not really be taught, they were by definition frustrating. They could be frustrating in another way, as John Bartlow Martin discovered in the course of teaching for ten years at the Medill School of Journalism at Northwestern while writing his biography of Adlai Stevenson. He found his students neither very good nor very serious. Wearied of correcting their faulty articles, he made up rubber stamps saying "awkward," "says little," "what mean?" and on some pages stamped as many words as had been written. His overall view of the experience was decidedly glum: "When I started teaching, I was, by and large, on the students' side. But after a few years, after all the unmet deadlines and broken appointments, after all the superficial interviews and sloppy drafts dashed off at the last minute, I found myself approaching each new student somewhat warily. . . . Some found magazine writing all but impossible. Some could not do penetrating interviewing, many had trouble conceptualizing the story, nearly all had trouble organizing their material. Most of their writing was disappointing. . . . I taught my course to fifty-four students each year; if I found one or two who had a chance of making it as a writer, I counted it a good year."[29]

From a student standpoint, disenchantment with classroom instruction could as easily point in the opposite direction. Jack London claimed in *John*

Barleycorn that before he could succeed as a writer he had to unlearn nearly everything high school teachers and university professors had taught him. When he first realized this he was indignant; later he understood that his teachers simply had no knowledge of "the trick of successful writing" in the present day. "They knew all about 'Snow Bound' and 'Sartor Resartus'; but the American editors of 1899 did not want such truck. They wanted the 1899 truck, and offered to pay so well for it that the teachers and professors of literature would have quit their jobs could they have supplied it."[30] Paul Gallico remembered taking every writing class he could at Columbia University and becoming "saturated with the rules and regulations of storycraft, the mechanics and mathematics of construction," then teaching the very same things to small groups outside the university. "Why my students went for it," he noted, "and ever paid me money, or what good they got out of it, I shall never know. The whole thing makes me shudder with shame today."[31]

five

If books and magazines for writers together with conferences, courses, and degree programs gave authorship a semblance of professional standing, so too did the organization of author societies. In 1882 a seven-member group that included such stalwarts as Edward Eggleston, Richard Watson Gilder, Brander Matthews, and E. C. Stedman founded the Authors Club in New York, essentially a social gathering of literary gentlemen. The Society of Authors in Britain, established in 1884 and directed by the novelist Walter Besant, offered a model of more militant purpose after Besant's articles in the *Forum* in 1892 vigorously outlined efforts to gain fair play for writers in the marketplace. Besant wrote: "It is not greed of gold, my friends, that inspires the men who form our company to band together, but the determination to get justice, if it can be got, and, when it is got, to maintain and defend it."[32] But the American counterparts formed in the 1880s and 1890s lacked aggressive leadership and swiftly faded in importance, and it was not until the formation of the Authors League of America in 1912, with Ida Tarbell and Hamlin Garland among its founders, that writers had a vigilant group voice and, in its *Bulletin,* a muscular publication.

From offices in Greenwich Village the organization concentrated on such matters as better copyright provisions, the protection of the various serial rights of published work, and legal and market information. Arthur Train, another of the founders, characterized the League as "merely hard-working young writers" who "wanted an equitable share in the proceeds of our labors." However, when the opportunity arose in 1916 for formal affiliation with the American Federation of Labor, the majority of members shied away from the implication of trade-union status. "I like to think that my writing is an attempt at expressing something in terms of an art," Hamlin Garland remarked loftily, "not in terms of a trade."[33]

Several organizations followed under the umbrella of the League, all devoted to particular writing crafts—Authors Guild, Dramatists Guild, Newspaper Guild, Screen Writers Guild, Radio Writers Guild—though none attained the prominence of Britain's Society of Authors or leadership matching that of Besant and his successor, George Bernard Shaw. The most ambitious effort to organize American writers was waged by the novelist James M. Cain just after World War II with what he called the American Authors' Authority. Cain wanted a centralized authority that would stoutly represent writers in negotiating contracts and in legal disputes—a "massively powerful organization" with "a full-time tough mugg at the head of it."[34] While writers had little quarrel with Cain on this score, they took issue with his insistence that they assign all copyrights to the organization. Cain's view was that author groups were inevitably weak because they sought to organize writers rather than manage their properties; only through holding copyrights in a central legal repository and leasing rather than selling rights could writers secure enough clout in the marketplace.

Cain traveled and spoke tirelessly to drum up support for his idea. When it failed to materialize, in part due to political infighting between writers on the political left and right as well as the anti-communist furor of the postwar years, Cain placed ultimate blame on the writing community. To H. L. Mencken he complained that writers as a breed had almost no sense of basic questions that arose from their work. For Hollywood columnist Hedda Hopper he added that writers were impossible to organize: "Plumbers, yes, or scene shifters, or electric chair operators. In these will be found some sense, some comprehension of the solidarity they owe each other. But writers . . . are idiots and may be expected not only to turn on each other at every conceivable point, but to pursue any whacky idea that catches their fancy, regardless of whether it is in their own interest or not."[35] Richard Fine, who has unraveled the complex history of the AAA, generally sides with Cain's sour view, arguing that the failure of the organization points to an abiding hollowness at the core of conceptions of writing as a profession: "In 1946, and continuing to this date, writers have suffered a crisis of professional identity, and this fact more than any other accounts for their singular lack of success in pressing their claims to a share of the profits from their work commensurate with their contribution. Unable to create a true profession, writers invariably fall back on the cult of the individual and wrap themselves in the quasi-sacred notion that writing is a 'calling.' Unable to organize to protect their own economic interests in a society that values those interests above all else, writers have become diminished players in the literary marketplace, and in American culture as a whole."[36]

six

The increased role of literary agents beginning in the 1880s and '90s had far greater impact on the professional and economic life of writers than literary associations.[37] Agents had appeared in England roughly a half century before, and informal agents, friends or lawyers or relatives, had long been a feature of literary life, acting as buffers between authors and publishers. One of the first professional English agents, A. P. Watt, with Rudyard Kipling and W. B. Yeats as clients, had in the 1880s taken on a beleaguered Bret Harte. The former Western sensation had fallen far from the halcyon year of 1871 when he signed a contract with Boston's Fields, Osgood and Company, publishers of the *Atlantic* and *Every Saturday,* for $10,000 for a year's exclusive right to his poems and sketches.[38] Now, relieved of the patronage of his consular position and living in England while trying to make his way on a freelance basis, he needed someone to take charge of his production. Watt did. He marketed Harte's stories to the highest bidder, placed them in top English and American periodicals, and saw to it that book publication quickly followed. An important successor of Watt, James B. Pinker, handled work with equal skill for Henry James and was the English agent for Stephen Crane.

In America, James Lawson, a Scot by birth and accountant by trade, acted as an informal agent as early as the 1820s, serving the interests of Poe, William Cullen Bryant, and William Gilmore Simms, among others, taking no fees and presenting himself as a gentlemanly advocate benefiting both author and publisher. In Poe's series on New York's literati, Lawson was treated to a brief sketch, Poe noting that he had written little yet "few men have more ardently at heart the welfare of American letters."[39] The position of the first important professional agent in the country is generally accorded to Paul Revere

Reynolds, a Harvard-educated Bostonian who had studied under William James and pursued an editing career before stumbling upon his life's work in New York.[40]

Reynolds first served as an agent for English publishers, scouting for material and placing English writing in the American market. Eventually he realized that his contacts in American publishing would serve the interests of native writers and began marketing American material, charging his clients a ten-percent commission for his services. His business developed slowly. Many publishers resisted agents on the grounds that they fractured cordial relations with authors and tempted them to jump from house to house in pursuit of financial gain. Writers also resisted, holding that agents could do no more for them in the marketplace than they could do for themselves.

By 1904, in business for twelve years, Reynolds was still drawing most of his work from English connections. But an increasing number of American writers were turning to agents, and the following year Reynolds took a young associate into his office, Harold Ober, who would become an important agent in his own right. In time Reynolds included among his clients Hamlin Garland, Stephen Crane, Ida Tarbell, Willa Cather, James Branch Cabell, Booth Tarkington, Richard Harding Davis, and F. Scott Fitzgerald. By the time his son joined the agency in 1927 it was a thriving business.

Reynolds maintained formal, distant relations with writers and editors, conducting most of his business by letter. When he forwarded a manuscript to an editor it was accompanied by a terse note that simply identified the work and set a price. He refrained from praising the material he represented on the grounds that accolades from an agent were pointless, and only rarely was he willing to bargain about price. Typical was a note sent to the editor of the *Saturday Evening Post* accompanying the novel of a popular writer of the day:

> Dear Mr. Lorimer,
>   I am enclosing a novel by Henry Kitchell Webster entitled *The Man With the Scarred Hand.* I will sell you the serial rights for $30,000.
>   Yours sincerely, [41]

When he made a sale Reynolds, averse to using the telephone, sent his authors a telegram.

Among his important services for clients was negotiating advance payment against future earnings for books and serials, funds that could help support a writer between books. Of 367 novels Reynolds handled in the ten-year period from 1910 to 1920, fifty-seven percent received advances. He was also able to negotiate for many clients royalty rates better than the standard ten percent.[42] Perhaps his most crucial service was help with subsidiary rights. Frank Norris in 1902 listed the bewildering thicket of possibilities for a successful novel:

> First it is serialized either in the Sunday press or, less probably, in a weekly or monthly. Then it is made up into book form and sent over the course a second time. The original publisher sells sheets to a Toronto or Montreal house and a Canadian edition reaps a like harvest. It is not at all unlikely that a special cheap cloth edition may be bought and launched by some large retailer either of New York or Chicago. Then comes the paper edition, with small royalties it is true, but based upon an enormous number of copies, for the usual paper edition is an affair of tens of thousands. Next the novel crosses the Atlantic, and a small sale in England helps to swell the net returns, which again are added to—possibly—by the "colonial edition" which the English firm issues. Last of all comes the Tauchnitz edition, and with this (bar the improbable issuing of later special editions) the exploitation ceases. Eight separate times the same commodity has been sold, no one of the sales militating against the success of the other seven, the author getting his fair slice every time.[43]

Added to the list in the 1920s was the recycling possible through books clubs—and there were further rights for adaptation to stage, screen, and radio.

Reynolds did not hold his clients to binding contracts, and consequently they were free to leave him as they wished. But he was not above soliciting business. He went after Richard Harding Davis with the appeal that he could make him the best-paid magazinist in the country, and succeeded in getting Davis a top rate of $3,000 per story from the newspaper Sunday editions.[44] He likewise dangled money in front of Tarkington, who agreed to let Reynolds handle some of his work while reserving to himself the right to market serial versions of his novels with magazines. Reynolds accepted the unusual arrangement but kept urging Tarkington to reconsider: "I want to say if you have a new serial coming along, I do not see why it wouldn't be business for you to say to me, 'I sold my last serial for so much money. If you can get me more, and enough more to make it worth while, I will pay you a commission. Otherwise not.' I think 'The Flirt' could have been sold for more money than you got for it, from what I learn, and if there is more money floating around here I think it is a mistake for us to let it float. Don't you?"[45]

For a decade Reynolds served as Willa Cather's agent for stories and the serial rights to her novels, but although the fees he commanded greatly pleased her she eventually drifted away, leaving her work in the hands of the new publishing firm of Alfred Knopf. After she won the Pulitzer Prize for fiction in 1923 Cather was in demand by the magazines and Reynolds tried to lure her back to story work, largely to no avail. Before book publication of her hugely successful novel *Death Comes for the Archbishop* in 1927, he handled magazine serialization, finally making a sale to the *Forum* for a modest $3,000 after failing to place it with other magazines for $15,000.[46] For Tarbell, Reynolds held out the prospect of increased income if whe wrote more often for the women's magazines. Put off at first by his persistence, she eventually learned that the agent could indeed bring in more than she expected. "You will be the salvation of my old age!" she happily informed him.[47] Reynolds also courted London, who was not adverse to using his services, especially for work he was not able to peddle successfully himself. In 1912 he sent the agent a story that had nearly run the gamut of the slick market: "Please find inclosed herewith 'Told in the Drooling Ward.' Since I shall be away for six months, you will have to sell it for anything you can get. . . . [It] has already been submitted to *Saturday Evening Post, The Cosmopolitan, Nation's Review, McClure's, Everybody's, Sunday Magazine, Woman's Home Companion, Collier's Weekly,* and *Success."*[48]

In the case of Fitzgerald, it was the writer who sought out the agent. At the beginning of his career he was able to place stories with magazines such as *Smart Set* and *Scribner's* but he turned to Reynolds in an effort to break into the better-paying pages of the *Saturday Evening Post.* The agent succeeded on a grand scale, with Fitzgerald's stories of young love in high society that began appearing in the magazine in 1919 eventually bringing in as much as $4,000 each. Fitzgerald was soon recommending Reynolds to other writers as "the best in New York—The Post people come to see him every week,"[49] but when Ober, who had handled Fitzgerald's work for Reynolds, left in 1928 to start his own firm the writer was quick to go with him. At the end of his career Fitzgerald broke with Ober when the agent refused to continue advancing him money for stories, maintaining to Maxwell Perkins at Scribner's that he preferred to deal personally with editors. His regard for Ober, however, remained high and he wished only a "peaceful cleavage." He "has always treated me fairly and generously and is above reproach as an agent," he told Perkins, and added: "I have not, nor will ever say, nor *could* say anything against him either personally or professionally."[50]

Agents also worked the low end of Grub Street, and here their services could be perfunctory. Ed Bodin specialized in the seedier pulps and would market any story handed him for a flat $1 fee. But at the other end of the street Erd Brandt of the well-regarded Brandt and Brandt firm functioned nearly as a co-author, as one of his clients, John R. Tunis, fondly remembered. In the 1920s and '30s Tunis was selling regularly in the New York magazine article market with the benefit of Brandt's editorial sense. "He knew where to smell out an article idea," Tunis recalled, "how to doctor up a feeble plot, how to encourage a writer in those moments of black despair when he wishes he had been an honest fellow and gone into his father-in-law's wholesale soap business." The agent was equally adept at cracking the whip, pointing out in the face of Tunis's authorial laments that no one had forced him to go into the writing business. With a particular article Brandt, later a senior editor of the *Saturday Evening Post,* would work with Tunis until it was whipped into presentable magazine shape. "His was not exactly an easy school," Tunis noted with admiration. "You wrote, you rewrote, you worked over a lead a dozen times or more, changing it or the ending until he felt it was right. All the time Erd kept saying: 'I still think we have something there.' Or, 'Suppose we do this. . . .' It was usually 'we.' He insisted on pretending it was your work, not his."[51]

A further service provided by most agents was keeping track of unsold work. The Brandt agency maintained a "B-file" of such manuscripts for each client while looking for marketing opportunities. When Carl Brandt of the agency placed Stephen Vincent Benét's *Selected Works* with the Book-of-the-Month Club in 1941 it had the effect of making Benét's work hot items with magazine editors. After Brandt pulled out an old story from the B-file and sold it to the *Saturday Evening Post* for $1,750, he wired Benét, "I fear they are unaware it is not fresh from the mill," and later added, "Personally, I feel a little like the cat, who has not only eaten the canary, but has had a bottle of cream all to himself!"[52] A few months later Brandt dusted off another Benét story and sold it to *Redbook* (the former *Red Book*) for $800.

seven

Agents of the caliber of Reynolds, Ober, and Erd and Carl Brandt were clearly of crucial importance to writers, as no one knew better than Jack London, ever alert to the inner workings of the marketplace. "The big majority of the stuff written by well-known writers in England and America to-day," he remarked in 1908, "is 'hawked' by their literary agents. There is no writer to-day, of importance, who does not use, either steadily or sporadically, literary agents for the sale of his work." London's qualifiers—well-known writers,

writers of importance—pointed, on the other hand, to the limitations of agents as far as writers were concerned. Agents were in business to make money, and writers who had already established their names with editors and publishers were the dependable moneymakers. With few exceptions, beginning writers had to market their work on their own; only when they began making regular sales were they sufficiently attractive to be taken on by agents. Here was the frustrating paradox for writers: they first had to function as their own literary agents; once they met with a measure of success, they paid someone a commission to do the same work. London again: "All stuff sold to the magazines is handled just precisely like merchandise. It doesn't matter whether Reynolds does the hawking, or Mrs. Ninetta Eames does the hawking, or Jack London does the hawking; it is handled as merchandise."[53]

One way or another, a writer's work had to be "hawked," yet most writers arrived at the conclusion that agents, if and when they could be secured, could do the job more effectively. Agents knew the marketplace, knew how to match a writer's work with an editor's needs, knew it was to their advantage as much as to a writer's to wring the last dollar from subsidiary rights. And not least, they could function for prized clients as bankers of last resort, providing emergency funds against earnings from future work. Crane, who met Reynolds at a party given by Irving Bacheller in 1896 and was happy to turn over his affairs to the agent ("I will allow you ten percent on the sales and refer everything to you, giving you the clear field which is your right"),[54] was soon pleading with him to "for Christ's sake get me some money quick here by cable."[55] Reynolds obliged. In a later period Ober provided a similar service for Paul Gallico, seeing to his debts, paying his life insurance, wiring him funds abroad. In turn, Gallico was quick to whip out work, telling the agent, "You know me, I do anything for money."[56]

For some writers, though, hawking their work directly had its benefits. Nina Wilcox Putnam, a popular author of humorous fiction, for a number of years sold material through Harold Paget, an agent whose name had come to her attention while she worked as a manuscript reader for the publishing firm she married into, G. P. Putnam's Sons. When she wrote a story in slang and wanted it sent to the *Saturday Evening Post,* Paget balked, insisting the story was not the *Post's* type and he would not make a fool of himself by submitting it. "I'd rather resign as your agent than do so," he told her. "Personally, I think it a very inferior story." Putnam was troubled. Paget had, as she put it, "hand-nursed my literary career to such an extent that he believed I could not do without him, and he almost had me thinking so, too." But she made an appointment to see Churchill Williams, a *Post* editor who each Thursday came to New York to see agents and authors, and hand-delivered her manuscript. On Monday she received an acceptance, agreed to a handsome fee, and accepted an invitation to meet in Philadelphia with the editor in chief, Lorimer, to discuss future work.[57]

Marijane Meaker took another approach. As a young writer in New York at the start of the 1950s and unable to get her stories and articles published or find an agent, she set up shop as her own agent, printing stationery and circulating as the work of clients her own work under pseudonyms. She had an editorial job at the time with Fawcett Publications and on lunch breaks, as she remembered, she "visited editors and talked about Laura Winston (who wrote slicks for women's magazines), Mamie Stone (who wrote confessions), Edgar Stone, her 'husband' (who wrote detective stories), and Winslow Albert (who wrote articles). . . . They were all me."[58] One day a letter came from the *Ladies' Home Journal* addressed to Marijane Meaker, Literary Agent, saying they would buy a Laura Winston story for $750. Meaker went on from her first published story to have a successful career in paperback originals as Vin Packer and young adult fiction as M. E. Kerr.

Now and then writers found marketing methods that circumvented not only the need for agents but mainline publishers. Harold Bell Wright, one of the great stars of the popular fiction boom that extended up to World War II, is a spectacular case in point. After the publication of his second novel in 1907, *The Shepherd of the Hills,* Wright retired from the ministry of the Church of the Disciples and gave himself to writing, following the vein of didactic religious views conveyed through sentimental storytelling that had been mined earlier by Charles Sheldon and E. P. Roe—"the ministry of print," as Frank Luther Mott called it.[59] Wright had already established a close relationship with a Chicago mail-order bookseller, Elsbery W. Reynolds, whose Book Supply Company published his first novel, *That Printer of Udell's;* with Wright's subsequent books, author and publisher joined in an advertising blitz. For *The Calling of Dan Matthews* in 1909, $48,000 was plunged into advertising, a considerable sum for the time. It worked. The novel, as well as Wright's two earlier books, sold in vast quantities, the Book Supply Company now placing its wares directly in book outlets as well as selling through the mail. *The Eyes of the World,* published in 1914 with a promotion budget of $100,000, was soon selling 8,000 copies a day, according to advertising copy. *When a Man's a Man* was announced in 1916—the Wright-Reynolds combine, with Wright now owning half the firm, followed a regular two-year cycle in publishing—another $100,000 promotion blitz resulted in advance sales reaching the 600,000 mark.

Full-page advertisements in newspapers and magazines was the main marketing strategy of Wright and Reynolds. A lesser but effective device was the placing of a postcard in each novel bearing quotations from the work and with instructions that the reader could send it to a friend, endorsing Wright's work as "one of the best I have ever read." Booksellers were supplied with stacks of the cards and collectors sought out the entire series. Wright and Reynolds also were quick to sell the rights to the novels for tent-show dramatizations, banking that those seeing the plays would purchase the books.[60] The various strategies succeeded into the 1920s, when reader interest dipped; Wright's greatest vogue had been prior to World War I, and by the time of his last book in 1942 his market had dried up entirely. Overall, his nineteen books sold some ten million copies, placing him in the top rank of best-selling authors in the first quarter of the twentieth century.

Vigorous as they were, the promotions ploys of Reynolds and Wright seem restrained when compared with those Bantam Books used on behalf of one of Max Brand's successors in western fiction, Louis L'Amour, who made his name in the 1950s and '60s with paperback originals. In 1980, now the dominant figure in westerns and a hardcover author, Bantam dispatched him on a wide-ranging journey aboard "The Louis L'Amour Overland Express," a luxury customized bus leased from a company that normally sent bands and rock singers on motorized tours. For three weeks he covered the country, meeting fans and signing copies of his seventy-five works then available (leading to a quip that the most valuable book in New York after L'Amour had passed through was any one he had written but not autographed). A continuing Bantam gimmick was the offer to readers of free wall calendars that featured the dashing covers of L'Amour's books. As with efforts on behalf of Wright, the promotions worked magnificently. At the height of their appeal L'Amour's books sold at a rate of fifteen to twenty thousand copies a day.[61]

Of course writers like Wright and L'Amour, as their sales figures attest, were in publishing leagues of their own. The books of typical authors of the period were launched without fanfare and as often as not slid quickly into oblivion—a disappointment but hardly a surprise. The regular paydays needed by independent writers were to be found more in magazine publication than in books (a situation developed in more detail in the following chapter). Scott Fitzgerald hoped the name he established with stories in the *Saturday Evening Post* and other popular magazines would carry over to his novels, boosting their sales, but as Matthew J. Bruccoli has pointed out, the two novels that sold best appeared before Fitzgerald's top period as a *Post* writer. In 1929 eight stories for the magazine earned him $31,000 while royalties on seven books brought in a total of only $31.77.[62] Fitzgerald was far from a typical writer but his experience in the marketplace, with magazines his main source of continuing income, was ordinarily the case for professional writers.

Ten

GATEKEEPERS

Dominant Editors in the
Glory Days of Magazines

It is the first business of an editor to make
other men write—not to write himself.
—George Horace Lorimer

one

Paul Revere Reynolds's early work as an agent was directed to books. As the magazine market grew ever more lucrative, the work shifted, and by 1927, as his son recalled, "the agency's great business consisted of selling the work of American writers to American magazines."[1] Magazines were where the money was, and the work in highest demand in the magazines was fiction. Large-circulation slicks dominated the high end of the market, carrying six stories or more in each issue together with novelettes and a serial novel. At the other end of the financial scale were over a hundred pulp magazines equally devoted to fiction. Popular fictioneers were able to command top fees in the $5,000 range for stories and $50,000 or better for serials. Reynolds sold work everywhere but no market compared with the weekly *Saturday Evening Post,* which printed some 250 stories and twenty to twenty-five serial novels a year and took roughly a fourth of all its fiction from his agency.

Throughout Reynolds's long career as a literary agent, which extended to his death in 1944, and on into the early 1960s the *Post* remained the most magnetic magazine market in the land. To appear regularly in its pages as the author of either fiction or nonfiction was to reach a point of well-paid professional success midway between the syndicates, Sunday newspapers, and pulp magazines on the one hand and the sober literary and intellectual journals on the other. Because it was so attractive, competition was fierce, making the *Post* as maddening a market as it was magnetic. Writers who met repeated rejection were tempted to believe that only name authors were accepted or only authors represented by influential agents like Reynolds—or tempted to reject the magazine entirely as hopelessly middlebrow or worse. Upton Sinclair, his hack-writing days behind him, fulminated for them all when he said of the *Post* that its "stuff is as standardized as soda crackers; originality is taboo, new ideas are treason, social sympathy is a crime, and the one virtue of man is to produce larger and larger quantities of material things."[2] For writers who did manage to appear regularly in its pages the *Post* could be maddening in another way: it bound them within a writing manner that had proven popular and that the magazine was reluctant to alter. Soon after he broke into the *Post* with stories Scott Fitzgerald was complaining that he would "go mad if I have to do another debutante, which is what they want."[3]

What the *Post* wanted from Fitzgerald and other writers it usually got. The magazine was simply unavoidable—as much an American staple, Isaac Marcosson remarked, as wheat.[4] Will Irwin figured that during the magazine's golden years three-quarters of the professional writers in the country who aimed for popular markets gave it first choice for their latest and finest work.[5]

The gatekeeper, the most powerful editor in the land, was George Horace Lorimer. He flourished at a time in which editors stayed in their positions for lengthy periods and placed an individual stamp on their magazines, becoming nearly as well known as the publications themselves. In 1925 the photographer Doris Ulmann caught something of the importance of magazine editors with a handsome limited-edition book of forty-three portraits accompanied by brief commentaries written by the editors. Along with Lorimer, most of the major figures of the day were represented: Frank Crowninshield of *Vanity Fair,* Robert H. Davis of *Munsey's,* Norman Hapgood of *Hearst's International,* Ray Long of *Cosmopolitan,* Ellery Sedgwick of the *Atlantic,* Robert Bridges of *Scribner's,* George Jean Nathan and H. L. Mencken of the *American Mercury.* In his commentary Mencken sounded a characteristically sour note, if a surprising one given the homage the book paid to magazine editors, by observing that the best contemporary thought was not found in magazines but in books: "Books I read constantly, as every other curious man reads them, and not infrequently I get sound information out of them or stimulating entertainment. But who ever got information or entertainment in any real and solid sense, save as a sort of miracle, out of a magazine?" Lorimer, on the other hand, the editor of the most popular magazine of all, stoutly defended the ordinary fare of mass periodicals: "Those critics who complain most loudly about the popular magazines are kept out not because their work is so good, but because it is so bad; because, though they can tear a novel to pieces in ten minutes, they cannot write one in ten years."[6]

two

The son of a notable evangelical minister in Boston, Lorimer left college for a successful business career with the Armour packing company in Chicago, then after a failed business venture of his own switched to newspaper work with Boston papers. When he learned that Cyrus H. K. Curtis had purchased the *Post* and was hunting for an editor, he sought the job and was promptly hired in 1898 for the unlikely position, given his background, of literary editor. When Lorimer came on the scene Curtis was searching not only for an editor but for a way to distinguish the nearly moribund weekly from his successful monthly, the *Ladies' Home Journal,* under the direction of Edward Bok. In Lorimer, who swiftly became the *Post's* editor in chief, he had the right man in the right place. What Lorimer lacked in magazine experience he made up for in ideas and a firm vision of the magazine's audience, one national in scope and composed of average citizens with average interests. As one student of the magazine has noted, Lorimer "would, in fact, invent the average American—some compound of nineteenth-century values and twentieth-century opportunities."[7]

In a two-page house ad appearing six months after he became editor, Lorimer set out in detail the "Post's Plans for 1900." As a magazine rather than a news weekly, the *Post* would feature a blend of timely articles, poetry, humor, reviews, and fiction. Dominating the mix, the magazine's fiction would avoid the "abnormal" and mirror instead the "healthy appetite" of its readers; it would not "force upon its readers stories for which they do not care." Although the *Post's* contributors included some of the country's foremost writers, Lorimer insisted his pages were equally open to unknown contributors. No story, he declared, "is accepted simply because it was written by a man who has been made famous by something else; and none is declined for the sole reason that the author has his reputation in front instead of behind him. The readers of the Post have indorsed this policy with no uncertain voice, and it will be continued."[8]

To make good on his promises Lorimer made the *Post* inescapably inviting to professional writers. There were no in-house staff writers and all work was submitted on a freelance basis. Fiction was read within seventy-two hours of receipt, the *Post* paid on acceptance rather than on publication, and its terms were more attractive than those offered by most magazines, including the fact that it purchased only North American rights and left writers free to market all others. Will Irwin fondly recalled the speed with which Lorimer arrived at his decisions: "I would post a short story on Monday afternoon, insuring its arrival at his office in the first mail on Tuesday. Either the rejected manuscript or a pleasant letter of acceptance would reach me on the first mail Thursday. If it was accepted, the following Tuesday brought the check and the proof."[9] Nina Wilcox Putnam thought Lorimer's policy of payment upon acceptance revolutionized the life of the professional writer, who was now treated as "a respectable citizen with rights and earning powers in full proportion to his or her ability. A decade hence the authors of America will probably erect monuments to him something like those raised in memory of Lincoln—only the slaves in this case will be starving writers, set free to enjoy their fame and their profits while they are still alive, through his far-sighted justice, and the example which his precedent has forced upon other editors all over the world."[10]

For nonfiction the *Post's* approach was necessarily different. Lorimer had strong ideas about the subjects he wanted covered and how they should be treated, which meant the magazine had to develop a dependable corps of writers, usually newspapermen or fiction writers who in time would build reputations as *Post* experts. While Lorimer's fiction policy bore fruit rapidly, bringing in material by such luminaries as Hamlin Garland, Bret Harte, Stephen Crane, Richard Harding Davis, and Rudyard Kipling, gathering a group of nonfiction specialists took longer, and in the meantime Lorimer secured articles by such famous men as ex-President Grover Cleveland and Senator Albert J. Beveridge. Eventually, skilled journalists like Sam Blythe, Isaac Marcosson, Irvin S. Cobb, Ernest Poole (who was also a *Post* fiction writer and whose 1917 book *His Family* won the first Pulitzer Prize given to a novel), Garet Garrett, Kenneth Roberts, and Will Irwin became household names through exposure in the magazine.

Lorimer had a special fondness for articles and stories about business, and when his writers were slow to warm to the subject he took up the pen himself. His "Letters from a Self-Made Merchant to His Son," the supposed correspondence between a Chicago meat packer and a son at Harvard, began running as an anonymous serial in the *Post* in 1901 and proved immensely popular. Circulation soared and the series eventually was published in book form (Lorimer's name appearing for the first time as the author), and widely translated around the world. Lorimer published two other books but it was editing the magazine that dominated his attention. He spent long hours at his desk, reading everything that would appear in the magazine, judging manuscripts by a simple standard: would the *Post's* audience like it? For all his efforts to attract and hold the best writers, he was, in Mary Roberts Rinehart's words, "a reader's editor, rather than a writer's. He knew what his audience wanted and he gave it to them."[11] The approach worked, with the magazine's circulation in the 1920s reaching 2,750,000.

Rinehart had graduated from the pulps to become one of the *Post's* premier fiction writers, in time commanding rates of $4,500 for stories and $60,000 for serials.[12] She was still at the beginning of her long attachment to the magazine when war broke out in Europe and she asked to become a correspondent; Lorimer agreed, paying her expenses and $1,000 for each article if she worked exclusively for the *Post*. By attaching herself to the Belgian Red Cross Rinehart was soon at the front lines and sending back riveting war dispatches as well as interviews with subjects ranging from Allied generals to the British royal family. Lorimer told her the articles helped boost the magazine's circulation by 50,000 a week. When she returned from the war the editor was equally quick to rekindle her enthusiasm for fiction. "War stuff is important and there are a lot of people who can write it and are writing it," he told her, "but there's only one lady who can write Tish and Deb and sich [*sic*] like things, and the country needs them quite as much as the other sort of thing right now."[13]

Eager as he was to print Rinehart's fiction, Lorimer had no hesitation in rejecting what he did not like. When he turned down a novelette, an irked Rinehart wrote him that she had accepted a $5,000 offer from *Cosmopolitan* "just in time to be obliged to refuse an offer from *McClure's* of seventy-five hundred, which is going some!" Unfazed, Lorimer replied: "So glad you have taken the money away from the Philistines and have added it to your own bankroll."[14]

Lorimer enthusiastically published Fitzgerald's flapper stories but could also turn him down cold. In June 1922 Fitzgerald told his agent, Harold Ober, that he had completed "a 25,000 word touring serial, humorous throughout, for the *Post*" that was based on the misadventures he and his wife encountered on a drive from Connecticut to Alabama in their Marmon roadster. When Lorimer rejected the serial, Fitzgerald calmly accepted the verdict. He told Ober he realized "The Cruise of the Rolling Junk" was not right technically, yet ever the practical professional he wanted to see if he could recycle the manuscript into something saleable. In time Ober sold a shortened version to *Motor* magazine for a modest $300.[15]

Ring Lardner was a prominent *Post* contributor, yet Lorimer turned down his story "The Golden Honeymoon"—a major miscalculation, as was his view that Lardner's readers expected him to stick to sports subjects. The rejection, said Dorothy Parker, "should send the gentleman down to posterity along with that little band whose members include the publisher who rejected *Pride and Prejudice,* the maid who lighted the hearth with the manuscript of Carlyle's *French Revolution,* and Mrs. O'Leary's cow."[16] Subsequently judged one of Lardner's better stories, "The Golden Honeymoon" was snapped up by *Cosmopolitan* for $1,500.

Will Irwin was a seasoned journalist who had also published short stories when Lorimer, wisely this time, suggested he have a "sustained go at fiction."[17] Irwin agreed. He had spent eight years roaming the country as a freelance magazine writer and considered himself as well connected to sources as anyone save the *Post's* Sam Blythe. At the same time he believed newspaper and magazine reporting was a job for the energetic young; it was time to settle down and make a living by never leaving his desk. When the *Post* regularly bought his fiction as well as some continuing nonfiction, Irwin concluded that Lorimer was an ideal editor. With fiction he made only small editorial changes needed to conform to the magazine's standards, and with proposals for nonfiction pieces he made decisions on the spot. Irwin recalled the typical process with the latter:

> I telephoned to Philadelphia for a half hour's appointment. Having arrived, I submitted my proposals. Number one—without a shade of hesitation he might say, "No—don't want that!" and he would give his reason. The same response, perhaps, to the second and the third. The fourth—
>
> "Yes, that looks promising. Tell me a little more." Sometimes in the middle of a sentence, he would cut me off with:
>
> "Yes, I'll take it. When can you get it in? Need any advance against expenses? All right, see the cashier!" And, there being a few minutes left of the half hour, he would use it in the gossip which he loved.[18]

But when Irwin grew restless with fiction and wanted to return to reporting in 1914 to cover the war in Europe for the *Post,* Lorimer balked. "Full up!" he was told. "Irvin Cobb, Sam Blythe, and Mary Rinehart applied ahead of you." Irwin went abroad instead for *Collier's* and the *American Magazine,* assuming—as did Lorimer—that the war would last no more than a few months. "One campaign—just one—and back to my desk," he told himself."[19] When the war dragged on Lorimer changed his mind, calling Irwin to Philadelphia and proposing that he become the *Post's* main correspondent in Europe. In return for raising his rates the magazine would get first crack at his fiction and his article ideas while Irwin would consider himself on call for ideas conceived by the magazine; further, he would not contribute articles to any other American magazine without permission. Irwin agreed, and the arrangement, making him in effect a staff writer with the magazine, lasted seven years. By 1923, when he ended his exclusive tie to the *Post,* Irwin was contributing mostly fiction. He and Lorimer had political differences over Irwin's determination to crusade in print for the League of Nations and Irwin defected to *Collier's,* which offered editorial freedom and more money. He remained hopeful that the *Post* would still buy his fiction and an occasional article unrelated to politics, and he told Lorimer that he was leaving the *Post* "with genuine personal regret. I have never had such agreeable business relations with any man."[20]

Lorimer's manner as an editor was firm and decisive at best, despotic and intimidating at worst. He was always, as some writers referred to him, the Boss. Jane Grant, the first wife of Harold Ross of the *New Yorker,* remembered an initially chilly audience with the Boss when she and a collaborator were summoned to Philadelphia after publishing articles in the *Post:*

> The great man sat at a desk at the end of a long room. The floor was covered with the thickest carpet I had ever walked upon, and before we had finished our journey down the length of the room, I felt as if I had done a day in the jungle. Our embarrassment was increased by his silence. Since no one else seemed willing to do so, I broke the stillness by looking out of the window and remarking, "Why, there's Faneuil Hall." My nervous remark did the trick, for Lorimer and Costain both laughed heartily, and Lorimer accused me of buttering him up because he was a native of Boston.[21]

Beyond the right to confer publication in the magazine, Lorimer's main tool of authority was money, and he handed it out with rigid control. The *Post's* rates were generous but Lorimer, not his contributors, determined them. He refused to be caught up in competitive bidding wars, nor could he be bullied by a writer's demand or moved by pleas of financial need. After trying, and failing, to nudge up his rates with the magazine, Will Irwin came to realize the central place of money in Lorimer's style of "absolute monarch" control: "He liked to confer bounty, not to have it screwed or wheedled out of him. Once, before I understood that peculiarity, I accompanied a manuscript with a letter asking for a raise in prices. The manuscript came back and the letter remained unanswered. Two or three more contributions, while accepted, drew the same old fee; then without further mention of the subject, he himself raised my price to a sum in excess of what I had asked."[22]

Over the years money matters caused defections by several of the *Post's* established names, usually when competing magazines dangled exclusive contracts or when Hollywood beckoned. When Churchill Williams of the *Post* wrote Jack London to inquire about his departure, London readily acknowledged the lure of big money for a freelancer: "Yes, it is a fact that I am tied up with *The Cosmopolitan* on a five-year contract that includes all my fiction, whether short stories or novels. Of course, you nor Lorimer can blame a fellow for falling for the big money, especially when said big money assures one's total fiction output for as long a period as five years. Any writer doing serial free lance stuff, is gambling all the time. More than one novel written by me in the past has entirely failed of serial publication."[23] Yet most writers who left the *Post* eventually returned, or wanted to, after their exclusive deals ran out. For his part, Lorimer could never fathom why a writer would give up the exposure the magazine provided; even a writer whose work had been rejected should wait patiently until the magazine again looked favorably on his production. All this was well understood by Mary Roberts Rinehart, who in 1931 sent Lorimer a detective novel even though she expected him to pay a reduced rate of $30,000. "I think I can get forty elsewhere," she told her husband, "but I want the *Post* audience. It is good business and has largely put me where I am."[24]

Even Lorimer's critics, those who pointed out the narrow gauge of his vision of America and the middling quality of much of the work he printed, grudgingly admired the high level of craftsmanship that was required to command the *Post's* attractive fees. There were only two classes of people, Bernard De Voto held in an article in the *Saturday Review of Literature* in 1937, who did not write for the *Post:* those who had independent means or satisfactory incomes from their other writing, and those who failed to meet Lorimer's standards. De Voto was thinking of the *Post's* fiction, which, like all fiction writing for the slick magazines, he considered a branch of the amusement industry. The purpose was simply entertainment through means of a good story.

Yet the immense technical skill that went into the fiction was a lesson for serious writers who imagined it easy to toss off a story for the *Post*. Writing for all the slicks was in fact "a craft which requires exactness, comprehension, flexibility of intelligence, and versatility of style," and within the limits of its story forms allowed a writer to "utilize all the shrewdness, humor, observation, intelligence, and skill that he possesses." In reality, De Voto concluded, "serious fiction in America owes the slicks a sizable debt for having made better writers of a considerable number of novelists."[25]

three

One of the *Post*'s main competitors during Lorimer's long reign was William Randolph Hearst's *Cosmopolitan*. The editor, Ray Long, dominated the monthly every bit as much as Lorimer the *Post*—so much so, *Fortune* magazine decided in an article in 1931, that "*Cosmopolitan* may accurately be described as the book that Mr. Long makes."[26] At the time of his death in 1935 the *New York Times* noted that Long was said to have known more American writers than any of his contemporaries with the possible exceptions of Lorimer and Robert Davis.

A former newspaperman who had edited *Red Book* before taking over in 1918 as the head of *Cosmopolitan* as well as editor in chief of all the Hearst magazines, Long engineered a determined raid on the *Post*'s stable of writers in the early twenties that drew off a number of prominent figures, among them London, Cobb, Lardner, and Peter B. Kyne. Money and long-term commitments were the enticements. "For your next six short stories," Long wrote to Lardner in 1924, "$3,000, or, for your next twelve short stories, to be delivered at intervals of not more that 45 days, $3,500."[27] Lorimer tried to remain unflappable over the defections, telling one of his writers that "Ray Long has been making the rounds of the Post men in an earnest endeavor to segregate those whom he considers the key writers; but I am not at all concerned about that as I have a stable full of exceedingly promising young colts." He added, referring to the money Long was casting about, "I have been, and always shall be, willing to go along on price except when that particular razor is selected in an effort to cut my throat."[28]

As an editor Long was believed to have an uncanny sense of popular literary taste, especially in fiction, which enabled him to keep pace with swings of public interest.[29] He himself disclaimed any special insight into the reading public, saying he was simply "an average American, with the reading taste of the average American."[30] He read some quarter-million words of manuscript each week and scoured the country and Europe for new writers. For each issue of *Cosmopolitan* he printed the best material he had on hand, never holding back for the future, and making all final judgments himself. Lincoln Steffens once sent him from Europe a story by Hemingway, then an unknown young journalist and fiction writer, called "My Old Man" that had strong echoes of Sherwood Anderson's work. Steffens admired the story enough to forward it on his own initiative, but his reputation as a writer did not carry enough weight to cause Long to buy.[31] (Lorimer also had a chance to print Hemingway's early work. In 1925 Hemingway sent him the story "The Undefeated" with a cover letter in which, trying to sell the editor on the work, he explained that he himself had "never read a real bull fight story, one written without bunk, from the inside by some one who really knew bull fighting."[32] Lorimer declined to buy.)

Later, Hemingway's name established, Long went after his work. When Maxwell Perkins brought up the possibility of serializing his current novel, *A Farewell to Arms,* in *Scribner's* magazine, Hemingway had to report that he had "quite gratuitously promised Ray Long I would let him have the first look at my next book if I decided to serialize it. I did this to shut them up when they were worrying me with propositions while I was working." He added that he preferred serializing in *Scribner's* if the difference in pay was "a few thousand—2 or 3."[33] In the end he stayed with *Scribner's,* telling Perkins that "I imagine when I see Ray Long or some of his under Rays I can fix it up with them as you suggest."[34]

At the time of the *Fortune* article in 1931, *Cosmopolitan's* monthly circulation stood at an impressive 1.7 million. The magazine was receiving some three thousand manuscripts a month, buying twenty to thirty, and paying rates up to $3,000 for articles, $5,000 for stories, and $40,000 for serials. Long himself was said to eclipse Lorimer and every other editor in the world in salary.[35] With *Red Book* Long had discovered the fiction of Edgar Rice Burroughs and James Oliver Curwood, and his list of name authors with *Cosmopolitan* included, among American writers, Booth Tarkington, Sinclair Lewis, Theodore Dreiser, Louis Bromfield, and Edna Ferber as well as London and Lardner. He also took credit for starting the vogue for "short short" stories in popular magazines. Long's stable of nonfiction writers was never as impressive. At the height of his power in 1931 and just after the appearance of the *Fortune* article, Long resigned, ostensibly to pursue a career in book publishing. His firm failed, and in 1935, while working as a screenwriter and editor in Hollywood, he took his own life. According to a front-page story in the *New York Times* about his death, Long had been despondent about the direction of his new career.

Long's successor on *Cosmopolitan*, Harry Payne Burton, had made his reputation at *McCall's*. A former feature writer for the Newspaper Enterprise Association syndicate in Cleveland, Burton had come to *McCall's* in 1921 with a mandate to enliven the women's magazine by bringing to its pages some of the star writers then appearing in other slick magazines. Among those he attracted were Tarkington, Mary Roberts Rinehart, Zane Grey, and Harold Bell Wright. Money was rarely an object. To Gene Stratton-Porter he paid out $75,000 for serial rights to a novel, and on the nonfiction side he gave Hendrick Willem Van Loon $30,000 for serial rights to the *Story of the Bible*. To Hemingway he made an offer in 1936 of $40,000 for serial rights to his next novel, $7,500 for long stories, $3,000 for short ones.[36] The approach worked, putting *McCall's* on the route to the three million in circulation it reached by 1940. When he replaced Long at *Cosmopolitan* during the Depression years Burton continued a policy of seeking out big names with big money. Sinclair Lewis's later novels appeared in the magazine, as did nonfiction by Ida Tarbell, in an editorial mix that in the thirties usually included a book-length novel, a novelette, six short stories, and eight or so nonfiction articles. By the 1940s *Cosmopolitan*'s circulation had picked up from a Depression dip and stood at the two-million mark.

four

After his retirement in 1936 Lorimer did consulting work for the *Reader's Digest*, the first of several *Post* editors to wind down their careers with the upstart periodical that in the 1920s and '30s amassed the largest circulation of any American magazine lacking pictures, fiction, or advertising.[37] The brainchild of DeWitt Wallace, like Lorimer the son of an eminent minister (who was also president of Macalester College in Minnesota), the *Reader's Digest* made its appearance in February 1922. Its sixty-four pages were devoted, as the cover proclaimed, to "Thirty-One articles each month [one for each day of the longest months] from leading magazines—each article of enduring value and interest, in condensed and compact form." The idea of a magazine sampler was not new but condensing reprints was—and, in the busy twenties and under competition for print from radio and the movies, it was an idea right for the time.

Major magazines had all begun to shorten articles and experiment with very brief short stories. What was unusual about the *Digest* was that it was devoted to fact in an age in which fiction flourished in periodicals. Wallace was convinced that the nation hungered most for information, and especially information of the self-improvement variety that could be served up painlessly. By 1926 the *Digest*'s circulation had reached twenty thousand and in the the next three years would increase an amazing tenfold. Soon foreign editions appeared together with an ancillary empire that included record and condensed-book clubs.

As the *Digest* grew in size and subscription list, editors (mostly experienced hands from other magazines) trooped to the headquarters in Pleasantville, New York, and later to a leafy campus-like setting in Chappaqua, for well-paid employment. Since it carried no advertising, the *Digest* was not required to make public its circulation, and Wallace made every effort to keep the magazine's success—and, as a result, the numbers of subscribers, actual or potential, he was drawing from the magazines he reprinted—veiled in secrecy. Eventually he turned to blanket fees with magazines for exclusive rights to reprint from their pages, an arrangement that brought in more money for the magazines while squeezing out potential *Digest* imitators. In the early years only William Randolph Hearst seems to have fully understood the *Digest* as a stiff competitor and refused to allow reprinting from any of his publications.

For writers the *Digest* was found money. Although they might squirm over editorial reduction of their work, an article in the magazine meant another paycheck without added effort, the reprint fee ordinarily split with the original publication. In the Depression years a good situation got better. As the economy took a toll on the magazines canvased by the *Digest,* the editors turned to two new kinds of material—reprints of articles actually conceived by *Digest* editors and planted in magazines with which it had a reprint agreement, and genuinely original articles. The first of the original pieces was a signed article in February 1933 by Henry Morton Robinson, a young English professor at Columbia who would become a *Digest* editor and a popular novelist.

In that year Charles W. Ferguson, an editor of religious books for the George H. Doran Company, sent a thank-you note to the *Digest* for a $12.50 check that had come to him as half of a reprint fee for an article in *Harper's*. Wallace responded by telling Ferguson the *Digest* meant to carry some original pieces and asked him for suggestions. The magazine eventually bought six articles from Ferguson and later he joined the staff, becoming an "originals" editor (as against "pickups" from other magazines) who oversaw the planting of articles.

The *Digest* would approach a client magazine with a story idea and offer to pay a writer's first-serial fee and expenses in return for reprint rights, which it also paid for, after the story was published. Ordinarily the writer came from a group approved by the *Digest* editors. At times the procedure worked the other way, a magazine proposing an article to the *Digest,* which then developed and paid all costs on the way to its "preprinting" in the magazine. For the *Digest,* planting articles was a way of getting the material it wanted while maintaining the pretense of being a reprint publication; equally important, it gave reprint material a gloss of importance by virtue of its prior appearance in respected magazines such as *Harper's,* the *Atlantic,* the *Nation,* and the *New Republic.* Despite a continuing decline in the number of American magazines, the *Digest* persevered in planting or preprinting articles until the middle 1970s, when the practice was stopped and originals, now making up most of the periodical's contents, were frankly presented as such.

The *Digest* was paying up to $2,500 for articles in the thirties and forties but attracting only a few of the country's top freelance writers. Some of the big names in its pages—Ida Tarbell, for one—were on the downside of their careers and happy for any exposure. Writing for the *Digest* meant accepting tight space limits and heavy editing; even in the early days of the magazine's existence it came to seem a comfortable but inescapably certain way of selling out. To bolster his roster of writers Wallace went after such prominent stylists as the *New Yorker's* E. B. White and Alexander Woollcott. Woollcott, who actually did some writing for the *Digest* and for a time was listed on the masthead as a roving editor, was once offered $24,000 for a year's work on a column to be composed of brief glimpses of American life. Woollcott died shortly thereafter but a regular column, "Life in These United States," would become a popular *Digest* feature.[38]

An equally improbable writer snared by Wallace was Max Eastman, the former radical editor of the *Masses* who had turned his back on communism and swung to the political right. An article in the *Digest,* "Socialism Does Not Gibe with Human Nature," brought down on him the wrath of left-wing intellectuals but there was consolation in the money Wallace waved in his direction. Eventually Eastman was invited to lunch at headquarters, where Wallace told him, "You write so beautifully that I'm sure you can write for us." When Eastman outlined a series called "Men with Ideas," Wallace instantly agreed and proposed that Eastman become a roving editor: "We will pay you a living wage, and we won't tell you whom to write about. You pick your own subjects, write as you please and send us your expense account."[39] Eastman never wrote the series but did become a *Digest* roving editor, a position—as he explained in his autobiography, *Love and Revolution*—that had nothing to do with editing the magazine but meant he was a "contributor on salary, a man actually paid money to roam the earth, and the libraries, and his mind if he has one, in search of exciting facts and bright ideas."[40]

Roving editors on monthly stipends was a Wallace inspiration introduced in 1940.[41] The first three—Barclay Acheson, Karl Detzer, Paul Palmer—appeared on the masthead that year, and by the 1960s the number had reached nineteen. Most worked within specific fields: Paul de Kruif, a research bacteriologist and the figure Sinclair Lewis had drawn on for his portrait of Martin Arrowsmith in *Arrowsmith,* was a prolific author of medical stories; Donald Culross Peattie was a resident naturalist; Francis Vivian Drake handled aviation stories. The roving editors did their own legwork and research, and the *Digest* had first call on articles, which were written to full length and left to in-house editors to check and condense. In addition to designated roving editors, Wallace kept other writers on retainers, building up a core of regulars meant to resemble those gathered by S. S. McClure and Lorimer.

If there was a stigma attached to writing for the *Digest,* the generous rates —whether in the form of monthly retainers, fees from pick-ups, or sales of originals—were always pleasant compensation. John R. Tunis, who ordinarily concentrated on sports stories, was sent by the *Saturday Evening Post* during World War II to do an article on Robert M. Hutchins of the University of Chicago. The fee was $1,200 plus $250 expenses. When the magazine turned down the finished article Tunis took it to the *Digest,* where it sold immediately, Wallace wiring him: "Best piece on education we ever received. Check for two thousand in the mail."[42] In 1948 *Harper's* paid $500 for a long article from John Bartlow Martin on a mine disaster in Centralia, Illinois, and played it as a lead story. When the *Digest* picked up the story for reprinting in condensed form Martin was paid $2,500.[43]

five

Given the yawning chasm between their publications, it could be expected that DeWitt Wallace and Harold Ross would find themselves at odds. The *New Yorker* had a reprint agreement with the *Reader's Digest* and its material was frequently picked up, a practice Ross frowned on though his writers, naturally enough, supported it. James Thurber, a *Digest* favorite, pointed out that the *Digest* paid five times more for reprint rights than Ross did for first-serial rights.[44] But whatever his writers thought, Ross resisted the *Digest*'s practice of planting articles, this despite the attractive fees it brought in and the fact the *Digest* actually used only a portion of the material it paid for from his and other magazines.

In 1944 Ross put his foot down entirely. A letter bearing his unique stamp went out to all *New Yorker* contributors announcing a total break with the *Digest*:

> The *Digest* started out as a reprint magazine but grew into something quite different. Nowadays a large proportion of its contents is frankly original with the *Digest* and not presented as reprint material; and of the stuff that is reprinted as reprint material much actually originates in the office of the *Digest* and then gets farmed out to some other magazine for first publication. The effect of this (apart from spreading a lot of money around) is that the *Digest* is beginning to generate a considerable fraction of the contents of American magazines. This gives us the creeps. . . . If the *Digest* wants to publish a magazine of original material, it should do so in a direct manner. We believe it should not operate through other publications to keep alive the reprint myth. We don't want to be in the position of receiving for consideration a manuscript that has already been bought and paid for by some one else, for we regard such a situation as unhealthy. We were willing to be digested, but we are not willing to be first supplied, then digested.[45]

In fact, the reprint agreement with the *Digest* had already been terminated by the *New Yorker*'s publisher, Raoul Fleischmann, and in the letter Ross may have been trying to justify the break and thereby placate unhappy writers who were losing reprint fees.[46] Whatever his reasoning, the letter was considered a high-minded stand for editorial independence, generating a wave of resistance to the *Digest* that caused other magazines to end reprint arrangements.

Writing for the *Digest* meant money whereas writing for the *New Yorker* meant money plus prestige. At first, though, it meant neither. The year the magazine began publishing, 1925, was a miraculous one in literary circles—the year of *The Great Gatsby, In Our Time, Soldier's Pay, Manhattan Transfer, The Professor's House, Arrowsmith,* and *An American Tragedy.* The *New Yorker,* on the other hand, was what Thurber termed the "outstanding flop of 1925."[47] But thanks to Fleischmann's persistence as the chief backer, the thin and undistinguished weekly survived its start and soon became one of the most glamorous periodical markets. Appearing in its pages meant a writer had passed muster with the most demanding of editors—first Ross, the founder and editor for twenty-five years, then William Shawn, his successor. It meant a writer could produce copy at once accurate, grammatical, clear, witty, and stylish. He could, in short, write.

Except in his success as an editor, Ross bore no resemblance to Lorimer or Wallace. He was a rough-hewn Westerner ("often as rude as a Fifth Avenue bus driver," one of his early writers said of him)[48] who had kicked around on newspapers and magazines before developing a weekly that prided itself on brisk urban sophistication. The *New Yorker's* prospectus outlined a magazine whose tone would be gay and satirical, and whose audience would be narrowly metropolitan; yet the magazine evolved into something more, a sophisticated literary magazine that printed the best reporting, fiction, humor, and criticism available. Unlike the *Saturday Evening Post* and the *Reader's Digest,* it was not edited for the taste and values of middle-class or middlebrow America—for, as Ross put it in the now-legendary remark in the prospectus, the old lady in Dubuque[49]—but for the taste and values of Ross himself and the skilled staff he assembled.

In the several accounts written of him Ross emerges as a quirky but instinctive editor who through trial and error and a good deal of confusion forged the magazine's blend of integrity, wit, and high style. Writers responded to him with anger and devotion, yet all seemed convinced that he understood and respected ability. "It was certainly not the least of Ross's talents," Shawn said of him, "that he was able to see talent in writers and artists before it was plainly visible to everyone. Also, he understood that talent developed more slowly in some than in others, and he was willing to wait. He gradually learned that the primary function of the magazine's editors, including him, was to create a structure and an atmosphere—a little world apart from the world—within which the writers and artists could fulfill themselves."[50] One of Shawn's many predecessors as the magazine's managing editor under Ross, Ralph Ingersoll, said of the founder that his "one amazing right instinct was the instinct for detecting what was phony. The magazine grew, a monument to thousands and thousands of tiny prejudices, nearly all of which are astonishingly worthy."[51]

Some of Ross's witty friends from the Algonquin Round Table had appeared in the prospectus as advisory editors but provided little help when the magazine began printing. Dorothy Parker sent a few things, but her "Constant Reader" book reviews would not begin appearing for two years. (According to Ray Long, Parker was "the most promising writer in the world" because ". . . she'll promise anything to any editor. She has such a kind heart that she can't refrain from promising them. But try to get her to deliver! Just try!")[52] Robert Benchley's theater criticism would come even later, as would Alexander Woollcott's "Shouts and Murmurs" page. Pressed for material, Ross called on agents, buttonholed friends and anyone with a manuscript or an idea, searched through newspapers and other magazines. In an era of high magazine rates, his at the start were low. But he had little fascination with name writers, even if he could have afforded them, and he opened the magazine to fresh talent. In time he found it—or it found him.

Among the first to team up with Ross on a regular basis was Morris Markey. A young reporter on the *New York World,* he was persuaded to handle a department called "In the News," in which he would write up intriguing or atmospheric bits and pieces ordinarily bypassed by the newspapers. At Ross's suggestion Markey later developed a press column examining New York's newspapers, "The Current Press," that evolved into "The Wayward Press," an acclaimed *New Yorker* department. "In the News" gave way to "A Reporter at Large," a title Markey thought up for factual articles generally told from the detached viewpoint of an implied observer and marked by a casual air together with some of fiction's mannerisms, a form of nonfiction writing that would deeply influence other magazines. For a long time the Reporter at Large pieces were written by Markey alone, the material gathered in an evening and written the next morning. As the pieces became longer and more involved, others tried their hand, and in time some of the magazine's best-known writers (A. J. Liebling, Joseph Mitchell, Philip Hamburger, E. J. Kahn, Jr., Brendan Gill, St. Clair McKelway) turned out its lengthy fact pieces.

John R. Tunis was one of the early writers who came looking for work. Ross already had someone writing sports but gave Tunis a chance to improve coverage, and in April 1925 his column, running up to a thousand words, began appearing in the back of the magazine. The pay was $50 a column. Tunis branched out into Reporter at Large pieces and Profiles—a form developed from the interview articles Isaac Marcosson had published in the *Saturday Evening Post* and that Alva Johnston would polish into another *New Yorker* specialty—for which his top pay into the early thirties was $200. His first Profile, about the football hero Red Grange, brought a note from Ross along with a check: "Excellent piece; somewhat exciting." The qualification gave him pause, but Tunis was ecstatic when he was offered a bonus of $200 whenever he sold the magazine six long stories in a twelve-month period. "It was earth-shaking," he remembered. "No editor had done this before."[53]

Like many a *New Yorker* writer after him, Tunis squirmed under Ross's tight editing, his copy coming back with scores of "wild-eyed curlicues with comments" in the margins. In his obsessive editing Ross resembled *Vanity Fair*'s Frank Crowninshield, who was said to edit his incoming mail before tossing it in the wastebasket. But while Crowninshield liked to dabble in fiction by supplying young writers with the elements of plots ("Take that vase. It is a rare porcelain and was formerly in a Buddhist temple in Burma. You steal it. Spies follow you. You smuggle it into Mexico. There you meet this young architect—you see, there's your plot!"),[54] Ross's passion was for facts. He insisted that everything be checked, and he had a maddening but effective way of making his writers explain the most ordinary matters. "Don't get" became an overly familiar Ross margin notation. Tunis was exasperated when his copy was returned for more work but usually admitted Ross was right. "Everyone learned the agony of creation," he remembered, "by submitting material to his none too tender mercies."[55]

Others in the early band of *New Yorker* regulars were Howard Brubaker, Lois Long, Elmer Davis, Robert Simon, G. F. T. Ryall, and Janet Flanner. Ring Lardner, who said (with tongue in cheek perhaps since at the time he was scrambling for money) he would rather write for the *New Yorker* at five cents a word than *Cosmopolitan* at a dollar, was an early contributor, writing relaxed autobiographical pieces and, later, his radio criticism. E. B. White, James Thurber, and Wolcott Gibbs joined as staff editors. John O'Hara appeared in 1928 when the magazine printed a two-hundred-word monologue he had submitted and for which he was paid $15. That year, age twenty-three and a New York newspaperman, O'Hara sold the magazine eleven more "casuals," Ross's catch-all term for brief prose pieces that did not appear in departments. After he was fired from his newspaper job O'Hara tried to catch on as a reporter for the Talk of the Town department, but it was as an author of casuals that he kept his connection with the magazine. In 1929 he had twenty-five accepted and the next year another twenty-one. Most were brief, often monologues, and essentially sketches, but they opened the way to the O'Hara short stories that came to epitomize the *New Yorker* style of thinly-plotted, understated, elliptical fiction. A biographer, Matthew J. Bruccoli, suggests that Ross and editors like Gibbs and Katharine Angell (who later married E. B. White) helped formulate such stories; in any case, O'Hara became the magazine's most prolific practitioner of the form, so much so that the *New Yorker* stamp on his stories made them virtually impossible to place in other magazines.[56]

Thurber had behind him a newspaper background and a period in France during which, after trying and failing to write a novel, he worked on the Paris edition of the *Chicago Tribune*. In New York in the summer of 1926 and sending short pieces to the *New Yorker*, he found them coming back with a speed that suggested the magazine had a rejection machine. Later he found that in effect it did, a man named John Chapin Mosher. According to Thurber, Mosher looked like a professor of English literature who hadn't approved of the writing of anyone since Sir Thomas Browne. "It was in the always slightly lunatic tradition of the *New Yorker*," Thurber wrote, "that he had been made first reader of the manuscripts of unknown writers. In the years that followed, we became friends, but I never had lunch with him that he didn't say, over his coffee, 'I must get back to the office and reject.'"[57]

Thurber broke the ice of rejection with a poem, then a satirical piece about a man who became famous after going around and around in a revolving door and setting a world endurance record.[58] He sold the magazine other pieces, but when he heard Ross was looking for staff members he stopped by the office and was hired. What Ross wanted was a "Jesus," or a managing editor, to run the editorial operation of the magazine with machine-like efficiency, a position for which Thurber was eminently unqualified, as he knew and Ross eventually realized. "Writers are a dime a dozen, Thurber," Ross insisted. "What I want is an editor." But Thurber wanted to write and Ross finally caved in. "All right then, if you're a writer, write! Maybe you've got something to say." As a writer Thurber went through another kind of ordeal with Ross. "Thurber's worked too long on newspapers," Ross complained. "He can't write Talk the way I want it. He'll always write journalese." Months went by before a Talk of the Town piece of Thurber's appeared without Ross's editorial tinkering, and even longer before his casuals and whimsical drawings became regular features of the magazine.

During its rocky early period the *New Yorker* offered some contributors stock in lieu of cash. When Tunis was made the offer in return for his $50-a-week sports column, he declined—a major blunder, he realized, when the magazine turned the corner to success. By 1934 it was receiving up to 1,200 manuscripts a week and eclipsing the *Saturday Evening Post* in the amount of advertising it carried. Its estimated profit for that year was $600,000, according to Ralph Ingersoll in a long, breezy, and mostly laudatory *Fortune* article in 1934 in which he neglected to mention that he had been the *New Yorker's* managing editor. The magazine's financial situation, Ingersoll pointed out, allowed it to boost the money it paid to contributors, but still it was not a place where writers were likely to get rich. He put the earnings of such top contrib-utor-editors as White and Thurber in the $11,000 range,[59] or somewhat more than popular *Saturday Evening Post* fictioneers could earn from two short sto-ries. For ordinary contributors the magazine could set its own rates since the work it wanted was not easily marketed elsewhere. Ingersoll thought the word rate actually equalled that of the *Post,* but since most *New Yorker* pieces were short (Profiles, the longest, running up to 3,600 words) and editing could be heavy (except, Ingersoll noted, for certain sacred cows), final payment was modest.

To insure an inner group of dependable contributors Ross eventually put his top fact writers on drawing accounts. As described by Dale Kramer, the system was not an entirely comfortable one:

> Writers and artists drew fixed weekly stipends or lump sums, as they chose, which were liquidated when contributions were accepted. This provided a degree of se-curity, and, for the larger producers at least, went a long way toward solving the free lance's problem. Some were not happy. They likened themselves to sharecrop-pers who go to the landlords for loans to pay grocery bills and repay them out of their crop—if they get a crop.
>
> Artists or writers whose crops didn't come in were left in debt. The magazine thus did not *guarantee* anything. If, for example, a writer were assigned to a profile and the material proved inadequate, he took the loss. A newspaper reporter would have drawn his salary no matter what happened. The strain of sitting at a type-writer, palms sweating, trying to work out of debt by being amusing, was too much for some and they cracked.[60]

Although Ross was lenient with drawing-account debt, writers who got few acceptances over a year or so were expected to drift off—and if acceptances came eventually to pay something on their accounts.

On the fiction side the *New Yorker* used another scheme to bind writers to it—a first-reading agreement whereby a writer gave the magazine the right of first refusal on all work in return for a yearly payment. Pay for acceptance de-pended on length and other variables, and Ross offered bonuses to writers who sold the magazine six stories in a year. John O'Hara, the magazine's prickly star of the short story ("Once you have finished a story," he advised a fellow writer, "there's only one way to improve it: tell the editor to go to hell"),[61] once agi-tated for a scheme in which he would be paid something even when his con-tributions were rejected. When Ross balked O'Hara left the magazine for a decade.[62] A writer of fact pieces, Geoffrey Hellman, who pushed Ross for higher pay (including, in *New Yorker* jargon, pay for "breakage," or stories that had not worked out), received from the editor a long memorandum that pointed out the perilous nature of professional writing despite the cushions the magazine provided:

> Writers are small-businessmen in the last analysis, manufacturing and selling their wares, and are subject to the lonely responsibilities and hazards of small-business-men. I don't see how it can be otherwise. I've been in the business of buying things from writers and artists for thirty years and have never worked out a workable scheme to pay writers' and artists' salaries, to remove them from the state of being a free-lance, or a small-businessman. . . . No other magazine has ever worked out a scheme for paying writers except by the piece. This magazine made an effort to beat this game a couple of years ago, an effort that will be a final one so far as I am concerned, I trust. Shawn worked out a scheme that guaranteed writers a certain income for exclusive services, and I approved it. It collapsed immediately. It was cried down by writers because of the exclusive services provision. . . . Writers want their independence, to a greater or less extent, or the right to it. I don't blame them for this. I am now glad the scheme failed, for it cleared the air, and convinced me once and for all that nothing can be done to better the cruel fundamentals of the magazine-writer relationship. . . . You don't have, you say, "much security." That is true, but who does? You have as much security as I have. There is no such thing as security, and that's that.[63]

When Shawn followed Ross as editor the magazine came close to provid-ing contributors with the security Ross had thought so chimerical. Shawn cre-ated a "literary empire," as one observer called it, of around 140 writers on contract, divided almost equally between writers of fiction and nonfiction.[64] Drawn individually, the contracts called for an annual stipend in return for which writers gave the magazine first refusal on all work, though for nonfic-tion writers rejections were rare since subjects were approved in advance. While at work writers had generous drawing accounts—in effect, weekly pay-checks if they chose—to meet living expenses. The amount of payment for accepted work was at Shawn's discretion—a matter of continuing rumor on the magazine, as it was in Ross's day, since no one knew for sure what others were getting—and there were bonuses for pieces the editor particularly liked. *New Yorker* writers, in Shawn's view, should not have to write for other mag-azines in order to make ends meet. Contract writers also came under the mag-azine's health, life insurance, and retirement plans, and they kept all proceeds from the sale of their work in the "aftermarkets" of books, movies, or an-thologies, with the magazine providing a staff to assist in such sales.

From a writer's standpoint, the only irritant in Shawn's warm embrace was that the purchase of a story or article did not lead immediately to publication. The editor was so obsessed, or so some believed, with building up a storehouse of work that years could pass before a piece actually appeared in print. At an Authors Guild seminar in 1985, E. J. Kahn, Jr., complained that due to the backlog of purchased material "it's almost impossible to get your pieces into the magazine no matter how good you may think they are, no matter how good the editors may think they are . . . and no matter how well they pay you for it." He added: "No matter how handsomely one may get paid for a piece that isn't published, the subject of the piece, particularly if it's a profile and one has spent days, hours, weeks, months bothering the hell out of a subject, the subject will never quite believe that you wrote the piece, that it got bought, that it got praised, and that it isn't going to run because there are fifty other writers competing for the space."[65]

six

"But if ever a magazine sounded like useless balls this one does," Ernest Hemingway wrote Maxwell Perkins at Scribner's in 1929. "Am doing it for Archy—how he got mixed up with them God knows."[66]

The magazine was Henry Luce's luxurious new business monthly *Fortune*, launched with regrettable timing in the year following the market crash, yet a success from the start. What Hemingway was doing was an article for the magazine on the economic aspects of Spanish bullfighting that would appear in March 1930 under the title "Bullfighting, Sport and Industry" with lavish illustration of paintings and etchings by Spanish artists. And Archy was his friend from Paris days, the poet Archibald MacLeish, who had just taken an editorial job with the magazine and had approached Hemingway about doing the article. The young writer had amply revealed his knowledge of bullfighting in newspaper articles for the *Toronto Star Weekly* and in his first novel, *The Sun Also Rises*.

Looking back, it is hard to square the involvement of writers like Hemingway and MacLeish with one of the entrenched organs of corporate culture. The "useless balls" remark suggests not only Hemingway's unbuttoned epistolary style but the traditional stance of writers to big business, let alone to "a romance of business magazine," as Hemingway would describe *Fortune* to Perkins.[67] But as MacLeish noted toward the end of his life, one had to keep in mind the difference between the magazine then and now. Then, infatuated with writers and good writing, it assembled one of the most talented staffs ever attached to an American magazine. Then, as another of its writers remarked, it was "a magazine of business—plus" that tried to acquaint the Philistine businessman with "worlds he never knew."[68]

In Hemingway's one-shot experience *Fortune* paid a solid Depression-period fee of $1,000 for 2,500 words of what turned out to be a flat account of the business of bullfighting. It was "written in journalese full of statistics," Perkins was told, and intentionally kept as "dull as possible," though there was possibility in the subject for something better,[69] as Hemingway would demonstrate later with his nonfiction treatise on the world of the corrida, *Death in the Afternoon*. MacLeish's staff job paid equally well. Henry Luce had followed the same path that had taken MacLeish to Hotchkiss and Yale, and although the two had never met Luce had presumably kept track of MacLeish's shift from a Boston law office to Paris and a full-time pursuit of poetry. When he was organizing *Fortune,* a solo venture after founding *Time* with Briton Hadden, he asked MacLeish to join the staff as one of the editors, meaning one of the in-house writers. MacLeish was interested but wanted to finish his long poem *Conquistador,* so Luce offered an arrangement that allowed him to work on the magazine long enough each year to pay his bills and have the rest of the time off for poetry. In October 1929 MacLeish joined *Fortune* at a salary of $5,000 for half-time work, and for the nine years he spent with the magazine his unusual arrangement with Luce held.

Behind the hiring was Luce's notion of proper writers for a business magazine. Originally he planned to use contributors with established reputations, then switched to the view that the magazine should be essentially staff written. In this, together with a lack of by-lines, it would resemble *Time,* though its stories would be longer and its prose better. "It will be brilliantly written," Luce said in outlining the magazine. "It will have *Time's* bursting-with-fact, economical, objective merits, but the language will be smoother, more sophisticated, which combination of virtues can be obtained because there will be far more time to assemble the facts, write, edit." The writers Luce wanted would be enthusiastic amateurs rather than experienced economic journalists, writers capable of looking beyond numbers to the excitement of commercial life and the personalities of the board rooms. "There are men who can write poetry," he declared, "and there are men who can read balance sheets. The men who can read balance sheets cannot write. That, happily with some exceptions, is the general rule." It was, he added, "easier to turn poets into business journalists than to turn bookkeepers into writers."[70] When MacLeish had informed Luce that he knew nothing about business, Luce replied that this was exactly why he wanted him for the magazine.

In addition to MacLeish, Luce hired fellow poets Russell Davenport and James Agee—and Hart Crane would also have a brief encounter with the magazine. Others who joined the staff for short or long periods were critics Dwight Macdonald, Louis Kronenberger, and Alfred Kazin; novelists James Gould Cozzens, Robert Cantwell, Charles Wertenbaker, and Green Peyton; the economist John Kenneth Galbraith; and such able journalists as Wilder Hobson, John Chamberlain, and Eric Hodgins (a Massachusetts Institute of Technology graduate who would become *Fortune*'s managing editor, its publisher, and in 1946 author of the popular novel *Mr. Blandings Builds His Dream House*). The likelihood of employment was increased by having gone to Luce's *alma mater,* but flair with words mattered more. Macdonald, a Yale product, remembered Luce's standard writing test in which a prospective staff member was "set at a desk, handed two fat wads of news clips and research on two different subjects, and told to write eight hundred words or so on each."[71]

There were no guidelines on how to write a *Fortune* article other than writing it well. Luce said in a memo: "We don't care much how it's written: it could be written sixteen different ways and still be a good *Fortune* story. Furthermore, it can be about almost anything from an essay on the Gold Standard to a description of the method of making tomato juice in Alaska. All we care is that it should be a knockout *Fortune* story." When he became the magazine's managing editor, Ralph Ingersoll simply told writers to "just put all the material about the same subject in the same place."[72] For the hapless, though, editorial criticism could be scathing. "This draft," Hodgins informed a writer, "*subtracts* from the sum total of human knowledge."[73]

MacLeish was *Fortune*'s star performer. "Just throw the switch and let her run" he maintained about the good copy he produced with ease.[74] In his *Fortune* career he wrote nearly a hundred stories on subjects ranging from apple pie to farm strikes to New York skyscrapers. "He arrived every morning at 9 a.m. on the dot," Hodgins recalled, "wrote (or thought) steadily all day long and left at 5:30, with reams of copy behind him. Most unpoetlike."[75] Agee was MacLeish's opposite, a slow, agonized, night-owl writer, but, as Hodgins noted, he "could do it—if he were watched like a hawk so that he would not disappear into some private dreamland."[76] Agee wrote stories about the Tennessee Valley authority, cockfighting, and commercial orchids, and in 1936 went into the Deep South with the photographer Walker Evans to investigate cotton tenancy for a series on poor Americans. The pair were gone two months, twice as long as the magazine intended; the report Agee wrote was not what the magazine had in mind either. It was ten times longer than asked for and, according to Macdonald, "pessimistic, unconstructive, impractical, indignant, lyrical, and always personal."[77] *Fortune* killed the article, but reworked by Agee it was published with Evans's photographs by Houghton Mifflin in 1941 as *Let Us Now Praise Famous Men* and in later years took on the stature of a nonfiction classic.

Macdonald, along with MacLeish one of *Fortune's* most ardent liberals, had an uneasy stay with the magazine from its first issue until 1936 when he resigned in protest over editorial changes in his final article of a controversial series about U.S. Steel.[78] "Thank God," he said about his always anonymous pieces in the magazine, "the readable junk I turned out at least didn't have my name on it"; on another occasion he quipped that as a writer he had "sold but not, with one large exception, out"—the exception being his years with *Fortune*.[79] In the *Nation* a year after he left *Fortune* Macdonald turned his wrath on the Luce empire. On *Fortune* a gap was widening, he insisted, between Luce's conservative views and the liberal attitude of *Fortune's* key writers. To write for the magazine one needed "literary ability plus some competence in handling masses of factual data," a combination of skills that Macdonald thought naturally bred liberal tendencies. After some political openness due to its Depression beginning, Luce had tried to shift *Fortune* to the right; if he prevailed, Macdonald warned, he could find himself with a magazine but no real writers.[80]

Hart Crane withdrew from the magazine for the more elemental reason that he failed to complete a usable *Fortune* article. After the publication of his long poem *The Bridge,* MacLeish and Davenport thought Crane would be the ideal writer for an article on the George Washington Bridge. Parker Lloyd-Smith, the magazine's first managing editor, agreed and met with Crane to discuss both the bridge article and a biographical piece on J. Walter Teagle, the president of Standard Oil. Crane set out on the projects with enthusiasm, enjoying the interviewing and the legwork, but when it came time to write the bridge article he was stopped cold. MacLeish was called in and the two worked out an outline but Crane still failed to produce. The Teagle article went only slightly better. "I managed to keep the oil king talking far beyond the time allotted," Crane wrote in a letter, "but when I came to write it up in typical *Fortune* style the jams gather by the hundred." He finished a draft of the article and sent it to the magazine, but when it was returned it disappeared, Crane claiming it was stolen from his mailbox. His *Fortune* career was over. "As things turned out with *Fortune*," Crane concluded, "I might better have surrendered earlier than I did, but at the time I thought the chances worth hazarding."[81]

James Gould Cossens could produce *Fortune* material but had little interest in doing so. He had written for the slick magazines, published novels, and had the good fortune of having a wife who was a literary agent with Brandt and Brandt when he joined *Fortune* in January 1938 on the invitation of Russell Davenport, the magazine's current managing editor, at a salary of $15,000. It was Cozzens's understanding that he had been brought in to improve the magazine's writing, but his work was altered by editors and only one story, on the Fuller Brush Company, appeared mostly as he wrote it. *Fortune*'s theory, he maintained, was "the more similes, the better or more colorful the writings." His contrary view was that "a simile is a boob trap. What it amounts to is that the writer, unable to think clearly enough or write well enough to say what he means, gets around the impasse by cutely changing the subject."[82] When he tendered his resignation after ten months on the job, thinking his presence was embarrassing for Davenport,[83] it was promptly accepted and Cozzens returned to fiction.

The quick exit from the magazine of writers like Crane and Cozzens was not untypical. In the words of Hodgins, "the parade of gifted men who joined the staff for four or five months and then resigned or had to be fired was a Grand Army of the Republic of Letters." It was the distinction between writing well and writing well under deadline pressure that usually sent otherwise competent writers out the magazine's revolving door. Hodgins recalled another MacLeish protege, the poet Schuyler Jackson, who had a prior problem: he could turn out prose as fine as Agee's but could not grasp the fact that attractive images failed to add up to an effective journalistic story. The heat of a deadline caused him to falter altogether. At last even MacLeish accepted the obvious about Jackson. He said: "He just can't bear down; his pelvis is too narrow."[84]

While *Fortune* paid attractive salaries, working conditions were difficult and expectations high. The new Chrysler Building gave the magazine a prestige New York address but the editorial space was kept cramped and spartan to remind writers and editors of the reason they had been hired. In the early days there were never enough typewriters and desks ("A desk, for Godsake!" Luce cried when Macdonald had requested one. "What's happened to the old log-cabin spirt that founded *Time*?").[85] Nor were there enough writers. There were infrequent outside contributions and now and then a writer was borrowed from *Time,* but for the most part the magazine was turned out by a handful of hard-pressed staff writers who relied on researchers—young women with even less business experience than the writers themselves—for gathering material. ("The theory of *Fortune*," Hodgins recalled, "was that every writer on its staff should be capable of turning out one good major story per month [with the average story running over ten thousand words in the magazine's early days] for eleven months of the year—and on the twelfth month he rested.")[86] Since the magazine didn't draw on a bank of finished articles and was largely put together on a month-to-month basis, chaos usually reigned as deadlines neared. In an attempt to stabilize the new magazine Luce turned to a "Jesus" discarded by Harold Ross.

The year the *New Yorker* began publication Ralph McAllister Ingersoll was an unemployed newspaperman and failed novelist who had published a book about Mexico and had a few magazine credits, including an article in the *Saturday Evening Post*.[87] He was also broke. When he learned through his agents, Brandt and Brandt, that Ross was hunting for staffers for his faltering magazine, he applied. Ross asked him to work up some short sketches before hiring him at $50 a week. Ingersoll soon found himself the senior staff member, then (as he put it) the "managing editor of facts," responsible for the Talk of the Town, most of the nonfiction and reporting, and seeing that the magazine got to press on time, with Katharine Angell, the "managing editor of fiction," handling casuals and fiction. Though most observers credited him with giving the magazine some operating order, in time Ingersoll slipped in Ross's estimation, as most of his managing editors did, and after five years on the job Ingersoll left—for a salary nearly twice what he was making on the *New Yorker* —to accept Luce's offer to join his new business magazine. "Hell, Ingersoll," Ross said when he learned, *"Fortune* was invented for you to edit."[88]

Ross was right. When he joined *Fortune* in the summer of 1930 Ingersoll shared the top job in an odd co-editor arrangement with Parker Lloyd-Smith, the two splitting the duties of getting out the magazine, but after Lloyd-Smith's suicide in September 1931 Ingersoll was solely in charge. He had developed the idea that monthly magazines were ideal journalistic mediums. While newspapers and weekly magazines were too pressed for time and books took too long to write and read, in a monthly, extensive research could be condensed into a single long article brought to life by a skilled writer. Ingersoll went to work to create the magazine he envisioned.

Together with Luce he changed procedures so that writers had more responsibility for articles and the support staff was improved, with researchers assigned to writers as editorial assistants. His main contribution was generating a stir of excitement in the editorial offices. Hodgins recalled coming to the Chrysler Building one evening at about eleven o'clock to show Ingersoll the rewrite of an article and being "flabbergasted to find every desk occupied and

all lights blazing. It was editorial high noon." "Within a half hour," Hodgins
went on, "he had read my draft and covered it with marginal scrawls—
'Good'; 'Dull'; 'Hit it harder'; 'Kill'; etc. I asked Ingersoll when he wanted me
to rework it. 'Right now, for Christ's sake,' he said. So I sat down at a secre-
tary's typewriter outside his office and went to work. I finished about 2:30
a.m."[89]

Many of his writers found Ingersoll an overbearing personality and harsh
taskmaster. When a writer faltered on a story Ingersoll abruptly switched it to
another to finish or rewrite. Yet with writers who failed to measure up altogether he could find ways to let them down gently, as he did with one writer
he turned away yet recommended to *Time:* "Your manuscript failed to convince us that you have the special and unique flair which we are hunting for—
that flair which might have brought you to the top earning brackets of
Fortune in a few years. There is nothing to reproach yourself about if you
haven't got it. What we are looking for is not exclusively writing but a strange
combination of talents which would be useful to no other magazine in the
world . . . if you like, we are looking for a certain kind of freak to join our
menagerie."[90]

Agee, who Ingersoll acknowledged as "the best word-bird on the floor,"[91]
presented a different problem. In 1934 Ingersoll assigned him an article on the
American roadside, and Agee spent two months traveling the country's high-
ways. After he returned to the office and seemed about to take another two
months to write the article, Ingersoll intervened. When Agee's copy suddenly
turned up in galleys, Hodgins asked Ingersoll why it was not late. "I had to go
down one evening and take eight thousand words off the top of Jim's desk and
send them to the printer," Ingersoll told him. "They were *great.*" "I don't
think Jim knows that," Hodgins said. "Jim is still in his office writing like hell
and I think it's still on 'The Great American Roadside.' I don't think Jim
knows the issue is closed." Ingersoll asked him to tell Agee what had happened, and Hodgins did. Agee simply replied "Oh," but that night, Hodgins
noted, "I am sure James Agee must have cursed Ingersoll in fifty languages."[92]

Ingersoll considered himself a writer as well as an editor and found time for
several pieces, assigning himself subjects and fact-gathering travel that interested him. A story on the King Ranch in Texas in December 1933 was considered a model of the kind of business story Luce wanted for the magazine. An
in-depth story on the business of burlesque helped make Gypsy Rose Lee na-
tionally known—and enhanced Ingersoll's already rich reputation as a man
about town. His 1934 profile of the *New Yorker* ruffled feathers on Ross's mag-

azine with its disclosure of salary figures. Two years later the *New Yorker* retaliated with a profile of Luce. Written by Wolcott Gibbs, it depicted Luce as an "ambitious, gimlet-eyed, Baby Tycoon," famously parodied *Time*'s manner of backward-running sentences causing the mind to reel, and returned the favor of announcing salary figures.[93] (A two-part profile of Ingersoll in 1942, also from Gibbs's nimble hand, was generally tame and generally favorable.)

When Ingersoll was elevated to general manager of Time Inc. in 1935 Luce credited him in a press release as "largely responsible for the development of the scope, efficiency and literary standards of *Fortune*'s editorial organization."[94] Later, while still general manager, he became publisher of *Time* and had a major hand in the development of *Life* magazine. But his strong suits were as an editor and a writer, not as manager and publisher, and in 1939 he parted company with the Luce empire.

Meanwhile, *Fortune*'s glow for writers had dimmed. MacLeish's departure in 1938 to become the first curator of the Nieman Foundation at Harvard marked the end of that heady period when it was home to poets, novelists, and critics—a time when it was a magazine of business "plus." MacLeish seemed to speak for most of the early band of writers when he informed Luce of his disenchantment with the current direction of the magazine: "I will admit (with resentment) that Fortune is not the association of mutually assisting journalists it was for five or six very exciting years. I will admit (without enthusiasm) that it is now a part of a publishing enterprise in which not more than a dozen or so people know each other's names and not more than half that many wish each other well enough to stand by each other in the only work that finally counts—the writing of the journal."[95]

seven

"The Luce organization," Alfred Kazin remarked, "had a hilarious respect for *writers*."[96] If the respect faded with corporate success, it had a celebrated if ill-fated carryover in the continuing career of Ralph Ingersoll. With the *New Yorker* and *Fortune* he had helped bring other men's ideas into being; *PM*, on the other hand, was his from the ground up. The central conception was as simple as it was doomed: to create a tabloid daily newspaper that carried no advertising and read like a magazine, thereby reforming through its powerful example the essential nature of American journalism.

Ingersoll wanted to bring to the newspaper innovations that had been pioneered by magazines: better paper and printing, improved photography and layout, extensive background research. The biggest change would be found in the writing. The traditional news story was shaped like an inverted pyramid, the information set down in order of importance so the story could be cut easily from the end. "But I wanted my stories told as writers would tell them," Ingersoll said. "I wanted to return to the classical form of beginning, middle and end. Moreover, I was confident that it could be done—and was even commercially practical because Time Inc. had made fifty million dollars rewriting newspaper stories into miniature compositions and giving them new dimensions."[97]

In a sixty-one page memorandum outlining the tabloid—eventually to become a classic document in the annals of American journalism—Ingersoll maintained that newspapers lacked a genuine regard for writing. They were turned out by young men and old hacks who were worked too hard and paid too little. Real writing talent had long since been drained off by the possibility of serious money elsewhere, as Ingersoll specified in graphic economic detail. In advertising, writers could make $10,000 to $50,000 a year; in fiction, $15,000 to $50,000 from the magazines and "as big a plum as $100,000 a year in as silly a pie as pulp magazine writing"; in nonfiction magazine writing, $10,000 to $50,000. In newswriting, however, "a really talented writer, as a grade A reporter on a big metropolitan paper, may expect to earn $75 a week."

Some writing talent still survived on newspapers—it had to if *PM* was to come into being—and Ingersoll's plan would allow a saving remnant of young journalists to employ their ability by freeing the form of newswriting and allowing the pursuit of truth as they saw it rather than as owners saw it. He also planned to recruit well-known creative writers and magazine writers and, as he put it, "young men graduating yearly from Universities (from which most of *Time*, *Fortune* and the *New Yorker's* staffs were recruited). These men need training, guidance, practical education. But you can train, guide and educate a real writer whereas you can not teach merely well educated men how to write."[98] The result, as Ingersoll proclaimed it, would be a new kind of newspaper that imitated no existing paper.

When Luce declined to back the venture financially, Ingersoll raised the needed money himself and *PM* began publishing on June 18, 1940. What happened thereafter is a complex story surviving in several versions. *PM* attracted many talented writers but never enough. With the *New Yorker* and *Fortune* Ingersoll had gone from a weekly to a monthly, both of them publications that could be put out with a small core of dedicated workers; now he had reversed his field, publishing six days a week and needing a large staff. If *PM* had been a weekly, he came to believe, it would have posed no problem. "But *PM* wasn't. Every week there were not one but six issues to be conceived, researched, written, edited and fitted together. Never having successfully done it, I have no absolute answer, but in my opinion, to create a newspaper even approximately fulfilling *PM*'s prospectus would take not five or ten exceptional, superior writers and editors, but no less than fifty really first-class craftsmen—and we never came even within shooting distance of getting that many together at one time."[99]

Less than three months after it began publication Ingersoll was forced to give up ownership of *PM* to Marshall Field, one of his main backers. He remained on with the paper as editor but his time was more and more taken up with writing. In the period before American entry into World War II his extensive and strong reporting from Europe urged involvement, and—as Captain Ralph Ingersoll—his 1943 book *The Battle Is the Payoff* was a Book-of-the-Month Club choice and one of the war's first best sellers (Ingersoll turning over rights to the U.S. Army, which then allowed him to keep a half-cent royalty on every copy sold). As the war ended another book appeared, *Top Secret,* which gave Ingersoll's controversial account of the war's military strategy, and he tried to resume control of the newspaper he had long left in other hands. But in 1946 differences with Marshall Field on a variety of fronts—including whether *PM* should carry advertising, as Field wanted and Ingersoll resisted—caused Ingersoll to finally cut his ties with the newspaper he had founded. Shortly thereafter, eight years after it began publishing, *PM* entered journalism history.

eight

The glory days of big-circulation magazines and dominant editors lingered on into the postwar period. The tumultuous sixties saw a successful new publishing venture in *Rolling Stone,* while editors like Harold Hayes at *Esquire* and Willie Morris at *Harper's* gained attention by injecting fresh life into older publications. At *Saturday Review* Norman Cousins turned a staid literary journal into a general culture magazine with circulation approaching 700,000.[100] But already the landscape of the periodical world was shifting. Costs were rising and there was increased competition from special-interest publications and from television. Print culture itself was in decline. Soon some of the biggest slicks followed the pulps into oblivion: *Collier's* in 1957; the *Saturday Evening Post* in 1969; *Look* and *Life*[101] at the beginning of the seventies. For independent writers another period of adjustment was at hand. Once again they had to scramble to find new markets—the stern requirement that had marked the lives of writers for hire since Poe and Willis first took up the pen.

Epilogue

SWEET DEAL

Writing for Hire in a New Age

I stay home and write poems—and essays, stories,
text-books, children's books, biography. . . . Work?
—Donald Hall

one

Two months after Howells's "The Man of Letters as a Man of Business" appeared in *Scribner's* in 1893, the magazine took issue with one of his passing remarks. Presumably written by the editor, Edward L. Burlingame, an item in the Point of View section quoted Howells to the effect that magazines, however much they might enrich writers, crowded out "pure literature" with their typical mixture of "two-thirds popular science, politics, economics, and the timely topics which I will call contemporanics," and consequently had the effect of narrowing the field of literary activity. In *Scribner's* view, Howells simply had it wrong. Magazines wanted all the pure literature they could get; they would happily be what Howells called "altogether literary." The problem was that not enough quality literary material was produced to fill the quality magazines, and never had been. *Scribner's* pointed out that even in the past, when the field was as yet uncrowded with rival publications, magazines such as the *Atlantic* abounded in contemporanics while printing what pure literature was to be had.

As to the charge that magazines narrowed the literary industry, *Scribner's* challenged Howells for an instance of a writer rejected solely on the grounds that space was lacking for pure literature. In Howells's own case, the magazine doubted his work had ever been limited by the pages given over to, say, popular science. Moreover, the magazine held that pay for pure literature was better than that for lesser material, indicating its value to magazines. The one area where *Scribner's* found common ground with Howells was in the sense, implied by his comments, of a general decline in literary quality. If Howells meant, *Scribner's* concluded, that "magazines must, for the present, do without the highest form of pure literature except in very moderate quantities, he would say what is true of them as of the whole time." It was only the erroneous notion that pure literature was unwanted that the magazine resisted.[1]

Even at the time, the *Scribner's* spat with Howells must have seemed a tempest in a teapot—the sort of airy literary debate prestige magazines still indulged in while the popular periodical press went its profitable way. Today it has about it the haze of ancient history. We can barely glimpse a magazine world in which writers and editors quibbled in print over the amount of space given to pure literature as against contemporanics—or over whether or not serious writers were squeezed out by the editorial formulas of mass magazines. For us, serious literary activity is confined almost wholly to high-culture periodicals, contemporanics is nearly all there is in the surviving magazines, and the print world in general has shriveled in importance.

Reasons for this are not part of my subject, nor questions of what took place when. From an independent professional writer's point of view, the death of the *Saturday Evening Post* on January 10, 1969, effectively, if crudely, marks the end of the golden age of print. With the magazine's passing went a major weekly market that, even if one failed to make its pages, proclaimed the possibilities of professional writing in a way matched by no other single publication. Well before its actual death, however, the *Post* was in precipitous decline,[2] and with it the great age of the writing game.

In 1962 Hartzell Spence, a freelancer of twenty-two years with twelve books and over 150 articles to his credit, surveyed the field of professional writing in a *Saturday Review of Literature* article and reached somber conclusions. Spence guessed that only two hundred independent writers remained, down in a generation from at least two thousand. When he took up freelancing in 1940, a yearbook listed 529 general magazines that took work from independent writers, with 69 of them weeklies in need of a regular supply of material. Most carried fiction as well as nonfiction. In the same yearbook for 1962 he found 104 general markets, three of them weeklies, one a bi-monthly, the rest monthlies. In just over twenty years the market had shrunk 80 percent. Yet the situation was even darker than the numbers indicated, for the trend in the remaining general magazines was toward coordinated and staff-written issues. Even the *Saturday Evening Post* now listed a number of staff writers, and the serial novel was gone from its pages along with much of its former short fiction.

Television, apparently once the freelancer's savior, also had gone the way of salaried staff writers. Occasionally a fictional story became the basis of a series or a thriller was given a one-shot adaptation, but this was rare, and there was no nonfiction market in television, with documentaries all staff-produced. Save for an occasional blockbuster sale, movies were no more realistic a market for writers than in the past. As for book publishing, it was given over to corporate moneymen with eyes fixed on accounting ledgers. Spence wrote: "Publishers no longer ask their editors, 'Is the manuscript good?' Instead, they ask, 'Will it make a book club, rate a magazine preview, sell to stage or movies, go big in paperback later, and how many foreign translations can you expect?'"

Amid the litany of decline, where was the freelancer left? In Spence's view he was writing fewer magazine pieces, though polishing them more, and very little fiction. He was ghosting autobiographies ("of famous illiterates"), collaborating on "as told to" biographies, and turning out corporate histories. There also was some continuity writing for comic strips and some bootlegging of scripts to salaried TV writers. And some ("in fact many") writers were not working at all but hustling for paying jobs. In this Spence included himself. "By the way," he ended the article, "if you know of any obscure college that needs a teacher of the practical writing crafts, and could use a fellow with twenty-two years of experience in writing for all of the mass media, let me know. I may be available shortly."[3]

two

Murray Teigh Bloom, a freelancer whose career began at the same time as Spence's, in the 1940s, remembers the period extending into the 1970s in a different light. It was "delightful professionally and financially" for writers. If the *Reader's Digest* was an especially difficult market, as Spence mentions, Bloom points out that it nonetheless paid splendid rates, and he recalls getting a monthly stipend—beginning in the early 1960s—for a first look at his article ideas. Also from the magazine came hefty Christmas bonuses based on the number of articles a writer got into print during the year.[4]

Of course even in its best days writers had differing experiences on Grub Street—and Grub Street itself was always in flux, hostage to publishing fads and fickle public taste. Independent writers, naturally disposed to insecurity, often feared the end was at hand. With the close of the great decade of the sporting life in the 1930s, John R. Tunis solemnly concluded that "sports were finished and I began to wonder whether I was finished as a writer too."[5] Although the remark was typical, the reality was that the writing game in sports and other areas continued to beckon, and still does, with only the conditions changing for each new generation of writers. The central change at the present moment is that story papers, pulp and slick magazines, newspaper syndicates, and newspaper Sunday editions have all vanished, or very largely so, as important paying markets for independent writers. What remains, with exception here and there, is mostly book writing—or just the reverse of the situation that once confronted Poe, Willis, and the first generation of American writers for hire.

The American Society of Journalists and Authors, an organization of freelance nonfiction writers, currently lists about 800 members, and professional writers of fiction and nonfiction swell the ranks of the Authors Guild, the Poetry Society of America, PEN, the National Writers Union, and the various writer groups devoted to genres. Books and magazines for writers still abound—and still sing the siren song of living by words alone. One such magazine, alive at this writing, bears the no-nonsense name *Writing for Money*. A guidebook put out by the magazine has an equally direct title: *How to Make $1,000 a Week as a Freelance Writer*. If organizations and publications point to the continuing allure of the writing game, social science survey data give some indication of the underlying reality. In 1980 the Authors Guild Foundation sponsored a study that was conducted by Columbia University's Center for the Social Sciences, the results of which were subsequently published in a 1986 book called *The Wages of Writing*.[6] Based on the responses of 2,241 authors (meaning authors of at least one published book, fiction or nonfiction), the survey found, among other things, the following:

> —The median income of authors in 1979 was $4,775.
> —The typical author had an hourly writing income of $4.90.
> —The typical author received 98 cents of every writing dollar from books, with the remaining two cents from articles and scripts.
> —Nearly half of the authors had a regular paid position besides writing.

On the other side of the ledger were findings of a more encouraging nature from the standpoint of independent writing:

—Ten percent of authors had a writing income of more than $45,000, five percent more than $80,000.

—One-fifth of genre fiction writers, the most lucrative form of writing, earned at least $50,000 in 1979.

—Social or education backgrounds of authors had no discernible effect on writing income.

In addition, a majority of part-time authors said they found writing more satisfying than their regular jobs, with nearly half saying they would happily give up their other work if they could equal their present income by full-time writing.

three

Accounts of the writing life continue to appear—accounts, to repeat a point made in the prologue, by and about those not-quite-common writers who have found a measure of success and for whom there is some record of their labors—and continue to portray it, in Gustave Flaubert's terms, as a delicious thing whether performed well or badly.[7] What follows is a sampling of such reports, all issuing from Grub Street in its current dress.

Donald Hall is an unlikely figure, a poet of literary distinction who does not earn the bulk of his living in the classroom. In *Life Work* (1993) he recounts the decision in 1975 to abandon a tenured teaching position at the University of Michigan and move with his wife, the poet and essayist Jane Kenyon, to a farmhouse in New Hampshire to take up the life of an independent writer. In the years that followed he experienced the usual panic over money matters yet plugged along, taking long periods to complete his poems while spinning out a steady stream of children's books, baseball books, textbooks, edited anthologies, essays, reviews, magazine pieces—and relying on the poet's standby of public lectures and readings. He learned the freelancer's secret of selling every piece as many times as possible—and learned, too, to turn over some labor to others, typists and word processors and researchers, opening time for his own work. He writes about his current practice: "Sometimes two researchers work for me at once; always two or three people type. On my staff, as it were, no one works more than a few hours a week, but the staff's labor saves me hours by the dozen—freeing me to work, helping me to manufacture the best day."[8]

As described in an interview, Hall typically begins a work day with poems, then switches to prose or literary chores:

> I get up at 4:30 or 5:00, feed the cat, start the coffee, drive two miles to where I can tug a copy of *The Boston Globe* out of the bundle, then return home to drink coffee and eat breakfast reading the paper. Then I get to work. First thing, I work on poems—because I am hardest on myself earliest in the day; I don't let myself get away with anything. After poems I work on prose—or on editions, or on proof-reading, or on research. Then I dictate the day's writing onto a tape, which my helpers type up in the afternoon to be fresh tomorrow morning. Lunch comes at 11:00 followed by a brief nap, followed by fairly desultory labors. Early afternoon is low-energy—usually with a burst of writing late on, at 4:00 or 5:00.[9]

The result is an impressive productivity in which he averages four books a year, counting revised editions of old books—and, figuring every scrap turned out, about one published item a week, year in and year out. At the end of *Life Work,* Hall, now in his sixties and in weakened health, tells of slowing down, yet only to the extent of resisting long-term projects in favor of short stories, short poems, children's books, short books like his memoir about work, and brief essays for periodicals. As he remarks in a subsequent book, an essay collection, as a freelance writer he must continue to work in a variety of forms and "approach the same material from two (or seven) points of style and view. No one blames Cezanne for returning to the same rocks and the same town-scape. I claim a writer may do a scene again from another angle, in a different season, with new light at another time of day." Such inventive reshuffling is reason for pride. It is the freelancer's nimble dance of survival, bringing with it the "thrill and conceit of doing it oneself, of self-support by shrewdness like the entrepreneur's and the con man's."[10]

At the far end of Grub Street from a figure of literary standing like Hall is "Tex" W. Dixon, a pseudonym adopted for the occasion by a writer from Austin, Texas, who disclosed in a magazine article that under the name Franklin W. Dixon, pinned to it by the Stratemeyer Syndicate, he is one of the ghosts keeping alive the Hardy Boys series. The terms of authorship, now conducted with Mega-Books of New York, are unchanged: true identities remain secret (to fellow ghosts as well as readers); all rights are signed away to the company; writers are paid a flat fee per book. The process of creation is equally unchanged from assembly-line days.

Story ideas, first discussed with an editor, must be approved by Mega-Books. Then the author produces a detailed chapter outline, the work of a week; this accepted, the actual writing begins, the work of about a month.

"Tex" Dixon reports that his editor, who also functions as a travel writer for the *New York Times,* is demanding. So is the authors' guide produced by Mega-Books, which urges writers to give characters distinctive personalities and plot crimes that are realistic and dangerous. Violent death can take place but with no gory details, sex is outlawed, and every chapter must end in a cliffhanger, usually some sort of physical danger, with resolution in the first paragraphs of the following chapter.

The adventures of Joe and Frank Hardy are aimed at adolescents but the essential writing task is the same as for any effective mystery story: quick pacing, crisp dialogue, exact description, and as much plot plausibility as one can manage. The work takes an experienced hand, and "Tex" Dixon says his has twenty years of practice. He wonders whether "dreaming up boys' adventure tales comes rather easily to me. I'm supposed to be a serious writer; what does this propensity say about my emotional and aesthetic maturity?" But he dismisses the question ("But then again, who cares?") and slips into modest pride that he can manufacture a couple of Hardy books a year as one of the ten to fifteen ghosts around the country that keep the series going. He says of his writing: ". . . when I'm 'in the zone,' so to speak, I'm as oblivious to the rest of the world as I'd be if I were writing *War and Peace.* Coming to the climactic moment of my most recent Hardy tale, I even found myself getting teary when Joe's life was in danger and Frank was desperately trying to save him. Something about brotherly love must have gotten to me."[11]

Writing boys' adventure books is small change compared with the lucrative vein of women's romance novels, yet another arena in which production-line fictioneers find an ongoing market. In the early 1970s Avon Books let it be known through notices in writers' magazines that it was looking for paperback originals, with the predictable result that the sky rained manuscripts. Kathleen Woodiwiss's *The Flame and the Flower* had been rejected by a number of hardcover houses, but plucked from the slush pile (because, an editor recalled, at 200,000 words it was the largest manuscript) and published in 1972 it sold in the millions. When success was repeated with another slush-pile discovery (the manuscript came in addressed to "The Editor of *The Flame and the Flower*"), Rosemary Rogers's *Sweet Savage Love,* Avon was off and running with a string of popular romance novels by and for women.[12]

What was new was not the genre, though the content now was often more openly erotic, but the shift in the direction of paperback originals from mostly male-centered adventure and suspense fiction toward romance, a field of opportunity reopened by a declining number of mass magazines featuring such material. At the end of the 1970s romance fiction from Avon and its competitors—the genre separated into subspecies offering variety in time period of stories, locale, age of heroines, degrees of reality and sexuality [13]—constituted upwards of half of the American paperback market. By then a Canadian firm, Harlequin, was inundating the market with a line of sweetly chaste originals promoted with an emphasis on brand loyalty. Readers were encouraged to buy Harlequin Romances rather than particular authors or titles, safe in the knowledge that they were getting consistent value for their money.

When Harlequin decided to test the waters with romances using American rather than foreign settings, Janet Dailey was the writer in the right place at the right time. She had worked for six months on a Texas novel, *No Quarter Asked,* before sending it to Harlequin, where it was snapped up without revision and published in 1976. Dailey rushed back to her typewriter after that first sale to begin a series of romances set in each of the fifty states. She produced manuscript pages at a rate of fifteen to twenty-five a day while leaving research details and domestic chores to her husband, with the result that the novels came out at a dizzying rate. In 1980, a year only slightly more productive than most, there were thirteen.

As described in sixty-five biographical portraits in Kathryn Falk's 1982 book *Love's Leading Ladies,* romance writers following in the wake of Woodiwiss, Rogers, and Dailey are usually beginners or part-timers rather than professionals when they break into the field.[14] Competition is keen regardless of experience. Harlequin is said to receive over a thousand unsolicited manuscripts a month, accepting about one percent, while some houses consider only work submitted through literary agents. And like all production-line fictioneers, romancers must work within exacting specifications as to setting, characterization, tone, plot, and length. But for those who can master the requirements and produce acceptable manuscripts the rewards are enticing. According to an article in *Forbes* magazine in 1982, first-time authors could expect advances of $6,000 and eight percent royalties for 55,000-word manuscripts. "Nearly all titles that make it into print have a similar sales appeal," the article added, "so that might work out to a gross income of $30,000. A real pro can turn out ten books annually and afford to live as well as most corporate executives."[15]

For male adventure and suspense writers in the real pro category the situation is less rosy, as E. Howard Hunt, author of dozens of hardcover and paperback originals, indicated in a 1985 article. Under his writing regimen it takes eight weeks to produce a novel ("a reasonable average for a work of fiction") and four days to edit it—a total of sixty days. Assuming a $10,000 advance, the hourly rate of pay is $20.83—or less than the wage of a TV repairman. "But the TV repairman can work 360 days a year," Hunt noted, "not just in sixty-day segments. For the writer must recharge his mental cells, scrape up new ideas for his next book, and cope with the details of daily living before he can start anew." There are, of course, chances of added income from reprint deals and the sale of various subsidiary rights. "But rarely are those rights converted into cash. What keeps most writers going is the hope that some day the big pot of gold will be his. But, it's really a lottery. Professionals write because they want to write, or feel an irrepressible urge—the *cacoethes scribendi*—to do so, hoping to be adequately rewarded for their effort."[16]

Hunt's view of the present-day writing situation is exactly that which professional writers have always employed to explain their trade—an irrepressible itch to put words on paper, resulting in at least a living wage. John Jerome leans on it as well in *The Writing Trade* (1992), a detailed record of a generic year in the life of a freelancer specializing in nonfiction. The year is 1989 and Jerome is a thoroughgoing Grub Street professional. He longs, nevertheless, to free himself from what he calls the "special-interest ghetto" of writing "category books," and a main concern running through his account is how a soon-to-be-published book will fare. *Stone Work,* a book about country life, is simply a "noncategory" book, and if it sells well enough Jerome hopes to interest other publishers in such books. If it fails ("if it drops silently into the great abyss, as happens with ninety-eight percent of the fifty thousand titles that are published every year") he will have to return to writing books about sports and popular science, categories for which his enthusiasm has dimmed. He recalls that his first book, the *Sports Illustrated Book of Skiing,* was turned out in 1971 for a flat fee of $2,000 and was "no fun to do at all."[17]

In 1989 Jerome is in his thirtieth year as a professional writer, his twentieth as a freelancer. He lives in rural western Massachusetts with a wife who also writes and edits. In his salaried days he edited and wrote for single-interest magazines (*Car and Driver, Skiing*), and he still turns out essays each year for the *Complete Runner's Day-by-Day Log and Calendar,* described as a glorified desk calendar, though one that sells up to 70,000 copies a year. As the new year opens he has finished a quarter of the essays needed for the next edition, is awaiting galleys of *Stone Work,* has to tinker with the reissue of an earlier book, and has reluctantly agreed to write some magazine pieces. This scheduled work will bring in two-thirds of the year's income; for the rest he will have to scramble, as he usually has in a career that has resulted in eight books and some two hundred articles. Now, in his middle fifties, books are his main interest, with articles written only for ready money. The book at hand, *The Writing Trade,* is ideal since it is a book about writing. "I've always," Jerome says, "been much more interested in writing than in any of the subjects I was writing about."[18]

As he understands himself, Jerome is a contemporary version of Howells's clever authors of acceptable work—or as he phrases it: "I am a competent but essentially invisible writer, proof that one can earn a living from writing for years without ever breaking into the public consciousness."[19] His book is a month-by-month account of the ebb-and-flow of such a writer's year: work, domestic life, money worries, possible book proposals, more work. While completing *The Writing Trade* he needs to develop another book proposal, secure a contract and with it an advance, sustaining the financial flow of a free-lancer's life. Midway through the book Jerome receives the first copy of *Stone Work,* and thereafter the reception of the published book becomes a continuing concern. Early reviews are positive and his hopes soar. Finally, the book sells only 6,300 copies, and at the end of the year Jerome is stuck at the same level of the writing game, a survivor but only barely.

Yet books—the hope they sustain as well as the income they generate—remain his central concern. As Jerome sums up the situation, the problem with magazine writing is that it "lives on ideas that take a month to produce (think up, sell to the editor, research, write, get past the editor again, revise, pass through fact-checking) and pay about half a month's expenses. And never build any equity at all. Books at least hold out the hope of continuing income." And further: "There are thousand-dollar ideas (magazine pieces), thirty-thousand-dollar ideas (most books that have a chance of succeeding), million-dollar ideas (forget books, these are properties, marketed rather than written)." What he needs to live and work in the immediate future is one of those $30,000 book ideas. The return will not equal that of a local tradesman but—in the familiar salute of the independent professional writer to the quality of his existence no matter the current state of the print world—his life will be better. "I have a sweet deal," Jerome says. "I certainly don't want to do anything else."[20]

NOTES

Prologue: Clever Authors of Acceptable Work

Epigraph: Alexis de Tocqueville, *Democracy in America,* ed. Phillips Bradley (New York: Knopf, 1953), 2:61.

1. William Dean Howells, "The Man of Letters as a Man of Business," *Scribner's* 14 (October 1893): 431–32. An edited version of the article is reprinted in Howells's *Literature and Life* (New York: Harper and Brothers, 1911), 1–35. Hamilton Wright Mabie, a literary light of lesser brilliance, a year earlier had noticed the existence of a class of writers whose ranks had swelled with the expansion of literary activity at the beginning of the nineties: "If there are not, as of old, a few writers of very high rank, whose work has something approaching the touch of finality, there are an increasing number of well-furnished and thoroughly equipped men and women whose work, in its range and sincerity, indicates a general advance in skill, culture, and taste." "A Year's Literary Procution," *Forum* 10 (February 1892): 799.

2. Howells, "The Man of Letters as a Man of Business," 444.

3. Upton Sinclair, "The Confessions of a Young Author," *Independent,* November 20, 1902, 2748. The article was published anonymously, Sinclair wishing—as he pointed out in the article—to protect his future earning power with editors.

4. Robert V. Hudson, *The Writing Game: A Biography of Will Irwin* (Ames: Iowa State University Press, 1982), vii.

5. Wallace Stegner, *The Uneasy Chair: A Biography of Bernard De Voto* (Garden City, N.Y.: Doubleday, 1974), 340.

6. Gore Vidal, "The Romance of Sinclair Lewis," *New York Review of Books,* October 8, 1992, 14.

7. "The Post's Plans for 1900," *Saturday Evening Post,* December 30, 1899, 574.

8. Jack London to Esther Anderson, December 11, 1914, *The Letters of Jack London,* ed. Earle Labor, Robert C. Leitz III, and I. Milo Shepard (Stanford, Calif.: Stanford University Press, 1988), 3:1389.

9. Cyril Connolly, *The Unquiet Grave* (New York: Harper and Brothers, 1945), 1.

10. Milton E. Flower, *James Parton, The Father of Modern Biography* (Durham, N.C.: Duke University Press, 1951), 185.

11. *Jack London: Novels and Social Writings* (New York: Library of America, 1982), 726.

12. The actual figure for Fitzgerald's magazine sales, $106,585, is given by Matthew J. Bruccoli in the introduction to *The Price Was High: The Last Uncollected Stories of F. Scott Fitzgerald* (New York: Harcourt Brace Jovanovich, 1979), xi.

13. William Faulkner to Harold Ober, August 20, 1945, *Selected Letters of William Faulkner,* ed. Joseph Blotner (New York: Random House, 1977), 199.

14. Jacqueline Rose, *The Haunting of Sylvia Plath* (Cambridge, Mass.: Harvard University Press, 1992), 9. Plath's remark is quoted on p. 171, one of several passages in which she speaks of ambition as a popular writer.

15. Jonathan Raban, *For Love & Money: A Writing Life, 1969–1989* (New York: Harper and Row, 1989), 19–20.

16. Howells, "The Man of Letters as a Man of Business," 429.

17. Kenneth S. Lynn, *William Dean Howells: An American Life* (New York: Harcourt Brace Jovanovich, 1971), 4–5.

18. Martha Dickinson Bianchi, *The Life and Letters of Emily Dickinson* (Boston: Houghton Mifflin, 1924), 82–83.

19. Irvin S. Cobb, *Exit Laughing* (Indianapolis: Bobbs-Merrill, 1941), 319.

20. William Charvat, *The Profession of Authorship in America, 1800–1870,* ed. Matthew J. Bruccoli (Columbus: Ohio State University Press, 1968), 3.

21. William Charvat, *Literary Publishing in America, 1790–1850* (Philadelphia: University of Pennsylvania Press, 1959), 7–8.

22. Nigel Cross, *The Common Writer: Life in Nineteenth-Century Grub Street* (New York: Cambridge University Press, 1985), 91, 4–5.

23. James H. Collins, "The American Grub Street," *Atlantic* 98 (November 1906): 636, 643.

24. W. Jackson Bate, *Samuel Johnson* (New York: Harcourt Brace Jovanovich, 1977), 190 n.

25. Bate, *Samuel Johnson,* 190, 189. Paul Fussell maintains of Johnson in his Grub Street period that "although he was of this world, he always transcended it. He used the conventions and mechanisms of Grub Street—writing rapidly, writing to order, writing in a standard genre—to generate literature, happily defined by Ezra Pound as 'news that stays news.'" Paul Fussell, *Samuel Johnson and the Life of Writing* (New York: Harcourt Brace Jovanovich, 1971), 17.

26. Bate, *Samuel Johnson,* 212. The bracketed explanation is Bate's.

27. Pat Rogers, *Grub Street: Studies in a Subculture* (London: Methuen, 1972), 399. Rogers explores in exhaustive detail both the historical and metaphorical implications of the term.

28. Tocqueville, *Democracy in America,* 2:55.

29. Charvat, *The Profession of Authorship in America,* 77.

30. Charvat, *Literary Publishing in America,* 38.

31. *Works of Samuel Johnson* (New Haven, Conn.: Yale University Press, 1970), 2:457.

Chapter One: Light Artillery
of the Intellect

Epigraph: "The Literary Life of Thingum Bob, Esq.," *Collected Works of Edgar Allan Poe,* ed. Thomas Ollive Mabbott (Cambridge, Mass.: Harvard University Press, 1978), 3:1145.

1. Frank Luther Mott, *A History of American Magazines* (New York: Appleton, 1930), 1:586.

2. Kenneth Silverman, *Edgar A. Poe: Mournful and Never-Ending Remembrance* (New York: HarperCollins, 1991), 305. For Poe's life and work I follow this account together with the documentary biography by Dwight Thomas and David K. Jackson, *The Poe Log: A Documentary Life of Edgar Allan Poe, 1809–1849* (Boston: G. K. Hall, 1987).

3. Poe to George W. Eveleth, December 15, 1846, *The Letters of Edgar Allan Poe,* ed. John Ward Ostrom (Cambridge, Mass.: Harvard University Press, 1948), 2:332.

4. Poe mentions his rate of pay, and Willis's, in a letter to Philip P. Cooke, April 16, 1846, *Letters,* 2:314. The total amount received for the series is given in John Ward Ostrom, "Edgar A. Poe: His Income as Literary Entrepreneur," *Poe Studies* 15 (June 1982): 5. Unless otherwise indicated, Poe's sales figures are taken from this study.

5. Edgar A. Poe, "Magazine-Writing—Peter Snook," *Broadway Journal,* June 7, 1845. The article is in a reprint of the publication (New York: AMS, 1965), 354–57. For more on Poe's work for the *Journal* see Burton R. Pollin, ed., *Writings in the* Broadway Journal: *Nonfiction Prose* (New York: Gordian Press, 1986).

6. *Edgar Allan Poe: Essays and Reviews* (New York: Library of America, 1984), 1036.

7. Passages from "The Literati of New York City" are taken from the reprinting of the series in *Edgar Allan Poe: Essays and Reviews,* 1118–222.

8. Poe to George W. Eveleth, December 15, 1846, *Letters,* 2:332.

9. Thomas and Jackson, *The Poe Log,* 473.

10. Raymond Williams examines the situation of English writers at this time in *The Long Revolution* (London: Penguin Books, 1965), 258–60.

11. Henry Mills Alden, *Magazine Writing and the New Literature* (New York: Harper and Brothers, 1908), 42.

12. Larzer Ziff, *Writing in the New Nation* (New Haven, Conn.: Yale University Press, 1991), 97.

13. Kenneth Silverman, *A Cultural History of the American Revolution* (New York: Crowell, 1976), 485.

14. Mott, *A History of American Magazines,* 1:197.

15. Ibid., 1:327.

16. For Willis's life and work I follow an early biography by Henry A. Beers, *Nathaniel Parker Willis* (Boston: Houghton Mifflin, 1885), and Cortland P. Auser, *Nathaniel P. Willis* (New York: Twayne, 1969).

17. "The Editor's Table," *American Monthly Magazine* 2 (April 1830): 67.

18. Thomas and Jackson, *The Poe Log,* 99.

19. Poe to John Neal, June 4, 1840, *Letters,* 1:137.

20. "The Editor's Table," *American Monthly Magazine* 1 (March 1830): 866.

21. Beers, *Nathaniel Parker Willis,* 98.

22. N. P. Willis, Preface to *Pencillings by the Way* (New York: Charles Scribner, 1852), x.

23. Beers, *Nathaniel Parker Willis,* 130.

24. Willis, *Pencillings by the Way,* 225.

25. Beers, *Nathaniel Parker Willis,* 139–40.

26. Robert E. Spiller, *The American in England* (New York: Henry Holt, 1926), 382.

27. Willis, *Pencillings by the Way,* 474, 475.

28. Ibid., 480.

29. Thomas and Jackson, *The Poe Log*, 505.

30. Yale's costs are given in Mott, *A History of American Magazines*, 1:513 n. 72.

31. Beers, *Nathaniel Parker Willis*, 262. Mott suggests Willis's magazine fees given above, taken from Beers's account, may be too high. See *A History of American Magazines*, 1:507 n. 43. Beers's figures presumably come from Willis's contemporary, Charles T. Congdon, who called Willis "the first magazine writer who was tolerably well paid." *Reminiscences of a Journalist* (Boston: James R. Osgood, 1880), 127.

32. N. P. Willis, Preface to *Hurry-Graphs; or Sketches of Scenery, Celebrities and Society, Taken From Life* (New York: Charles Scribner, 1851), iii–iv.

33. Congdon, *Reminiscences of a Journalist*, 354, 357.

34. Poe to James Russell Lowell, March 30, 1844, *Letters*, 1:246.

35. Allen Tate, "The Angelic Imagination," *The Man of Letters in the Modern World* (New York: Meridian Books, 1955), 118.

36. Silverman, *Edgar A. Poe*, 224.

37. Another anonymous tale may have appeared in Philadelphia's *Saturday Evening Post* in 1831. See Silverman, *Edgar A. Poe*, 87.

38. Poe to Thomas W. White, June 33, 1835, *Letters*, 1:63.

39. Poe to John C. McCabe, March 3, 1836, *Letters*, 1:86.

40. Silverman, *Edgar A. Poe*, 120–21.

41. Ibid., 132.

42. Ibid., 140.

43. Poe to Washington Irving, June 21, 1841, *Letters*, 1:162,

44. Beers, *Nathaniel Parker Willis*, 260.

45. Mott, *A History of American Magazines*, 1:508–9. The money figures given above are Mott's estimates, pp. 506–9.

46. Thomas and Jackson, *The Poe Log*, 320.

47. Poe to Frederick W. Thomas, May 25, 1942, *Letters*, 1:197.

48. Poe to Joseph Evans Snodgrass, April 1, 1841, *Letters*, 1:157.

49. For Poe's modest career as a solver of ciphers see Silverman, *Edgar A. Poe*, 152–53.

50. Poe's comments about the story all appear in a letter to Philip P. Cooke, August 9, 1846, *Letters*, 2:328.

51 Poe to Frederick W. Thomas, July 4, 1841, *Letters*, 1:172.

52. Lambert A. Wilmer, *Merlin*, ed. Thomas Ollive Mabbott (New York: Scholars' Facsimiles and Reprints, 1941), 33.

53. George E. Woodberry, *The Life of Edgar Allan Poe* (Boston: Houghton Mifflin, 1885), 2:2–3.

54. Poe to Charles Anthon, late October 1844, *Letters*, 1:270–71.

55. James Russell Lowell, "Our Contributors—No. XVII. Edgar Allan Poe," *Graham's* 27 (February 1845): 53, 50.

56. Thomas and Jackson, *The Poe Log*, 491.

57. Poe to Frederick W. Thomas, May 4, 1845, *Letters*, 1:286.

58. Poe to N. P. Willis, April 20, 1849, *Letters*, 2:436.

59. Thomas and Jackson, *The Poe Log*, 800.

60. Willis's article, "Edgar Poe," was reprinted in *Hurry-Graphs*, p. 249.

61. Thomas and Jackson, *The Poe Log*, 212.

62. George R. Graham, "The Late Edgar Allan Poe," *Graham's* 36 (March 1850): 226.

63. For example, see Michael Allen, *Poe and the British Magazine Tradition* (New York: Oxford University Press, 1969), 157–81.

64. William Charvat makes this point in *The Profession of Authorship in America*, p. 85: "His [Poe's] magazine project, like his tales and poems, was dream work, inspired by revulsion against the realities of American journalism."

65. Poe to James Russell Lowell, October 28, 1944, *Letters*, 1:265.

66. Edmund Wilson, "Thoughts on Being Bibliographed," *Classics and Commercials* (New York: Farrar, Straus, 1950), 112.

67. Daniel Hoffman, *Poe Poe Poe Poe Poe Poe Poe* (Garden City, N.Y.: Doubleday, 1972), xiii.

68. Congdon, *Reminiscences of a Journalist*, 357.

69. Poe was also recycling earlier work. In a brief comment on "Magazine Literature" in the *Evening Mirror* on February 12, 1845, he had made the same points and used the phrase "light artillery," contrasting it with "the Peace-Makers of the intellect."

70. *Edgar Allan Poe: Essays and Reviews*, 1414–15.

Chapter Two:
Cacoethes Scribendi

Epigraph: Madeleine B. Stern, *We the Women: Career Firsts of Nineteenth-Century America* (New York: Schulte, 1963), 39.

1. Poe to Henry Wadsworth Longfellow, May 3, 1841, *Letters*, 1:158.

2. J. Albert Robbins, "Fees Paid to Authors by Certain American Periodicals, 1840–1850," in *Studies in Bibliography*, ed. Fredson Bowers (Charlottesville: Bibliographical Society of the University of Virginia, 1949), 2:100.

3. Mott, *A History of American Magazines*, 1:510, 511.

4. "The Pay for Periodical Writing," *Evening Mirror*, October 12, 1844, 2.

5. *Godey's Lady's Book* 50 (March 1855): 282.

6. Willis, "The Pay for Periodical Writing," 2.

7. Poe to Washington Irving, June 21, 1841, *Letters*, 1:162–63.

8. Joyce W. Warren, *Fanny Fern: An Independent Woman* (New Brunswick, N.J.: Rutgers University Press, 1992), 93. The exact date of the letter is not given. I generally follow this biography for Fanny Fern's life and work.

9. Willis, "The Pay for Periodical Writing," 2.

10. *Edgar Allan Poe: Essays and Reviews*, 1335–36.

11. James D. Hart, *The Popular Book* (New York: Oxford University Press, 1950), 97.

12. Russel Nye, *The Unembarrassed Muse: The Popular Arts in America* (New York: Dial, 1970), 26.

13. Charvat, *The Profession of Authorship in America*, 113. For a full account of Longfellow's literary earning see chapters 8 and 9 of this work.

14. Charvat, *The Profession of Authorship in America*, 125.

15. Nye, *The Unembarrassed Muse*, 93–94.

16. Longfellow's lines provided the title for a collection of newspaper and periodical verse, *The Humbler Poets*, published in 1885 and reprinted in a second edition in 1888.

17. Gordon S. Haight, *Mrs. Sigourney* (New Haven, Conn.: Yale University Press, 1930), 36. I follow this biography for Sigourney's life and work.

18. For more on the vogue of annuals and gift books see Hart, *The Popular Book*, 88–89.

19. Haight, *Mrs. Sigourney*, 109.

20. Ibid., 129.

21. Ibid., 99.

22. For Stephens' life and work I follow Stern, *We the Women: Career Firsts of Nineteenth-Century America*, 29–54.

23. Although he found her style too involved and her sentences too long, Poe put such faults down to the "effervescence of high talent, if not exactly of genius." About her physical characteristics he remarked that she was "tall and slightly inclined to *embonpoint*—an English figure." *Edgar Allan Poe: Essays and Reviews*, 1160.

24. Charles J. Peterson, "Our Contributors—No. XV. Mrs. Ann S. Stephens," *Graham's* 26 (November 1844): 234.

25. The notice appears in a reprint of the Beadle version of the novel published in New York by Benjamin Blom in 1971.

26. Stern, *We the Women*, 36.

27. Ibid., 50.

28. Peterson, "Our Contributors—No. XV. Mrs. Ann S. Stephens," 234.

29. M. S. McKinney, "In the Twilight of Poetry," *Saturday Evening Post*, December 31, 1898, 426.

30. Anna B. Warner, *Susan Warner* (New York: Putnam's, 1909), 282.

31. For these and sales figures of other popular women writers of the 1840s and 1850s see Hart, *The Popular Book*, 93–97.

32. Nye, *The Unembarrassed Muse*, 25.

33. "The Model Husband" is reprinted in *Ruth Hall and Other Writings*, ed. Joyce W. Warren (New Brunswick, N.J.: Rutgers University Press, 1986), 215–16.

34. The claim is substantiated in Warren, *Fanny Fern*, 104.

35. J. C. Derby, *Fifty Years among Authors, Books and Publishers* (New York: G. W. Carleton, 1884), 213. The sales figure is given as 70,000 in Hart, *The Popular Book*, 93.

36. Warren, *Fanny Fern*, 109.

37. "Fresh Leaves" is reprinted in *Ruth Hall and Other Writings*, 290–91.

38. Warren, *Fanny Fern*, 121.

39. Derby, *Fifty Years among Authors, Books and Publishers*, 213.

40. Fanny Fern, *Ruth Hall*, in *Ruth Hall and Other Writings*, 134.

41. Warren, *Fanny Fern*, 145.

42. Derby, *Fifty Years among Authors, Books and Publishers*, 203.

43. Susan Coultrap-McQuin, *Doing Literary Business: American Women Writers in the Nineteenth Century* (Chapel Hill: University of North Carolina Press, 1990), 74.

44. Fred Lewis Pattee, *The Feminine Fifties* (New York: D. Appleton-Century, 1940), 187.

45. Mary Noel, *Villains Galore. . . The Hey-day of the Popular Story Weekly* (New York: Macmillan, 1954), 155.

46. Warren, *Fanny Fern,* 149.

47. Fanny Fern, *Folly as it Flies* (New York: G. W. Carleton, 1868).

48. Noel, *Villains Galore,* 91.

49. James L. Ford, *The Literary Shop and Other Tales* (New York: Chelsea, 1899), 27.

50. Noel, *Villains Galore,* 184.

51. Ford, *The Literary Shop,* 8.

52. Ibid., 28.

53. John Tebbel and Mary Ellen Zuckerman, *The Magazine in America, 1741–1990* (New York: Oxford University Press, 1991), 24.

54. For Alcott's career as a thriller novelist see Madeleine B. Stern, Introduction to *A Double Life: Newly Discovered Thrillers of Louisa May Alcott,* ed. Madeleine B. Stern (Boston: Little, Brown, 1988), 3–29. Stern has assembled an omnibus volume of Alcott's thrillers in *Louisa May Alcott Unmasked: Collected Thrillers* (Boston: Northeastern University Press, 1995).

55. Louisa M. Alcott, *Little Women* (Boston: Little, Brown, 1900), 291–92. Published originally by Roberts Brothers in two parts in 1868 and 1869.

56. James Parton, ed., *Eminent Women of the Age* (Hartford, Conn.: S. M. Betts, 1868), 219.

57. Like Fanny Fern and Gail Hamilton, Grace Greenwood was a pen name, that of Sara Jane Lippincott. For an attempt at explaining the vogue of pen names among women writers of the time see Ann Douglas, *The Feminization of American Culture* (New York: Knopf, 1977), 186. See also Ann D. Wood, "The 'Scribbling Women' and Fanny Fern: Why Women Wrote," *American Quarterly* 23 (Spring 1971): 17–18.

58. Parton, *Eminent Women of the Age,* 84.

59. Ibid., 207.

60. H. Augusta Dodge, ed., *Gail Hamilton's Life in Letters* (Boston: Lee and Shepard, 1901), 1:107–8.

61. Ibid., 1:118.

62. Ibid., 1:139.

63. Ibid., 1:411.

64. Ibid., 1:275.

65. Ibid., 2:1065.

66. Ibid., 1:410.

67. Ibid., 1:384.

68. Gail Hamilton, "My Book," reprinted in *Gail Hamilton: Selected Writings,* ed. Susan Coultrap-McQuin (New Brunswick, N.J.: Rutgers University Press, 1992), 126–27.

69. Dodge, *Gail Hamilton's Life in Letters,* 1:412.

70. John Tebbel, *Between Covers: The Rise and Transformation of Book Publishing in America* (New York: Oxford University Press, 1987), 62.

71. Dodge, *Gail Hamilton's Life in Letters,* 2:643

72. Gail Hamilton, *A Battle of the Books* (Cambridge, Mass.: Riverside Press, 1870), 285, 286, 288.

73. Dodge, *Gail Hamilton's Life in Letters,* 2:1020–21.

Chapter Three: Laying Pipes

Epigraph: Gilbert Patten, "Dime-Novel Days," *Saturday Evening Post*, March 7, 1931, 52. The first part of the two-part article appeared on February 28. The quotation is from an acecdote about Ingraham's manner of writing adventure fiction.

1. *American Notes: Rudyard Kipling's West,* ed. Arrell Morgan Gibson (Norman: University of Oklahoma Press, 1981), viii–ix.

2. Tebbel, *Between Covers*, 71.

3. Ralph Admari, "Ballou, the Father of the Dime Novel," *The American Book Collector* 4 (September–October 1933): 121.

4. Noel, *Villains Galore*, 32.

5. Ibid., 53.

6. Ibid., 33.

7. The first dime novel appeared under the imprint of Irwin P. Beadle and Company, with the firm subsequently known simply as Beadle and Company. Prior to 1860 it was known as Beadle and Adams.

8. Albert Johannsen, *The House of Beadle and Adams and Its Dime and Nickel Novels* (Norman: University of Oklahoma Press, 1950), 1:4–5. I follow this massive study for subsequent details about dime novels and their authors.

9. Jay Monaghan, *The Great Rascal: The Life and Adventures of Ned Buntline* (Boston: Little, Brown, 1952), 250.

10. Henry Nash Smith, *Virgin Land: The American West as Symbol and Myth* (Cambridge, Mass.: Harvard University Press, 1970), 106.

11. George C. Jenks, "Dime Novel Makers," *Bookman* 20 (October 1904): 112.

12. The letterhead is reproduced in Johannsen, *The House of Beadle and Adams*, 2:295.

13. Patten, "Dime-Novel Days," *Saturday Evening Post*, March 7, 1931, 60.

14. Gary Scharnhorst and Jack Bales, *The Lost Life of Horatio Alger, Jr.* (Bloomington: Indiana University Press, 1985), 38. Unless noted otherwise, I follow this account for Alger's life and work.

15. Scharnhorst and Bales, *The Lost Life of Horatio Alger, Jr.*, 62.

16. Nye, *The Unembarrassed Muse*, 62.

17. John Tebbel, *From Rags to Riches: Horatio Alger, Jr., and The American Dream* (New York: Macmillan, 1963), 141.

18. Ibid., 142.

19. Scharnhorst and Bales, *The Lost Life of Horatio Alger, Jr.*, 144.

20. Mott, *Golden Multitudes*, 158, 159.

21. I follow Patten's account of his career in his two-part article in 1931 in the *Saturday Evening Post*. Essentially the same information material is covered in less detailed form in what was later published as Patten's autobiography, *Frank Merriwell's "Father,"* ed. Harriet Hinsdale and Tony London (Norman: University of Oklahoma Press, 1964).

22. Patten, "Dime-Novel Days," *Saturday Evening Post*, February 28, 1931, 125.

23. Jenks, "Dime Novel Makers," 111.

24. Patten, "Dime-Novel Days," *Saturday Evening Post*, February 28, 1931, 126.

25. Edward W. Bok, "Literary Factories," *Publishers Weekly*, August 13, 1892, 231.

26. William G. Patten, "Experiences with Publishers," *Writer* 3 (March 1889): 59–60.

27. Quentin Reynolds, *The Fiction Factory or From Pulp Row to Quality Street* (New York: Random House, 1956), 90. Ormond Smith's original letter to Patten, outlining the series, is given in Christine Bold, *Selling the Wild West: Popular Western Fiction, 1860–1960* (Bloomington: Indiana University Press, 1987), 5.

28. Patten, "Dime-Novel Days," *Saturday Evening Post*, March 7, 1931, 57

29. James M. Cain, "The Man Merriwell," *Saturday Evening Post*, June 11, 1927, 129.

30. After the deaths of the founders of the firm, Francis Street in 1883 and Francis S. Smith in 1887, Smith's two sons took over the operation.

31. Cain, "The Man Merriwell," 132.

32. "For It Was Indeed He," *Fortune* 9 (April 1934): 87. This unsigned article is the major source of information about Stratemeyer and his secretive syndicate. It is relied on in Carol Billman, *The Secret of the Stratemeyer Syndicate* (New York: Ungar, 1986).

33. The formation date is variously given as 1906 to 1908. The syndicate was incorporated in 1910.

34. Billman, *The Secret of the Stratemeyer Syndicate*, 26.

35. *Tom Swift and His Giant Magnet* (New York: Grosset and Dunlap, 1932), 216.

36. Roger Garis, *My Father Was Uncle Wiggily* (New York: McGraw-Hill, 1966), 8.

37. Ibid., 83–84.

38. Ibid., 168–69.

39. Tebbel, *Between Covers*, 301.

40. Judy Klemesrud, "100 Books," *New York Times*, April 4, 1968, 52.

41. "All you need," a pulp editor noted, "is some credit from a dealer in pulp paper and from a printer, and an arrangement with a distribution company. You can promise to pay authors after publication. You can pay the printing and paper bills when the check for sold copies comes in from the distributor." Robert Kenneth Jones, *The Shudder Pulps: A History of the Weird Menace Magazines of the 1930s* (New York: New American Library, 1978), 115.

42. Lee Server examines the world of pulp fiction under the following headings: horror and fantasy; adventure (including Western); private eye; romance and sex; hero; weird menace; science fiction. *Danger Is My Business: An Illustrated History of the Fabulous Pulp Magazines* (San Francisco: Chronicle Books, 1993).

43. Mabie, "A Year's Literary Production," 797.

44. Mott, *A History of American Magazines*, 4:2.

45. Nye, *The Unembarrassed Muse*, 210.

46. Allan R. Bosworth, "The Golden Age of Pulps," *Atlantic* 208 (July 1961): 57–60.

47. Harold Brainerd Hersey, *Pulpwood Editor* (New York: Frederick A. Stokes, 1937), 32–33, 130–31. For a brief, unflattering account of Hersey's editorial career ("Hersey was what you call an 'idea man,' and the problem was that most of his ideas were no good"), see Server, *Danger Is My Business*, 30–31.

48. *The Autobiography of Upton Sinclair* (New York: Harcourt, Brace and World, 1962), 50.

49. Ibid., 50–51.

50. Sinclair, "The Confessions of a Young Author," 2750.

51. I generally follow Rinehart's account of her writing life in her autobiography, *My Story* (New York: Farrar and Rinehart, 1931; rev. ed., 1948). A biographer suggests the claim

of financial necessity was largely a proper Victorian mask for what was simply burning ambition to write. Jan Cohn, *Improbable Fiction: The Life of Mary Roberts Rinehart* (Pittsburgh: University of Pittsburgh Press, 1980), 30–31.

52. Rinehart, *My Story*, 86.

53. Mary Roberts Rinehart, *Writing Is Work* (Boston: The Writer, Inc., 1939), 12. First published as an article in the *Saturday Evening Post*, March 11, 1939, for which Rinehart was paid $1,500.

54. Rinehart, *Writing Is Work*, 14, 22.

55. Rinehart, *My Story*, 90.

56. Irvin S. Cobb recalled that "Lorimer and Davis, in the matter of spying out fresh talent, were the Christopher Columbuses of their day. And they were twin Burbanks when it came to the nuturing and cultivation of the same." *Exit Laughing*, 116.

57. Robert H. Davis, "A Woman of Some Importance," *Mary Roberts Rinehart: A Sketch of the Woman and Her Work* (New York: George H. Doran [no date]), 36.

58. Cohn, *Improbable Fiction*, 220.

59. Mary Roberts Rinehart, "Thoughts," *Ladies' Home Journal*, May 1931, 179. Rinehart added: "But do not be misled by the diagram! A logical and consistent crime story is still a most difficult undertaking." See also Mary Roberts Rinehart, "The Detective Story," in *Mary Roberts Rinehart: A Sketch of the Woman and Her Work*, 39–42.

60. Actually, Rinehart had received an advance payment from Bobbs-Merrill a month after *The Circular Staircase* began appearing in *All-Story*—and the publisher was already putting the story in type when the final magazine installment appeared. Cohn, *Improbable Fiction*, 44.

61. John J. McAleer, *Royal Decree: Conversations with Rex Stout* (Ashton, Md.: Pontes Press, 1983), 3.

Chapter Four: The Precious Over-Note

Epigraph: Frank Gruber, *Zane Grey* (New York: World, 1970), 152. The passage is from a diary Grey kept in 1919 while writing his novel *Wanderer of the Wasteland*.

1. Carlton Jackson, *Zane Grey*, rev. ed. (Boston: Twayne, 1989), 12. For Grey's life and work I follow this account, Gruber's *Zane Grey*, and Grey's sketch of his career, "My Own Life," *Zane Grey: The Man and His Work* (New York: Harper and Brothers, 1928), 1–19. The latter appeared originally as an article, "Breaking Through: The Story of My Own Life," *American Magazine* 98 (July 1924): 13 ff.

2. Unless indicated otherwise, all Grey's remarks as well as those made to him are taken from "My Own Life."

3. The larger-than-life exploits of Charles Jesse Jones are recounted in Robert Easton and Mackenzie Brown, *Lord of Beasts: The Saga of Buffalo Jones* (Tucson: University of Arizona Press, 1961). For an opposing view of Jones's career see Richard A. Bartlett, *Yellowstone, A Wilderness Besieged* (Tucson: University of Arizona Press, 1985), 340.

4. Robert H. Boyle, "The Man Who Lived Two Lives in One," *Sports Illustrated*, April 29, 1968, 78.

5. Gruber, *Zane Grey*, 84.

6. For more of Grey's astonishing publishing record see Hart, *The Popular Book,* 219.

7. Jackson, *Zane Grey,* 124.

8. Ibid., 126.

9. William F. Nolan, *Max Brand: Western Giant* (Bowling Green, Ohio: Bowling Green State University Popular Press, 1985), 2. For most details of Faust's life and work I follow Robert Easton, *Max Brand, The Big "Westerner"* (Norman: University of Oklahoma Press, 1970). See also William Bloodworth, Introduction to *The Collected Stories of Max Brand,* ed. Robert and Jane Easton (Lincoln: University of Nebraska Press, 1994), xi–xx.

10. John Schoolcraft, ed., *The Notebooks and Poems of "Max Brand"* (New York: Dodd, Mead, 1957), 49.

11. Ibid., 22.

12. Easton, who recounts the anecdote, points out that some believe Faust worked on the story for a couple of days before submitting it to Davis. Similarly, Gruber says the story was a serial and was written in "a very few days." Frank Gruber, *The Pulp Jungle* (Los Angeles: Sherbourne Press, 1967), 121–22.

13. Schoolcraft, *Notebooks and Poems,* 35.

14. John Schoolcraft, "Bohemian Days on Grub Street," in Nolan, *Max Brand,* 28–29.

15. Schoolcraft, *Notebooks and Poems,* 39.

16. Gruber, *Zane Grey,* 108.

17. Schoolcraft, *Notebooks and Poems,* 71.

18. Easton, *Max Brand,* 68.

19. Schoolcraft, *Notebooks and Poems,* 39.

20. Ibid., 38.

21. Ibid., 151, 187.

22. Ibid., 85.

23. Ibid., 68.

24. Easton, *Max Brand,* 199. Heinie was Faust's nickname.

25. Steve Fisher, "A Farewell to Max Brand," in Nolan, *Max Brand,* 42.

26. Ibid., 227.

27. Ibid., 263.

28. Hersey, *Pulpwood Editor,* 127.

29. Paul R. Reynolds, *The Middle Man: The Adventures of a Literary Agent* (New York: William Morrow, 1972), 41. Reynolds ranks Jones as a dazzling three-cent-a-word pulp writer.

30. Server, *Danger Is My Business,* 12–13.

31. "Burks of the Pulps," *New Yorker,* February 15, 1936, 12–13. Burks is the subject of a chapter, "The Speed Merchant of the Pulps," in Jones, *The Shudder Pulps,* 83–95.

32. Gruber, *The Pulp Jungle,* 29. My account of Gruber's career is drawn from his memoir. Burks himself failed to move on to better work. According to Lee Server, he finally lost interest in writing and disappeared from New York, surfacing years later in Chicago as a spiritualist giving psychic readings for a fee. In a not dissimilar vein, L. Ron Hubbard, who labored in a variety of pulp genres in the 1930s and '40s and also served as president of the New York chapter of the American Fiction Guild, moved on to found the Church of Scientology. *Danger Is My Business,* 137, 128.

33. Gruber, *The Pulp Jungle,* 67.

34. Ibid., 77.

35. Joseph T. Shaw, ed., *The Hard-Boiled Omnibus: Early Stories from Black Mask* (New York: Simon and Schuster, 1946), vi, vii.

36. Gruber, *The Pulp Jungle,* 177, 179, 184.

37. Ibid., 116.

38. Robert W. Fenton, *The Big Swingers* (Englewood Cliffs, N.J.: Prentice-Hall, 1967), 40. For Burroughs life and work I follow this biography and especially Irwin Porges, *Edgar Rice Burroughs: The Man Who Created Tarzan* (Provo, Utah: Brigham Young University Press, 1975).

39. Fenton, *The Big Swingers,* 41. Through a printing error the name first appeared as Norman Bean.

40. Porges, *Edgar Rice Burroughs,* 5–6.

41. Ibid., 123–24, 125.

42. Alva Johnston, "How to Become a Great Writer," *Saturday Evening Post,* July 29, 1939, 7, 6. The other lessons were: be a disappointed man; achieve no success at anything you touch; lead an unbearably drab and uninteresting life; hate civilization; learn no grammar; read little; write nothing; have an ordinary mind and commonplace tastes, approximating those of the great reading public.

43. Porges, *Edgar Rice Burroughs,* 342.

44. Nye, *The Unembarrassed Muse,* 273.

45. Kyne described his business and investment activities in "I Used to Be a Business Man," *American Magazine* 115 (June 1933): 58 ff.

46. Introduction to *My Story That I Liked Best,* ed. Ray Long (New York: International Magazine Company, 1925), 7.

47. Sinclair Lewis once previewed *Babbitt* for H. L. Mencken with a tongue-in-cheek remark that acknowledged the range and popularity of Kyne's work. "In certain ways," he said, "it seems to be different both from The Sheik, and the better works of Ethel M. Dell and Peter B. Kyne." Mark Schorer, *Sinclair Lewis: An American Life* (New York: McGraw-Hill, 1961), 291.

48. Long, *My Story That I Like Best,* 54, 53.

49. Cobb, *Exit Laughing,* 129.

50. Ibid., 333.

51. The number of Judge Priest stories is put at "forty-odd" in Wayne Chatterton, *Irvin S. Cobb* (Boston: Twayne, 1986), 94.

52. Rinehart, *My Story,* 148.

53. Ibid.

54. Both quoted passages appear in Cohn, *Improbable Fiction,* 219.

55. Robert Polito, *Savage Art: A Biography of Jim Thompson* (New York: Knopf, 1995), 340. For Thompson's life and work, here and again in chapter 8, I follow this account.

56. Tebbell, *Between Covers,* 434.

57. The figures are given in Kenneth C. Davis, *Two-Bit Culture: The Paperbacking of America* (Boston: Houghton Mifflin, 1984), 155.

58. Tebbell, *Between Covers,* 434.

59. Thomas L. Bonn, *Heavy Traffic and High Culture: New American Library as Literary Gatekeeper in the Paperback Revolution* (Carbondale: Southern Illinois University Press, 1989), 21.

60. E. Howard Hunt, "A Writer's Life," *Books at Brown* 33 (1986): 128.

61. Thomas L. Bonn, *Undercover: An Illustrated History of American Mass Market Paperbacks* (New York: Penguin, 1982), 50.

62. Polito, *Savage Art*, 342.

63. Ibid., 344.

64. Ibid.

65. Ibid., 384.

66. M. E. Kerr, *Me Me Me Me Me* (New York: Harper Trophy, 1983), 212. M. E. Kerr, a play on the surname of Marijane Meaker, was, like Vin Packer, one of the author's pen names. For her work as Packer see Jon L. Breen, "The Novels of Vin Packer," ed. Jon L. Breen and Martin Harry Greenberg, *Murder Off the Rack: Critical Studies of Ten Paperback Masters* (Metuchen, N.J.: Scarecrow Press, 1989), 55–69.

67. Polito, *Savage Art*, 387.

68. Ibid., 392.

69. Ibid., 4.

Chapter Five: Sublime Tramps

Epigraph: *Martin Eden* in *Jack London: Novels and Social Writings*, 794–795.

1. Julian Hawthorne, "American Magazines and Authors," *Belford's Monthly* 1 (June 1888): 29.

2. Julian Hawthorne, "Journalism the Destroyer of Literature," *Critic* 48 (February, 1906): 171.

3. Frank Luther Mott, *American Journalism, A History: 1690–1960*, 3d ed. (New York: Macmillan, 1962), 201.

4. William Dean Howells, *Years of My Youth* (New York: Harper and Brothers, 1916), 141.

5. James Parton, "Journalism as a Profession for Young Men," *Writer* 21 (May 1888): 105, 106.

6. Norman Hapgood, *The Changing Years* (New York: Farrar and Rinehart, 1930), 117.

7. Samuel G. Blythe, *The Making of a Newspaper Man* (Philadelphia: Henry Altemus, 1912), 236.

8. A. B. Guthrie, Jr., *The Blue Hen's Chick* (New York: McGraw-Hill, 1965), 196.

9. *Mark Twain: Roughing It* (New York: Library of America, 1984), 746, 862. I draw here on material developed at more length in an article, "Journalism, Writing, and American Literature" (Occasional Paper No. 5, April 1987, Gannett Center for Media Studies [now the Freedom Forum Media Studies Center]), and in a book, *Hemingway's Art of Nonfiction* (New York: St. Martin's, 1990), chap. 1.

10. *The Kingdom of Art: Willa Cather's First Principles and Critical Statements, 1893–1896*, ed. Bernice Slote (Lincoln: University of Nebraska Press, 1966), 332.

11. Gertrude Stein, *The Autobiography of Alice B. Toklas* (New York: Harcourt, Brace, 1933), 262.

12. Ernest Hemingway to Gertrude Stein and Alice B. Toklas, November 9, 1923, *Ernest Hemingway: Selected Letters, 1917–1961*, ed. Carlos Baker (New York: Scribner's, 1981), 101.

13. Howells, *Years of My Youth*, 143.

14. *Theodore Dreiser: A Selection of Uncollected Prose,* ed. Donald Pizer (Detroit: Wayne State University Press, 1977), 73.

15. For Davis's career I follow Arthur Lubow, *The Reporter Who Would Be King: A Biography of Richard Harding Davis* (New York: Scribner's, 1992).

16. Roger Garis, *My Father was Uncle Wiggily,* 87–88.

17. David Graham Phillips, *The Great God Success* (Ridgewood, N.J.: Gregg Press, 1967), 11, 13, 84. The book appeared originally in 1901 under the pseudonym John Graham. For Phillips's career I follow Abe Ravitz, *David Graham Phillips* (New York: Twayne, 1966).

18. Christopher P. Wilson, *The Labor of Words: Literary Professionalism in the Progressive Era* (Athens: University of Georgia Press, 1985), 156.

19. For Terhune's life and work I follow his autobiographical account in *To the Best of My Memory* (New York: Harper and Brothers, 1930).

20. Terhune, *To the Best of My Memory,* 105.

21. Cobb, *Exit Laughing,* 127.

22. Terhune, *To the Best of My Memory,* 148.

23. Ibid., 174–75.

24. Ibid., 183.

25. Ibid., 200. Ray Long tells how the Lad stories began in "Over a Bottle of Scotch," *20 Best Short Stories in Ray Long's 20 Years as an Editor* (New York: Ray Long & Richard S. Smith, 1932), 372–73.

26. Terhune, *To the Best of My Memory,* 213, 215.

27. Ibid., 234, 239.

28. Ibid., 218.

29. The story sale is mentioned in Schorer, *Sinclair Lewis,* 217. On the same page Schorer remarks that "a close reading of *Dad* does not enable one to isolate one man's prose from the other's in the general wash of it." I follow Schorer's biography for Lewis's years as a journalist and hack writer.

30. Terhune, *To the Best of My Memory,* 195.

31. Sinclair Lewis, "I'm an Old Newspaperman Myself," *The Man from Main Street,* ed. Harry E. Maule and Melville H. Cane (New York: Random House, 1953), 91.

32. Schorer, *Sinclair Lewis,* 154

33. Ibid., 156.

34. Jack London to Cloudesley Johns, October 24, 1899, *The Letters of Jack London,* ed. Earle Labor, Robert C. Leitz III, and I. Milo Shepard (Stanford, Calif.: Stanford University Press, 1988), 1:118.

35. The exchange of letter between Lewis and London is in *Letters from Jack London,* ed. King Hendricks and Irving Shepard (New York: Odyssey Press, 1965), 483–85. The plot summary is given on p. 485 n. l.

36. Schorer, *Sinclair Lewis,* 171.

37. Ibid., 186.

38. Ibid., 197.

39. Dorothy Thompson to Rose Wilder Lane, July 28, 1932, *Dorothy Thompson and Rose Wilder Lane: Forty Years of Friendship,* ed. William Holtz (Columbia: University of Missouri Press, 1991), 131.

40. Sinclair Lewis, "Literature as a Business," in *The Man from Main Street,* 194.

41. Andrew Sinclair, *Jack: A Biography of Jack London* (New York: Harper and Row, 1977), 168. Unless indicated otherwise, I follow this account of London's life and work.

42. London to Anna Strunsky, July 24, 1901, *The Letters of Jack London,* 1:250. Christopher P. Wilson takes note of London's disdain for regular newspaper and magazine work in *The Labor of Words,* p. 97.

43. London to Cloudesley Johns, December 22, 1900, *Letters,* 1:226.

44. London to Emanuel Haldeman-Julius, May 21, 1913, *Letters,* 3:1172.

45. *Jack London: Novels and Social Writings,* 794–95.

46. London to S. S. McClure, April 10, 1906, *Letters,* 2:570.

47. Jack London, "Getting into Print," *No Mentor but Myself: A Collection of Articles, Essays, Reviews, and Letters,* ed. Dale L. Walker (Port Washington, N.Y.: Kennikat, 1979), 55. The article appeared originally in the *Editor* in 1903.

48. *Jack London: Novels and Social Writings,* 63.

49. London to the *Youth's Companion,* January 7, 1899, *Letters,* 1:41–42.

50. London to Cloudesley Johns, November 21, 1899, *Letters,* 1:127.

51. London to Elwyn Hoffman, June 17, 1900, *Letters,* 1:194.

52. London to Anna Strunsky, February 3, 1900, *Letters,* 1:151–152. As it turned out, Johns eventually did live up to his words. He withdrew the story from *Munsey's* when the unrevised version was accepted by the *Puritan,* a women's magazine also published by Frank Munsey. See *Letters,* 1:148 n. 5.

53. James Lundquist, *Jack London: Adventures, Ideas, and Fiction* (New York: Ungar, 1987), 44.

54. Jack London, "The Question of a Name," in *No Mentor But Myself,* 19.

55. Peter Lyon, *Success Story: The Life and Times of S. S. McClure* (New York: Scribner's, 1963), 158.

56. James Oliver Curwood, *Son of the Forests* (Garden City, N.Y.: Doubleday, Doran, 1930), 92. Curwood's autobiography, left unfinished at his death, was completed by Dorothea A. Bryant. I follow this sketchy work and Judith A. Eldridge, *James Oliver Curwood* (Bowling Green, Ohio: Bowling Green State University Popular Press, 1993), for Curwood's life and work.

57. Curwood, *Son of the Forests,* 190.

58. Eldridge, *James Oliver Curwood,* 55.

59. Curwood, *Son of the Forests,* 196.

60. Eldridge, *James Oliver Curwood,* 76.

61. Ray Long, "Jim Curwood," *Bookman* 66 (November 1927): 289–290.

62. Eldridge, *James Oliver Curwood,* 136. Peter B. Kyne was another writer published in book form by the magazine.

63. Long, *20 Best Short Stories in Ray Long's 20 Years as an Editor,* 209.

64. Ibid., 209, 211.

Chapter Six: Writing for the Millions

Epigraph: S. S. McClure, *My Autobiography* (New York: Frederick A. Stokes, 1914), 234–35.

1. London to Cloudesley Johns, September 12, 1899, *Letters,* 1:110.

2. *Jack London: Novels and Social Writings,* 725–26.

3. Elmo Scott Watson, *History of Auxiliary Newspaper Service in the United States* (Champaign, Ill.: Illini Publishing Company, 1923), 22. Watson expanded his pioneering study of syndicates into a master's thesis at Northwestern University that was published in revised form in 1935 as a supplement to *The Publishers' Auxiliary.* The work is available through University Microfilms, Ann Arbor, Michigan, under the title *A History of Newspaper Syndicates in the United States, 1865–1935.* I was unable to draw upon Charles A. Johanningsmeier's *Fiction and the American Literary Marketplace: The Role of Newspaper Syndicates in America, 1860–1900* (New York: Cambridge University Press, 1997), a study that appeared as my book was in production. This is the most thorough account to date of the origin, development, and subsequent decline of the literary syndicates, though unlike Watson's work it is concerned mainly with syndicates that offered fiction and treats a narrower range of time. For the development of fiction syndicates in England see Cross, *The Common Writer,* 208–9.

4. Elmo Scott Watson, *History of Auxiliary Newspaper Service in the United States,* 22–23.

5. *Sinclair Lewis: Babbitt* (New York: Library of America, 1992), 587, 601.

6. McClure, *My Autobiography,* 168.

7. Cross, *The Common Writer,* 208.

8. Lyon, *Success Story,* 55–56.

9. Ibid., 57.

10. Ibid., 58.

11. Ibid., 71.

12. Howells, "The Man of Letters as a Man of Business," 441. When Howells reprinted the article in *Literature and Life* in 1911 he removed material about newspaper syndicates, perhaps reasoning that they had declined in importance.

13. Ibid.

14. Hamlin Garland, *Roadside Meetings* (New York: Macmillan, 1930), 341.

15. Lyon, *Success Story,* 78, 80.

16. Bok describes the start of his syndicate in *The Americanization of Edward Bok* (New York: Scribner's, 1923), 78ff.

17. Ford, *The Literary Shop,* 299–305, 166.

18. Richard H. Waldo, "The Genius of S. S. McClure," *Editor and Publisher,* July 21, 1934, 80.

19. Garland, *Roadside Meetings,* 307.

20. "Editorial Notes," *McClure's,* January 1898, 289.

21. Ellery Sedgwick, *The Happy Profession* (Boston: Little, Brown, 1946), 139.

22. McClure, *My Autobiography,* 234–35.

23. Mary E. Tomkins, *Ida M. Tarbell* (New York: Twayne, 1974), 30. For Tarbell's life and work I follow this study, Kathleen Brady, *Ida Tarbell: Portrait of a Muckraker* (New York: Seaview/ Putnam, 1984), and Tarbell's autobiography, *All in the Day's Work* (New York: Macmillan, 1939).

24. Tarbell, *All in the Day's Work,* 86

25. Tarbell gives the figure in her autobiography. Kathleen Brady sets it at the amount Tarbell had settled upon with newspaper editors, $6, or some four words per penny. *Ida Tarbell,* 56.

26. Tarbell, *All in the Day's Work*, 100.

27. R. W. Stallman, *Stephen Crane* (New York: George Braziller, 1968), 87.

28. Stephen Crane to Hamlin Garland, November 15, 1894, *The Correspondence of Stephen Crane*, ed. Stanley Wertheim and Paul Sorrentino (New York: Columbia University Press, 1988), 1:79. In *Success Story* (p. 129, note) Lyon says McClure kept the manuscript for nine months. I generally follow this work and Stallman's biography for Crane's association with McClure.

29. Irving Bacheller, *From Stores of Memory* (New York: Farrar and Rinehart, 1938), 110.

30. Bacheller recalled his syndicate operation in both *From Stores of Memory* and *Coming Up the Road: Memories of a North Country Boyhood* (Indianapolis: Bobbs-Merrill, 1928).

31. Mott, *Golden Multitudes*, 203–4.

32. Bacheller, *Coming Up the Road*, 278–79.

33. Willa Cather, "When I Knew Stephen Crane," in *The World and the Parish: Willa Cather's Articles and Reviews, 1893–1902*, ed. William M. Curtin (Lincoln: University of Nebraska Press, 1970), 2:776–77. Cather's recollection, written on the occasion of Crane's death in 1900, is possibly heightened with invention. On this point see Christopher Benfey, *The Double Life of Stephen Crane* (New York: Knopf, 1992), 121.

34. Bacheller, *From Stores of Memory*, 111.

35. Crane to S. S. McClure, January 27, 1896, *Correspondence*, 1:193.

36. Lyon, *Success Story*, 140.

37. Crane to Paul Revere Reynolds, October [no day] 1897, *Correspondence*, 1:305.

38. London to George P. Brett, March 7, 1907, *Letters*, 2:675.

39. Crane to Paul Revere Reynolds, October [no day] 1897, *Correspondence*, 1:305–6.

40. Crane to Paul Revere Reynolds, October 20, 1898, *Correspondence*, 2:380.

41. Crane to Paul Revere Reynolds, January 27, 1899, *Correspondence*, 2:422.

42. Porges, *Edgar Rice Burroughs*, 158.

43. Burton Rascoe, *We Were Interrupted* (Garden City, NY: Doubleday, 1947), 66.

44. Penelope Niven, *Carl Sandburg* (New York: Scribner's, 1991), 331. For an account of the political turmoil surrounding the poet's brief time in Europe, see Philip R. Yannella, *The Other Sandburg* (Jackson: University Press of Mississippi, 1996).

45. Rascoe, *We Were Interrupted*, 72.

46. For Oscar Odd McIntyre's odd career, including the renowned inaccuracy of his syndicated column, see Charles B. Driscoll, *The Life of O. O. McIntyre* (New York: Greystone Press, 1938). Driscoll was the column's editor.

47. John N. Wheeler, "Selling Other Men's Brains," *Saturday Evening Post*, March 10, 1928, 16.

48. Wheeler, "Selling Other Men's Brains," 48.

49. Hemingway's Spanish journalism is examined in William Braasch Watson, "Hemingway's Spanish Civil War Dispatches," *Hemingway Review* 7 (Spring 1988): 4–13. The article introduces a special issue of the journal devoted to Hemingway in the Spanish war.

50. See Carlos Baker's assessment in *Ernest Hemingway: A Life Story* (New York: Scribner's, 1969), 329, and Phillip Knightley's in *The First Casualty* (New York: Harcourt, Brace, 1975), 212–14.

51 John N. Wheeler, *I've Got News for You* (New York: Dutton, 1961), 183.

52. Wheeler, *I've Got News for You*, 139.

53. Wheeler, "Selling Other Men's Brains," 52.

Chapter Seven: Sporting Life

Epigraph: Ring Lardner, *Lose with a Smile* (New York: Scribner's, 1933), 79. The passage is taken from lyrics written by the outfielder-songwriter Danny Warner.

1. For Patten's few predecessors in sports fiction see Michael Oriard, *Dreaming of Heroes: American Sports Fiction, 1868–1980* (Chicago: Nelson-Hall, 1982), 27.

2. For Herbert's life and work I follow Luke White, Jr., *Henry William Herbert and the American Publishing Scene, 1831–1858* (Newark, N.J.: Carteret Book Club, 1943). See also William S. Hunt, *Frank Forester: A Tragedy in Exile* (Newark, N.J.: Carteret Book Club, 1933).

3. The remark appears in a review of *Twice-Told Tales, Edgar Allen Poe: Essays and Reviews,* 578.

4. White, *Henry William Herbert,* 27. Fay was a New York lawyer who wrote a best-selling novel, *Norman Leslie,* that Poe ridiculed in a review. In a letter soliciting information for the Literati series, Poe asked: "Is Herbert living in N.Y?—if so, where?" Poe to Evert A. Duyckinck [?], January 30, 1846, *Letters,* 2:313.

5. John F. Reiger, *American Sportsmen and the Origins of Conservation,* rev. ed. (Norman: University of Oklahoma Press, 1986), 28.

6. Poe to Lydia H. Sigourney, November 16, 1842, *Letters,* 1:187.

7. Robbins, "Fees Paid to Authors by Certain American Periodicals, 1840–1850," 101.

8. Some of Grey's outdoor writing is collected in *The Best of Zane Grey, Outdoorsman,* ed. George Reiger (Harrisburg, Penn.: Stackpole Books, 1992).

9. Gruber, *Zane Grey,* 180. A recent critic holds that Grey's outdoor exploits "were not merely recreational, they kept him alive in every sense: psychically, physically, creatively." Jane Tompkins, *West of Everything: The Inner Life of Westerns* (New York: Oxford University Press, 1992), 165.

10. Upton Sinclair, *Money Writes!* (New York: Albert and Charles Boni, 1927), 18.

11. I draw here on my account of Hemingway's *Esquire* letters in *Hemingway's Art of Non-fiction,* 64.

12. Baker, *Hemingway,* 271. Hemingway's personal library contained four of Grey's angling books, according to Michael S. Reynolds in *Hemingway's Reading, 1910–1940* (Princeton, N.J.: Princeton University Press, 1981), 132.

13. John Raeburn, *Fame Became of Him: Hemingway as Public Writer* (Bloomington: Indiana University Press, 1984), 46.

14. Ernest Hemingway, "Monologue to the Maestro: A High Seas Letter," *By-Line: Ernest Hemingway,* ed. William White (New York: Scribner's, 1967), 214.

15. Weber, *Hemingway's Art of Non-fiction,* 65.

16. Gruber, *Zane Grey,* 36.

17. Henry Steele Commager, "When Majors Wrote for Minors," *Saturday Review of Literature,* May 10, 1952, 45.

18. Robert Cantwell, "A Sneering Laugh with the Bases Loaded," *Sports Illustrated,* April 23, 1962, 74.

19. "William Heyliger," *The Junior Book of Authors,* ed. Stanley J. Kunitz and Howard Haycraft, 2nd rev. ed. (New York: H. W. Wilson, 1951), 161.

20. William Heyliger, "Writing Fiction for Boys," *Fiction By Its Makers,* ed. Francis X. Talbot, S.J. (New York: America Press, 1928), 185.

21. On this point see the comment by the pulp editor Harold Hersey in *Pulpwood Editor*, 192.

22. John R. Tunis, *A Measure of Independence* (New York: Atheneum, 1964), 287.

23. Ibid., 116.

24. Ibid., 175.

25. Ibid., 157.

26. Darwin Payne, *The Man of Only Yesterday: Frederick Lewis Allen* (New York: Harper and Row, 1975), 136.

27. Tunis, *A Measure of Independence*, 190–91.

28. Ibid., 215.

29. Leverett T. Smith, Jr., "John R. Tunis's American Epic; or, Bridging the Gap between Juvenile and Adults Sport Fiction," *The Achievement of American Sport Literature: A Critical Appraisal*, ed. Wiley Lee Umphlett (Cranbury, N.J.: Associated University Presses, 1991), 47.

30. I follow Gallico's accounts of his writing life in the introductions to *Confessions of a Story Writer* (New York: Knopf, 1947) and *Further Confessions of a Story Writer* (Garden City, N.Y.: Doubleday, 1961).

31. Gallico, *Further Confessions of a Story Writer*, 13.

32. Gallico, *Confessions of a Story Writer*, 251.

33. Ibid., 233–34.

34. In a foreword to the book, Wheeler made no mention of the collaboration, saying only that Mathewson "always. . . has been a student and something of a writer" and the book was a "true tale of Big Leaguers, their habits and their methods of playing the game, written by one of them." Christy Mathewson, *Pitching in a Pinch* (New York: Stein and Day, 1977), xv. This reprinting of the 1912 book has an introduction by the sportswriter Red Smith.

35. Wheeler, *I've Got News For You*, 13.

36. London to George Hough Perry, February 4, 1915, *Letters*, 3:1421.

37. For Lardner's life and work I mainly follow Jonathan Yardley, *Ring: A Biography of Ring Lardner* (New York: Random House, 1977).

38. Van Loan, for example, is credited with contacting Lorimer on Lardner's behalf in Issac F. Marcosson, *Before I Forget* (New York: Dodd, Mead, 1959), 111, and the story is repeated in Oriard, *Dreaming of Heroes*, 333 n. 16. Ring Lardner, Jr., says his father discussed the idea of the story with Van Loan and that Van Loan, who wrote for the *Post*, probably told Lorimer to be on the lookout for the finished work. He adds that Lorimer promptly accepted the story for $250. *The Lardners* (New York: Harper Colophon Books, 1977), 87. See also the version in George W. Hilton, *The Annotated Baseball Stories of Ring W. Lardner, 1914–1919* (Stanford, Calif.: Stanford University Press, 1995), 7.

39. Yardley, *Ring*, 163.

40. Virginia Woolf, "American Fiction," *The Moment and Other Essays* (New York: Harcourt, Brace, 1948), 123.

41. An astonished Scott Fitzgerald remarked about Lardner's treatment of his work: "My God! he hadn't even saved them—the material of *How to Write Short Stories* was obtained [by Max Perkins of Scribner's] by photographing old issues of magazines in the public library!" Yardley, *Ring*, 267.

42. Yardley, *Ring*, 225.

43. Yardley, *Ring,* 254–55. Yardley adds that the $100,000 figure was the equivalent in the late 1970s—the period of his biography—of $500,000.

44. In late 1928 Lardner came back to newspapering for a brief stint with "Ring's Side," a four-times weekly column in the *New York Morning Telegraph*. Another comeback followed in 1931 with a short-lived syndicate column called "Night Letter from Ring Lardner."

45. Yardley, *Ring,* 314.

46. Lardner, *Lose with a Smile,* 4, 80.

47. "Over the Waves," *New Yorker,* June 18, 1932, 30.

48. F. Scott Fitzgerald, *The Crack-Up* (New York: New Directions, 1956), 36, 38.

49. Hersey, *Pulpwood Editor,* 195.

Chapter Eight: Facts of the Matter

Epigraph: Bernard De Voto, "On the Writing of History," *Chicago History* 2 (Winter 1950–51): 314–15.

1. McClure, *My Autobiography,* 244–45.

2. Sedgwick, *The Happy Profession,* 143–44.

3. Irwin, *The Making of a Reporter,* 148.

4. Charvat, *Literary Publishing in America,* 75.

5. John Higham with Leonard Krieger and Felix Gilbert, *History* (Englewood Cliffs, N.J.: Prentice-Hall, 1965), 241.

6. Charvat, *Literary Publishing in America,* 77–78.

7. Robert Underwood Johnson, *Remembered Yesterdays* (Boston: Little, Brown, 1923), 213. Grant agreed to write the articles for $500 apiece but the sum was voluntarily doubled by the magazine.

8. Arthur John, *The Best Years of the* Century (Urbana: University of Illinois Press, 1981), 128.

9. Johnson, *Remembered Yesterdays,* 215.

10. Mott, *A History of American Magazines,* 3:469.

11. Higham, *History,* 70.

12. The dispute is discussed in Flower, *James Parton* , 24. I follow this biography for Parton's life and work.

13. "James Parton's Rules of Biography," *McClure's* 1 (June 1893): 59.

14. Though not without its difficulties. Under Massachusetts law, the marriage was illegal, and when Parton was made aware of this he petitioned the legislature and a bill was passed to legalize the union. The governor then vetoed the bill, and enough votes could not be gathered to override the action. "James Parton," *Critic,* October 24, 1891, 219–20.

15. Flower, *James Parton,* 82.

16. Ibid., 118, 120–21.

17. Ibid., 176.

18. Ibid., 199.

19. Lyon, *Success Story,* 135.

20. Ibid., 220.

21. Tarbell, *All in the Day's Work,* 161.

22. Ibid., 159–60.

23. McClure, *My Autobiography*, 221.

24. Ibid., 243, 240.

25. Tarbell, *All in the Day's Work*, 205.

26. Brady, *Ida Tarbell*, 125.

27. Ibid., 133.

28. Ibid., 152.

29. Tarbell, *All in the Day's Work*, 241.

30. Higham, *History*, 75.

31. Michael Kammen, *The Lively Arts: Gilbert Seldes and the Transformation of Cultural Criticism in the United States* (New York: Oxford University Press, 1996), 127. In the passage Seldes is recalling his work as a critic of the popular arts but Kammen remarks that he "has in mind his work on American history as well."

32. I follow the account of Allen's life and work in Payne, *The Man of Only Yesterday*.

33. "Frederick Lewis Allen Is Dead; Editor Wrote 'Only Yesterday,'" *New York Times*, February 14, 1954, 1. For Allen's influence on professional historians and also the limitations of his journalistic methods see Kenneth S. Lynn, "Only Yesterday," *American Scholar* 49 (Autumn 1980): 513–18.

34. Tunis, *A Measure of Independence*, 232.

35. "Hendrik Van Loon Dies in Home at 62," *New York Times*, March 12, 1944, 37.

36. For the genesis and publication of *The Story of Mankind* I follow Walker Gilmer, *Horace Liveright: Publisher of the Twenties* (New York: David Lewis, 1970), 32–33. Burton Rascoe tells a different story in *We Were Interrupted*, pp. 90–91:

> The *Story of Mankind* was Liveright's first big financial success as publisher, and this success was entirely due to [Horace] Liveright's tenacity of belief in his hunches. He had published a series of children's books, in which Van Loon had retold the story of the development of civilization in simple language and had illustrated them himself. They had all been costly failures, but Liveright kept on bringing them out because he, personally, liked them and they had taught him what he did not know about the origin, evolution, history, and progress of civilization, and also because his two young children liked them. He got the idea of printing and binding them in one volume for the general trade under the title *The Story of Mankind*. And the rest is book-selling history; it became a sensational best seller; it paid Liveright's overhead for the year and put Van Loon into the high-income brackets—hitherto a poverty-stricken ex-professor of history at Cornell.

37. Rascoe, *We Were Interrupted*, 90, 91.

38. Gilmer, *Horace Liveright*, 202.

39. *New York Times*, March 12, 1944, 37.

40. Henry Seidel Canby, *American Memoir* (Boston: Houghton Mifflin, 1947), 297.

41. "Mortality in Writers," *Saturday Review of Literature*, March 18, 1944, 14.

42. Crane to John Phillips, December 30, 1985, *Correspondence*, 1:160–61.

43. "Finally," De Voto wryly noted in the acknowledgments for his first Western history, *The Year of Decision: 1846*, "I acknowledge that I could not possibly have written the book if I had not had periodic assistance from Mr. John August." Wallace Stegner, De Voto's

biographer, notes that John August was a pseudonym for De Voto's magazine fiction, first used in 1926, resurrected in 1934, and thereafter supporting his "serious work ever since." Stegner adds: "There was not an artistic bone in August's body, not a single aesthetic corpuscle in his blood. He was all pro, and he provided the security that other historians got from academic tenure and other novelists from foundation grants." Later, fiction and John August abandoned, De Voto supported his historical work with light essays for *Woman's Day* and other magazines under the name Cady Hewes. Richard Dye, Fairley Blake, and Frank Gilbert were additional De Voto pen names. Stegner, *The Uneasy Chair*, 236–37, 332, 341–42. See also Stegner's introduction to *The Letters of Bernard De Voto* (Garden City, N.Y.: Doubleday, 1975), xi.

44. De Voto, "On the Writing of History," 314.

45. For Cain's work on the novel that eventually became *Mignon* I follow the account given in Roy Hoopes, *Cain* (New York: Holt, Rinehart and Winston, 1982).

46. Ibid., 431.

47. Ibid.

48. Ibid., 441.

49. Ibid., 454.

50. Ibid., 464.

51. Ibid., 477.

52. Kenneth Roberts, *I Wanted to Write* (Garden City, N.Y.: Doubleday, 1949), 78.

53. Isaac F. Marcosson, *Adventures in Interviewing* (New York: Dodd, Mead, 1939), 63. The book was first published in 1919.

54. Although Lorimer and Roberts were equally xenophobic, the editor felt it necessary to edit out some of his star reporter's more blatant remarks. See Jack Bales, *Kenneth Roberts* (New York: Twayne, 1993), 21–25. For added detail on the Lorimer-Roberts relationship see Richard Cary, "Roberts and Lorimer: The First Decade," *Colby Library Quarterly* 6 (September 1962): 106–29.

55. Roberts, *I Wanted to Write*, 148. Blythe's retirement was brief, and he was soon contributing more political and personal articles to the *Post*.

56. Ibid., 130.

57. Ibid., 170.

58. Ibid., 188.

59. Ibid., 204.

60. Tebbel, *George Horace Lorimer*, 95.

61. Roberts, *I Wanted to Write*, 225.

62. Ibid., 235.

63. John Bartlow Martin, *It Seems Like Only Yesterday* (New York: Morrow, 1986), 28–29. In their veneer of fact Martin's true-crime stories for Chicago pulps bore some resemblance to the detective books turned out in Chicago between 1874 and 1884 by Allan Pinkerton, founder of the detective agency bearing his name, and described in Frank Morn, *"The Eye That Never Sleeps": A History of the Pinkerton National Detective Agency* (Bloomington: Indiana University Press, 1982), 80–88. Based on actual cases of the agency, the stories (with such plodding titles as *The Bank Robbers and the Detective* and *The Expressman and the Detective*) were meant to upgrade the image of detectives in general and

the Pinkerton agency in particular while correcting a romantic view of investigative work that was the stuff of pulp fiction. But because the agency's early criminal records were destroyed in the Chicago fire, Allan Pinkerton drew his material from memory; the result was that fictional dramatization tended to dominate historical fact. Usually criminals in the stories were known from the start, with the accounts concentrating on ways of tracking them down and developing evidence for conviction. Of course Pinkerton himself could not spare time from his prospering agency to write sixteen books over the course of the decade. His method was to dictate case information to a stenographer who in turn passed his notes to a professional writer, with Pinkerton then editing the final manuscript. In 1876 alone Pinkerton kept four writers busy in his employ.

64. *The Saturday Evening Post Treasury,* ed. Roger Butterfield (New York: Simon and Schuster, 1954), 507.

65. Martin, *It Seems Like Only Yesterday,* 344.

66. For Macfadden's adventures in true-crime publishing see Robert Ernst, *Weakness Is a Crime: The Life of Bernarr Macfadden* (Syracuse, N.Y.: Syracuse University Press, 1991), 83–84.

67. Polito, *Savage Art,* 191, 192.

68. Ibid., 198.

69. Ibid., 190.

Chapter Nine: Brass Tacks

Epigraph: Irvin S. Cobb, *Exit Laughing,* 319.

1. London, *Martin Eden,* 626–27.

2. London to Cloudesley Johns, February 22, 1899, *Letters,* 1:47.

3. London to Mabel Applegarth, [editors' date: December 31, 1898], *Letters,* 1:35–36.

4. London to Cloudesley Johns, September 6, 1899, *Letters,* 1:108.

5. An advertisement for the magazine is included at the end of *1001 Places to Sell Manuscripts,* ed. William R. Kane, 9th ed. (Ridgewood, N.J.: The Editor Company, 1913).

6. London to Churchill Williams, May 20, 1913, *Letters,* 3:1171.

7. *500 Places to Sell Manuscripts,* ed. James Knapp Reeve (Franklin, Ohio: The Chronicle Press, 1894), 7, 52.

8. London to Ralph Kasper, January 3, 1913, *Letters,* 3:1110. London may have taken the "501" from the title of subsequent editions of the book. Cf. *1001 Places to Sell Manuscripts* in the following paragraph.

9. *1001 Places to Sell Manuscripts,* 7.

10. William W. Cook, *The Fiction Factory* (Ridgewood, N.J.: The Editor Company, 1912), 29. For a brief discussion of the book and Cook's career as a fictioneer see Bold, *Selling the Wild West,* 19 ff.

11. The magazine was started with a partner, Robert Luce, whom Hills eventually bought out.

12. William J. Fowler, "Hints to Newspaper Writers," *Writer* 1 (September 1887): 109.

13. London to Mabel Applegarth, December 31, 1893, *Letters,* 1:36.

14. London to Cloudesley Johns, March 24, 1900, *Letters,* 1:175.

15. Mott, *A History of American Magazines,* 4:430. Mott devotes a chapter to the *Black Cat,* pp. 428–31.

16. "The 'Volunteer Manuscript': Plain Talk to the Ambitious Amateur," *The Literary Criticism of Frank Norris,* ed. Donald Pizer (Austin: University of Texas Press, 1964), 141, 143.

17. Sinclair, *Money Writes!,* 20.

18. Fanny Fern, "Literary People," *Folly as it Flies,* 276.

19. Nancy A. Walker, *Fanny Fern* (New York: Twayne, 1993), 100.

20. Curwood, *Son of the Forests,* 213.

21. Kenneth Roberts, "The Truth About a Novel," *For Authors Only and Other Gloomy Essays* (Garden City, N.Y.: Doubleday, Doran, 1935), 178, 187–88.

22. Roberts, *I Wanted to Write,* 1, 353.

23. Rinehart, *My Story,* 407, 408.

24. Roberts, *I Wanted to Write,* 3.

25. Ibid., 64–65.

26. Heywood Broun, "Professor George Pierce Baker," *Collected Edition of Heywood Broun,* ed. Heywood Hale Broun (New York: Harcourt, Brace, 1941), 116.

27. D. G. Myers, "The Rise of Creative Writing," *Journal of the History of Ideas* 54 (April 1993): 293. I follow Myers's account of Foerster's primary place in the development of writing programs.

28. Myers, "The Rise of Creative Writing," 277 n.3.

29. Martin, *It Seems Like Only Yesterday,* 314–15.

30. *Jack London: Novels and Social Writings,* 1058.

31. Gallico, *Further Confessions of a Story Writer,* 10.

32. Walter Besant, "The Work of the British Society of Authors," *Forum* 13 (March 1892): 106.

33. Both quotations appear in Richard Fine, *James M. Cain and the American Authors' Authority* (Austin: University of Texas Press, 1992), 62, 66. For a concise description of the formation of writer organizations see pp. 60–77.

34. For details of the Authority I follow Fine's *James M. Cain and the American Authors' Authority.* The quotation appears as an epigraph on p. 81.

35. Hoopes, *Cain,* 411.

36. Fine, *James M. Cain and the American Authors' Authority,* 243.

37. The essential information about agents is found in James G. Hepburn, *The Author's Empty Purse and the Rise of the Literary Agent* (London: Oxford University Press, 1968). James L. W. West in *American Authors and the Literary Marketplace since 1900* (Philadelphia: University of Pennsylvania Press, 1988) has a detailed chapter about the rise of agents.

38. A biographer, Richard O'Connor, notes that the contract was "said to be the most lucrative ever offered an American writer." *Bret Harte, A Biography* (Boston: Little, Brown, 1966), 145.

39. *Edgar Allan Poe: Essays and Reviews,* 1180.

40. Paul R. Reynolds gives a brief account of his father's career in *The Middle Man,* pp. 13–32.

41. Reynolds, *The Middle Man,* 25.

42. Daniel H. Borus, *Writing Realism: Howells, James, and Norris in the Mass Market* (Chapel Hill: University of North Carolina Press, 1989), 55.

43. Frank Norris, "Fiction Writing as a Business," *The Literary Criticism of Frank Norris,* 150.

44. Borus, *Writing Realism,* 55.

45. West, *American Authors and the Literary Marketplace,* 90. *The Flirt* was Tarkington's most recent serial.

46. Reynolds, *The Middle Man,* 26–27.

47. Brady, *Ida Tarbell,* 225.

48. London to Paul R. Reynolds, February 6, 1912, *Letters,* 2:1066.

49. F. Scott Fitzgerald to Thomas Boyd, June 23, 1924, *Correspondence of F. Scott Fitzgerald,* ed. Matthew J. Bruccoli and Margaret M. Duggan (New York: Random House, 1980), 143.

50. Fitzgerald to Maxwell Perkins, July 19, 1939, *Correspondence,* 537.

51. Tunis, *A Measure of Independence,* 176–77. Brendan Gill remembered that Carl Brandt of the firm was equally adept at doctoring stories for the magazine market: "Smiling and intent, punctuating his sentences with a series of grunted 'm-m-m?'s, he would say, 'Why don't you bring in a little dog just here, m-m-m?, who then gets run over by a car?' Or, 'Why not have the boy start hitchhiking out West, m-m-m?, and then turn back, m-m-m?, because he hears his father's sick?'" Although he submitted to it, Gill found the agent's aid "tiresome, because it had so little to do with what I thought of as the sacred act of writing." Brendan Gill, *Here at* The New Yorker (New York: Random House, 1975), 157.

52. West, *American Authors and the Literary Marketplace,* 98.

53. London to Ninetta Eames, October 26, 1908, *Letters,* 2:759. Ninetta Eames, the foster mother of London's second wife, functioned as what London called his "California Agent" while he was on an ocean voyage.

54. Crane to Paul Revere Reynolds, October [no date] 1897, *Correspondence,* 1:305.

55. Crane to Paul Revere Reynolds, October 20, 1898, *Correspondence,* 2:380.

56. West, *American Authors and the Literary Marketplace,* 98.

57. Nina Wilcox Putnam, *Laughing Through* (New York: Sears, 1930), 300–304.

58. Kerr, *Me Me Me Me Me,* 209.

59. Mott, *Golden Multitudes,* 227. I follow below Mott's discussion of Wright's career, pp. 225–33. For an account of the elaborate mechanism Wright used in constructing his novels see Clair Kenamore, "A Curiosity in Best-Seller Technique," *Bookman* 47 (July 1918): 538–44.

60. Nye, *The Unembarrassed Muse,* 39–40.

61. For the promotion of L'Amour and his sales figures see Robert L. Gale, *Louis L'Amour,* rev. ed. (New York: Twayne, 1992), 8–10. Authorial bus tours live on. In the summer of 1996 Knopf sent the Gothic novelist Anne Rice on a forty-city, fifty-five-day bus tour to promote *Servant of the Bones,* a work with an initial printing of one million copies.

62. *F. Scott Fitzgerald on Authorship,* ed. Matthew J. Bruccoli (Columbia: University of South Carolina Press, 1966), 13. Bruccoli speculates that Fitzgerald's peak magazine rate of $4,000 in 1929 would be worth $32,000 to $40,000 in 1996 dollars.

Chapter Ten: Gatekeepers

Epigraph: Marcosson, *Adventures in Interviewing,* 63.

1. Reynolds, *The Middle Man,* 17.

2. Sinclair, *Money Writes!* 68.

3. Scott Donaldson, *Fool for Love: F. Scott Fitzgerald* (New York: Congdon and Weed, 1983), 101.

4. Marcosson, *Adventures in Interviewing,* 53.

5. Will Irwin, *The Making of a Reporter* (New York: Putnam's, 1942), 186.

6. Doris Ulmann, *A Portrait Gallery of American Editors* (New York: William Edwin Rudge, 1925), 108, 96.

7. Jan Cohn, *Creating America: George Horace Lorimer and the* Saturday Evening Post (Pittsburgh: University of Pittsburgh Press, 1989), 28. For Lorimer's career with the *Post* I follow this work and John Tebbel, *George Horace Lorimer and* The Saturday Evening Post (Garden City, N.Y.: Doubleday, 1948).

8. "The Post's Plans for 1900," 574–75.

9. Irwin, *The Making of a Reporter,* 185.

10. Putnam, *Laughing Through,* 305. Although it got a good deal of attention for doing so, the *Post* under Lorimer was far from the first periodical to pay on acceptance. The *Century* under Richard Watson Gilder, for example, paid in this manner in the latter years of the nineteenth century. It also notified writers of the receipt of manuscripts, returned rejected manuscripts even when authors forgot to include postage, and went so far in the direction of tactful treatment of contributors that it sent rejection notices in plain envelopes, acceptances with the magazine's official stationery. John, *The Best Years of the* Century, 147.

11. Cohn, *Creating America,* 277.

12. Rinehart's top payment for a serial, however, $75,000, came from Hearst's *Good Housekeeping.* Cohn, *Improbable Fiction,* 209.

13. Tebbel, *George Horace Lorimer,* 58.

14. Cohn, *Improbable Fiction,* 101.

15. Matthew J. Bruccoli, Introduction to *The Cruise of the Rolling Junk* (Bloomfield Hills, Mich.: Bruccoli Clark, 1976) [no page number given].

16. Lardner [Jr.], *The Lardners,* 4.

17. Irwin, *The Making of a Reporter,* 204.

18. Ibid., 185–86.

19. Ibid., 204.

20. Cohn, *Creating America,* 177.

21. Jane Grant, *Ross,* The New Yorker, *and Me* (New York: Reynal, 1968), 135. Thomas Costain was a *Post* editor and later a successful writer.

22. Irwin, *The Making of a Reporter,* 186.

23. London to Churchill Williams, June 3, 1913, *Letters,* 3:1182.

24. Cohn, *Creating America,* 276. Cohn adds that Lorimer eventually paid $50,000 for the serial when it was lengthened to six installments.

25. Bernard De Voto, "Writing for Money," *Saturday Review of Literature,* October 9, 1937, 3, 20, 22.

26. "The *Cosmopolitan* of Ray Long," *Fortune* 3 (March 1931): 49.

27. Donald Elder, *Ring Lardner* (Garden City, N.Y.: Doubleday, 1956), 219.

28. Tebbel, *George Horace Lorimer,* 82–83.

29 Frank Luther Mott thought Long had only ordinary success in turning up new writers and preferred name authors. *A History of American Magazines,* 4:503.

30. Long, Introduction to *20 Best Short Stories in Ray Long's 20 Years as an Editor,* xi.

31. Kenneth S. Lynn, *Hemingway* (New York: Simon and Schuster, 1987), 184. Long also rejected Hemingway's story "Fifty Grand," which made the rounds of the *Saturday Evening Post, Scribner's,* and *Collier's* before it was bought by the *Atlantic* in 1927 for $350, Hemingway's biggest short story sale to that point in his career. Long included the story in *20 Best Short Stories in Ray Long's 20 Years as an Editor* as an example of how editors go wrong.

32. Hemingway to George Horace Lorimer, January 21, 1925, *Selected Letters,* 148.

33. Hemingway to Maxwell Perkins, September 28, 1928, *Selected Letters,* 286.

34. Hemingway to Maxwell Perkins, October 11, 1928, *Selected Letters,* 289. During the thirties, after Long's departure from the magazine, *Cosmopolitan* printed some of Hemingway's work.

35. "The *Cosmopolitan* of Ray Long," 49. Burton Rascoe said Long's salary (as editorial director of all the Hearst magazines) was reputedly $300,000. *We Were Interrupted,* 103. In an article at the time of his death the *New York Times* put Long's salary and bonuses during his *Cosmopolitan* period at about about $180,000 a year. *New York Times,* July 10, 1935, 1.

36. Carlos Baker, who recounts the offer, adds that Burton bought "The Short Happy Life of Francis Macomber" for $5,000. *Ernest Hemingway,* 284.

37. For the creation and operation of the *Digest* I follow John Heidenry, *Theirs Was the Kingdom: Lila and DeWitt Wallace and the Story of the* Reader's Digest (New York: Norton, 1993), 75. Heidenry gives the date of Lorimer's retirement as 1932.

38. And one for which the present-day version of the magazine solicits contributions of "true, unpublished stories from your own experience, revealing *adult* human nature and providing appealing or humorous sidelights on the American scene." Maximum length is three hundred words, with payment upon publication of $400. The *Digest* also solicits short humor items for other departments of the magazine, payment specified, but makes clear the fact that it neither reads nor returns unsolicited article-length manuscripts.

39. Heidenry, *Theirs Was the Kingdom,* 135.

40. Max Eastman, *Love and Revolution* (New York: Random House, 1964), 641–42.

41. The origin of roving editors is discussed in James Playsted Wood, *Of Lasting Interest: The Story of the* Reader's Digest (Garden City, N.Y.: Doubleday, 1967), 91–102.

42. Tunis, *A Measure of Independence,* 255. The article was planted in the *Christian Science Monitor* before reprinting in the *Digest.*

43. Martin, *It Seems Like Only Yesterday,* 68.

44 James Thurber, *The Years with Ross* (Boston: Little, Brown, 1959), 164.

45. Heidenry, *Theirs Was the Kingdom,* 193, 197.

46. Heidenry makes this suggestion in *Theirs Was the Kingdom,* p.196.

47. Thurber, *The Years with Ross,* 20. Lorimer claimed he threw the initial issue across the room in disgust, and Frank Crowninshield of *Vanity Fair,* after thumbing through the first issue, told a writer that his magazine had nothing to fear. Thomas Kunkel, *Genius in Disguise: Harold Ross of* The New Yorker (New York: Random House, 1995), 100.

48. Tunis, *A Measure of Independence*, 157.

49. The prospectus is reprinted in Kunkel, *Genius in Disguise*, 439–41.

50. Brendan Gill, *Here at* The New Yorker, 391.

51. Ralph Ingersoll, "*The New Yorker*," *Fortune*, 10 (August 1934): 82. The article did not carry Ingersoll's by-line.

52. "Blame Dorothy Parker," *20 Best Short Stories in Ray Long's 20 Years as an Editor*, 528.

53. Tunis, *A Measure of Independence*, 157, 159.

54. The plot is spun in a two-part *New Yorker* profile of Crowninshield written by Geoffrey T. Hellman that appeared in the issues of September 19 and 26, 1942. For Crowninshield's manner as an editor see also George H. Douglas, *The Smart Magazines* (Hamden, Conn.: Archon Books, 1991), 100–104.

55. Tunis, *A Measure of Independence*, 159, 160. For an account of the continuation of the magazine's diligent fact checking during the Shawn years ("If sometimes the *New Yorker's* checking department seemed a little dense, especially when they questioned the facts of poems, I was grateful") see Donald Hall, *Principal Products of Portugal* (Boston: Beacon Press, 1995), 263–65.

56. Matthew J. Bruccoli, *The O'Hara Concern* (New York: Random House, 1975), 74.

57. Thurber, *The Years with Ross*, 33.

58. According to a biographer, the satire was written after Thurber's wife decided he was taking too long to write his freelance pieces and suggested he give each one just forty-five minutes. Thurber set an alarm clock to meet the deadlines. Neil A. Grauer, *Remember Laughter: A Life of James Thurber* (Lincoln: University of Nebraska Press, 1994), 32.

59. Thurber later called the estimate of his annual income "somewhat magnified." *The Years with Ross*, 216.

60. Kramer, *Ross and* The New Yorker, 217.

61. Bruccoli, *The O'Hara Concern*, 85.

62. The dust-up with O'Hara is described by Gill in *Here at* The New Yorker, p. 275. Bruccoli thinks the amount O'Hara wanted was $200. *The O'Hara Concern*, 190. For more on the magazine's byzantine manner of compensating fact and fiction writers see Kunkel, *Genius in Disguise*, 319–24.

63. Gill, *Here at* The New Yorker, 361.

64. Shawn's contract system is described in Gigi Mahon, *The Last Days of* The New Yorker (New York: McGraw-Hill, 1988), 69–70. For details of how the system worked with one writer, Frank O'Connor, for twenty years a major contributor of stories to the magazine, see Michael Steinman, *The Happiness of Getting It Down Right: Letters of Frank O'Connor and William Maxwell, 1945–1966* (New York: Knopf, 1996), 38.

65. Mahon, *The Last Days of* The New Yorker, 71–72. In another illustration of the magazine's cushy treatment of its writers, Kahn recalled a time in the sixties when routinely they were allowed to travel first class on foreign flights. E. J. Kahn, Jr., *Year of Change: More About* The New Yorker *& Me* (New York: Viking, 1988), 111.

66. Hemingway to Maxwell Perkins, December 15, 1929, *Selected Letters* , 317.

67. Hemingway to Maxwell Perkins, December 15, 1929, *Selected Letters,* 317.

68. Eric Hodgins, *Trolley to the Moon* (New York: Simon and Schuster, 1973), 406. Because of its Depression start, it has been argued, *Fortune* in its early days had more of a serious sociological bent than Luce had intended for a celebration-of-business magazine. See Laurence Bergreen, *James Agee* (New York: Dutton, 1984), 117.

69. Hemingway to Maxwell Perkins, December 15, 1929, *Selected Letters,* 317.

70. Robert T. Elson, *Time Inc.: The Intimate History of a Publishing Enterprise, 1923–1941* (New York: Atheneum, 1968), 130, 137. Lincoln Steffens had similar ideas earlier. As editor of a New York newspaper, the *Commercial Advertiser,* he looked for aspiring writers rather than experienced journalists. He hired young people out of college and tried them out during summers when regular staff members were on vacation, maintaining he "had use for any one who, openly or secretly, hoped to be a poet, a novelist, or an essayist." Lincoln Steffens, *The Autobiography of Lincoln Steffens* (New York: Harcourt, Brace, 1931), 314. James L. Baughman says Luce turned to young writers straight from college after job offers were rejected by some business correspondents with New York newspapers. *Henry R. Luce and the Rise of the American News Media* (Boston: Twayne, 1987), 69.

71. Dwight Macdonald, "Against the Grain," *Writing for* Fortune (New York: Time Inc., 1980), 152.

72. Bergreen, *James Agee,* 119, 122.

73. Robert E. Herzstein, *Henry R. Luce* (New York: Scribner's, 1994), 60.

74. Scott Donaldson, *Archibald MacLeish: An American Life* (Boston: Houghton Mifflin, 1992), 194.

75. Hodgins, *Trolley to the Moon,* 383.

76. Ibid.

77. William Stott, *Documentary Expression and Thirties America* (New York: Oxford University Press, 1973), 262. Stott describes in detail the birth and death of Agee's article at *Fortune.*

78. Macdonald said about the article that Luce and the magazine's managing editor, Ralph Ingersoll, "junked it and substituted a clumsy piece [written by Ingersoll] that blunted or deleted" the sharpest points made in the article. Macdonald, *Writing for* Fortune, 155. Robert Elson says the article was not used because Macdonald had written an opinion piece. However, Ingersoll told Luce that Macdonald's opinion was an informed one, and he suggested the magazine change policy and allow such pieces, possibly with bylines. *Time Inc.,* 254.

79. Macdonald, *Writing for* Fortune, 151; Dwight Macdonald, *Discriminations: Essays and Afterthoughts, 1938–1974* (New York: Grossman, 1974), 171.

80. Dwight Macdonald "'Fortune' Magazine," *Nation,* May 8, 1937, 528.

81. Crane's brush with *Fortune* is described in John Unterecker, *Voyager: A Life of Hart Crane* (New York: Farrar, Straus and Giroux, 1969), 635–37.

82. Cozzens's time at Fortune is described in Matthew J. Bruccoli, *James Gould Cozzens: A Life Apart* (New York: Harcourt Brace Jovanovich, 1983), 139–41. Cozzens is quoted on p. 140.

83. Another *Fortune* writer of the period remembered Cozzens's exit differently—the result of "coming apart under the pressures of monthly journalism." Robert Coughlan, "A Collection of Characters," *Writing for* Fortune, 76.

84. Hodgins, *Trolley to the Moon,* 384.

85. Bergreen, *James Agee,* 118.

86. Hodgins, *Trolley to the Moon,* 383.

87. For Ingersoll's life and work I follow Roy Hoopes, *Ralph Ingersoll* (New York: Atheneum, 1985).

88. Hoopes, *Ralph Ingersoll,* 80.

89. Hodgins, *Trolley to the Moon,* 348–49.

90. Hoopes, *Ralph Ingersoll,* 100.

91. Hodgins, *Trolley to the Moon,* 442.

92. Ibid., 445.

93. Gibbs collected the profile in *More in Sorrow* (New York: Henry Holt, 1958), 3–19.

94. Hoopes, *Ralph Ingersoll,* 128.

95. MacLeish to Henry R. Luce, July 20, 1938, *Letters of Archibald MacLeish, 1907–1982,* ed. R. H. Winnick (Boston: Houghton Mifflin, 1983), 291–92.

96. Alfred Kazin, *New York Jew* (New York: Vintage Books, 1979), 88.

97. Hoopes, *Ralph Ingersoll,* 228. I follow this work for *PM's* complex history.

98 Ingersoll's memorandum is reprinted as an appendix in Hoopes, *Ralph Ingersoll,* 396–403. The quoted passages appear on pp. 399 and 403.

99. Hoopes, *Ralph Ingersoll,* 229.

100. The success of the *Saturday Review* (formerly the *Saturday Review of Literature*) was short lived. After a decade of decline, it died in 1982. See Tebbel and Zuckerman, *The Magazine in America,* 251. Hayes's reign at *Esquire* is told in Carol Polsgrove, *It Wasn't Pretty, Folks, but Didn't We Have Fun?* (New York: Norton, 1995). Willie Morris recounts his time at *Harper's* in *New York Days* (Boston: Little, Brown, 1993).

101. *Life* was later revived by Time Inc. as a monthly.

Epilogue: Sweet Deal

Epigraph: Donald Hall, *Life Work* (Boston: Beacon Press, 1993), 3.

1. "The Point of View," *Scribner's Magazine* 14 (December 1893): 791–92.

2. For an account of the magazine's final stumbling years see Otto Friedrich, *Decline and Fall* (New York: Harper and Row, 1970).

3. Hartzell Spence, "The Bent and Blunted Free Lance," *Saturday Review of Literature,* November 10, 1962, 63 ff.

4. Letter to author.

5. Tunis, *A Measure of Independence,* 240.

6. Paul W. Kingston, *The Wages of Writing: Per Word, Per Piece, or Perhaps* (New York: Columbia University Press, 1986).

7. Used as the epigraph to this book, Flaubert's words come from a letter written while he was in the midst of *Madame Bovary.* He added: "But when I think of these marvelous pleasures I have enjoyed [as a writer] I am tempted to offer God a prayer of thanks—if only I knew he could hear me! Praised be the Lord for not creating me a cotton merchant, a vaudevillian, a wit, etc.!" Letters written at the same period amply portray the other, miserable side of the writing life. Gustave Flaubert to Louise Colet, December 23, 1853, *The Selected Letters of Gustave Flaubert,* ed. Francis Steegmuller (New York: Vintage Books, 1957), 163.

8. Hall, *Life Work,* 50

9. Joan Fry, "Donald Hall," *Poets & Writers* 22 (September/October 1994): 40.

10. Hall, *Principal Products of Portugal,* 267, 270.

11. "Tex" W. Dixon, "Ghost Story," *Texas Monthly* 23 (September 1995): 60–64.

12. Avon's entry into romance originals is described in Davis, *Two-Bit Culture*, 361–63.

13. The distinctions are Margaret Ann Jensen's in *Love's $weet Return: The Harlequin Story* (Bowling Green, Ohio: Bowling Green State University Popular Press, 1984), 62.

14. Kathryn Falk, *Love's Leading Ladies* (New York: Pinnacle Books, 1982). Each entry in this paperback original ends with the author's favorite recipe.

15. Barbara Rudolph, "Heartbreak comes to Harlequin," *Forbes,* March 29, 1982, 51.

16. Hunt, "A Writer's Life," 124. The article is the text of talk by Hunt on the occasion of presenting his papers to the library of his *alma mater,* Brown University.

17. John Jerome, *The Writing Trade: A Year in the Life* (New York: Viking, 1992), 3, 68.

18. Jerome, *The Writing Trade,* 6. For another recent book about writing by a productive professional writer, this one in the manner of a how-to manual, see Richard Rhodes, *How to Write: Advice and Reflections* (New York: William Morrow, 1995).

19. Jerome, *The Writing Trade,* 3.

20. Ibid., 139–40.

SOURCES

Admari, Ralph. "Ballou, the Father of the Dime Novel." *The American Book Collector* 4 (September–October 1933): 121–29.

Alcott, Louisa May. *Little Women.* Boston: Little, Brown, 1900.

Alden, Henry Mills. *Magazine Writing and the New Literature.* New York: Harper and Brothers, 1908.

Allen, Michael. *Poe and the British Magazine Tradition.* New York: Oxford University Press, 1969.

Auser, Cortland P. *Nathaniel P. Willis.* New York: Twayne, 1969.

Bacheller, Irving. *Coming Up the Road: Memories of a North Country Boyhood.* Indianapolis: Bobbs-Merrill, 1928.

———. *From Stores of Memory.* New York: Farrar and Rinehart, 1938.

Baker, Carlos. *Ernest Hemingway: A Life Story.* New York: Scribner's, 1969.

———, ed. *Ernest Hemingway: Selected Letters, 1917–1961.* New York: Scribner's, 1981.

Bales, Jack. *Kenneth Roberts.* New York: Twayne, 1993.

Bate, W. Jackson. *Samuel Johnson.* New York: Harcourt Brace Jovanovich, 1977.

Baughman, James L. *Henry R. Luce and the Rise of the American News Media.* Boston: Twayne, 1987.

Beers, Henry A. *Nathaniel Parker Willis.* Boston: Houghton Mifflin, 1885.

Benfey, Christopher. *The Double Life of Stephen Crane.* New York: Knopf, 1992.

Bergreen, Laurence. *James Agee.* New York: Dutton, 1984.

Besant, Walter. "The Work of the British Society of Authors." *Forum* 13 (March 1892): 95–106.

Bianchi, Martha Dickinson. *The Life and Letters of Emily Dickinson.* Boston: Houghton Mifflin, 1924.

Billman, Carol. *The Secret of the Stratemeyer Syndicate.* New York: Ungar, 1986.

Blotner, Joseph, ed. *Selected Letters of William Faulkner.* New York: Random House, 1977.

Blythe, Samuel. *The Making of a Newspaper Man.* Philadelphia: Henry Altemus, 1912.

Bok, Edward W. "Literary Factories." *Publishers Weekly* (August 13, 1892): 231.

———. *The Americanization of Edward Bok.* New York: Scribner's, 1923.

Bold, Christine. *Selling the Wild West: Popular Western Fiction, 1860–1960.* Bloomington: Indiana University Press, 1987.

Bonn, Thomas L. *Undercover: An Illustrated History of American Mass Market Paperbacks.* New York: Penguin, 1982.

———. *Heavy Traffic and High Culture: New American Library as Literary Gatekeeper in the Paperback Revolution.* Carbondale: Southern Illinois University Press, 1989.

Borus, Daniel H. *Writing Realism: Howells, James, and Norris in the Mass Market.* Chapel Hill: University of North Carolina Press, 1989.

Bosworth, Allan R. "The Golden Age of Pulps." *Atlantic* 208 (July 1961): 57–60.

Boyle, Robert H. "The Man Who Lived Two Lives in One." *Sports Illustrated* (April 29, 1968): 69–82

Brady, Kathleen. *Ida Tarbell: Portrait of a Muckraker.* New York: Seaview/Putnam, 1984.

Brand, Max. *The Untamed.* New York: Dodd, Mead, 1919.

Breen, Jon L., and Martin Harry Greenberg. *Murder Off the Rack: Critical Studies of Ten Paperback Masters,* Metuchen, N.J.: Scarecrow Press, 1989.

Broun, Heywood Hale, ed. *Collected Edition of Heywood Broun.* New York: Harcourt, Brace, 1941.

Bruccoli, Matthew J., and Margaret M. Duggan. *Correspondence of F. Scott Fitzgerald.* New York: Random House, 1980.

Bruccoli, Matthew J. *James Gould Cozzens: A Life Apart.* New York: Harcourt Brace Jovanovich, 1983.

———. *The O'Hara Concern.* New York: Random House, 1975.

———, ed. *F. Scott Fitzgerald on Authorship.* Columbia: University of South Carolina Press, 1996.

———, ed. *The Price Was High: The Last Uncollected Stories of F. Scott Fitzgerald.* New York: Harcourt Brace Jovanovich, 1979.

"Burks of the Pulps." *New Yorker* (February 15, 1936): 12–13.

Cain, James M. "The Man Merriwell." *Saturday Evening Post* (June 11, 1927): 13 ff.

Canby, Henry Seidel. *American Memoir.* Boston: Houghton Mifflin, 1947.

Cantwell, Robert. "A Sneering Laugh with the Bases Loaded." *Sports Illustrated* (April 23, 1962): 67–76.

Cary, Richard. "Roberts and Lorimer: The First Decade." *Colby Library Quarterly* 6 (September 1962): 106–29.

Charvat, William. *Literary Publishing in America, 1790–1850.* Philadelphia: University of Pennsylvania Press, 1959.

———. *The Profession of Authorship in America, 1800–1870.* Ed. Matthew J. Bruccoli. Columbus: Ohio State University Press, 1968.

Chatterton, Wayne. *Irvin S. Cobb.* Boston: Twayne, 1986.

Cobb, Irvin S. *Exit Laughing.* Indianapolis: Bobbs-Merrill, 1941.

Cohn, Jan. *Creating America: George Horace Lorimer and the* Saturday Evening Post. Pittsburgh: University of Pittsburgh Press, 1989.

———. *Improbable Fiction: The Life of Mary Roberts Rinehart.* Pittsburgh: University of Pittsburgh Press, 1980.

Collins, James H. "The American Grub Street." *Atlantic* 98 (November 1906): 634–43.

Commager, Henry Steele. "When Majors Wrote for Minors." *Saturday Review of Literature* (May 10, 1952): 11 ff.

Congdon, Charles T. *Reminiscences of a Journalist.* Boston: James R. Osgood, 1880.

Connolly, Cyril. *The Unquiet Grave.* New York: Harper and Brothers, 1945.

Cook, William W. *The Fiction Factory.* Ridgewood, N.J.: The Editor Company, 1912.

"The *Cosmopolitan* of Ray Long." *Fortune* 3 (March 1931): 49–55.

Coultrap-McQuin, Susan. *Doing Literary Business: American Women Writers in the Nineteenth Century.* Chapel Hill: University of North Carolina Press, 1990.

————, ed. *Gail Hamilton: Selected Writings.* New Brunswick, N.J.: Rutgers University Press, 1992.

Cross, Nigel. *The Common Writer: Life in Nineteenth-Century Grub Street.* New York: Cambridge University Press, 1985.

Curtin, William M., ed. *The World and the Parish: Willa Cather's Articles and Reviews, 1893–1902.* 2 vols. Lincoln: University of Nebraska Press, 1970.

Curwood, James Oliver. *Son of the Forests.* Garden City, N.Y.: Doubleday, Doran, 1930.

Davis, Kenneth C. *Two-Bit Culture: The Paperbacking of America.* Boston: Houghton-Mifflin, 1984.

De Voto, Bernard. "On the Writing of History." *Chicago History* 2 (Winter 1950–51): 313–15.

————. "Writing for Money." *Saturday Review of Literature* (October 9, 1937): 3 ff.

Derby, J. C. *Fifty Years among Authors, Books and Publishers.* New York: G. W. Carleton, 1884.

Dixon, "Tex" W. "Ghost Story." *Texas Monthly* 23 (September 1995): 60–64.

Dodge, H. Augusta, ed. *Gail Hamilton's Life in Letters.* 2 vols. Boston: Lee and Shepard, 1901.

Donaldson, Scott. *Fool for Love: F. Scott Fitzgerald.* New York: Congdon and Weed, 1983.

————. *Archibald MacLeish: An American Life.* Boston: Houghton Mifflin, 1992.

Douglas, Ann. *The Feminization of American Culture.* New York: Knopf, 1977.

Douglas, George H. *The Smart Magazines.* Hamden, Conn.: Archon Books, 1991.

Driscoll, Charles B. *The Life of O. O. McIntyre.* New York: Greystone Press, 1938.

Eastman, Max. *Love and Revolution.* New York: Random House, 1964.

Easton, Robert. *Max Brand, The Big "Westerner."* Norman: University of Oklahoma Press, 1970.

Easton, Robert, and Mackenzie Brown. *Lord of Beasts: The Saga of Buffalo Jones.* Tucson: University of Arizona Press, 1961.

Easton, Robert, and Jane Easton, eds. *The Collected Stories of Max Brand.* Lincoln: University of Nebraska Press, 1994.

Elder, Donald. *Ring Lardner.* Garden City, N.Y.: Doubleday, 1956.

Eldridge, Judith A. *James Oliver Curwood.* Bowling Green, Ohio: Bowling Green State University Popular Press, 1993.

Elson, Robert T. *Time Inc.: The Intimate History of a Publishing Enterprise, 1923–1941.* New York: Atheneum, 1968.

Erisman, Fred. "The Strenuous Life in Practice: The School and Sports Stories of Ralph Henry Barbour." *Rocky Mountain Social Science Journal* 7 (April 1970): 29–37.

Ernst, Robert. *Weakness Is a Crime: The Life of Bernarr Macfadden.* Syracuse, N.Y.: Syracuse University Press, 1991.

Falk, Kathryn. *Love's Leading Ladies.* New York: Pinnacle Books, 1982.

Fenton, Robert W. *The Big Swingers.* Englewood Cliffs, N.J.: Prentice-Hall, 1967.

Fern, Fanny. *Folly As It Flies.* New York: G. W. Carleton, 1868.

Fine, Richard. *James M. Cain and the American Authors' Authority.* Austin: University of Texas Press, 1992.

Fitzgerald, F. Scott. *The Crack-Up.* New York: New Directions, 1956.

———. *The Cruise of the Rolling Junk.* Bloomfield Hills, Mich.: Bruccoli Clark, 1976.

Flower, Milton E. *James Parton, The Father of Modern Biography.* Durham, N.C.: Duke University Press, 1951.

"For It Was Indeed He." *Fortune* 9 (April 1934): 86 ff.

Ford, James L. *The Literary Shop and Other Tales.* New York: Chelsea, 1899.

Fry, Joan. "Donald Hall." *Poets & Writers* 22 (September/October 1994) : 38–51.

Fussell, Paul. *Samuel Johnson and the Life of Writing.* New York: Harcourt Brace Jovanovich, 1971.

Gale, Robert L. *Louis L'Amour.* Rev. ed. New York: Twayne, 1992.

Gallico, Paul. *Confessions of a Story Writer.* New York: Knopf, 1947.

———. *Further Confessions of a Story Writer.* Garden City, N.Y.: Doubleday, 1961.

Garis, Roger. *My Father was Uncle Wiggily.* New York: McGraw-Hill, 1966.

Garland, Hamlin. *Roadside Meetings.* New York: Macmillan, 1930.

Gibson, Arrell Morgan, ed. *American Notes: Rudyard Kipling's West.* Norman: University of Oklahoma Press, 1981.

Gill, Brendan. *Here at* The New Yorker. New York: Random House, 1975.

Gilmer, Walker. *Horace Liveright: Publisher of the Twenties.* New York: David Lewis, 1970.

Graham, George R. "The Late Edgar Allan Poe." *Graham's* 36 (March 1850): 226.

Grant, Jane. *Ross,* The New Yorker, *and Me.* New York: Reynal, 1968.

Grauer, Neil A. *Remember Laughter: A Life of James Thurber.* Lincoln: University of Nebraska Press, 1994.

Grey, Zane. "Breaking Through: The Story of My Own Life." *American Magazine* 98 (July 1924): 13 ff.

Gruber, Frank. *The Pulp Jungle.* Los Angeles: Sherbourne Press, 1967.

———. *Zane Grey.* New York: World, 1970.

Guthrie, A. B., Jr. *The Blue Hen's Chick.* New York: McGraw-Hill, 1965.

Haight, Gordon S. *Mrs. Sigourney.* New Haven, Conn.: Yale University Press, 1930.

Hall, Donald. *Life Work.* Boston: Beacon Press, 1993.

Hamilton, Gail. *A Battle of the Books.* Cambridge, Mass.: Riverside Press, 1870.

Hapgood, Norman. *The Changing Years.* New York: Farrar and Rinehart, 1930.

Hart, James D. *The Popular Book.* New York: Oxford University Press, 1950.

Hawthorne, Julian. "American Magazines and Authors." *Belford's Monthly* 1 (June 1888): 25–33.

———. "Journalism the Destroyer of Literature." *Critic* 48 (February 1906): 166–71.

Heidenry, John. *Theirs Was the Kingdom: Lila and DeWitt Wallace and the Story of the Reader's Digest.* New York: Norton, 1993.

Hendricks, King and Irving Shepard, ed. *Letters from Jack London.* New York: Odyssey Press, 1965.

Hepburn, James G. *The Author's Empty Purse and the Rise of the Literary Agent.* London: Oxford University Press, 1968.

Hersey, Harold Brainerd. *Pulpwood Editor.* New York: Frederick A. Stokes, 1937.

Herzstein, Robert E. *Henry R. Luce.* New York: Scribner's, 1994.

Higham, John. *History.* Englewood Cliffs, N.J.: Prentice-Hall, 1965.

Hills, William H. "The Idea of *The Writer.*" *Writer* 1 (April 1887): 16–17.

Hilton, George W., ed. *The Annotated Baseball Stories of Ring W. Lardner, 1914–1919.* Stanford, Calif.: Stanford University Press, 1995.

Hinsdale, Harriet and Tony London, ed. *Frank Merriwell's "Father."* Norman: University of Oklahoma Press, 1964.

Hodgins, Eric. *Trolley to the Moon.* New York: Simon and Schuster, 1973.

Hoffman, Daniel. *Poe Poe Poe Poe Poe Poe Poe.* Garden City, N.Y.: Doubleday, 1972.

Holtz, William, ed. *Dorothy Thompson and Rose Wilder Lane: Forty Years of Friendship.* Columbia: University of Missouri Press, 1991.

Hoopes, Roy. *Cain.* New York: Holt, Rinehart and Winston, 1982.

———. *Ralph Ingersoll.* New York: Atheneum, 1985.

Howells, William Dean. "The Man of Letters as a Man of Business." *Scribner's* 14 (October 1893): 429–45.

———. *Years of My Youth.* New York: Harper and Brothers, 1916.

Hudson, Robert V. *The Writing Game: A Biography of Will Irwin.* Ames: Iowa State University Press, 1982.

Hunt, E. Howard. "A Writer's Life." *Books at Brown* 33 (1986): 122–38

Hunt, William S. *Frank Forester: A Tragedy in Exile.* Newark, N.J.: Carteret Book Club, 1933.

Irwin, Will. *The Making of a Reporter.* New York: Putnam's, 1942.

Jackson, Carlton. *Zane Grey.* Rev. ed. Boston: Twayne, 1989.

Jenks, George C. "Dime Novel Makers." *Bookman* 20 (October 1904): 108–14.

Jensen, Margaret Ann. *Love's $weet Return: The Harlequin Story.* Bowling Green, Ohio: Bowling Green State University Popular Press, 1984.

Jerome, John. *The Writing Trade: A Year in the Life.* New York: Viking, 1992.

Johanningsmeier, Charles A. *Fiction and the American Literary Marketplace: The Role of Newspaper Syndicates in America, 1860–1900.* New York: Cambridge University Press, 1997.

Johannsen, Albert. *The House of Beadle and Adams and Its Dime and Nickel Novels.* 2 vols. Norman: Univeristy of Oklahoma Press, 1950.

John, Arthur. *The Best Years of the* Century. Urbana: University of Illinois Press, 1981.

Johnson, Robert Underwood. *Remembered Yesterdays.* Boston: Little, Brown, 1923.

Johnston, Alva. "How to Become a Great Writer." *Saturday Evening Post* (July 29, 1939): 5 ff.

Jones, Robert Kenneth. *The Shudder Pulps: A History of the Weird Menace Magazines of the 1930s.* New York: New American Library, 1978.

Kahn, E. J., Jr. *Year of Change: More About* The New Yorker *& Me.* New York: Viking, 1988.

Kammen, Michael. *The Lively Arts: Gilbert Seldes and the Transformation of Cultural Criticism in the United States.* New York: Oxford University Press, 1996.

Kazin, Alfred. *New York Jew.* New York: Vintage Books, 1979.

Kenamore, Clair. "A Curiosity in Best-Seller Technique." *Bookman* 47 (July 1918): 538–44.

Kerr, M. E. *Me Me Me Me Me.* New York: Harper Trophy, 1983.

Kingston, Paul W. *The Wages of Writing: Per Word, Per Piece, or Perhaps.* New York: Columbia University Press, 1986.

Klemesrud, Judy. "100 Books." *New York Times* (April 4, 1968): 52 ff.

Knightley, Phillip. *The First Casualty.* New York: Harcourt Brace, 1975.

Kunitz, Stanley J. and Howard Haycraft, ed. *The Junior Book of Authors.* 2d rev. ed. New York: H. W. Wilson, 1951.

Kunkel, Thomas. *Genius in Disguise: Harold Ross of* The New Yorker. New York: Random House, 1995.

Kyne, Peter B. "I Used to be a Business Man." *American Magazine* 115 (June 1933): 58 ff.

Labor, Earle, Robert C. Leitz, and I. Milo Shepard, ed. *The Letters of Jack London.* 3 vols. Stanford, Calif.: Stanford University Press, 1988.

Lardner, Ring, Jr. *The Lardners.* New York: Harper Colophon Books, 1977.

Lardner, Ring. "Over the Waves." *New Yorker* (June 18, 1932): 30–33.

———. *Lose with a Smile.* New York: Scribner's, 1933.

Lewis, Sinclair. *Babbitt.* New York: Library of America, 1992.

Lichtenstein, Nelson. "Authorial Professionalism and the Literary Marketplace." *American Studies* 19 (Spring 1978): 35–53.

"The Literary Aspirant." *Independent* 52 (April 26, 1900): 997–1000.

London, Jack. *Novels and Social Writings.* New York: Library of America, 1982.

Long, Ray, ed. *My Story That I Liked Best.* New York: International Magazine Company, 1925.

———. "Jim Curwood." *Bookman* 66 (November 1927): 289–91.

———, ed. *20 Best Short Stories in Ray Long's 20 Years as an Editor.* New York: Ray Long and Richard S. Smith, 1932

Lowell, James Russell. "Our Contributors—No. XVII. Edgar Allan Poe." *Graham's* 27 (February 1845): 49–53.

Lubow, Arthur. *The Reporter Who Would Be King: A Biography of Richard Harding Davis.* New York: Scribner's, 1992.

Lundquist, James. *Jack London: Adventures, Ideas, and Fiction.* New York: Ungar, 1987.

Lynn, Kenneth S. *Hemingway.* New York: Simon and Schuster, 1987.

———. "Only Yesterday." *American Scholar* 49 (Autumn 1980): 513–18.

———. *William Dean Howells: An American Life.* New York: Harcourt Brace Jovanovich, 1971.

Lyon, Peter. *Success Story: The Life and Times of S. S. McClure.* New York: Scribner's, 1963.

Mabbott, Thomas Ollive, ed. *Collected Works of Edgar Allan Poe.* 3 vols. Cambridge, Mass.: Harvard University Press, 1978.

Mabie, Hamilton Wright. "A Year's Literary Production." *Forum* 12 (February 1892): 797–806.

Macdonald, Dwight. "Fortune" Magazine. *Nation* (May 8, 1937): 527–30.

———. *Discriminations: Essays and Afterthoughts, 1938–1974.* New York: Grossman, 1974.

Mahon, Gigi. *The Last Days of* The New Yorker. New York: McGraw-Hill, 1988.

Marcosson, Issac F. *Adventures in Interviewing.* New York: Dodd, Mead, 1939.

———. *Before I Forget.* New York: Dodd, Mead, 1959.

Martin, John Bartlow. *It Seems Like Only Yesterday.* New York: Morrow, 1986.

Mary Roberts Rinehart: A Sketch of the Woman and Her Work. New York: George H. Doran [no date].

Maule, Harry E., and Melville H. Cane, ed. *The Man from Main Street.* New York: Random House, 1953.

McAleer, John J. *Royal Decree: Conversations with Rex Stout.* Ashton, Md.: Pontes Press, 1983.

McClure, S. S. *My Autobiography.* New York: Frederick A. Stokes, 1914.

McKinney, M. S. "In the Twilight of Poetry." *Saturday Evening Post* (December 31, 1898): 486.

Monaghan, Jay. *The Great Rascal: The Life and Adventures of Ned Buntline.* Boston: Little, Brown, 1952.

Morn, Frank. *"The Eye That Never Sleeps": A History of the Pinkerton National Detective Agency.* Bloomington: Indiana University Press, 1982.

Mott, Frank Luther. *American Journalism, A History: 1690–1960.* Rev. ed. New York: Macmillan, 1962.

———. *Golden Multitudes.* New York: Macmillan, 1947.

———. *A History of American Magazines.* 5 vols. New York: Appleton, 1930.

Myers, D. G. "The Rise of Creative Writing." *Journal of the History of Ideas* 54 (April 1993): 277–97.

"*The New Yorker.*" *Fortune* 10 (August 1934): 73 ff.

Niven, Penelope. *Carl Sandburg.* New York: Scribner's, 1991.

Noel, Mary. *Villains Galore . . . The Hey-day of the Popular Story Weekly.* New York: Macmillan, 1954.

Nolan, William F. *Max Brand: Western Giant.* Bowling Green, Ohio: Bowling Green State University Popular Press, 1985.

Nye, Russel. *The Unembarassed Muse: The Popular Arts in America.* New York: Dial, 1970.

O'Connor, Richard. *Bret Harte, A Biography.* Boston: Little, Brown, 1966.

O'Meara, Stephen. "Does it Pay to be a Reporter?" *Writer* 1 (April 1887): 14–15.

Oriard, Michael. *Dreaming of Heroes: American Sports Fiction, 1868–1980.* Chicago: Nelson-Hall, 1982.

Ostrom, John Ward. "Edgar A. Poe: His Income as Literary Entrepreneur." *Poe Studies* 15 (June 1982): 1–7.

———, ed. *The Letters of Edgar Allan Poe.* 2 vols. Cambridge, Mass.: Harvard University Press, 1948.

Parton, James. "James Parton's Rules of Biography." *McClure's* 1 (June 1893): 59–62.

———. "Journalism as a Profession for Young Men." *Writer* 21 (May 1888): 103–6.

———, ed. *Eminent Women of the Age.* Hartford, Conn.: S. M. Betts, 1868.

Pattee, Fred Lewis. *The Feminine Fifties.* New York: D. Appleton-Century, 1940.

Patten, Gilbert. "Dime-Novel Days." *Saturday Evening Post* (February 28 and March 7, 1931): 6 ff.; 33 ff.

Patten, William G. "Experiences with Publishers." *Writer* 3 (March 1889): 59–60.

Payne, Darwin. *The Man of Only Yesterday: Frederick Lewis Allen.* New York: Harper and Row, 1975.

Peterson, Charles J. "Our Contributors—No. XV. Mrs. Ann S. Stephens." *Graham's* 26 (November 1844): 234–36.

Phillips, David Graham. *The Great God Success.* Ridgewood, N.J.: Gregg Press, 1967.

Pizer, Donald, ed. *The Literary Criticism of Frank Norris.* Austin: University of Texas Press, 1964.

———, ed. *Theodore Dreiser: A Selection of Uncollected Prose.* Detroit: Wayne State University Press, 1977.

Poe, Edgar Allan. *Essays and Reviews.* New York: Library of America, 1984.

———."Magazine-Writing—Peter Snook." *Broadway Journal* (New York: AMS Reprint, 1965): 354–57.

Polito, Robert. *Savage Art: A Biography of Jim Thompson.* New York: Knopf, 1995.

Porges, Irwin. *Edgar Rice Burroughs: The Man Who Created Tarzan.* Provo, Utah: Brigham Young University Press, 1975.

Putnam, George Haven. "Authors' Complaints and Publishers' Profits." *Forum* 12 (September 1891): 62–77.

Putnam, Nina Wilcox. *Laughing Through.* New York: Sears, 1930.

Raban, Jonathan. *For Love & Money: A Writing Life, 1969–1989.* New York: Harper and Row, 1989.

Raeburn, John. *Fame Became of Him: Hemingway as Public Writer.* Bloomington: Indiana University Press, 1984.

Rascoe, Burton. *We Were Interrupted.* Garden City, N.Y.: Doubleday, 1947.

Ravitz, Abe. *David Graham Phillips.* New York: Twayne, 1966.

Reiger, George, ed. *The Best of Zane Grey, Outdoorsman.* Harrisburg, Penn.: Stackpole Books, 1992.

Reiger, John F. *American Sportsmen and the Origins of Conservation.* Rev. ed. Norman: University of Oklahoma Press, 1986.

Reynolds, Paul R. *The Middle Man: The Adventures of a Literary Agent.* New York: William Morrow, 1972.

Reynolds, Quentin. *The Fiction Factory or From Pulp Row to Quality Street.* New York: Random House, 1956.

Rinehart, Mary Roberts. *My Story.* Rev. ed. New York: Farrar and Rinehart, 1931.

———. "Thoughts." *Ladies' Home Journal* (May 1931): 3 ff.

———. *Writing Is Work.* Boston: The Writer, Inc., 1939.

Robbins, J. Albert. "Fees Paid to Authors by Certain American Periodicals, 1840–1850." In *Studies in Bibliography,* ed. Fredson Bowers, 95–104. Charlottesville: Bibliographical Society of the University of Virginia, 1949.

Roberts, Kenneth. *For Authors Only and Other Gloomy Essays.* Garden City, N.Y.: Doubleday, Doran, 1935.

———. *I Wanted to Write.* Garden City, N.Y.: Doubleday, 1949.

Rogers, Pat. *Grub Street: Studies in a Subculture.* London: Methuen, 1972.

Rose, Jacqueline. *The Haunting of Sylvia Plath.* Cambridge, Mass.: Harvard University Press, 1992.

Rudolph, Barbara. "Heartbreak Comes to Harlequin." *Forbes* (March 29, 1982): 50–51.

Scharnhorst, Gary and Jack Bales. *The Lost Life of Horatio Alger, Jr.* Bloomington: Indiana University Press, 1985.

Schoolcraft, John, ed. *The Notebooks and Poems of "Max Brand."* New York: Dodd, Mead, 1957.

Schorer, Mark. *Sinclair Lewis: An American Life.* New York: McGraw-Hill, 1961.

Sedgwick, Ellery. *The Happy Profession.* Boston: Little, Brown, 1946.

Server, Lee. *Danger Is My Business: An Illustrated History of the Fabulous Pulp Magazines.* San Francisco: Chronicle Books, 1993.

Shaber, Sarah R. "Hemingway's Literary Journalism: The Spanish Civil War Dispatches." *Journalism Quarterly* 57 (Autumn 1980): 420 ff.

Shaw, Joseph T., ed. *The Hard-Boiled Omnibus: Early Stories from Black Mask.* New York: Simon and Schuster, 1946.

Silverman, Kenneth. *A Cultural History of the American Revolution.* New York: Crowell, 1976.

———. *Edgar A. Poe: Mournful and Never-Ending Remembrance.* New York: HarperCollins, 1991.

Sinclair, Andrew. *Jack: A Biography of Jack London.* New York: Harper and Row, 1977.

Sinclair, Upton. *The Autobiography of Upton Sinclair.* New York: Harcourt, Brace and World, 1962.

———. "The Confessions of a Young Author." *Independent* 54 (November 20, 1902): 2748–52.

———. *Money Writes!* New York: Albert and Charles Boni, 1927.

Slote, Bernice, ed. *The Kingdom of Art: Willa Cather's First Principles and Critical Statements, 1893–1896.* Lincoln: University of Nebraska Press, 1966.

Smith, Henry Nash. *Virgin Land: The American West as Symbol and Myth.* Cambridge, Mass.: Harvard University Press, 1970.

Spence, Hartzell. "The Bent and Blunted Free Lance." *Saturday Review of Literature* (November 10, 1962): 63 ff.

Spiller, Robert. *The American in England.* New York: Henry Holt, 1926.

Stallman, R. W. *Stephen Crane.* New York: George Braziller, 1968.

Steffens, Lincoln. *The Autobiography of Lincoln Steffens.* New York: Harcourt, Brace, 1931.

Stegner, Wallace. *The Uneasy Chair: A Biography of Bernard De Voto.* Garden City, N.Y.: Doubleday, 1974.

———, ed. *The Letters of Bernard De Voto.* Garden City, N.Y.: Doubleday, 1975.

Stein, Gertrude. *The Autobiography of Alice B. Toklas.* New York: Harcourt, Brace, 1933.

Stern, Madeleine B. *We the Women: Careers of Nineteenth-Century America.* New York: Schulte, 1963.

———, ed. *Double Life: Newly Discovered Thrillers of Louisa May Alcott.* Boston: Little, Brown, 1988.

———, ed. *Louisa May Alcott Unmasked: Collected Thrillers.* Boston: Northeastern University Press, 1995.

Stott, William. *Documentary Expression and Thirties America.* New York: Oxford University Press, 1973.

Tarbell, Ida. *All in the Day's Work.* New York: Macmillan, 1939.

Tate, Allen. *The Man of Letters in the Modern World.* New York: Meridian Books, 1955.

Tebbel, John. *Between Covers: The Rise and Transformation of Book Publishing in America.* New York: Oxford University Press, 1987.

———. *From Rags to Riches: Horatio Alger, Jr., and The American Dream.* New York: Macmillan, 1963.

———. *George Horace Lorimer and* The Saturday Evening Post. Garden City, N.Y.: Doubleday, 1948.

Tebbel, John, and Mary Ellen Zuckerman. *The Magazine in America, 1741–1990.* New York: Oxford University Press, 1991.

Terhune, Albert Payson. *To the Best of My Memory.* New York: Harper and Brothers, 1930.

Thomas, Dwight, and David K. Jackson. *The Poe Log: A Documentary Life of Edgar Allan Poe, 1809–1849.* Boston: G. K. Hall, 1987.

Tompkins, Jane. *West of Everything: The Inner Life of Westerns.* New York: Oxford University Press, 1992.

Thurber, James. *The Years with Ross.* Boston: Little, Brown, 1959.

Tocqueville, Alexis. *Democracy in America.* Ed. Phillips Bradley. 2 vols. New York: Knopf, 1953.

Tomkins, Mary E. *Ida Tarbell.* New York: Twayne, 1974.

Tunis, John R. *A Measure of Independence.* New York: Atheneum, 1964.

Twain, Mark. *Roughing It.* New York: Library of America, 1984.

Ulmann, Doris. *A Portrait Gallery of American Editors.* New York: William Edwin Rudge, 1925.

Umphlett, Wiley Lee, ed. *The Achievement of American Sport Literature: A Critical Appraisal.* Cranbury, N.J.: Associated University Presses, 1991.

Unterecker, John. *Voyager: A Life of Hart Crane.* New York: Farrar, Straus and Giroux, 1969.

Vidal, Gore. "The Romance of Sinclair Lewis." *New York Review of Books* (October 8, 1992): 14–20.

Waldo, Richard H. "The Genius of S. S. McClure." *Editor and Publisher* (July 21, 1934): 80 ff.

Walker, Dale L., ed. *No Mentor but Myself: A Collection of Articles, Essays, Reviews, and Letters.* Port Washington, N.Y.: Kennikat, 1979.

Walker, Nancy A. *Fanny Fern.* New York: Twayne, 1993.

Warner, Anna B. *Susan Warner.* New York: Putnam's, 1909.

Warren, Joyce W. *Fanny Fern: An Independent Woman.* New Brunswick, N.J.: Rutgers University Press, 1992.

———, ed. *Ruth Hall and Other Writings.* New Brunswick, N.J.: Rutgers University Press, 1986.

Watson, Elmo Scott. *History of Auxiliary Newspaper Service in the United States.* Champaign, Ill.: Illini Publishing Company, 1923.

———. *A History of Newspaper Syndicates in the United States, 1865–1935.* Chicago [no publisher], 1936.

Watson, William Braasch. "Hemingway's Spanish Civil War Dispatches." *Hemingway Review* 7 (Spring 1988): 4–13.

Weber, Ronald. *Hemingway's Art of Non-fiction.* New York: St. Martin's, 1990.

———. "Journalism, Writing, and American Literature." Occasional Paper No. 5, Gannett Center for Media Studies (April 1987).

Wertheim, Stanley, and Paul Sorrentino, ed. *The Correspondence of Stephen Crane.* 2 vols. New York: Columbia University, 1988.

West, James L. W. *American Authors and the Literary Marketplace since 1900.* Philadelphia: University of Pennsylvania Press, 1988.

Wheeler, John N. *I've Got News for You.* New York: Dutton, 1961.

_____. "Selling Other Men's Brains." *Saturday Evening Post* (March 10, 1928): 16 ff.

White, Luke, Jr. *Henry William Herbert and the American Publishing Scene, 1831–1858.* Newark, N.J.: Carteret Book Club, 1943.

White, William, ed. *By-Line: Ernest Hemingway.* New York: Scribner's, 1967.

Williams, Raymond. *The Long Revolution.* London: Penguin Books, 1965.

Willis, Nathaniel Parker. "Authors Pay in America." *Evening Mirror* (October 10, 1844): 2.

_____. *Hurry-Graphs; or Sketches of Scenery, Celebrities and Society, Taken From Life.* New York: Charles Scribner, 1851.

_____. "The Pay for Periodical Writing." *Evening Mirror* (October 12, 1844): 2.

_____. *Pencillings by the Way.* New York: Charles Scribner, 1852.

Wilmer, Lambert A. *Merlin.* Ed. Thomas Ollive Mabbott. New York: Scholars' Facsimiles and Reprints, 1941.

Wilson, Christopher P. *The Labor of Words: Literary Professionalism in the Progressive Era.* Athens: University of Georgia Press, 1985.

Wilson, Edmund. *Classics and Commercials.* New York: Farrar, Straus, 1950.

Winnick, R. H., ed. *Letters of Archibald MacLeish, 1907–1982.* Boston: Houghton Mifflin, 1983.

Wood, Ann D. "The 'Scribbling Women' and Fanny Fern: Why Women Wrote." *American Quarterly* 23 (Spring 1971): 3–24.

Wood, James Playsted. *Of Lasting Interest: The Story of the* Reader's Digest. Garden City, N.Y.: Doubleday, 1967.

Woodberry, George E. *The Life of Edgar Allan Poe.* 2 vols. Boston: Houghton Mifflin, 1885.

Woolf, Virginia. *The Moment and Other Essays.* New York: Harcourt, Brace, 1948.

Writing for Fortune. New York: Time Inc., 1980.

Yardley, Jonathan. *Ring: A Biography of Ring Lardner.* New York: Random House, 1977.

Zane Grey: The Man and His Work. New York: Harper and Brothers, 1928.

Ziff, Larzer. *Writing in the New Nation.* New Haven, Conn.: Yale University Press, 1991.

INDEX

A Note about the Author

RONALD WEBER is Professor of American Studies at the University of Notre Dame. He has published several books about American writing, including *The Literature of Fact: Literary Nonfiction in American Writing* and *Seeing Earth: Literary Responses to Space Exploration* (both with Ohio University Press). He is the editor of *The Reporter as Artist: A Look at the New Journalism Controversy.*